Advances in Entrepreneurial Economics and Sustainable Development - Volume 1

Climate-Smart Innovation

Social Entrepreneurship and Sustainable Development in the Environmental Economy

Advances in Entrepreneurial Economics and Sustainable Development

Series Editor: Elena G Popkova (*MGIMO University, Russia*)

Published:

Vol. 1 *Climate-Smart Innovation: Social Entrepreneurship and Sustainable Development in the Environmental Economy*
edited by Elena G Popkova, Natalia G Vovchenko & Olga V Andreeva

Advances in Entrepreneurial Economics and Sustainable Development - Volume 1

Climate-Smart Innovation

Social Entrepreneurship and Sustainable Development in the Environmental Economy

editors

Elena G Popkova
MGIMO University, Russia

Natalia G Vovchenko
Rostov State University of Economics, Russia

Olga V Andreeva
Rostov State University of Economics, Russia

World Scientific

NEW JERSEY • LONDON • SINGAPORE • BEIJING • SHANGHAI • HONG KONG • TAIPEI • CHENNAI • TOKYO

Published by

World Scientific Publishing Co. Pte. Ltd.
5 Toh Tuck Link, Singapore 596224
USA office: 27 Warren Street, Suite 401-402, Hackensack, NJ 07601
UK office: 57 Shelton Street, Covent Garden, London WC2H 9HE

Library of Congress Cataloging-in-Publication Data
Names: Popkova, Elena G., editor. | Vovchenko, Natalia G., editor. |
Andreeva, Olga V. (Economist), editor.
Title: Climate-smart innovation : social entrepreneurship and sustainable development in the environmental economy / editors, Elena G. Popkova, MGIMO University, Russia, Natalia G. Vovchenko, Rostov State University of Economics, Russia, Olga V. Andreeva, Rostov State University of Economics, Russia.
Description: New Jersey : World Scientific, [2023] | Series: Advances in entrepreneurial economics and sustainable development ; volume 1 |
Includes bibliographical references and index.
Identifiers: LCCN 2022032897 | ISBN 9789811264245 (hardcover) |
ISBN 9789811264252 (ebook) | ISBN 9789811264269 (ebook other)
Subjects: LCSH: Social entrepreneurship. | Social responsibility of business. |
Sustainable development.
Classification: LCC HD60 .C528 2023 | DDC 658.4/08--dc23/eng/20220829
LC record available at https://lccn.loc.gov/2022032897

British Library Cataloguing-in-Publication Data
A catalogue record for this book is available from the British Library.

For any available supplementary material, please visit
https://www.worldscientific.com/worldscibooks/10.1142/13082#t=suppl

Desk Editors: Nimal Koliyat/Geysilla Jean

Typeset by Stallion Press
Email: enquiries@stallionpress.com

https://doi.org/10.1142/9789811264252_fmatter

Preface

The book focuses on a systemic study of climate-smart innovations in social entrepreneurship in the unity of climate risks of entrepreneurship and innovative responses to them in support of sustainable development of the ecological economy, which is consistently disclosed in four parts of the book. The first part outlines climate risks and green innovations of social entrepreneurship in the ecological economy.

The second part forms the scientific vision of institutional provision and financial support of social entrepreneurship for the sustainable development of the ecological economy. The third part reflects climate-smart manufacturing innovations for resource-efficient social entrepreneurship. The fourth part reveals the climate-smart innovations of environmental marketing and green logistics of social entrepreneurship in support of sustainable development of territories.

The novelty and uniqueness of the book are underscored by the fact that it highlights a previously unknown angle of climate change risk management in entrepreneurship. In this new perspective, the subject of risk management is social entrepreneurship, and the tool is climate-smart innovation.

The book is intended for scientists interested in the economics of climate change. For them, the book forms a theoretical and methodological platform for climate risk management in social entrepreneurship in support of sustainable development of the ecological economy through climate-smart innovations. The book is also of interest to subjects of social entrepreneurship, for whom the book offers applied recommendations for implementing climate-smart innovations in support of sustainable development of the ecological economy.

https://doi.org/10.1142/9789811264252_fmatter

About the Editors

Elena G. Popkova, Doctor in Economics, is a Professor at MGIMO University, Moscow, Russia, and the founder of the Institute of Scientific Communications, Volgograd, Russia. Scientific interests of Prof. Popkova include economic growth, sustainable development, social entrepreneurship, globalization, humanization of economic growth, developing countries, the institutionalization of society development, development planning, strategic planning, knowledge economy, digital economy, and Industry 4.0. Dr. Popkova has more than 350 publications and is a member of the editorial board of the *International Journal of Economic Policy in Emerging Economies* (Scopus, WoS) and the *International Journal for Quality Research* (Scopus, WoS). Prof. Popkova was awarded the Emerald "Literati Awards" in the "Highly Commended Paper Award" for 2020. She is the editor of the *Advances in Research on Russian Business and Management* book series published by Information Age Publishing (USA) (Scopus,WOS).

Olga V. Andreeva, PhD in Economics, is the Head of the Center for Strategic Studies of Socio-Economic Development of Southern Russia at Rostov State University of Economics (RSUE); Associate Professor of the Department of Finance; and Public Representative of the Agency for Strategic Initiatives on the Environment and Climate. In 1996 she graduated from Rostov State Academy of Economics with a degree in Finance and Credit. In 2002, she defended her PhD thesis to the Dissertation Council of the Rostov State University of Economics on the topic: "Sources of financing medical services in modern Russia." In 2006, she became an Associate Professor. Her pedagogical experience spans 25 years, and she has been working at the Department of Finance since 1996. Dr. Andreeva's research interests include sustainable development, green economy, and ESG agenda, with more than 10 scientific papers published in the leading journals including *E3S Web of Conferences, Fundamental Research, CITISE, Social Entrepreneurship and Corporate Social Responsibility*, and *Financial Economy*.

Natalia G. Vovchenko, Doctor of Economics, is an economist and the Vice-Rector for Research and Innovation. She is a 1990 graduate of the Rostov-on-Don Order of the Badge of Honor of the Institute of National Economy, specializing in Industrial Planning. Her specialty is "Accounting, Control and Analysis of Economic Activity." In 1994, she defended her PhD thesis to the Dissertation Council of Rostov State University on the topic "Land Reform and Improvement of Relations of Agrarian Nature Management in the Conditions of Market Formation." Her scientific supervisor was Professor V.N. Ovchinnikov, Doctor of Economics. In 2002, she became an Associate Professor. In 2006, she defended her D.Sc thesis to the dissertation Council of the Rostov State University of Economics on the topic "The Impact of Financial Globalization Processes on the Transformation of the Financial System of Russia." Her scientific consultant was Prof. Vladimir Zolotarev, Doctor of Economics. In 2015, she was awarded the academic title of professor. She has a teaching experience spanning 31 years.

https://doi.org/10.1142/9789811264252_fmatter

Contents

https://doi.org/10.1142/9789811264252_fmatter

Introduction

Climate Change as a Challenge to the Sustainable Development of the Ecological Economy and Response to It in Social Entrepreneurship

Elena G. Popkova

MGIMO University, Moscow, Russia
E.Popkova@inno.mgimo.ru

Sustainable development of the ecological economy presupposes a balance between economic activity and environmental protection. Entrepreneurship is a key actor in the ecological economy because it accumulates most resources and carries out the most large-scale transformative and utilizing activities. Social entrepreneurship refers to those business entities guided in their activities by the Sustainable Development Goals (SDGs). Climate change brings high entrepreneurial risks with it, the management of which in social entrepreneurship as a driver of growth of the ecological economy involves the management of the interests of society, putting them above commercial interests.

Climate risks of entrepreneurship are associated with increased uncertainty and reduced accuracy of forecasts of economic activity, with the need to transform the organization and management of entrepreneurship, and with higher costs with a natural decline in the efficiency of entrepreneurship. A promising response of social entrepreneurship to the challenge of climate change is climate-smart innovation, a feature and advantage of which is the reliance on "smart" technology in adapting to climate change. As with all innovations, it is advisable to classify and consider them in the context of the following three entrepreneurial processes.

First, it is necessary to consider organizational and managerial innovations. As the climate changes, the organizational structure and management practices of social entrepreneurship must be restructured. To introduce climate-smart innovations in entrepreneurship, government support is required through the development of institutions. The public digital infrastructure must be prepared to implement ever more advanced climate-smart innovations continually. The regulatory environment for entrepreneurship must be continually modernized to regulate (delineate the legal field) and stimulate social entrepreneurship innovation. In this regard, the implementation of SDG 16 is essential to achieve climate resilience in social entrepreneurship and the development of the ecological economy.

When managing climate-smart innovations in social entrepreneurship, financing these innovations is important. A high level of corporate social (environmental) responsibility alone is not enough to implement climate-smart innovations — considerable financial support is also required. In this case, the difficulty is that social entrepreneurship, in many cases, acquires non-commercial features and is therefore limited in its ability to attract investment in innovation.

Therefore, it is necessary to use flexible market mechanisms to manage investment flows, particularly integration processes in entrepreneurship. Collaboration with universities and networking in technoparks, innovation networks, and environmental clusters offers great opportunities for uniting green finance in support of climate-smart innovation in social entrepreneurship. It is also necessary to develop institutions for lending to social entrepreneurship as sources of "green" finance. Consequently, it is necessary to implement SDG 17 to introduce climate-smart innovations in social entrepreneurship in support of a sustainable ecological economy.

Second, it is necessary to consider production and technological innovations. The transformational activities of social entrepreneurship are highly susceptible to climate risks because climate change reduces the availability of natural resources and changes their quality. The impact of climate risks on social entrepreneurship is most pronounced and clear in agriculture. Climate-smart innovations support food security and thus contribute to the realization of SDG 2.

Climate-smart innovations in social entrepreneurship in industries aimed at managing these risks are related to improving the resource efficiency of entrepreneurial processes. The core of the resource efficiency of climate-smart innovations is energy efficiency because energy is a basic natural resource required in virtually all transformational processes. Simultaneously, smart technologies are characterized by increased energy consumption. This causes a contradiction in the nature of climate-smart innovations, which have to balance low power with high output. The above contradiction is resolved in social entrepreneurship in the orientation toward SDG 7.

Third, it is necessary to consider marketing and sales innovations. There is a clear link between social entrepreneurship and the territory in which it carries out its production and distribution processes. Resilient communities, cities, and regions developed through the implementation of SDG 11 create market incentives for climate-smart innovation in social entrepreneurship. This, in turn, supports responsible production and consumption in the territory of social enterprise, contributing to the realization of SDG 12. Consequently, climate-smart innovations ensure the cyclical development of the ecological economy, increasing its sustainability in each new cycle of development.

Climate-smart innovations should support climate change (SDG 13) and biodiversity conservation (SDGs 14 and 15) in the area where they are located. Moreover, they should encourage local communities to take initiatives in these areas. Marketing innovations are related to the use of smart technologies to study public opinion and identify consumer preferences for climate risk management in a given territory. Marketing is also designed to publicly highlight the benefits to local communities of climate-smart innovations introduced by social entrepreneurship. Innovations in logistics are designed to reshape value chains to make them more climate-resilient. Green value chains are critical to a sustainable climate economy.

Thus, climate-smart innovations of social entrepreneurship encompass a wide range of entrepreneurial processes and represent a special form of change management. This book details the current best practices of climate risk management in social entrepreneurship, particularly in the COVID-19 pandemic and crisis, and based on case studies of smart cities in the countries of the Eurasian Economic Union (EAEU) located in Eastern Europe and Central Asia. The practice of implementing climate-smart innovations in social entrepreneurship is rethought and refined from the perspective of ESG principles.

The book's purpose is to systematically explore climate-smart innovations in social entrepreneurship in the unity of climate-smart entrepreneurship risks and innovative responses to them in support of a sustainable ecological economy. The classification of climate-smart innovations presented according to the Theory of Innovation determined the book's logic and structure. The first part of the book examines climate risks and green innovations of social entrepreneurship in the ecological economy.

The second part is devoted to institutional provision and financial support of social entrepreneurship for the sustainable development of the ecological economy. The third part reveals climate-smart innovations in manufacturing for resource efficiency in social entrepreneurship. The fourth part identifies climate-smart innovations of environmental marketing and green logistics of social entrepreneurship to support the sustainable development of territories.

The book's novelty lies in the fact that it reflects the climate risks of current entrepreneurship and forms scientific and methodological support for highly effective risk management, one of the promising directions of which, according to the book, is climate-smart innovations. The book's contribution to the literature is that it takes a comprehensive look at the totality of entrepreneurial processes in which climate risk is managed. In this way, the book offers a holistic and practical guide to climate-smart innovation in social entrepreneurship.

The book is unique in that it reveals a new angle of climate change risk management in entrepreneurship — through the prism of social entrepreneurship, the distinguishing feature of which is a non-commercial (socially-oriented) approach to implementing climate-smart innovations whose new property becomes responsibility (sustainability). With this distinction, social entrepreneurship improves business performance and supports the sustainability of the ecological economy with climate-smart innovations.

The primary target audience for this book is scientists studying climate change, sustainable ecological economies, and social entrepreneurship. In the book, they will find a systemic theoretical concept and methodological framework for climate risk management in social entrepreneurship to support a sustainable ecological economy through climate-smart innovation.

The book is multidisciplinary because it is prepared at the junction of different fields of scientific knowledge. Therefore, the book is of interest to representatives of the economics of climate change, environmental economics, business economics, innovation economics, regional economics, finance, government and corporate management in the economy, risk management, and marketing.

Practicing experts are an additional target audience for the book. In this book, government regulators of entrepreneurship will find the authors' recommendations for improving government regulation of social entrepreneurship for climate risk management and sustainable development of the ecological economy. Social entrepreneurs will find a systemic view on how to organize entrepreneurial processes to achieve high climate resilience, as well as applied recommendations for implementing climate-smart innovations.

Part 1

Climate Risks and Green Innovations of Social Entrepreneurship in the Ecological Economy

https://doi.org/10.1142/9789811264252_0001

Chapter 1

The Mediating Impact of Innovation on Green Entrepreneurship Practices and Sustainability

Denis S. Ushakov[*,†,¶], **Daria G. Ivanova**[‡,‖], **Eteri D. Rubinskaya**[‡,**] **and Khodor Shatila**[§,††]

[†]*College of Hospitality Industry Management Suan Sunandha Rajabhat University, Bangkok, Thailand*
[‡]*Rostov State University of Economics, Rostov-on-Don, Russia*
[§]*Sagesse University, Furn El Chebbak Baabda, Lebanon*
[¶]*fintaliano@yandex.ru*
[‖]*ivanova753@yandex.ru*
[**]*eteri-rubinskaya@mail.ru*
[††]*info1@iprocares.com*

Abstract: Green entrepreneurs are now recognized as major driving forces in the move toward a greener economy. Developing a "green" economy is becoming increasingly popular as a way to balance economic growth with environmental protection. As a result, entrepreneurs in the green economy are swapping varying degrees of rigidity between their company activity, environmental philosophy, and larger settings. The findings of this investigation have a number of practical and theoretical ramifications. Instead of promoting and legitimizing green

[*]Corresponding author.

entrepreneurship, political action should concentrate on actively modifying the socio-technological environment of the economy and institutions in a way that expedites and maintains the discursive hegemony of green entrepreneurship over economic development. Environmental entrepreneurs — especially "visionary champions," "innovative opportunists," and "bioneers" — need to be used to their fullest extent to achieve environmental sustainability.

Keywords: Innovations; Green economy; Green entrepreneurship; Ecopreneurship.

1.1. Introduction and Background

When it came to the business world, the word "entrepreneurship" was not anything new. It is a novel approach to running a firm. If we want to comprehend emerging trends in entrepreneurship, we need to define the term "entrepreneur" accurately [9]. To succeed as an entrepreneur, one must be able to combine the aspects of invention, creativity, opportunity, and commercialization. Businesses have become more popular because of entrepreneurs' ability to continually come up with something new (innovation) and exploit resources from their environment to their advantage (creative) [12]. People began to use money instead of barter as a means of trading products with the development of quantifiable instruments for transferring items. As a result, entrepreneurs began to focus on making money as their primary goal. In business, money became the primary issue (selling and buying). Therefore, many individuals have begun to pay greater attention to social concerns such as poverty, health challenges, hunger, and other basic needs. As their goals entail achieving financial and social objectives, they are referred to as "social entrepreneurs."

Green entrepreneurs are now recognized as major driving forces in the move toward a greener economy. Developing a "green" economy is becoming increasingly popular as a way to balance economic growth with environmental protection [1,5]. As a result, entrepreneurs in the green economy are swapping varying degrees of rigidity between their company activity, environmental philosophy, and larger settings [8,14].

However, green innovation and entrepreneurship research has remained finitely focused and apolitical. Entrepreneurs, in particular, face enormous challenges in the field of green innovation (e.g., green packing and green marketing). In fact, promoting environmentally friendly and forward-thinking corporate practices is becoming more popular.

Eco-innovation facilitators are organizations that support businesses in the eco-innovation process by offering inspiration, motivation, guidance, and other specific assistance, generally by acting as an intermediary between two and more parties [11].

A comprehensive review of the literature suggests that innovation intermediaries may help maintain sustainability in a variety of ways. As a result of this demand, a variety of functions were performed: the articulation of demand (searching for information and opportunities, anticipatory planning, diagnostics based on needs/knowledge gaps), creation of networks (selection of collaborators, forming of business connections), and the development of organizational capacity (training and competence building through management/technical incubation) [4,9]. Sustainable innovation intermediaries might include one or more actors who concentrate on implementing sustainability principles into these services to assist the formation of niche experiments or regime subsystems. Sustainability may be promoted in several ways through intermediaries [7,12].

One of the examples is an incubator, which, as a kind of intermediary, requires tenants to achieve specific climate adaptation or mitigation performance criteria, as well as larger environmental, social, economic, and governance considerations. In certain cases, incubators required tenants to satisfy particular sustainability requirements, such as green building, solar and wind energy, energy storage, energy efficiency, and the smart grid [15].

Brem, van den Bergh, and Sivash examined how incubators in Germany, Finland, and Sweden have influenced sustainable entrepreneurship by requiring prospective tenants to include sustainability indicators in their business plans and goals [2,13,15]. A glut of applications meant that certain incubators could be more selective about the quality of their sustainability ideas since there were more applicants than seats available.

Consequently, each entrepreneur working in the incubator was responsible for implementing sustainability into their company's business strategy. To guarantee that sustainability concepts are included in projects and business strategies, a sustainability specialist, coordinator, or team should engage with the intermediary and its entrepreneurs. The institution should also require environmental monitoring and reporting from the intermediary.

1.2. Literature Review

A mediated-moderated model was used to study [6] the relationship between social networking sites and green entrepreneurship goals. Ajzen's theory of planned behavior and Shepero's model of entrepreneurial intents were used in the research.

The study's design shows that risk propensity and self-efficacy influence the association between social networking sites and green entrepreneurship aspirations, whereas subjective norms further regulate the relationship between self-efficacy and green entrepreneurship intentions.

Data was gathered from 500 participants using a well-designed and self-administered questionnaire. The partial least squares path modeling (PLS-SEM) was used to evaluate the data and test hypotheses. The research results show that there is a positive and substantial relationship between social networking sites and green entrepreneurship goals via the indirect influence of risk propensity and self-efficacy [3].

According to the results of the moderating effect study, self-efficacy and green entrepreneurial goals were unaffected by subjective standards. Academic and practical consequences for government officials, politicians, and entrepreneurial educational institutions may be derived from the results of this research. Green innovation (GI) practices are examined in the research of [12] to see whether stakeholders' perspectives have an impact on GI practices, which, in turn, have an impact on environmental and organizational performance (OP).

The sample size of 515 replies necessitated a quantitative approach. Random sampling was employed to collect data from the respondents. A closed-ended questionnaire was used to gather data from industrial and service enterprises in the Punjab region of Pakistan. In this case, partial least square analysis was used using a structural equation model. Our results showed that stakeholders' perceptions of GI practices are positively and significantly related. There is a strong correlation between GI habits and environmental and OP factors. Moderating effects were shown to have a statistically significant but unfavorable impact. Several contributions and decision-making insinuations may be gleaned from [16].

Humanity faces tremendous problems in the 21st century due to environmental deterioration and global warming. As a result, companies increasingly use more environmentally friendly production processes and procedures. Green practices and long-term success are inescapable outcomes for companies.

The work by Wang *et al.* [16] aimed to construct a complete model by merging the natural resource-based view (NRBV) and triple bottom line (TBL) frameworks. The impact of three factors, namely green absorptive capacity (GAC), sustainable human capital (SHC), and organizational support (OS), on the GRIN (Green Innovation) of small and medium-sized enterprises (SMEs) from the manufacturing sector was examined.

All three pillars of TBL sustainability (environmental, economic, and social) were considered in light of the potential repercussions of GRIN. The research sample was 304 Saudi Arabian businesses, who were randomly selected to participate in the study using a questionnaire. Using smart PLS 3.0 software, structural equation modeling (SEM) was used to examine the correlations between variables to ensure validity and reliability. Small and medium-sized businesses were classified into two categories to better understand the distinctions between the two groupings [10].

As a result, firm size was incorporated as a moderator in the suggested model, and multi-group analysis (MGA) was conducted. According to the findings, GAC, SHC, and OS positively impact GRIN in SMEs. Additionally, the findings show that GRIN had a substantial influence on all three indicators of long-term sustainability in performance. According to the MGA, there are substantial discrepancies between medium-sized and small enterprises when it comes to GAC-GRIN relationships. Environmental performance was more closely associated with medium-sized enterprises than small ones. This is a one-of-a-kind investigation that has consequences for the real world and academia. Scholars, marketers, and politicians may find this study useful because it presents an integrated model for sustainability [5].

The goal of the research conducted by Méndez-Picazo *et al.* [8] is to explore the influence of knowledge management components on green innovation (i.e., knowledge acquisition, distribution, and responsiveness). Furthermore, the research aims to examine how environmental consciousness in SMEs in the United Arab Emirates (UAE) affects these interactions. Two informants from each company's top 388 managers made up the sample of 194 SMEs in Abu Dhabi, UAE. Random sampling was utilized in this cross-sectional investigation. A statistical induction technique was used to adopt the positivist approach. Researchers employed previously validated measuring scales to assess the research components. Smart partial least squares structural equation modeling (PLS-SEM) 3.0 was used to analyze the data quantitatively [7].

According to the research findings, information acquisition, knowledge distribution, and knowledge responsiveness are all positively and significantly linked to green innovation. Data shows that environmental awareness acts as a mediator between information distribution and green innovation. In the link between information acquisition and knowledge responsiveness with regard to green innovation, environmental awareness did not play a mediating function [2].

One of the most critical components of green innovation is the ability to manage information efficiently. Though knowledge management is critical for long-term success, literature on the subject is scarce. The findings of this research have practical relevance for the executives of SMEs. A company's ability to grasp and apply the value of knowledge management may be aided by environmental awareness and green innovation. They may become eco-innovative environmentally, commercially, and socially.

Few studies explore the impact of knowledge management aspects (knowledge acquisition, distribution, and responsiveness) on green innovation in UAE SMEs.

1.3. Green and Sustainable Entrepreneurial Intention

People's buying patterns have changed considerably as the human population expanded rapidly; this fact had a direct and an indirect effect on people's health. Due to these developments, pollution and climate change have increased, and animal populations have decreased. According to [11], human and systemic levels of service quality have been affected by global climate change throughout time.

Consumers' opinions and investments in environmental causes have altered as a result of changes in the climate and the market. Entrepreneurship had its genesis in the 17th century. This term has a wide range of meanings and uses in different contexts. According to Sivash *et al.* [13], this concept was generally adopted when a company started making money. Others see entrepreneurship as a means of creating new products and services to satisfy their customers' desires."

There has been considerable evolution in the concept of green entrepreneurship, although it remains a relatively young phenomenon. As the global environment changes, businesses are also reacting by emphasizing sustainability and environmental issues.

In a study, entrepreneurs Muo *et al.* (2020) take advantage of this situation, invest, and take risks. Experts have concentrated on green entrepreneurship and environmental challenges in the last several decades. A solution to economic and social issues caused by climate change is possible and is already being pushed as a green business solution.

According to another study, "green" business has also reduced deforestation and improved environmental quality. Green entrepreneurship is becoming more popular among university graduates, and their hopes to pursue it are also rising. According to Richard *et al.* [12], the long-term viability of green entrepreneurship depends on human and environmental factors.

A bigger effect is exerted by other surrounding components, such as public universities and vocational schools that aid students with interest in green business. Additional benefits, such as increased employment and other social and economic advantages, may be gained by governments where the idea of green entrepreneurship has been successfully implemented. Governments and politicians have taken note of these and other advantages.

It is believed that green business may lead to rapid economic and social development. Consequently, according to Van den Bergh [15], they are worried about the potential risks such as not being able to remain sustainable. Despite this, it can transform low-production units into high-performance processes.

The last several decades saw considerable interest in green entrepreneurship. An increase in green entrepreneurship may be on the horizon due to an ever-increasing need for new businesses and entrepreneurs.

Entrepreneurs generate economic activity and income possibilities for themselves and the country by founding and developing viable company ideas, which create money for both parties. Many technological and scientific developments have been pioneered by entrepreneurs who have also played a significant role in generating employment and keeping businesses competitive.

There has been much change in the world of green business, and social media has emerged as the primary source of information. Current and relevant information may be found on various social networking sites. Facebook and Twitter are more effective in providing quick and reliable information in times of disaster or tragedy.

With the growth of social networking sites like Facebook and Twitter, people have grown more conscious of environmental issues, which has led to a rise in environmental awareness. People younger than 30 years are increasingly interested in green businesses because of the efforts of social media and social networking sites to promote a better and greener environment [16].

1.4. Methodology

A systemic questionnaire was used to generate hypotheses, which were then tested empirically using a data-gathering tool. Student demographic data is included as an independent variable for social networking sites, known as "generic evaluations," in the "first section." Green entrepreneurship aspiration is a dependent variable in the second phase of the research. In the third section, we looked at the connections between the last three variables (innovation, sustainability, and green entrepreneurship practices).

A total of 300 people took part in the survey, all of them were students at educational institutions in Lebanon and Russia. At least 300 samples must be used in this sample size to estimate the *C*-coefficient correctly. The research participants were selected using a convenience sample. As a result of the convenience sampling method, researchers may rapidly and conveniently gather data from a considerable number of individuals.

For structural equation modeling, a minimum sample size of 300 has been employed and recommended by a number of studies. Consequently, this research used a sample size of 300 as the basic minimum. The data was analyzed using SPSS.

Among other things, just one variable must be considered to ensure that each collection of objects is easily understood and distinguishable from the others.

Two experts were invited to improve the material, and interviews with four professional experts were conducted after they completed the in-depth content validity investigation of the measurement items. After everything was completed and approved, the survey included the opinion of academic and professional specialists. All variables' internal consistency and composite dependability ranged from 0.823 to 0.915, indicating a high level of dependability across the board.

The data was gathered via a seven-point survey, which, according to a Likert scale, ranged from 0 (strongly disagree) to 7 (strongly agree). Company size (number of employees) and age served as the only controls (years of operation).

1.5. Results

1.5.1. *Regression 1: The Relationship Between Green Entrepreneurship Practices and Innovation*

Referring to Table 1.1, we can note that the Pearson coefficient (PE) scored 0.863 between green entrepreneurship practices (GEP) and sustainability, which means that every unit of increase in GEP leads to an 86.3% increase in CI.

Referring to Table 1.2, we note that this model scored 63.5%, which means that the relationship between GEP and sustainability is 63.5% and that 36.5% of the variables affecting sustainability had not been addressed in this model.

Referring to Table 1.3, we can note that GEP scored a *P*-value (0.00), *T*-test (10.997), and *B* (0.735). It means that there is a direct relationship between GEP and sustainability, and for every one-unit increase in GEP, sustainability increases by 73.5%.

Table 1.1. Correlations between variables.

		Green entrepreneurship practices	**Sustainability**
Green entrepreneurship practices	Pearson correlation	1	0.863**
	Sig. (2-tailed)		0.000
	N	300	300
Sustainability	Pearson correlation	0.863**	1
	Sig. (2-tailed)	0.000	
	N	300	300

Note: **Correlation is significant at the 0.01 level (2-tailed).

Table 1.2. Model summary-1.

Model	***R***	***R* square**	**Adjusted *R* square**	**Std. error of the estimate**
1	0.735[a]	0.503	0.500	0.760

Note: [a]Predictors: (Constant), social networking sites, and climate innovation.

Table 1.3. Model summary-2.

Model B		Unstandardized coefficients		Standardized coefficients	*T*	Sig.
		B	Std. error	Beta		
1	(Constant)	1.062[a]	0.253		4.203	0.000
	Green entrepreneurship practices	0.687	0.062	0.735	10.997	0.000

Note: [a]Dependent variable: Climate innovation.
Source: Compiled by the authors based on SPSS Version 20.

1.5.2. *Regression 2: Mediation Effect of Innovation on the Relationship Between Green Entrepreneurship Practices and Sustainability*

Referring to Table 1.4, we can note that GEP tends to impact sustainability by 61.3% and that innovation tends to impact sustainability by 32.1% in a positive way.

Referring to Table 1.5, we note that *R* is 87.3%, which increased from Regression 1 (73.5%). This means that innovation mediates the relationship between GEP and sustainability by 13.8%.

Referring to Table 1.6, we can note that GEP scored *P* value (0.00), *T*-test (6.565), and B (0.334); innovation scored *P* value (0.00), *T*-test (7.644), and B (0.596). Thus, innovation tends to mediate the relationship between GEP and Innovation in a positive way.

1.5.3. Political Practice and Green Entrepreneurship/ Technological Eco-Innovation

In the absence of political action, the transition to more sustainable technological regimes is very unlikely to occur, develop, or function. Green entrepreneurship rhetoric interacts with the framework of a sustainable economy and political engagement. As a result of this dynamic relationship, politics directly influence the formulation and execution of this discourse.

Developing regulatory and fiscal tools and incentives (e.g., energy efficiency mandates, market-based instruments) is the first step in promoting and functionalizing this discursive connection (e.g., tax exemptions and reductions, carbon emission trading schemes for green and energy

Table 1.4. Correlations between variables.

		Green entrepreneurship practices	Innovation	Sustainability
Green entrepreneurship practices	Pearson correlation	1	0.831**	0.613**
	Sig. (2-tailed)		0.000	0.000
	N	300	300	300
Innovation	Pearson correlation	0.831**	1	0.321**
	Sig. (2-tailed)	0.000		0.000
	N	300	300	300
Sustainability	Pearson correlation	0.613**	0.321**	1
	Sig. (2-tailed)	0.000	0.000	
	N	300	300	300

Note: **Correlation is significant at the 0.01 level (2-tailed).

Table 1.5. Model summary-1.

Model	*R*	*R* square	Adjusted *R* square	Std. error of the estimate
1	0.873[a]	0.598	0.593	0.708

Note: [a]Predictors: (Constant), social networking sites and climate innovation.

Table 1.6. Model summary-2.

	Model B	Unstandardized coefficients		Standardized coefficients	*T*	Sig.
		B	Std. error	Beta		
1	(Constant)	0.841[a]	0.210		4.016	0.000
	Green entrepreneurship practices	0.453	0.069	0.334	6.565	0.000
	Innovation	0.451	0.059	0.596	7.644	0.000

Note: [a]Dependent variable: Climate innovation.

efficiency technology adoption, etc.). Governments must find the most cost-effective methods to implement policy and regulations to achieve market reform and change in economic behavior. For the creation of new policy instruments, a cost-benefit analysis is necessary.

Many believe that the government has a role in promoting green economic behavior because low-carbon solutions are not always practical. Another way politics influences the development and integration of environmental entrepreneurship is via government involvement. There are many instances of this, such as sponsoring technical eco-innovations, encouraging the use of environmentally-friendly goods, greening ecologically unfriendly industries, and raising conversations about the need to become carbon-neutral in economic operations.

It is possible to mainstream green entrepreneurship via political action, including collecting and preserving essential knowledge and disseminating and educating green business ideas. This issue is currently being extensively studied in Europe; it is becoming increasingly popular in specific fields of study, such as green entrepreneurship and ecological economics. Ecopreneurship is becoming more common in entrepreneurship textbooks and curricula. More and more colleges and universities, including business institutions, are offering courses and units in environmental entrepreneurialism to their students.

1.6. Discussion

The findings of this investigation have a number of practical and theoretical ramifications. Instead of promoting and legitimizing green entrepreneurship, political action should concentrate on actively modifying the socio-technological environment of the economy and institutions in a way that expedites and maintains the discursive hegemony of green entrepreneurship over economic development. Environmental entrepreneurs — especially "visionary champions," "innovative opportunists," and "bioneers" — need to be used to their fullest extent to achieve environmental sustainability.

The creation of effective finance arrangements should be supported to promote green business growth and sustainable technology-based spin-offs from existing institutions. Innovations in renewable energy should be encouraged. To support and mainstream green companies in the long term, policymakers should also focus on financial instruments and tax incentives at the start-up stage. As a result, state-owned and government-funded institutions are compelled by law to adjust their objectives to support firms in the alternative energy industry.

Green firms might benefit from the lending missions of these groups, even if they "may not necessarily require that the funds be deployed to finance positive net present value projects or that loans be returned at market rates." They may also utilize a portion of their profits to achieve political objectives, such as promoting green growth Muo *et al.* (2020, pp. 85–89).

Public (and private) investment for green entrepreneurs in a given country directly impacts the country's capacity for a sustainable economic transformation. European countries have an essential role in enabling and promoting technological eco-innovations. Eco-entrepreneurship and eco-venture can help hasten the transition to a low-carbon, green economy that is in line with European environmental and technology policies that foster eco-innovation.

The experiences of ecopreneurs are critical to the development of policy frameworks because of their knowledge and expertise in ecopreneurship. It is imperative that government support for green entrepreneurship be maintained so that current players are challenged and encouraged to invest in sustainable energy technologies, therefore becoming more environmentally engaged. Political action is crucial to the overthrow of present unsustainable technological systems.

1.7. Research Implications

We hope that our findings will serve as a basis for future studies that examine the relationship between microeconomic innovation (ecoentrepreneurship) and macroeconomic change, as well as the limitations of technology-based green entrepreneurialism when it comes to building green economies historically and epistemologically.

Comparing European governments' financing programs for eco-tech enterprises across countries is another intriguing area of research. For green entrepreneurship and innovation ventures, this information might benefit policymakers and investors. A thorough examination of the long-term feasibility and extent of the use of low-carbon technology is necessary. Instead of concentrating on isolated and small-scale scenarios, it is necessary to conduct empirical studies of green firms and eco-innovations. There are several ways in which the activities of ecopreneurs stem from the interplay between internal and external factors; visionary advocates like ecopreneurs enforce their green values; and unique individuals are molded by external elements.

Further research is required to better understand how green entrepreneurship and a more sustainable economy are linked. Theories and models now in use are based on speculative assumptions rather than empirical evidence, and the existing literature is heavy on conjecture rather than evidence-based research. The link between green entrepreneurship and the sustainable economy must be made relevant to the future of capitalist/economic development via extensive empirical and conceptual work.

We believe that it is necessary to examine how the apparent benefits of low carbon technologies are compared to their actual environmental costs, even before they are widely used, if at all. There are still many unsolved uncertainties concerning the environmental impact of green and energy-efficient technologies.

Green technology is rejected to prevent environmental degradation and the unsustainable use of (material and energy) resources, and energy efficiency technology is related to complicated choices between direct, indirect, systematic, and rebound consequences.

For the sake of a more holistic and strategic approach to climate change, future research should focus on the downsides of low-carbon technology and how to handle them and pave the way for upstream solutions. It is possible to overestimate the beneficial effects of creating innovative and green technologies that are important to a sustainable economy by concentrating just on technology.

References

1. Al-Qudah AA, Al-Okaily M, Alqudah H. The relationship between social entrepreneurship and sustainable development from economic growth perspective: 15 'RCEP' countries. *Journal of Sustainable Finance and Investment*, 2021; 2(192): 44–61. DOI: 10.1080/20430795.2021.1880219
2. Brem A. Linking innovation and entrepreneurship-literature overview and introduction of a process-oriented framework. *International Journal of Entrepreneurship and Innovation Management*, 2011; 14(1): 6–35. DOI: 10.1504/IJEIM.2011.040820
3. Ebrahimi, P. and Mirbargkar, S. M. Green entrepreneurship and green innovation for SME development in market turbulence. *Eurasian Economic Review*, 2017; 7(4).

4. Galindo-Martín MA, Castaño-Martínez MS, Méndez-Picazo MT. The relationship between green innovation, social entrepreneurship, and sustainable development. *Sustainability.* 2020; 12(11): 4467. DOI: 10.3390/su12114467
5. George G, Merrill RK, Schillebeeckx SJD. Digital sustainability and entrepreneurship: How digital innovations are helping tackle climate change and sustainable development. *Entrepreneurship: Theory and Practice*, 2021; 45(5): 999–1027. DOI: 10.1177/1042258719899425
6. Habib MA, Bao Y, Ilmudeen A. The impact of green entrepreneurial orientation, market orientation and green supply chain management practices on sustainable firm performance. *Cogent Business and Management*, 2020; 7(1): 1743616. DOI: 10.1080/23311975.2020.1743616
7. Hussain I, Nazir M, Hashmi SB, di Vaio A, Shaheen I, Waseem MA, Arshad A. Green and sustainable entrepreneurial intentions: A mediation-moderation perspective. *Sustainability*. 2021; 13(15): 8627. DOI: 10.3390/su13158627
8. Méndez-Picazo MT, Galindo-Martín MA, Castaño-Martínez MS. Effects of sociocultural and economic factors on social entrepreneurship and sustainable development. *Journal of Innovation and Knowledge*, 2021; 6(2): 69–77. DOI: 10.1016/j.jik.2020.06.001
9. Mukonza C. An analysis of factors influencing green entrepreneurship activities in South Africa. In: Atewamba C, Yong Ngondjeb D (Eds.) *Inclusive Green Growth.* Cham, Switzerland: Springer Nature; 2020. pp. 47–67. DOI: 10.1007/978-3-030-44180-7_3
10. Muo, I. and Azeez, A. Organisational green behavioural change: The role of change management. *International Journal of Entrepreneurial Knowledge*, 8(1), 34–48, 2020.
11. Passaro R, Scandurra G, Thomas A. The emergence of innovative entrepreneurship: Beyond the intention — Investigating the participants in an academic SUC. *International Journal of Innovation and Technology Management*, 2017; 14(5): 1750025. DOI: 10.1142/S0219877017500250
12. Richard M, Olatunji F, Samuel T. Green entrepreneurship and employment generation in a developing nation: The Nigerian case. *Journal of Humanities, Arts and Social Science,* 2021; 5(1): 81–88. DOI: 10.26855/jhass.2021.01.009
13. Sivash O, Ushakov D, Ermilova, M. Investment process resource provision in the agricultural sector. *IOP Conference Series: Earth and Environmental Science*, 2019; 272(3): 032118. DOI: 10.1088/1755-1315/272/3/032118
14. Ushakov D, Vinichenko M, Frolova E. Environmental capital: A reason for interregional differentiation or a factor of economy stimulation (the case of Russia). *IOP Conference Series: Earth and Environmental Science*, 2019; 272(3): 032111. DOI: 10.1088/1755-1315/272/3/032111

15. Van den Bergh JCJM. Environmental and climate innovation: Limitations, policies and prices. *Technological Forecasting and Social Change*, 2013; 80(1): 11–23. DOI: 10.1016/j.techfore.2012.08.004
16. Wang H, Khan MAS, Anwar F, Shahzad F, Adu D, Murad M. Green innovation practices and its impacts on environmental and organizational performance. *Frontiers in Psychology*, 2021; 11: 553625. DOI: 10.3389/fpsyg.2020.553625

https://doi.org/10.1142/9789811264252_0002

Chapter 2

Social Entrepreneurship and Climate Innovation: The Mediating Effect of Norms and Self-Efficacy

Denis S. Ushakov[*,†,¶], **Elima A. Israilova**[‡,‖], **Daria G. Ivanova**[‡,**] **and Khodor Shatila**[§,††]

[†]*College of Hospitality Industry Management Suan Sunandha Rajabhat University, Bangkok, Thailand*
[‡]*Rostov State University of Economics, Rostov-on-Don, Russia*
[§]*Sagesse University Furn El Chebbak Baabda, Lebanon*
[¶]*fintaliano@yandex.ru*
[‖]*elimarsue@mail.ru*
[**]*ivanova753@yandex.ru*
[††]*info1@iprocares.com*

Abstract: There has been a growing interest in identifying the elements that influence economic success in the wake of impact of a recession. One of the most important goals for policymakers is to ensure that the economy grows steadily, increasing employment and ensuring social welfare. Our research significantly contributes to the field by testing the

[*]Corresponding author.

link between social entrepreneurship and sustainable development from an economic growth viewpoint. The research considers several kinds of entrepreneurship (social and traditional). It also provides a model that examines the contribution of social entrepreneurship to sustainable development using two primary dimensions: embryonic and operational social entrepreneurial activity and operational social entrepreneurial activity that contributes to the achievement of social goals. To achieve the goal of sustainable development, this research incorporates latent factors such as social entrepreneurship, innovation, and institutional features. The findings of this research show that it is critical to build methods that encourage long-term sustainability. In this context, identifying the most critical indicators that directly impact long-term growth will be beneficial. Since sustainable development has become one of the most important goals to satisfy current demands without compromising the value of other goals, the decision-makers should concentrate on inspiring sustainable development.

Keywords: Innovations; Green economy; Social entrepreneurship; Sustainable development; Ecopreneurship.

2.1. Introduction

There has been a growing interest in identifying the elements influencing economic success in the wake of the recession's impact on the economies of nations. One of the most important goals for policymakers is to ensure that the economy grows at a steady pace, increasing employment and social welfare. Many studies, such as [1], have been conducted to identify the variables contributing to economic development, including inventions, human capital, entrepreneurship, etc. Additional nations and more qualitative factors have been included in empirical investigations as statistical knowledge has grown [3,10].

Among the many probable factors, inventions and entrepreneurship have received the most attention in the literature, with institutions playing a role in certain cases.

There is no difficulty in development from the first viewpoint because technical advancement may lead to environmental limits. According to this position, regarding the economic development, prosperity, and success of businesses, innovation plays a major role in encouraging innovation in the production processes of organizations [11,12].

2.1.1. *The Relationship Between Green Innovation, Social Entrepreneurship, and Sustainable Development*

A key purpose of economic policy is to promote economic development, which positively affects job creation and overall well-being. Entrepreneurship and innovation have been shown to play a significant influence in achieving this goal during the last several decades [5]. However, the degradation in environmental quality caused by policies aimed at promoting growth has led to the consideration of alternate goals, such as sustainable development, that are more in line with environmental protection [8].

For this reason, it is critical to identify the conditions eliciting their response. This research examines traditional and social entrepreneurship, innovation, and green innovation. Institutions are thought to impact both forms of entrepreneurship by generating legal and economic settings [9]. Given the bidirectional causality, this study also examines the relationship between the two forms of entrepreneurship and institutions. Using this information, we will be able to craft policies that promote sustainable growth [6].

As a first step, we will look at the connection between forms of entrepreneurship, innovation, sustainable development, and the relationship between social/traditional entrepreneurship and institutions [11]. It is possible to compare the end goal route coefficients in both circumstances, which can be useful for developing economic strategies [1]. Using the partial least squares (PLS) method, an empirical study is conducted on data from 20 member nations of the Organization for Economic Cooperation and Development (OECD) [10].

2.1.2. *Impact of Green Entrepreneurship Orientation on Environmental Performance: The Natural Resource-Based View Perspective*

Several challenges need to be dealt with to ensure the long-term viability and sustainability of environmental entrepreneurship. To maximize the influence of green innovation performance (GIP) on environmental performance, green entrepreneurship orientation (GEO) aims to harmonize their interactions with the external environment (EP). The research explores the impact of the green entrepreneurship approach on GIP and EP using a natural resource-based perspective [13].

Additionally, the influence of Managerial Environmental Concerns (MEC) on this connection is examined. Green Absorbative Capacity (GAC), Environmental Cooperation (EC), and MEC were shown to substantially impact GEO.

According to Wang, Khan, Anwar, Shahzad, Adu, and Murad, GEO positively impacted GIP and EP [14]. Thus, the link between green innovation and EP is mediated in part by GEO, which is GAC, EC, and management problems. The connection between GEO and EP is also moderated by MEC, which is an important factor. Firms with GEO must make sure that their green practices and environmental performance are sufficient to meet the needs of the external environment. The research also discussed the theoretical and practical ramifications of the findings [2].

2.2. Methodology

An empirical data collection tool was used to assess the hypotheses created using a structured questionnaire. An independent variable for social networking sites, "generic evaluative data," is included in the "first section," which begins with demographic information about students.

The second section includes a dependent variable for green entrepreneurial ambition. The relationship between the last three variables was discussed in the third part (self-efficacy, risk propensity, and subjective norm).

There were 300 respondents from Thai, Lebanese, and Russian universities.

To accurately estimate the *C*-coefficient, at least 300 samples have to be utilized in this sample size. A convenience sample was used to choose the study's participants. Researchers can collect as much information as possible from a large number of people quickly and easily when using the convenience sampling approach.

Many studies have used and suggested a minimum sample size of 300 for the computation of structural equation modeling analyses [4,7]. As a result, a sample size of 300 was utilized as the bare minimum in this investigation. Statistical Package for the Social Sciences (SPSS) was used to analyze the data.

To ensure that each set of items can be clearly understood and distinguished from the others, just one variable, among others, has to be considered. An in-depth content validity investigation of the measurement items was carried out by inviting two experts to enhance the material, followed by interviews with four professional experts.

Once everything had been completed and finalized, the input of academic and professional experts was integrated into the survey.

The internal consistency and composite reliability of all variables varied from 0.823 to 0.915, showing a high degree of dependability for all variables. Finally, the survey questions are reworked, and the final version is translated into English as a result. To achieve the research goal, the researchers altered the measurements used in previous studies and applied them to the industry scenario.

A seven-point survey was used to gather the information, which, according to a Likert scale, ranged from 0 (strongly disagree) to 7 (strongly agree).

2.3. Results

2.3.1. *Regression 1: Relationship Between Social Networking Sites and Climate Innovation*

Referring to Table 2.1, we can note that the Pearson coefficient (PE) scored 0.763 between social networking sites (SNS) and climate innovation (CI), which means that every unit increase in SNS increases CI by 76.3%.

Referring to Table 2.2, we can note that this model scored 63.5%, which means that the relationship between SNS and CI is 63.5% and that 36.5% of the variables affecting CI were addressed in this model.

Table 2.1. Correlation between social networking sites and climate innovations.

		Social networking sites	**Climate innovation**
Social networking sites	Pearson correlation	1	0.763**
	Sig. (2-tailed)		0.000
	N	300	300
Climate innovation	Pearson correlation	0.763**	1
	Sig. (2-tailed)	0.000	
	N	300	300

Note: **Correlation is significant at the 0.01 level (2-tailed).

Table 2.2. Model summary-1.

Model	*R*	*R* square	Adjusted *R* square	Std. error of the estimate
1	0.635[a]	0.403	0.400	0.860

Note: [a]Predictors: (Constant), social networking sites and climate innovation.

Table 2.3. Model summary-2.

Model		Unstandardized coefficients		Standardized coefficients		
		B	Std. error	Beta	*T*	Sig.
1	(Constant)	1.062[a]	0.253		4.203	0.000
	Social networking sites	0.687	0.062	0.635	10.997	0.000

Note: [a]Dependent variable: Climate innovation.
Source: Compiled by the authors based on SPSS Version 20.

Referring to Table 2.3, we can note that SNS scored a *P*-Value (0.00), *T*-Test (10.997), and *B* (0.635), which means that there is a direct relationship between SNS and CI, and for every unit increase in SNS, the CI increases by 63.5%.

2.3.2. *Regression 2: Mediation Effect of Norms on the Relationship Between Social Networking Sites and Climate Sustainability*

Referring to the Pearson correlation in Table 2.4, we can note that SNS tends to impact CI by 41.3% and that norms tend to impact CI by 32.1% in a positive way.

Referring to Table 2.5, we can note that *R* is 77.3%, which increased from Regression 1, which was 63.5%. This means that norms mediate the relationship between SNS and CI by 13.8%.

Referring to Table 2.6, we can note that SNS scored *P*-Value (0.00), *T*-Test (3.642), and B (0.234), and Norms scored *P*-Value (0.00), *T*-Test

Table 2.4. Correlations between variables.

		Social networking sites	Norms	Climate sustainability
Social networking sites	Pearson correlation	1	0.631**	0.413**
	Sig. (2-tailed)		0.000	0.000
	N	181	181	181
Norms	Pearson correlation	0.631**	1	0.321**
	Sig. (2-tailed)	0.000		0.000
	N	181	181	181
Climate sustainability	Pearson correlation	0.413**	0.321**	1
	Sig. (2-tailed)	0.000	0.000	
	N	181	181	181

Note: **Correlations significant at 0.01.

Table 2.5. Model summary.

R	*R* Square	Adjusted *R* Square
0.773[a]	0.598	0.593

Note: [a]Predictors: (constant), social networking sites, norms, climate sustainability, and innovation.

Table 2.6. Coefficients.

	Model	Unstandardized coefficients		Standardized coefficients		
		B	Std. Error	Beta	*T*	Sig.
1	(Constant)	0.841	0.210		4.016	0.000
	Social networking sites	0.253	0.069	0.234	3.642	0.000
	Norms	0.551	0.059	0.596	9.270	0.000

(9.270), and B (0.596). Thus, norms tend to mediate the relationship between SNS and CI in a positive way.

2.3.3. *Regression 3: Mediation Effect of Self-Efficacy on the Relationship Between Social Network Sites and Climate Sustainability*

Referring to the Pearson correlation in Table 2.7, we can note that SNS tends to impact CI by 63.1% and that self-efficacy tends to impact CI by 32.3% in a positive way.

Referring to Table 2.8 and the above tables, we can note that R increased from 63.5 in Regression 1 to 78.6% in Regression 3. Since R in this regression is higher than R in Regression 2 (77.3%), self-efficacy tends to have a higher mediation effect on the relationship between SNS and CI.

Referring to Table 2.9, we can note that SNS scored P-Value (0.00), T (3.578), and B (0.225), and self-efficacy scored P-Value (0.002) and T (3.112), and B (0.153). It can be noted that self-efficacy mediates the relationship between SNS and CI.

Table 2.7. Correlations between variables.

		Social network sites	**Self-efficacy**	**Climate innovation**
Social network sites	Pearson correlation	1	0.631**	0.416**
	Sig. (2-tailed)		0.000	0.000
	N	181	181	181
Self-efficacy	Pearson correlation	0.631**	1	0.323**
	Sig. (2-tailed)	0.000		0.000
	N	181	181	181
Climate innovation	Pearson correlation	0.416**	0.323**	1
	Sig. (2-tailed)	0.000	0.000	
	N	181	181	181

Note: **Correlations significant at 0.01.

Table 2.8. Model summary.

Model	***R***	***R* Square**
1	0.786[a]	0.618

Note: [a]Predictors: (constant), social networking sites, norms, climate sustainability, and innovation.

Table 2.9. Coefficients.

		Unstandardized coefficients		**Standardized coefficients**		
	Model	***B***	**Std. error**	**Beta**	***T***	**Sig.**
1	(Constant)	0.594	0.219		2.709	0.007
	Social network sites	0.243	0.068	0.225	3.578	0.000
	Self-efficacy	0.136	0.044	0.153	3.112	0.002

2.4. Discussion

Our research significantly contributes to the field by testing the link between social entrepreneurship and sustainable development from the viewpoint of economic growth. The research considers several kinds of entrepreneurship (social and traditional). It also provides a model that examines the contribution of social entrepreneurship to sustainable development using two primary dimensions: embryonic and operational social entrepreneurial activity and operational social entrepreneurial activity that contributes to the achievement of social goals. To achieve the goal of sustainable development, this research incorporates latent factors such as social entrepreneurship, innovation, and institutional features.

According to the findings of this research, it is critical to build methods that encourage long-term sustainability. In this context, identifying the most critical indicators that have a direct impact on long-term growth will be beneficial. Since sustainable development has become one of the most important goals to satisfy current demands without compromising the value of other goals, the decision-makers should concentrate on inspiring sustainable development.

Two key variables should be considered while writing about entrepreneurship: social and conventional entrepreneurship. The research demonstrated a favorable correlation between social entrepreneurship and sustainable development after considering the validity and reliability of all measurements employed in the study model. In this situation, the assessment was also conducted to identify the impact of innovation on sustainable development as a second key element.

The research also discovered that institutions had a beneficial indirect influence on creativity. The research found that socio-cognitive qualities and entrepreneurship in the context of the moderating influence of economic institutions positively impact sustainable development. Research on social entrepreneurship has traditionally focused on the individual and the pro-social motivations of social entrepreneurs. However, newer studies have moved away from this emphasis and instead focused on the collaborative dynamics of this field.

As a result of this research, the emphasis on social entrepreneurship as an alternative to conventional economic growth will be increased. Furthermore, it is essential to consider the right methods for sustainable development, particularly those connected to social entrepreneurship.

To achieve the main goal of sustainable development, the researchers recommend considering some actions that stimulate entrepreneurs, such as tax advantages that can be introduced to those entrepreneurs for motivating them to establish more useful projects and thus obtain financing in a better way, which further supports economic growth.

Banks, governments, and other financial institutions may be more willing to work with them if they take this step, making it easier for them to borrow money or form a partnership to get it. On the other hand, market dimensions and all information related to these dimensions are important for entrepreneurs. The role of entrepreneurs as a means for small and medium-sized enterprises (SMEs) to access international markets can be promoted by entrepreneurs' focus on sustainable development. Institutional arrangements are a key consideration for entrepreneurs, and they should be considered. Governments may decide to encourage sustainable development by fostering innovative SMEs worldwide.

Our major goal was to investigate five concepts: social networking sites, green entrepreneurial goals, risk propensity, subjective norm, and self-efficacy, all of which are related to the global green wave. According to several studies, the green entrepreneurial purpose is directly linked to the use of Facebook.

Green business innovations are also favorably influenced by the mediating factors (risk propensity and self-efficacy). Although many studies have failed to show a significant link between self-efficacy and green entrepreneurship intention, this is not the case here. There is no significant relationship between self-efficacy and green entrepreneurship intention because of the moderating variable (subjective norm).

As a result, the link between self-efficacy and subjective norms remains unaffected. The link between self-efficacy and green entrepreneurship intention weakens as the subjective norm rises. There is a strong connection between students' green entrepreneurship goals and their self-efficacy and risk propensity through social networking sites. Students' appreciation and influence on green businesses were shown to have a positive impact on their success.

2.5. Conclusion

Furthermore, the study found that university students are interested in squeezing the green theory if they participate in commercial speculations. Green entrepreneurship became more enticing to them because of their self-efficacy and risk-taking proclivities. Students believe that green entrepreneurial businesses are more effective because of the present changes in climate and the environment. University students also rely on the practical approach and context of the green entrepreneurial company. With the help of the government and private sector, Lebanon is spreading the green message to potential company owners. As a result, students are confident that starting a green firm will not be difficult. Green firms are a viable business model because of their commitment to growth and extensive knowledge in the area.

Environmental issues have been included in studies of variables that contribute to a country's success because of the country's difficult environmental state. Since the aim of social welfare may be achieved without harming future generations, sustainable development has taken precedence over the conventional economic growth goal. This includes identifying the variables that have an impact on achieving the stated goal to craft policies that encourage such long-term growth. Entrepreneurship and innovation are two aspects that have been considered in this research.

There has also been a shift in the way people think about environmental and sustainability issues as a result of economic development, as has been the case with economic growth. Consequently, we may see social entrepreneurship alongside conventional entrepreneurs that are interested in sustainable development because of the opportunities it provides to distinguish their goods and build a positive reputation among stakeholders.

2.6. Limitations

Due to the tiny sample size, any extrapolation of the conclusions of this study should be done with extreme caution. A preliminary study into green entrepreneurship is presented to examine the most important aspects that affect it.

Thus, new elements that may influence green entrepreneurship may be studied. Let us consider the absence of environmental awareness in the country's enterprises and governmental policies, as well as strategic planning. Aside from other points, the need for environmental education must be highlighted. According to the conclusions of this research, entrepreneurs should be encouraged to become more conscious of environmental issues through participating in the media, education, and colleges. As a result, funding for environmentally friendly initiatives must be given the top priority at the national level; research into environmentally friendly and sustainable goods and processes must be given financial assistance.

Innovations in general and green innovation have been examined when it comes to new ideas. They have been investigated in this example to see how they affect the defined goal and both forms of entrepreneurship. Innovations may have a good influence on a goal; in this situation, the impact of green innovation is less significant. Another aspect to consider is that social entrepreneurs have less influence on green innovation than regular ones, while entrepreneurs have a comparable, although slightly larger, impact on both.

As a consequence of these findings, the design of policies to foster sustainable development should concentrate on social entrepreneurship. There are three broad categories of acts that might be considered in this context. The first group is concerned with money. For social entrepreneurs, this means that they will be able to access conventional funding sources from banks via public sector guarantees given by credit institutions.

Certain tax benefits may be introduced to encourage the use of alternative sources of financing (e.g., crowdsourcing, business angels, etc.).

Efforts to make it easier for entrepreneurs to reach markets are taken, such as giving advice services and knowledge about market niches. The last set of measures comprises those that have to do with the law. Furthermore, to develop an appropriate legal and budgetary framework for social entrepreneurship, it is necessary to define the scope of social entrepreneurship's activities. There should be an emphasis on cultivating a culture of social enterprise in the school system, which would help young people integrate into the social economy.

Social entrepreneurs might benefit from creating platforms and institutions that allow them to share their experiences, access private markets, and increase the exposure of their work. Finally, education may be used to increase one's commercial acumen.

However, since the estimated findings reveal the biggest path coefficient for conventional entrepreneurship, institutions play an essential influence in this regard. As a result, the third set of suggested measures — improving the rule of law and regulatory quality — should be put in place to raise the incidence of social entrepreneurship. It was revealed that both forms of entrepreneurship had a comparable path coefficient in terms of sustainable development, although the social entrepreneurship model had a slightly higher path coefficient.

This tells us that businesspeople of this sort are more likely to take advantage of the possibilities offered by the variable in question. Conventional entrepreneurs have a significantly higher influence on institutions than social entrepreneurs.

This suggests that conventional entrepreneurship has a stronger impact on the institutional environment than social entrepreneurship. Introducing the steps mentioned above to encourage this kind of social entrepreneurship would be less likely if the opposite were true, which would leave an opportunity to support sustainable development better via social entrepreneurship underutilized. In terms of the study's shortcomings, the most significant one is the sheer volume of data analyzed. Many more factors might be considered in addition to those that have already been mentioned in the literature.

These financial factors may have shown how much importance the availability of financing had on the two forms of entrepreneurship. The study's findings would reveal whether or not the suggested financial measures to encourage social entrepreneurship should be put into action. The government's R&D policies and how they have influenced each form of entrepreneurship might also be included in this discussion. As a matter of fact, the structural disparities across nations might be considered while designing policy in light of these conditions. Expanding the sample size would need the availability of data on social entrepreneurship in other countries.

2.7. Implications

The findings of this research shed light on many influences on green business ambitions. Government and business leaders may utilize the data to set standards to encourage green business practices on social media platforms, which will benefit the whole community. To instill green entrepreneurial aspirations in the next generation, city planners should utilize social media to spread awareness about the proper usage of social media. Understanding the methodology employed and offered in this research is critical to a better understanding of the linkages investigated here and their implications for business leaders. Greening SNS, the study's primary goal, may assist produce outstanding entrepreneurs, economic growth, and a better neighborhood.

References

1. Al-Qudah AA, Al-Okaily M, Alqudah H. The relationship between social entrepreneurship and sustainable development from economic growth perspective: 15 'RCEP' countries. *Journal of Sustainable Finance and Investment*, 2021; 2(192): 44–61. DOI: 10.1080/20430795.2021.1880219
2. Brem A. Linking innovation and entrepreneurship-literature overview and introduction of a process-oriented framework. *International Journal of Entrepreneurship and Innovation Management*, 2011; 14(1): 6–35. DOI: 10.1504/IJEIM.2011.040820
3. Faucher A. Linking innovation and entrepreneurship-literature overview and introduction of a process-oriented framework. *International Journal of Entrepreneurship and Innovation Management*, 2011; 14(1): 6–35. DOI: 10.1504/IJEIM.2011.040820
4. Galindo-Martín MA, Castaño-Martínez MS, Méndez-Picazo MT. The relationship between green innovation, social entrepreneurship, and sustainable development. *Sustainability*, 2020; 12(11): 4467. DOI: 10.3390/su12114467
5. George G, Merrill RK, Schillebeeckx SJD. Digital sustainability and entrepreneurship: How digital innovations are helping tackle climate change and sustainable development. *Entrepreneurship: Theory and Practice*, 2021; 45(5): 999–1027. 10.1177/1042258719899425

6. Habib MA, Bao Y, Ilmudeen A. The impact of green entrepreneurial orientation, market orientation and green supply chain management practices on sustainable firm performance. *Cogent Business and Management*, 2020; 7(1): 1743616. DOI: 10.1080/23311975.2020.1743616
7. Hussain I, Nazir M, Hashmi SB, di Vaio A, Shaheen I, Waseem MA, *et al.* Green and sustainable entrepreneurial intentions: A mediation-moderation perspective. *Sustainability*, 2021; 13(15): 8627. DOI: 10.3390/su13158627
8. Méndez-Picazo MT, Galindo-Martín MA, Castaño-Martínez MS. Effects of sociocultural and economic factors on social entrepreneurship and sustainable development. *Journal of Innovation and Knowledge*, 2021; 6(2): 69–77. DOI: 10.1016/j.jik.2020.06.001
9. Mukonza C. An analysis of factors influencing green entrepreneurship activities in South Africa. In: Atewamba C, Yong Ngondjeb D (Eds.) *Inclusive Green Growth.* Cham, Switzerland: Springer Nature; 2020, pp. 47–67. DOI: 10.1007/978-3-030-44180-7_3
10. Passaro R, Scandurra G, Thomas A. The emergence of innovative entrepreneurship: Beyond the intention — Investigating the participants in an academic SUC. *International Journal of Innovation and Technology Management*, 2017; 14(5): 1750025. DOI: 10.1142/S0219877017500250
11. Sivash O, Ushakov D, Ermilova M. Investment process resource provision in the agricultural sector. *IOP Conference Series: Earth and Environmental Science*, 2019; 272(3): 032118. DOI: 10.1088/1755-1315/272/3/032118
12. Ushakov D, Vinichenko M, Frolova E. Environmental capital: A reason for interregional differentiation or a factor of economy stimulation (the case of Russia). *IOP Conference Series: Earth and Environmental Science*, 2019; 272(3): 032111. DOI: 10.1088/1755-1315/272/3/032111
13. Van den Bergh JCJM. Environmental and climate innovation: Limitations, policies and prices. *Technological Forecasting and Social Change*, 2013; 80(1): 11–23. DOI: 10.1016/j.techfore.2012.08.004
14. Wang H, Khan MAS, Anwar F, Shahzad F, Adu D, Murad M. Green innovation practices and its impacts on environmental and organizational performance. *Frontiers in Psychology*, 2021; 11: 553625. DOI: 10.3389/fpsyg.2020.553625

https://doi.org/10.1142/9789811264252_0003

Chapter 3

Sequestration Industry in the Climate Innovation Development Framework: A Cluster Approach

Sergey G. Tyaglov[*,†,§], **Margarita A. Skvortsova**[†,¶], **Tatyana V. Miroshnichenko**[‡,||] **and Pavel A. Degtyarev**[†,‡,**]

[†]*Rostov State University of Economics, Rostov-on-Don, Russia*
[‡]*Sochi Institute (Branch) of the Peoples' Friendship, University of Russia, Sochi, Russia*
[§]*tyaglov-sg@rambler.ru*
[¶]*skvortsovamargarita1988@mail.ru*
[||]*shuruhina.tv@rudn-sochi.ru*
[**]*economfak@rudn-sochi.ru*

Abstract: The chapter focuses on the issues of the sequestration industry's development. The authors consider the prerequisites for the formation of this industry within the framework of the international environmental and economic agenda, including the study of the impact of the carbon tax on the export policy of Russia and the EU member countries. The chapter proposes the fundamental mechanisms and tools to reduce the negative impact of carbon-intensive industries on environmental systems and the financial losses of market participants from the

[*]Corresponding author.

introduction of additional environmental taxes and fees. Based on the analysis of the best practices of foreign countries, the authors propose a concept for the formation and development of the sequestration industry in Russia, determine the timing of the implementation of the main activities, and indicate the economic effects of the introduction of new green approaches to the scientific and technical policy of Russia.

Keywords: Sequestration industry; Carbon polygon; Carbon farm; Green socio-economic cluster.

3.1. Introduction

Global warming has been on the world community's agenda over the years. In Russia, the average rate of warming is 2.5 times higher than in the rest of the world. To combat global warming, countries have set targets and implemented measures that potentially lead to a reduction in carbon-intensive Russian exports and discrimination against carbon-intensive products in world markets. In the context of external challenges of transboundary carbon regulation, it is necessary to envisage and implement measures to support domestic manufacturing companies and exporters of carbon-intensive products, providing the creation of effective tools to reduce the carbon emissions footprint of companies. This chapter aims to identify possible measures aimed at supporting Russian companies in the context of introducing the cross-border carbon mechanism of the EU.

The stated topic is based on its presentation within the framework of theoretical and methodological provisions on sustainable development, the green economy, the cluster concept, and multidisciplinary research on the climate agenda outlined in the works of Russian and foreign scientific schools and scientists. Carbon polygons and carbon farms were chosen as the research object as elements of the sequestration industry system that can advance the solution of the climate agenda through the implementation of innovations. We analyzed the results of expert assessments to calculate the potential level of return on investments made in activities aimed at reducing the carbon footprint of manufactured products. The use of analytical methods and research techniques (analysis, generalization, induction, deduction, and a systemic approach) allowed substantiating the author's point of view and the algorithm for developing the sequestration industry in Russia. The systematization of knowledge on the introduction of carbon taxes and fees by the EU in relation to Russian products based on the size of the so-called carbon footprint has been carried out. The risks and losses that may be incurred by enterprises specializing in the export of products have been assessed. Additionally, we defined the sectors of the economy that are most likely to suffer from the introduction of this regulation. We also outlined the main ways to overcome such risks and determined the role and importance of carbon polygons in the system of the sequestration industry. The key mechanisms for creating and operating carbon farms as green socio-economic clusters are proposed.

Based on the research, we proposed a model for the development of the sequestration industry in Russia by forming socio-economic clusters based on scientific institutions — i.e., carbon polygons — by attracting private investment in the creation of carbon farms, which allows ensuring economic effects from investments in research and development carried out at polygons. The calculation of earning capacity from such green projects was carried out in relation to private companies specializing in the export of carbon-intensive products to European countries and the Russian economy. The research materials can be used and considered in the work of government officials and members of the business community to minimize the losses caused by the transboundary carbon tax and ensure the socio-economic development of territories suitable for carbon polygons and farms.

3.2. Methods

The methodological basis of this research includes general and special scientific methods, such as comparison, analogy, synthesis, analysis, induction, deduction, and the integrative method. Applying a system-structural analysis, we investigated the structural elements of the sequestration industry system developed in the USA. Using the analogy method, we provided recommendations for forming green socio-economic clusters in Russia.

Based on information obtained from open sources, a study was made of various regulatory policy instruments to reduce CO_2 emissions. Despite their diversity, it is possible to form the following main models using the methods of analysis and synthesis.

The first model is associated with the formation and regulation by the state of the market for the circulation of emission quotas for CO_2 emissions. This model is used in the USA and China.

The second model is the introduction of a special carbon tax, as is used by the EU and some Asian countries [11].

What they have in common is that they are mechanisms of state policy that are introduced "from above" and mandatory for business entities.

Additionally, we can single out one more model, which is initiated by the economic environment independently and operates based on the economic efficiency of companies. This model is called voluntary carbon offsetting. It represents an offset on a voluntary basis for reducing emissions based on implementing sectoral investment projects. An example is a reduction in the use of chemical fertilizers by agricultural producers or the transition of industrial production to alternative energy sources to reduce greenhouse gas emissions into the environment.

Participation in such schemes is attractive for companies for several reasons. First, it increases the attractiveness of the enterprise in the eyes of investors. Second, it provides the possibility of obtaining extra profit by strengthening its position in certain regional sales markets.

The described model is widely applied in the field of forestry and land use.

For the purposes of this research, we analyzed open sources containing information on the structure of greenhouse gas emissions by sectors in Russia, which allows us to conclude that it has remained relatively stable over the past decades, while most of the emissions traditionally come from the energy sector. The results of the analysis are presented in Table 3.1.

To form a list of industries most exposed to economic risks from the introduction of a cross-border carbon tax, information was collected and systematized on the volume of greenhouse gas emissions in Russia, depending on the sector of the economy (Table 3.2).

Thus, the economic effect of the introduction of the carbon tax proposed by the EU can affect almost half of the export flow of Russian products to Europe.

The greatest damage will be caused to the oil and gas sector, the metallurgical and coal industries, and agriculture. According to BCG experts, adopting the baseline scenario for introducing a carbon tax of $30 per ton of greenhouse gas emissions, the amount of losses could be about $1.5–2.4 billion annually for oil and gas enterprises, $0.3 billion annually for companies exporting non-ferrous metals, and $0.7 billion for ferrous metallurgy and coal industry. KPMG experts estimated the losses from the introduction of this tax at €33 billion in total for 2025–2030 [21].

Table 3.1. Ranking of countries by CO_2 emissions in 2020 (top 10).

No.	Country	Volume of emissions, mln. tons per year	Share in total emissions, %
1	China	9899.3	30.7
2	USA	4457.2	13.8
3	India	2302.3	7.1
4	Russian Federation	1482.2	4.6
5	Japan	1027.0	3.2
6	Iran	678.2	2.1
7	Germany	604.9	1.9
8	Republic of Korea	577.8	1.8
9	Saudi Arabia	570.8	1.8
10	Indonesia	545.4	1.7

Source: Compiled by authors based on Statistical Review of World Energy 2021 [4].

Table 3.2. Greenhouse gas emissions in the Russian Federation by industries (fields).

		Volume of emissions, bln. tons				Share, %	
No.	Industry	1990	2000	2010	2019	1990	2019
1	Energy	2.6	1.5	1.7	1.8	80.6	78.9
2	Production and manufacturing	0.3	0.2	0.2	0.2	8.9	11.0
3	Agriculture	0.3	0.1	0.1	0.1	8.7	5.7
4	Wastes	0.1	0.1	0.1	0.1	1.9	4.4
	Total	3.3	1.9	2.1	2.2	100.0	100.0

Source: Compiled by the authors based on the Bulletin on current trends in the Russian economy [1].

3.3. Results

The EU has been at the forefront of the international climate agenda for decades. Simultaneously, the period of the most active actions in this area falls in recent years. Earlier, everything was limited to framework conventions and agreements (e.g., the Paris Climate Agreement, the purpose of which was to keep the growth of the average temperature of the planet [34]). Nowadays, the EU moved to specific measures to combat greenhouse gas emissions posing a threat to climate [36]. Having set an ambitious goal to achieve carbon neutrality of the EU countries by 2050 as part of the European Green Deal [32] strategy, the European Commission intends to introduce a cross-border carbon regulation mechanism (Carbon Border Adjustment Mechanism) [10]. This mechanism involves introducing additional fees on goods imported into the territory of the EU member states from countries with a lower level of climate regulation. This assumes the calculation of the carbon footprint along the entire value chain of imported products.

Considering that the basis of Russia's economy is the export of hydrocarbon raw materials (about a third of all Russian exports go to the EU), as well as goods created on its basis, such a measure will inevitably lead to multi-billion losses for the most prominent Russian companies, the upcoming cross-border tax may affect 42% of the total export flow from Russia to Europe.

The situation is aggravated by the fact that, in addition to European countries, the USA and China also announced plans to achieve carbon neutrality [9]. Moreover, the largest investment funds and investors, as well as insurance companies, intend to withdraw their assets from oil, coal, and gas projects [28]. Control over carbon emissions is tightened even in the field of civil aviation.

The above circumstances can cause serious damage to certain large Russian corporations and endanger the stability of the Russian economy. In the future, manufacturers of metallurgical, petrochemical, and cement products, as well as the producers of agricultural goods, will face the need to pay a high border carbon fee in the European market and in the markets of countries that are partners of the EU.

Considering the latest trends in world practice, one of the most promising and effective methods of fighting climate change is the so-called decarbonization of the economy. On one hand, the essence of this technique is to reduce the carbon footprint, which is inherent in one way or another in almost all goods, products, or services. The main goal of this approach is to reduce greenhouse gas emissions into the atmosphere and thereby reduce its temperature. On the other hand, decarbonization also implies a set of technologies that reduce the concentration of greenhouse gases by extracting already emitted substances from the atmosphere, which will also slow down the process of heating the planet.

In this regard, the issue of developing a comprehensive program aimed at the decarbonization of industry in Russia becomes relevant.

When developing it, one should consider the huge potential of Russia to reduce greenhouse gas emissions and increase their absorption at the expense of another natural resource — Russian forests and agricultural land. The first step in implementing a comprehensive program should be the formation of an institutional framework, its regulatory consolidation, and methodological support. The second stage should envisage specific measures to monetize the implementation of projects.

The analysis of scientific publications on the issues considered in this research shows that the issues of the sequestration industry are extremely poorly covered in the domestic literature. Simultaneously, related aspects of the considered issues are widely represented; there are a fairly large number of works devoted to the development of the "green economy," sustainable development based on the best available technologies, organizing interaction between scientific institutions and organizations of the real sector of the economy on the principles of public-private partnership, which allows forming a sufficient theoretical and methodological basis for further study of the issue.

For example, the issues of implementing environmental projects at industrial enterprises to ensure the sustainable development of the territories of Kuzbass were the subject of research by Shevchuk *et al.* [31].

Mechanisms for the transformation of regional strategies according to an innovation-oriented scenario, models of formation and development in the regions of the post-industrial and green economy, tools for modernizing the regional economy based on energy-efficient, and the best available technologies are widely covered in the scientific works of Potravny [29], Lipina [37], Tyaglov and Kunetsov [23].

The effectiveness of interaction between scientific institutions and industrial enterprises and its role in preventing and minimizing the negative impact of economic activity on the environment, and the modernization and improvement of energy efficiency of the Russian economy, as well as certain regions, are considered in the works of such scientists as Burkin [7], Saulin [30], Medvedev *et al.* [25], Fiofanov [13], Klimenko [20], Bogatyrev *et al.* [3], Avdeeva *et al.* [2], Budovich and Startseva [5].

The theoretical developments outlined in the above works can be used as the basis for decisions included in the comprehensive program of decarbonization of the Russian economy. Additionally, we should also consider the experience of those countries that have already begun to work in this area: conducting deals with emission quotas in the USA and China, introducing carbon taxes in Asia and Europe [8]. Moreover, a variety of international emission control systems based on sectoral principles are developing at an accelerated pace (e.g., the Corsia system in the field of aviation), as well as voluntary offsetting systems for reducing emissions and voluntary carbon offsetting.

The sequestration industry involves the creation or use of facilities that absorb carbon dioxide from the atmosphere. Recently, projects in the field of forestry and land use have become increasingly popular. Thus, the owners of land plots covered with plants capable of absorbing large amounts of carbon dioxide and other greenhouse gases could be included in the system of circulation of emission quotas [24]. In the practice of foreign countries, the certification procedure for farms is already being applied. According to the results of this procedure, the farm is assigned the status of a participant in the quota trading system, which gives the right to sell compensatory quotas that exempt importers from paying a carbon tax.

As for the essence of such quotas, they correspond formally to securities, with face value calculated in CO_2 utilized (tons) [33]. The mechanism for the circulation of emission quotas on the market consists in determining the upper threshold for greenhouse gas emissions at the state level with the subsequent issuance of emission permits to enterprises. If an enterprise in the course of its production activities exceeds the limit specified for it in the permit, the enterprise may purchase additional volume from the state or other participants in the emission quota market. In both cases, the greater the volume of additional emissions, the higher the company's costs.

An example is the European Emissions Trading System (ETS), which is currently one of the leaders in this market, covering about 40% of CO_2 emissions. The cost of emissions allowances in this trading system indicated a significant increase: starting from 20 euros per ton of CO_2 in the period before the COVID-19 pandemic to 50 euros for the current year. According to some experts, the cost of one ton of CO_2 could reach at least 100 euros by 2030. According to various estimates, the total volume of the international carbon trading market is about $100 billion [14]. Accordingly, if the forecasted cost of 100 euros per ton is reached by 2030 and the total volume of the world market proportionally increases, the carbon industry has every chance of becoming one of the leading industries in the global economy.

Along with the institution of the market for the circulation of emission quotas, we highlight a mechanism for the tax regulation of enterprises whose activities are associated with greenhouse gas emissions into the atmosphere. The carbon tax acts as a kind of climate regulator, the essence of which is to establish a certain fee at the state level based on one unit of emissions [16].

It should be noted that trading in emission quotas has become more widespread in world practice compared to the use of a carbon tax. Simultaneously, for several reasons, it is impossible to unequivocally assert that it is more effective.

One of the advantages of the system of trading in quotas is the establishment of restrictions — the maximum volume of emissions for enterprises, which allows for forming a forecast of the volume of emissions. However, the price of permits is set in accordance with the law of demand and is subject to fluctuations depending on market conditions. The instability in prices for quotas reduces the ability of enterprises to predict their costs and, as a result, reduces the investment activity of companies. From this point of view, a carbon tax is more predictable and provides enterprises with the ability to accurately calculate the cost of paying it based on a known tax rate.

The carbon market is currently going through a growth stage and may, in the near future, become quite a serious competitor to the oil and gas markets, which have repeatedly experienced serious crises over the past ten years [22,23].

In this situation, the development of carbon farming, the demand for which in international markets is now in the growth stage, is of particular interest. This issue was investigated by specialists from Texas A&M University, who determined the profitability of forest owners and farmers in the case of the implementation of environmentally sound land management practices in their activities.

While conceptually supporting international environmental trends and principles for many years, Russia has not taken active steps in this direction until recently. The introduction of a carbon tax by the European Union threatens the already unstable markets for hydrocarbon fuels.

The first step in the current environmental agenda should be obtaining objective information on the state of greenhouse gas emissions in Russia; such information must be verified and recognized by international control systems. This information can be obtained from specially created carbonic polygons, which represent a part of the territory of the forest zone with a unique ecosystem, or agricultural land or sea area, where scientists are developing and testing technologies that allow for remote or ground-based monitoring of greenhouse gas emissions, including CO_2, as well as monitoring other factors influencing climate change, including using the artificial intelligence [15].

Carbon polygons provide measurement and calculation of emission and absorption of carbon dioxide. The technologies used at carbon polygons allow identifying industries or areas with the longest and most dangerous carbon footprint. Moreover, as a result of constant observations, they can provide information on the dynamics of the deterioration or improvement of climate safety in a particular industry or a settlement.

The first carbon polygon in Russia was created in the Kaluga Region, within the borders of the Ugra National Park on the territory of agricultural purposes with an area of about 600 hectares. In 2020, the Voronezh State University of Forestry and Technologies, named after G. F. Morozov, also received financial support from the Ministry of Education and Science of the Russian Federation to create an engineering center specializing in the implementation of projects to reduce harmful emissions from enterprises in the industrial sector. Financing is aimed at creating a carbon polygon and a carbon farm, which will ensure the implementation of the results of the research into economic activities.

In 2021 at the site of the St. Petersburg International Economic Forum, an agreement was signed on cooperation between the Tyumen State University, the Tyumen Region, and PJSC SIBUR Holding to create a carbon station for monitoring climate-active gases.

In total, within the framework of a pilot project approved by the Russian Ministry of Education and Science, it is planned to create carbon polygons in seven regions of the Russian Federation in the near future: the Chechen Republic, Krasnodar Territory, Novosibirsk Region, Kaliningrad Region, Sverdlovsk Region, Tyumen Region, and Sakhalin Region. The creation of carbon polygons will be carried out by universities with the active support of federal and regional authorities, scientific institutions, and commercial structures.

As we can see, the creation of carbon polygons in Russia follows the already well-known path of public–private partnership by combining the efforts of the government, educational or scientific institutions, and business. A similar approach is used to create world-class scientific and educational centers [6].

In the foreseeable future, the number of carbon polygons should increase by at least 50. Their creation is of great importance for scientific research and developing a green economy in Russia.

Currently, not only representatives of government agencies and the scientific community But also oil and gas industry enterprises have begun to show considerable interest in climate projects in Russia. For example, Sibur and Gazpromneft entered into a joint project with the West Siberian Research and Education Center as industrial partners. Additionally, Sibur, following the sustainable development strategy until 2025, supported the project to create a carbon station in the Voronezh Region.

The establishment of such partnerships in the direction of the environmental agenda leads to the following conclusions:

(1) Large Russian companies are consciously moving from the model of aggressive consumption of natural resources to the model of forming a green economy, including by reducing the anthropogenic impact on the climate.
(2) Businesses perceive the project to decarbonize the economy as a certain market opportunity. In this regard, it is worth dwelling in more detail on the issue of carbon farms, which, unlike polygons, are not exclusively scientific projects but are more commercial in nature.

Thus, the creation of carbon farms can be proposed as the next step in developing the sequestration industry. Their purpose is to organize the absorption of carbon dioxide on an industrial scale through natural ecological systems (e.g., forests) or artificially created plantations of specially selected plant varieties. Agricultural lands can also be used as carbon farms, where, through the use of special agricultural technologies, the processes of cultivating agricultural crops for subsequent processing and marketing are combined with the processes of conservation of atmospheric carbon in the soil [27].

In practice, carbon farms work out technologies developed at carbon polygons, considering the specifics of the area and the difference in latitudes and types of ecosystems.

Thus, being an inherently commercial project, farms provide cost-effectiveness for the costs invested in scientific research conducted at carbon polygons.

It can be said with confidence that the sequestration industry is one of the promising areas of development for Russia for several decades to come [12]. This is primarily due to the fact that Russia has vast territories suitable for carbon farms and carbon polygons.

It should be noted that carbon farms do not have to be located in close proximity to carbon polygons. To launch such projects, optimize the staffing of employees, and reduce transport costs, they can be placed on the same territory. However, in the future, in the case of successful development of the sequestration industry, proximity is not necessary.

New carbon farms are opened worldwide every year. However, the sequestration industry has just begun to form as an independent industry. For this reason, Russia has every chance to become a world leader in this field by placing carbon farms throughout its territory.

It is necessary to create an integrated network of carbon polygons, which could provide the functions of points of attraction and coordination of carbon farms and enterprises of the sequestration industry.

Considering the carbon polygons already created and planned to be created in the near future, as well as the most favorable factors for locating new objects in the sequestration industry, it is proposed to create a network of carbon farms on the territory of Russia (Table 3.3).

The creation of carbon farms or plantations within the territories indicated in Table 3.3 will increase carbon dioxide absorption by at least two times. The easiest and most effective way to create a carbon farm is to grow trees. Considering the geographical features of Russia, the creation of a network of carbon farms in the format of forest complexes is possible almost throughout its entire territory [18].

The main goal of carbon farms is to make a profit. The scientific and expert community is actively engaged in assessing the potential total profit of Russian producers from participation in projects related to the implementation of activities aimed at absorbing CO_2. If the sequestration policy is effectively implemented, Russia has every chance of becoming a world leader in projects aimed at reducing greenhouse gas emissions into the atmosphere and annually receiving at least $50 billion in additional income.

The study “Battle for the climate: carbon farming as Russia’s stake” considers the creation of carbon farms as an effective and profitable way to form CO_2 emission reduction units. According to calculations made by the RSPP, the income of the Russian Federation from CO_2 trading could be compared with the value of hydrocarbon exports [19].

The profitability of a carbon farm is directly proportional to its size because the larger its territory, the more carbon dioxide will be absorbed, and, accordingly, more emission quotas could be realized. Simultaneously, a vast territory requires more care, more maintenance costs, increased

Table 3.3. Subjects of the Russian Federation that are the most favorable for the placement of carbon farms, considering the type of creation.

No.	Region	Company	Industry	Carbon farm type
1	Kaliningrad Region	Lukoil-Kaliningradmorneft (LLC)	Hydrocarbon production	Water complex, peat bog
2	Moscow Region	Zagorsk Pipe Plant	Metallurgy	Forest complex
3	Krasnodar Region	Neftegazindustriya, Slavyansk Eco, Neftebitum-KGNK, RN-Tuapse Refinery	Oil refining	Water complex
4	Sverdlovsk Region	SinTZ, Kiberstal	Metallurgy	Forest complex
5	Tyumen Region	Surgutneftegaz, Gazprom	Oil and gas industry	Forest complex
6	Novosibirsk Region	Industrial Group "MAIR," Novosibirsk Metallurgical Plant, Novosibirsk Plant of Chemical Concentrates	Metallurgy, chemical industry	Forest complex
7	Sakhalin Region	Sakhalin Oil Company, Sakhalin Energy, Boshnyakovsky coal mine	Oil and gas industry, coal mining industry	Water complex
8	Voronezh Region	Voronezhsintezkauchuk, Voronezh Tire Plant	Chemical industry	Agricultural complex
9	Republic of Tatarstan	Special economic zone of industrial-production type Alabuga	Mechanical engineering	Agricultural complex
10	Chechen Republic	Chechenneftekhimprom, Grozneftegaz	Oil and gas industry	Agricultural complex
11	Republic of Bashkortostan	ANK Bashneft, Salavatnefteorgsintez, Selena-Neftekhim	Petrochemical industry	Forest complex, Agricultural complex

(*Continued*)

Table 3.3. (*Continued*)

No.	Region	Company	Industry	Carbon farm type
12	Khanty-Mansi Autonomous District – Yugra	Lukoil, Magma Oil Company, RN-Yuganskneftegaz	Oil and gas industry	Forest complex
13	Yamalo-Nenets Autonomous Area	Gazprom, Novatek	Oil and gas industry	Forest complex
14	Tomsk Region	Tomskneft, Sibur	Oil production	Forest complex
15	Leningrad Region	Tverskoy excavator	Mechanical engineering	Forest complex
16	Tver Region	Tver Carriage Works, Pozhtekhnika		Forest complex
17	Kursk Region	Mikhailovsky GOK, Kurskrezinotekhnika, Khimvolokno, Kurskoblnefteprodukt	Metallurgy, petrochemical industry	Forest complex
18	Tambov Region	Roskhimzashchita, Kotovsky paint and varnish factory	Chemical industry	Agricultural complex
19	Rostov Region	Southern Coal Company, Taganrog Metallurgical Plant, Aluminum Metallurg Rus	Coal mining industry, Metallurgy	Agricultural complex
20	Ulyanovsk Region	Metallokonstruktsiya, Ulyanovsknefteprodukt	Metallurgy, oil industry	Forest complex
21	Chuvash Republic	Khimprom	Chemical industry	Forest complex
22	Altai Territory	Altai-koks, Barnaultransmash, Sibenergomash	Coal mining industry, mechanical engineering	Forest complex
23	Kemerovo Region	Evraz (Iron and Steel Works)	Metallurgy	Forest complex

Table 3.3. (*Continued*)

No.	Region	Company	Industry	Carbon farm type
24	Krasnoyarsk Region	Achinsk Oil Refinery, Krasnoyarsk Biochemical Plant, Kansk Bioethanol	Oil industry, chemical industry	Forest complex
25	Primorye Territory	Spasskcement, Terekhovsky Concrete Products Plant	Chemical industry	Agricultural complex, Water complex

Source: Compiled by the authors based on data retrieved from the Ministry of Science and Higher Education of the Russian Federation [26].

staff salaries, and more equipment used to cultivate the territory. Additionally, it is required to constantly carry out fire prevention measures, control pests and diseases, plant new varieties of plants and tree species, and carry out other agrotechnical measures. In fact, it is not too different from the maintenance of a conventional farm or forestry. Managing a carbon farm also requires certain qualifications and an effective investment policy.

Nowadays, there are large-scale plans in Russia only for the creation of carbon polygons. There are currently practically no carbon farms, and the procedure for their creation is also not fixed in the legislation. However, it is possible to offer variants of territories for their placement already now. The most optimal region for this is the European-Ural region of Russia. The carbon dioxide absorption capacity of the forests in this area is about two tons of CO_2 per one hectare per year.

As mentioned above, "canned" carbon dioxide has a certain price in the emission allowance market.

The quota implementation mechanism is as follows. First, when creating a carbon farm, one needs to calculate and confirm the amount of CO_2 it absorbs. Next, such a farm could receive carbon status and start selling quotas or carbon credits to those enterprises that need to increase their ecological status.

The organization of the absorption of one ton of carbon dioxide at a carbon farm costs 5 euros, and its market value is about 15 euros.

Simultaneously, the average fine in Europe is about 30 euros per ton. Accordingly, such a business offer could be attractive.

Carbon farms are already operating in the USA and Australia. Thus, as part of a partnership agreement between the US Department of Agriculture and Chevrolet, the latter purchased about 40,000 quotas from several dozen pasture owners who will use no-till technologies on their farms.

The implementation of this mechanism in Russia is impossible until the definition of the legal status of the carbon farm, the procedure for its certification, the status of emission allowances, which, in fact, is a type of securities, the order of their circulation in the market, and the mechanism of exemption of enterprises from environmental taxes and fees.

According to Russian scientists from the Chelyabinsk State University and the Russian Academy of Sciences, the total volume of CO_2 absorption in Russia from forest areas alone could amount to about 250 million tons annually. According to the Organization for Economic Cooperation and Development (OECD), the fee for one ton of CO_2 emissions is at least 30 euros.

Thus, subject to the appropriate status, forests located on the territory of Russia can bring about 7.5 billion euros in income. Simultaneously, improving the quality of management of these territories will double the profitability and ensure the prosperity of carbon farms created in such territories.

The state policy of Russia considers current trends. The Government of the Russian Federation issued a decree approving a list of initiatives for socio-economic development until 2030, which includes, among other things, a project on low-carbon development policy, the responsible executor of which is the Ministry of Economic Development of Russia.

This strategy aims to achieve carbon neutrality while ensuring sustainable growth of the Russian economy.

The strategy includes measures aimed at stimulating the use of secondary energy resources; supporting the introduction and dissemination of new low-carbon and carbon-free technologies (including the capture, use, and utilization of carbon dioxide); making changes to customs, tax, and budget policies; developing green investment mechanisms and measures; and contributing to an increase in the absorptive capacity of ecosystems, including forests.

Moreover, starting from 2023, it is planned to introduce a mandatory carbon reporting system for enterprises.

It is assumed that the above measures can ensure the growth of the Russian economy and reduce CO_2 emissions by 60% by 2050, achieving full carbon neutrality by 2060.

To implement the strategy, the Government of the Russian Federation has already prepared draft regulations to limit greenhouse gas emissions and introduce low-carbon or green certificates meeting international standards.

Sakhalin has launched a pilot project to introduce a system for trading with quotas. The first transaction using the mechanism for trading emission quotas is expected to be completed in the middle of 2022.

Simultaneously, as long as there is no unified state system for measuring and evaluating greenhouse gas emissions in Russia, the EU has the opportunity to calculate the carbon footprint of products manufactured in Russia in maximum values. Currently, the rules for organizing and conducting monitoring of atmospheric air quality are valid only in 12 cities of Russia on an experimental basis.

Assessing the possible risks of introducing a carbon border tax by the EU, businesses also take additional measures to reduce the carbon footprint in products and increase investment in low-carbon and energy-saving technologies.

Tatneft has been taking measures to reduce greenhouse gas emissions since 2019. It has even joined the international project Science Based Targets initiative. The company's ambitious plans include achieving 100% carbon neutrality by 2050 (i.e., 10 years earlier than the national indicator). Gazprom and Severstal are also among the Russian companies pursuing energy efficiency and energy-saving policy within the framework of the environmental management system.

However, the above measures are of a private nature and cannot be considered as elements of the climate regulation regime system until a unified all-Russian standard for accounting for greenhouse gas emissions is introduced. Accordingly, the key direction of the state policy in the field of the green economy should be the course toward introducing a standardization system for accounting for greenhouse gas emissions.

The implementation of the described set of measures will allow ensuring that the value of Russian exports under the EU carbon tax will exceed 300 billion rubles by 2025 and attract more than 600 billion rubles of private investment in the implementation of green projects in the Russian economy.

An accompanying task that ensures the effective implementation and high-quality implementation of state policy in this area is the training of personnel for the sequestration industry that is emerging in Russia, including ensuring the functioning of the environmental monitoring system. Without this, the transition of the economy to a green course will be challenging. During the development of the sequestration industry, new professions and specialties related to the environmental agenda and the use of innovative technologies in biology, ecology, and nature management may appear. Accordingly, a transformation of the personnel training system will be required, which can be ensured only if the efforts of educational and scientific institutions, businesses, and the government are combined.

3.4. Discussion

The cluster approach to organizing the economic space of territories based on the principles of public–private partnership has proved its effectiveness in creating world-class scientific and educational centers, industrial clusters, and technology parks. By compact placement of cluster members within the same territory, this approach allows creating conditions for the concentration of resources and reducing transaction costs [36]. While in the classical sense, costs are often understood as the logistics costs associated with the delivery of raw materials to the place of further processing, production, and delivery of finished products to points of sale, as well as the costs associated with transactions between market participants, in current conditions, the costs of reducing environmental damage to the territory where a large industrial production is located should inevitably be attributed to the costs of producers.

Accordingly, the formation of carbon polygons and carbon farms is most appropriate in those areas where there are large enterprises of coal mining, metallurgical, oil and gas, and chemical industries.

In this regard, Russia already has all factors to successfully pursue a sequestration policy based on the cluster approach and the public–private partnership mechanism. An analysis of the location of large industrial enterprises related to the above industries, presented in Table 3.3, showed that most of them are already located on the territories adjacent to agricultural land, as well as within the forest and water complexes.

Accordingly, it is necessary to develop the model for forming the sequestration industry cluster and mechanisms for the interaction of its participants with each other, state bodies, and organizations at the federal and regional levels. The model of creation and functioning of the sequestration industry cluster can be represented as follows.

The following residents must represent the mandatory membership of the sequestration industry cluster:

(1) Scientific or educational institutions, on the basis of which the carbon polygon is formed;
(2) Large industrial enterprises of the region from among the companies most interested in the development of the sequestration industry, which, as a rule, belong to those industries that have the greatest negative impact on the environment, whose activities are associated with a significant amount of greenhouse gas emissions;
(3) A carbon farm created based on the principles and mechanisms of public–private partnership, which is engaged in the emission and trading of carbon quotas.

The role of the carbon polygon in this model is to calculate the carbon footprint of an industrial enterprise and the absorptive capacity of the carbon farm. Since the carbon polygon is a scientific institution, in this scheme, it is entrusted with the functions of developing an environmental agenda for the functioning of other members of the cluster.

The specifics of Russian legislation are such that territories suitable for carbon farms (e.g., forest lands and water bodies) cannot, as a rule, be transferred to private ownership. Thus, it is extremely important to note the role of the public sector in this scheme. As a measure necessary for the successful implementation of the project to create carbon farms and clusters of the sequestration industry, it is necessary to secure their special status in the legislation and a separate procedure for transferring state-owned territories for carbon farms.

Being the main source of environmental pollution, the enterprise is interested not so much in reducing the carbon footprint but in reducing the cost of paying environmental taxes and fees and increasing profits from the sale of its products. Thus, it can act as an investor in creating a carbon farm with the possibility of acquiring further emission quotas for this farm, which will significantly reduce the company's tax expenses. Subject to the introduction by the state of certain benefits and support measures for enterprises investing in the creation of carbon farms, their interest and investment in such projects could be increased.

3.5. Conclusion

The study of the prerequisites and conditions for developing the sequestration industry as a factor in the formation of green socio-economic clusters has led to the following conclusions.

The creation of green socio-economic clusters in the format of carbon farms in Russia follows the current trends of the international environmental agenda.

The threat of introducing a carbon tax leads Russia to the need to apply new mechanisms for accounting and evaluating the carbon footprint of Russian products and to search for and implement new solutions in the activities of companies exporting hydrocarbon raw materials and metallurgical products.

The creation of carbon polygons and farms will reduce the losses of Russian companies and improve the quality of ecosystems.

The authors propose a model for developing the sequestration industry in Russia through the formation of socio-economic clusters based on scientific institutions — i.e., carbon polygons — by attracting private investment in the creation of carbon farms, which will ensure the profitability of investments in research and development carried out at polygons.

The materials of this research could be used and considered in the work of public authorities and the activities of large Russian companies to minimize the losses caused by the cross-border carbon tax introduced by the EU.

The results presented in this research contain practical recommendations and allow us to outline key stages in studying the issue of creating green socio-economic clusters in forest areas and agricultural lands suitable for carbon polygons and farms.

References

1. Analytical Center for the Government of the Russian Federation. Ecology and Economics: The trend towards decarbonization. *Bulletin on Current Trends in the Russian Economy*. 2020; 66. Available from: https://ac.gov.ru/uploads/2-Publications/BRE/_October_web.pdf
2. Avdeeva IL, Golovina TA, Parakhina LV, Babich OV, Levin AM, Bushueva LI, *et al*. Public administration in the context of digital globalization. Orel, Russia; 2020.

3. Bogatyrev AV, Bubnova OY, Mironov NA, Elfimov OM. Economic security as a set of characteristics of the financial and economic activity of an enterprise (organization). *Economics: Yesterday, Today, Tomorrow*, 2020; 10(5A): 36–44.
4. British Petroleum. Statistical review of world energy. 70th ed. 2021. Available from: https://www.bp.com/content/dam/bp/business-sites/en/global/corporate/pdfs/energy-economics/statistical-review/bp-stats-review-2021-full-report.pdf
5. Budovich LS, Startseva YV. *St. Petersburg Innovative Economy: A Textbook*. St. Petersburg, Russia: Skifiya-print; 2020.
6. Burima LY. National market for greenhouse gas emissions as one of the country low-carbon development. *Bulletin of the Kama Social Institute*, 2020; 3(87): 84–94.
7. Burkin TA. Research and production cooperation as a factor of economic security. In: Ashmarina SI, Pavlova AV (Eds). *Actual Aspects of the Development of Modern Science*. Samara, Russia: Samara State University of Economics; 2019. pp. 31–34.
8. Chaturvedi RK, Raghubanshi AS, Singh JS. Carbon density and accumulation in woody species of tropical dry forest in India. *Forest Ecology and Management*, 2011; 262(8): 1576–1588. DOI: 10.1016/j.foreco.2011.07.006
9. Luo H, Sinha A, Sengupta T, Ghosh V. Carbon tax and energy innovation at crossroads of carbon neutrality: Designing a sustainable decarbonization policy. *Journal of Environmental Management*, 2021; 294: 112957.
10. Climate Analytics and New Climate Institute. Paris Agreement turning point. Wave of net zero targets reduces warming estimate to 2.1 °C in 2100. 2020. Available from: https://newclimate.org/wp-content/uploads/2020/12/CAT_2020-12-01_Briefing_GlobalUpdate_Paris5Years_Dec2020.pdf
11. Dang HP, Cheng JM, Rahimah A, Lin JYC, Truong-Dinh BQ, Glebanov PD, *et al*. What makes consumers willing to pay for carbon taxes–a view of terror management theory. *Sustainable Production and Consumption*, 2021; 28: 1192–1203. DOI: 10.1016/j.spc.2021.07.033
12. Ermakova EP. The development of the legal framework for “green” finance in Russia, the EU and China: A comparative legal analysis. *RUDN Journal of Law*, 2020; 24(2): 335–352. DOI: 10.22363/2313-2337-2020-24-2-335-352
13. Fiofanov OA. System of professional qualifications in the field of science. *Economics of Science*, 2019; 5(3): 185–196. DOI: 10.22394/2410-132X-2019-5-3-185-196
14. Galanina IA. Emission trading system as a tool for economic regulation of environmental management. *Bulletin of the Pacific State University*, 2021; 2(61): 195–202.
15. Ganieva IA, Koteev SV. Economic aspects of maintaining the carbon balance in agri-food systems in the production of products of the agro-industrial

complex. *Economics of Agriculture in Russia*, 2021; 8: 33–35. DOI: 10.32651/218-33

16. Gessen SM, Vorotnikov AM. Carbon polygons – a new scientific and educational project for the Arctic. *Arktika 2035: Topical Issues, Problems, Solutions*, 2021; 2(6): 98–104. DOI: 10.51823/74670_2021_2_98
17. Grushevenko E, Kapitonov S, Melnikov Y, Perdero A, Sheveleva N, Siginevich D. Decarbonization of the oil and gas industry: international experience and Russian priorities. Moscow, Russia: Energy Center of Moscow School of Management “Skolkovo”; 2021. Available from: https://energy.skolkovo.ru/downloads/documents/SEneC/Research/SKOLKOVO_EneC_Decarbonization_of_oil_and_gas_EN_22032021.pdf
18. Ivanov AY, Durmanov ND, Orlov MP, Piksendeev KV, Rovnov YE, Luksha PO, *et al*. The battle for climate: Carbon farming as a stake in Russia. Moscow, Russia: HSE University; 2021. Available from: https://tinyurl.com/mrx5ae97 (accessed on 01/10/2021).
19. Ivanova AY, Durmanova ND (Eds.) Battle for the climate: Carbon farming as Russia’s stake. Moscow, Russia: HSE University; 2021. Available from: https://ild.hse.ru/data/2021/05/26/1438213521/Битва%20за%20климат-карбоновое%20земледелие%20как%20ставка%20России.pdf
20. Klimenko TI. Assessment of the state of the field of industrial services in the Russian economy. *Management of Sustainable Development*, 2020; 2(27): 20–25.
21. KPMG. South Africa: Regulations implementing carbon tax. 2020 June 26. Available from: https://home.kpmg/us/en/home/insights/2020/06/tnf-south-africa-regulations-implementing-carbon-tax.html
22. Kuznetsov NG, Tyaglov SG, Ponomareva MA, Rodionova ND. Role of the best available technologies to develop the region’s innovative potential. *Economics and Management: Theory and Practice*, 2020; 6(3): 59–64.
23. Kuznetsov NG, Tyaglov SG, Ponomareva MA, Rodionova ND. The alternative energetics development as an important component of regional innovation systems in the context of the best available technologies implementation. *International Journal of Economic Policy in Emerging Economies*, 2020, 13(6): 648–662
24. Makeev YA. China’s greenhouse gas emissions trading and prospects for creating a global carbon market. *Bulletin of the Institute of Oriental Studies of the Russian Academy of Sciences*, 2021; 3(17); 67–74.
25. Medvedev VV, Pospekhov DV, Alyaev YV. The role of state scientific centers of the Russian Federation in the implementation of the national project “Science.” *Proceedings of the Institute of Engineering Physics*, 2019; 4(54): 124–127.
26. Ministry of Science and Higher Education of the Russian Federation. Carbon polygons. Available from: https://minobrnauki.gov.ru/action/poligony/

27. Morkovina SS, Panyavina EA, Shanin II, Avdeeva IA. Economic aspects of the organization of carbon farms on forest site. *Actual Directions of Scientific Research of the XXI Century: Theory and Practice*, 2021; 9(1): 17–25. DOI: 10.34220/2308-8877-2021-9-1-17-25
28. Pauwelyn J, Kleimann D. Trade related aspects of a carbon border adjustment mechanism. A legal assessment. Brussels, Belgium: European Parliament; 2020. DOI: 10.2861/095035
29. Potravny IM. Innovative approaches to the development of a green economy on the example of arctic settlements. *Ostrovskie Chteniya*, 2020; 1: 125–129.
30. Saulin AD. Innovative scientific and technical centers as a form of innovative territorial cluster. In: Krayukhina GA, Bagiev GL (Eds.) Management of innovation and investment processes and changes in the digital economy. *Proceedings of the II International Scientific and Practical Conference*. St. Petersburg, Russia: St. Petersburg State University of Economics; 2019, pp. 249–258.
31. Shevchuk AV, Panov AA, Efimov VI, Mekush GE. Strategic priorities of the environmental development of Kuzbass for the period until 2035. *Economics of Industry*, 2020; 13(3): 348–356. DOI: 10.17073/2072-1633-2020-3-348-356
32. Simionescu M, Păuna CB, Diaconescu T. Renewable energy and economic performance in the context of the European green deal. *Energies*, 2020; 13(23): 6440. DOI: 10.3390/en13236440
33. Stepanov IA, Galimova KZ. The price of carbon: theory and practice of regulation of greenhouse gas emissions. *Bulletin of Moscow University*, Series 6: Economy. 2021; 4: 95–116.
34. Tyaglov S, Sheveleva, A, Guseva T. Justification of the need and feasibility of switching to renewable energy sources for the implementation of sustainable development principles. *IOP Conference Series: Earth and Environmental Science*, 2019; 317(1): 012004. DOI: 10.1088/1755-1315/317/1/012004
35. Tyaglov SG, Sheveleva, AV, Shurukhina, TV, Guseva TB. Model for forming the interregional cluster of the alternative energy. *International Journal of Energy Economics and Policy*, 2019; 9(3): 373–378. DOI: 10.32479/ijeep.7958
36. Wirth AD. Global governance on climate change The Paris Agreement: A new component of the UN climate regime. *Bulletin of International Organizations: Education, Science, New Economy*, 2018; 12(4): 185–214. Available from: https://iorj.hse.ru/data/2018/01/15/1160391559/D.A.%20Wirth.pdf
37. Zaikov KS, Kondratov NA, Lipina SA, Bocharova LK. Organizational mechanisms for implementing Russia's Arctic strategy in the 21st century. *Arctic and North*, 2020; 39: 75–109. DOI: 10.37482/issn2221-2698.2020.39.75

https://doi.org/10.1142/9789811264252_0004

Chapter 4

Directions and Tools for Implementing the Principles of Sustainable Development in Russia

Sergey M. Nikonorov[*,†,¶], Konstantin V. Papenov[†,‖], Sergey G. Tyaglov[‡,] and Anastasia V. Sheveleva[§,††]**

[†]*Lomonosov Moscow State University, Moscow, Russia*
[‡]*Rostov State University of Economics, Rostov-on-Don, Russia*
[§]*MGIMO University, Moscow, Russia*
[¶]*nico.73@mail.ru*
[‖]*papenov-kv@yandex.ru*
[**]*tyaglov-sg@rambler.ru*
[††]*a_sheveleva@rambler.ru*

Abstract: The chapter analyzes the main directions and tools for implementing the principles of sustainable development in Russia. The aggravation of environmental and social problems, especially in the last two decades, has led to the actualization of the concept of sustainable development. At the present stage, almost all countries have already included sustainable development goals in their strategies and have achieved certain results in their implementation. According to the University of Cambridge Sustainability Report, in 2021, Finland, Sweden, and Denmark were the most effective in this area. In this

[*]Corresponding author.

rating, which includes 165 countries, Russia took only 46th place. In this regard, this chapter focuses on studying the tools introduced and planned for introduction in the near future to implement the principles of sustainable development in Russia. As a result, the authors proved that the priority areas for implementing the principles of sustainable development in Russia are reducing the negative impact on the environment and achieving carbon neutrality. The best available technologies and the environmental tax can become key tools in implementing these areas. The implementation of these areas and the use of the selected tools will allow Russia to make progress in achieving sustainable development goals and enter at least the top 20 leading countries in this direction.

Keywords: Concept of sustainable development; UN sustainable development goals; Decarbonization; Best available technologies; Environmental tax; Russia's carbon neutrality.

4.1. Introduction

The sustainable development mechanism is one of the priority areas for many Russian and international companies when developing business promotion strategies. Sustainable development implies a concept primarily focused on environmental protection, considering certain social aspects.

In the context of the global climate crisis, sustainability indicators have come to the fore: the ability of a company to accept new challenges and adequately respond to them becomes a considerable competitive advantage in these conditions; the inability to adapt a business to new challenges can be fatal.

Issues related to the development of the concept of sustainable development and the implementation of the UN Sustainable Development Goals (SDGs) are presented in the works of many specialists [4,8,9,15,20,21,23,24,30,37].

General aspects of the implementation of sustainable development goals in Russia are also discussed in many works [5,10,11,13,14,17,19, 31–33,36].

The tools for implementing the principles of sustainable development in Russia are considered in the works of a smaller number of authors [3,6,7,12,16,26–28,34]. However, the above works are devoted to a single tool, and a comprehensive analysis was not carried out, confirming the relevance and novelty of this research.

The research novelty also lies in the following. First, a critical analysis of the tools introduced and planned for introduction in the near future for implementing the principles of sustainable development in Russia was carried out, and their advantages and disadvantages were identified. Second, key directions for implementing the principles of sustainable development in Russia are proposed.

The research hypothesis is that the analysis of the directions and tools for implementing the principles of sustainable development in Russia is necessary to achieve carbon neutrality and improve the efficiency of companies.

The chapter aims to analyze the main directions and tools for implementing the principles of sustainable development in Russia, which will allow identifying the most priority and providing mutual benefit to the state and business. The research objectives are as follows:

- To substantiate the need to implement the UN sustainable development goals;
- To show what decarbonization activities and the main indicators for the implementation of its achievement are planned in Russia;
- To identify the tools that can help implement decarbonization.

4.2. Methods

To accomplish the tasks set in the introduction, a systemic approach was applied, allowing us to consider several diverse elements previously studied separately. Thus, the research was made of areas and tools that should ensure the implementation of the principles of sustainable development in Russia in the future.

The methods of generalization and synthesis of the obtained data allowed the authors to make the main conclusions.

4.3. Results and Discussion

The main directions for implementing the principles of sustainable development in Russia are laid down in the Strategy for the Social and Economic Development of Russia with a Low Level of Greenhouse Gas Emissions until 2050. This strategy assumes two scenarios — inertial and target (intensive) [1]. The target scenario is taken as a basis.

As a result, in the target scenario, annual economic growth rates remain above the world average until 2050 (up to 3% per year).

The implementation of the target scenario will require investments in reducing greenhouse gas emissions in the amount of about 1% of GDP in 2022–2030 and up to 1.5–2% of GDP in 2031–2050.

The measures envisaged by the target (intensive) scenario provide a reduction in gross emissions by 910 million tons of carbon dioxide equivalent by 2050 compared to the volume of emissions in the absence of such measures. The increase in absorption by 2050 provides an additional effect of up to 665 million tons of carbon dioxide equivalent.

Simultaneously, in the inertial scenario, emissions grow by 8% by 2030 and by 25% by 2050, with the absorptive capacity of forests unchanged, where the carbon intensity of the Russian economy will exceed the global average by 2050, and carbon neutrality will not be achieved.

The Strategy defines decarbonization measures and the main indicators for implementing its achievement.

Under the target scenario, it will be possible to grow the economy while reducing greenhouse gas emissions: by 2050, by 60% of the 2019 level, and by 80% of the 1990 level. Further implementation of this scenario will allow Russia to achieve carbon neutrality by 2060.

The following are envisaged as the main indicators of the implementation of the strategy:

- Volumes of total and sectoral greenhouse gas emissions;
- Volume and efficiency of energy production; indicators of energy efficiency in sectors of the economy;
- Indicators characterizing the carbon intensity of the economy;
- Indicators of the involvement of industries and government agencies in the implementation of the strategy;
- The volume and specific efficiency of investments in reducing greenhouse gas emissions and increasing absorption capacity (Table 4.1).

To achieve these indicators, it is planned to develop and apply the following instruments to Russian companies:

(1) Best Available Techniques (BAT);
(2) Environmental tax.

Table 4.1. Indicators of mass emissions and removals of greenhouse gases, mln. tons eq. CO_2.

Name of indicator	**Fact 2019**	**Plan 2030**	**Plan 2050**
Inertial scenario			
Greenhouse gas emissions	2119	2253	2521
Takeovers	–535	–535	–535
Net emissions	1584	1718	1986
Intensive scenario			
Greenhouse gas emissions	2119	2212	1830
Takeovers	–535	–539	–1200
Net emissions	1584	1673	630

Source: Compiled by the authors based on Ref. [1].

The BAT reform is a program for the modernization of industry through an influx of investments in its technological re-equipment under the threat of a multiple increase in environmental payments.

Thus, back in July 2014, the Federal Law "On amendments to the Federal law 'On Environmental Protection' and Certain Legislative Acts of the Russian Federation" was adopted. It revealed the concept of BAT and defined the categories of companies that should first of all switch to them, as well as the order and scope of their application [2].

In 2018, a separate Federal project "Introduction of the best available technologies" appeared in the national project "Ecology" with a deadline of December 21, 2024. However, it was frozen in the summer of 2020 due to the anti-crisis budget sequestration and then curtailed.

By the end of 2021, 51 BAT reference books have been developed.

By the end of 2022, the main polluters must obtain a minimum of 300 integrated environmental permits (IEPs), confirming that companies are doing everything they can to reduce emissions and discharges.

The preparation of an application for an IEP includes the following:

- Inventory of emission sources, calculation of standards for permissible emissions and discharges for substances of I and II hazard classes, technological standards, as well as standards of waste generation and limits on their disposal;

- Program for improving environmental efficiency and a draft program for industrial environmental control approved by the interdepartmental commission;
- A program for creating an automatic control system and a program for monitoring the state and pollution of the environment in the territories of waste disposal sites.

In Russia, the expert community is actively raising and discussing the issue of introducing an environmental tax. This tax will not increase the overall tax burden but will contribute to its redistribution within society and reduce environmental damage to nature.

Experts note that the introduction of an environmental tax is necessary to financially support the activities of the Government of the Russian Federation in the direction of greening the regions and provide conditions on the territory of the country for the implementation of the constitutional right of citizens to a favorable environment. Simultaneously, the state environmental policy does not provide a compromise solution to problems between the state and business. Compensatory payments by businesses for the negative impact on ecosystems established by the state are not comparable with the country's costs for financing programs for the protection and restoration of the environment. For example, in 2020, companies' environmental payments to the budget amounted to 382.8 billion rubles, while government spending on implementing the environmental protection program amounted to 68.7 billion rubles, i.e., almost 5.5 times less.

Thus, it is necessary to develop such a "theory of implementation" of economic mechanisms, which, on the one hand, will provide the state with financial resources for the implementation of state environmental programs and, on the other hand, will arouse business interest in creating effective environmentally balanced behavior when investing in environmental technologies.

Simultaneously, it is necessary to minimize the level of costs associated with the greening of territories and form a symmetrical relationship between government and business while reducing the level of technogenic pressure on the ecosystem. To reduce the economic damage from environmental pollution, it is necessary to improve microeconomic indicators (environmental costs of the enterprise, namely, adjusting profits when calculating the amount of the company's environmental obligations to compensate for environmental damage). Such actions will "translate" economic damage into internal costs of the company, reflecting directly on their business activities and stimulating the implementation of the best available technologies.

In today's conditions, it is possible to propose a model of green partnership as an effective mechanism. It will achieve a balanced relationship between government and business in the context of environmental protection (Figure 4.1).

The optimal level of environmental responsibility of business will be achieved at the intersection of the curves of interests of business and government at point A, when the level of environmental payments is higher than companies are willing to pay. It will become an incentive for companies to invest in modernizing technologies that reduce the anthropogenic impact on the environment. As a result, the corporate social responsibility of businesses will increase.

An incentive for Russian companies to actively implement the principles of sustainable development may be the introduction of a carbon tax by the EU countries — a fee for importing goods into the EU, the production of which is associated with considerable CO_2 emissions. In this case,

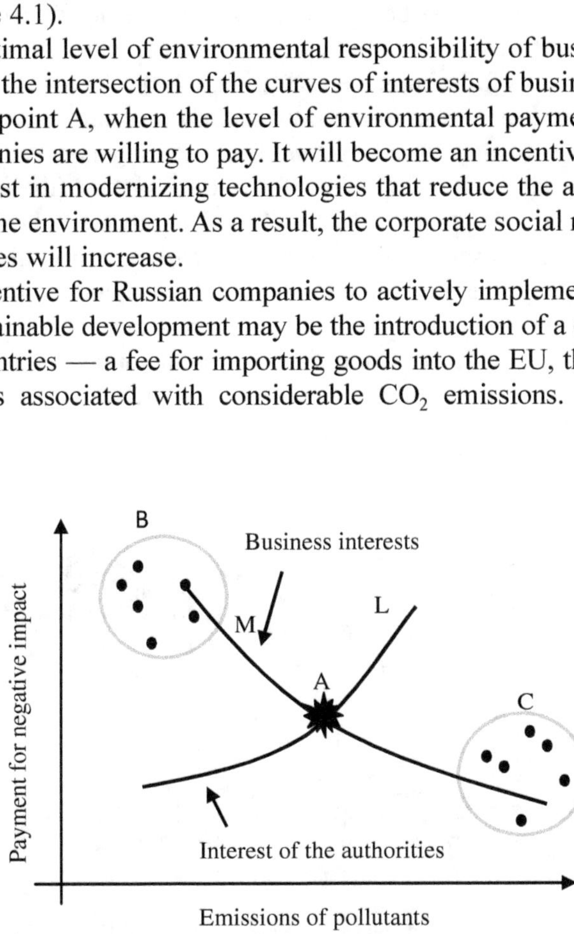

Fig. 4.1. Model of a green partnership between the state and business.

Notes: Curve L and point B — the area of interest of the authorities — compensation for environmental damage is much higher than harmful emissions; Curve M and point C — business interests — minimization of environmental costs with a significant amount of pollutant emissions; Point A — the balance of interests of business and government.

Source: Compiled by the authors based on Ref. [12].

importers of goods to the EU will buy special certificates and exchange them for the right to import carbon-intensive products. According to the project of the European Commission, the direct obligation to pay the tax will lie not on Russian residents but on companies importing relevant products into the EU, including traders. The EU carbon tax will primarily affect suppliers of fuel and energy resources, ferrous and non-ferrous metals, and fertilizers from Russia, which, when the tax begins to be levied at 100%, will pay more than 1 billion euros per year, and 24 billion euros by 2050 when the cross-border regulation project is fully implemented (Figure 4.2).

The response of Russia to the introduction of a carbon tax should be the introduction of a national system for assessing and accounting for carbon emissions, the development of a pricing system (the introduction of an internal environmental tax, which was mentioned above), and the introduction of concessional financing for decarbonization in the form of green financing or a return of the tariff, which was paid as internal tax.

As a reaction to the introduction of a carbon tax, Russian companies should form their own decarbonization system aimed at assessing the carbon intensity of their activities, systematically accounting for emissions in dynamics, developing a circular economy, and eliminating

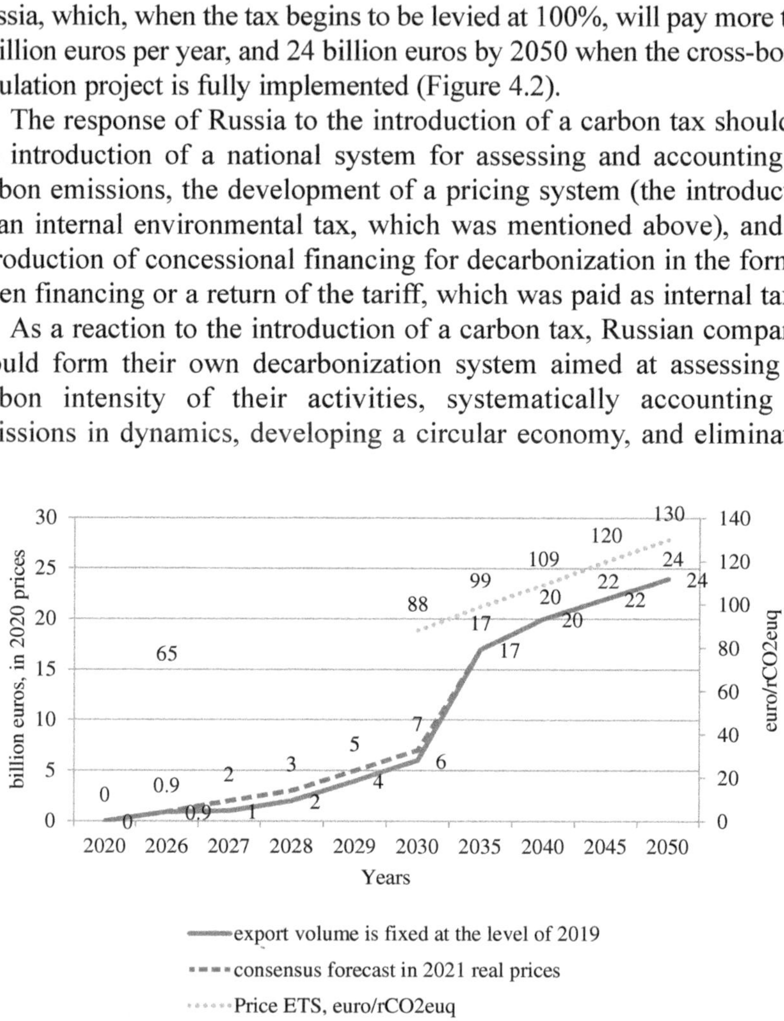

Fig. 4.2. Estimation of possible payments for cross-border carbon regulation for Russian export products to the EU, billion euros, in 2020 prices.

Source: Compiled by the authors based on Ref. [22].

emissions and replacing raw materials with less carbon-intensive ones. In this regard, companies should develop a clear decarbonization program and assign responsibility for its implementation; otherwise, they may suffer big losses.

Companies wishing to create and implement a more environmentally, socially, and commercially sustainable structure must have a complete package of necessary documentation and instructions. For this purpose, environmental, social, and governance criteria are applied, which together form the ESG strategy.

In this context, it should be noted that the idea of sustainable development and the ESG criteria are sometimes used as synonymous constructs. However, these are not identical concepts. Sustainability is a broader concept that does not consider any specific criteria or actions. At the same time, the ESG strategy is seen as a practical and comprehensive framework for building a sustainable business focused on meeting the needs and demands of stakeholders to increase the investment attractiveness of enterprises. Achieving sustainability is defined as the end goal and the ESG criteria as a plan of action and instructions.

The attraction of implementing ESG criteria lies in the specific environmental, social, and governance criteria required for the company's long-term prosperity. Moreover, it is a well-thought-out and promising strategy in all three aspects that is important for investors and clients. The environmental criterion implies that there is an answer to the question of what impact the company has on the environment. It covers issues such as the amount of carbon dioxide emissions, the efficiency of using all types of available resources, biodiversity, and waste disposal procedures, including the activities of state authorities authorized in regulation and environmental protection.

If a company lacks environmental responsibility, some investors may question the values of the enterprise, which is quite risky. On the other hand, if this criterion is met, there is an awareness that the company is actively developing, considers the peculiarities of contemporary business, and focuses on future trends, particularly in the field of ecology. Therefore, the environmental component is promising and risky for businesses.

Analyzing the social criterion, it is important to emphasize that it answers the question of how a particular company builds a policy of interaction with its employees, customers, suppliers, partners, and various communities. In this case, the attitude of the enterprise to employees, the available benefits, the amount of remuneration, and the results of the implementation of the company's social and corporate values are assessed. This criterion considers the issues of respect for the rights of employees and customer service, including social impact on the environment.

The social criterion is just as relevant as the environmental one. The corporate culture of the company and the interaction of employees and the employer are important indicators in the field of investment attractiveness and attracting new customers. However, if the enterprise has a large number of employees, there is a high risk of not meeting this criterion due to the dissatisfaction of individual employees or the prevalence of any other shortcomings. Therefore, various companies develop their own corporate policies and hire compliance specialists, which is necessary to implement the social criterion successfully.

The management indicator allows answering the question of how the enterprise is managed. This aspect involves the study of the executive management of a legal entity. Investors and clients evaluate stakeholder incentives, remuneration of board members, shareholders, available bonuses, issues of corruption, conflicts of interest, and transparency and hierarchy of management. The assessment of management under this criterion allows identifying various circumstances so that investors and clients can make the most accurate decisions based on the company's past, present, and future.

The considered criteria are quite promising and risky at the same time. However, they are important in the framework of the sustainable development goals formulated in the 2030 Agenda at the UN summit. The criteria are also remarkable because they are long-term strategic rather than short-term. They are also reflected in the Paris climate agreement, signed in December 2015. The criteria are in line with the objective of responsible consumption and production. Companies are called upon to move towards sustainable practices consistently and include relevant information in their reporting, which will reduce the negative impact on the environment, ensure effective interaction between the company and society, increase the transparency of doing business, and, as a result, improve certain operational and production performance indicators (Table 4.2).

Non-compliance with the principles of sustainable development by companies reduces the efficiency of their activities; worsens their reputation; and deprives them of investors, consumers, and partners.

Table 4.2. The impact of ESG principles on the activities of companies.

Activities of companies	The impact of ESG principles
Increases the income of the company's shareholders	Ban average of 2%
Production of goods and services is growing	By about 5%
Staff turnover is reduced	By 15–25%
The market valuation of EGS responsible companies becomes higher than that of competitors comparable in business scale	By 10–20%

Source: Compiled by the authors based on Ref. [25].

Simultaneously, the development of the principles of sustainable development can create several problems. Criteria scores may not always be accurate, and they are also not homogeneous. Thus, an accurate interpretation of the indicators is very important for investors and clients. Additionally, key performance indicators for implementing the principles do not always correspond to each other. A study by Miranda Partners [29] highlights that companies are only now starting to report sustainability key performance indicators. Some of them are more advanced in this process than others, which creates certain difficulties. Additionally, investors are not always committed to sustainable development criteria, claiming otherwise. This is also worth paying attention to.

Digital technologies, in particular big data, machine learning, artificial intelligence, 3D printing, cognitive analytics, the Internet of Things, robots, digital twins, visualization, and blockchain, can support and accelerate the achievement of the UN sustainable development goals. These digital technologies can end poverty, reduce maternal and infant mortality rates, encourage sustainable farming, provide jobs, increase universal literacy, make a significant contribution to combating climate change, and help companies reduce emissions. However, it should be noted that the use of digital technologies carries some threats; in particular, threats to privacy, cybersecurity, and inequality are expanding.

Recently, in the course of discussing issues of sustainable development, the concept of the "blue economy" has become increasingly widespread in the agenda of international organizations and the formation of national development strategies.

A general consensus on understanding the blue economy and harnessing the potential of the oceans for growth was first reached by countries at the 2012 Rio+20 UN Sustainable Development Conference. In 2015, the idea of the concept formed the basis for the definition of the UN Sustainable Development Goals; in particular, the 14th goal sounds like "conserve and sustainably use the oceans, seas, and marine resources for sustainable development" [35].

The term "blue economy" is used in relation to innovative ways of managing and using marine resources and creating new products through new non-traditional technologies. The blue economy concept proposes a shift from the traditional sectoral approach to ecosystem management, relying on policy instruments such as integrated coastal zone management, marine spatial planning, and the creation of marine protected areas.

A feature of the "blue economy" is the emphasis on the systemic and sustainable development of economic sectors related to the use of the resources of the world's oceans and seas. The sectors of the blue economy generally include industries related to the oceans, seas, and coasts, whether they are based directly on the marine environment (shipping, aquaculture, and energy production) or land (ports, shipyards, and algae production).

In itself, the development of this concept means that the importance of the oceans is recognized at the international level from the point of view of the further development of the world economic system. According to various estimates, the total value of the resources contained in the world's oceans is estimated at about $24 trillion. Additionally, the world's oceans absorb about a third of the amount of carbon dioxide produced by humankind, also providing food for more than a tenth of the world's population.

At the forefront of the considered concept is the ecosystem approach to management, which is replacing the more traditional industry approach. Within the framework of this approach, various tools are used, such as planning and managing the maritime space and coastal territories and the formation of a set of measures for their protection.

The concept of the blue economy offers many solutions to develop the ocean economy and reduce the cost of doing business while reducing the pressure on ecosystems: the development of innovation and green technologies, the introduction of new types of services and goods, the increase in the sustainability of traditional sectors, the development of alternative food products, and the development of additional useful resources [18].

The implementation of this approach is quite expensive. It should be understood that entry barriers are quite significant, but the return on invested assets is possible only in a reasonably long term, which necessitates the use of new tools and financing mechanisms (most often on a mixed basis), such as “blue” securities.

Simultaneously, even though investments in this area pay off for a relatively long time, investments in the blue economy still seem to be profitable because the amount of return received can be five times higher than the volume of investments, and in some areas of this type of activity — even in ten.

Blue economy financing can accelerate the adoption of responsible policies and business practices if based on global principles and standards.

4.4. Conclusion

The implementation of the principles of sustainable development becomes a necessary condition for the further strategic development of Russia, strengthening its position in the global economy. It is the basis for the strategies of Russian companies that seek to increase the efficiency of their activities and the level of their competitiveness in the world market.

The main directions for implementing the principles of sustainable development in Russia are reducing the negative impact on the environment and achieving carbon neutrality. The best available technologies and the environmental tax can become key tools in implementing these areas. Simultaneously, the use of these tools should be carried out within the framework of the green partnership model presented in the research, which aims to ensure a balanced relationship between government and business in the context of environmental protection. In this case, the government should introduce concessional financing for decarbonization in the form of green financing or a refund of the tariff paid as an internal tax. Russian companies should develop a clear decarbonization program and appoint those responsible for its implementation.

The ESG concept should form the basis for building a sustainable business, as a result of which the negative impact on the environment is reduced, the company’s effective interaction with society is ensured, business transparency is increased, and certain operational and production indicators of companies' activities are improved.

In recent years, the concept of the blue economy has played an important role in achieving sustainable development because healthy ocean ecosystems are more productive and are a prerequisite for the sustainable use of the oceans.

References

1. Government of the Russian Federation. Decree No. 3052-r "On approval of the strategy for the socio-economic development of the Russian Federation with low greenhouse gas emissions until 2050." Moscow, Russia; 2021 Oct 29.
2. Russian Federation. Federal Law No. 219-FZ "On Amendments to the Federal Law "On Environmental Protection" and Certain Legislative Acts of the Russian Federation." Moscow, Russia; 2014 July 21 [updated 2020 Jan 01].
3. Aleshkova IA. Ecological taxes as a means of achieving sustainable development: Search for an optimal model for the balance of environmental and economic principles. Social and humanitarian sciences. Domestic and foreign literature. Series 4: State and Law. 2021; 3: 94–108. DOI: 10.31249/rgpravo/2021.03.07
4. Bataeva BS, Kozhevina OV. Sustainable development: Ecological priorities of the transition to a green economy. *Russian Agricultural Economics*, 2017; 2: 80–87.
5. Batashova AF, Tkacheva OA, Popova EM, Barsukov SM. Implementation of the concept of sustainable development in Russia. *Druckerovsky Bulletin*, 2021; 3(41): 51–60. DOI: 10.17213/2312-6469-2021-3-51-60
6. Bekmurzaev ID, Nazhny VE, Abramov AK. Trends in the development and implementation of digital technologies for the implementation of sustainable development goals. *Economics and Entrepreneurship*, 2021; 1(126): 1428–1431. DOI: 10.34925/EIP.2021.126.01.281
7. Belyakova YM. Sustainable development mechanisms as a key factor in the development of public-private partnerships. *Issues of Risk Analysis*, 2021; 18(5): 72–78. DOI: 10.32686/1812-5220-2021-18-5-72-78
8. Bobylev SN, Kiryushin PA, Koshkina NR. New priorities for the economy and green finance. *Economic Revival of Russia*, 2021; 67(1): 152–166.
9. Bobylev SN. Sustainable development: A paradigm for the future. *World Economy and International Relations*, 2017; 61(5): 107–113. DOI: 10.20542/0131-2227-2017-61-3-107-113

10. Bobyleva SN, Kiryushina PA, Kudryavtseva OV. (Eds.). *Green Economy and Sustainable Development Goals for Russia*. Moscow, Russia: Lomonosov Moscow State University; 2019.
11. Danilov-Danilyan VI, Piskulova NA. (Ed.). *New Challenges in Sustainable Development for Russia and the World*. Newcastle upon Tyne, UK: Cambridge Scholars Publishing; 2018. Available from: https://publications.hse.ru/mirror/pubs/share/direct/242530981
12. Dyadik NV, Chapargina AN. Business and government: Environmental and economic responsibility in the Russian Arctic. *Arktika i Sever* [*Arctic and North*]. 2020; 41: 38–61. DOI: 10.37482/issn2221-2698.2020.41.38
13. Efremova MK, Neustroev SA. On the need to take climate change into account in the strategic documents of the Russian Government. *Arktika 2035: Topical Issues, Problems, Solutions*, 2021; 4(8): 12–20. DOI: 10.51823/74670_2021_4_12
14. Grachev VA, Kurysheva NI, Plyamina OV, Volkova II, Evseenkova TA, Lobkovskiy VA. Analysis of sustainable development factors in the implementation of the new climate commitments under The Paris Agreement by the Russian Federation. *Problems of Regional Ecology*, 2019; 5: 78–84. DOI: 10.24411/1728-323X-2019-17078
15. Isachenko TM, Medvedkova IA, Revenko LS, Platonova IN, Abdurakhman TKA, Abramova AV, *et al*. Modern international economic relations in the era of post-bipolarity. Moscow, Russia: MGIMO University; 2020.
16. Mazhorina MV. ESG-principles in international business and "sustainable contracts." *Actual Problems of Russian Law*, 2021; 16(12): 185–198. DOI: 10.17803/1994-1471.2021.133.12.185-198
17. Nikonorov SM, Baraboshkina, AV. The goals of sustainable development and the system of green finance in China and in Russia. *Management and Business Administration*, 2018; 2: 136–145.
18. Nikonorov SM, Papenov KV, Krivichev AI, Sitkina KS. Issues of the sustainable development measurement of the Arctic region. *Moscow University Economics Bulletin*, 2019; 4: 107–121.
19. Nikonorov SM, Tyaglov SG, Sitkina KS. Application of green financing of green economy in Russia. *Management and Business Administration*, 2021; 2: 54–61. DOI: 10.33983/2075-1826-2021-2-54-61
20. Nikonorov SM. Toward a "green" economy through "green" finance, bioeconomics and sustainable development. *Russian Political Science*, 2017; 3(4): 12–15.
21. Nozdreva RB, Konina NY, Burenin VA, Vasilyeva TN, Vasilyeva IV, Degtyareva OI, *et al*. *Contemporary Business: The Main Vectors of Development*. Moscow, Russia: MGIMO University; 2018.

22. Palikhova A. Carbon starvation: How Russia can adapt to the EU import tax. RBC. 2021 Oct 28. Available from: https://trends.rbc.ru/trends/green/cmrm/617a91d89a79477d74afe1e0
23. Revenko LS. (Ed.) *International Economic Relations: Pluralism of Opinions in An Era of Change*. Moscow, Russia: MGIMO University; 2017.
24. Revenko LS. (Ed.) *International Economic Relations: Realities, Challenges, and Prospects*. Moscow, Russia: MGIMO-University; 2019.
25. Sber.Pro. ESG is for a long time: What you need to know about the main letters of the outgoing year. 2021 Dec 24. Available from: https://sber.pro/publication/esg-eto-nadolgo-chto-nuzhno-znat-o-glavnykh-bukvakh-ukhodiashchego-goda
26. Sheveleva AV, Tyaglov SG. The practice of implementation of best available technologies in the Russian oil and gas complex. *Journal of Economic Regulation*. 2018; 9(4): 63–71. DOI: 10.17835/2078-5429.2018.9.4.063-071
27. Sheveleva AV. Evaluation of the prospects for creating an effective economic mechanism to stimulate the environmentally sustainable development of the oil and gas complex. *Journal of Economic Regulation*, 2015; 6(4): 94–102. DOI: 10.17835/2078-5429.2015.6.4.094-102
28. Sheveleva, AV. Best available technologies as a tool for reducing the negative impact of the oil and gas complex on the environment. *TerraEconomicus*, 2014; 12(2–3): 95–100.
29. Torreblanca M. What are the main limitations and criticisms of ESG investing? 2020 Feb 7. Available from: https://miranda-partners.com/what-are-the-main-limitations-and-criticisms-of-esg-investing/
30. Tyaglov S, Sheveleva A, Guseva T. Justification of the need and feasibility of switching to renewable energy sources for the implementation of sustainable development principles. *IOP Conference Series: Earth and Environmental Science*. 2019; 317: 012004. DOI: 10.1088/1755-1315/317/1/012004
31. Tyaglov SG, Ponomareva MA. Contemporary approaches to the formation of a system of indicators of sustainable development of the region. *Bulletin of the Plekhanov Russian University of Economics*. 2013; 6(60): 19–28.
32. Tyaglov SG, Sheveleva, AV, Rodionova, ND, Guseva, TB. Contribution of Russian oil and gas companies to the implementation of the sustainable development goal of combating climate change. *IOP Conference Series: Earth and Environmental Science. 2021*; 666: 022007. DOI: 10.1088/1755-1315/666/2/022007
33. Tyaglov SG. The principle of multi-level management of the sustainable development of the regional economy in terms of ensuring environmental and economic imperatives. *TerraEconomicus*, 2014; 12(2–3): 178–182.
34. Tyaglov, SG, Sheveleva AV. The role of corporate social responsibility as an institution for promoting the ideas of environmentally sustainable

development of oil and gas corporations. *Financial Research*, 2015; 4(49): 262–270.

35. United Nations. Sustainable Development Goals: Goal 14. [n.d.] Available from: https://sdgs.un.org/goals/goal14
36. Yunusov IA, Yunusov LA. Prospects for achieving Russia's sustainable development goals at the present stage. *Bulletin of the Academy*, 2020; 3: 142–150.
37. Zavyalova EB, Starikova EA. Defining business' contribution to the socially-oriented SDGs: Key trends and prospects. *Journal of Law and Administration*, 2018; 3(48): 107–120. DOI: 10.24833/2073-8420-2018-3-48-107-120

https://doi.org/10.1142/9789811264252_0005

Chapter 5

Study of the Status and Role of Social Entrepreneurship in the Sustainable Development of the Regional Economy

Vladimir M. Dzhukha[†], Mikhail A. Surzhikov[‡], Konstantin N. Mishchenko[*,§] and Julia A. Sedykh[¶]

Rostov State University of Economics, Rostov-on-Don, Russia
[†]dvm58@yandex.ru
[‡]2980135@mail.ru
[§]mishenkokn@mail.ru
[¶]serhides@mail.ru

Abstract: This chapter presents the results of research on the condition of social entrepreneurship and the potential of its involvement in solving the problems of sustainable development of the Rostov Region. Diagnostics of institutional conditions for implementing social-oriented and environmental business projects were also carried out. The social entrepreneurship sector is identified and determined considering the compliance of economic activities with the federal list, namely: (1) "education," (2) "activities in the field of health and social services," (3) "activities in the field of culture, sports, leisure and entertainment," and (4) "activities in the field of information and communication." The second group of industries closely related to eco-entrepreneurship and environmental protection is also analyzed separately.

[*] Corresponding author.

Keywords: Regional economy; Regional management; Social entrepreneurship sector; Eco-entrepreneurship; Sustainable development.

5.1. Introduction

Social entrepreneurship is currently considered as a tool for solving socially significant problems. On the one hand, in its essence, social entrepreneurship involves small and medium-sized enterprises (SMEs), the development of which is one of the priority goals of state and municipal government. On the other hand, social entrepreneurship is focused on social functions, which is also a priori the mission of the government. Thus, by facilitating the creation and development of the social entrepreneurship institution, the country obtains a double effect: employment of the population and the growth of the middle class through the creation of financially successful socially-oriented enterprises, as well as attracting targeted capital and resources to socially significant projects and social problems.

There are different points of view on social entrepreneurship presented in scientific research. The most common is the definition of social entrepreneurship as a socially-oriented activity [5,12] or activities aimed at solving acute social problems [6,7].

Safarov considers social entrepreneurship as an economic phenomenon based on entrepreneurial activity on the verge of charity [4].

Karibov defines social entrepreneurship as an entrepreneurial activity based on implementing the social responsibility of business and the social partnership of business and government in the region [10].

Arai and Burmistrova consider social entrepreneurship as innovative business models influencing social changes [16].

The study "Social entrepreneurship in Russia and in the world: practice and research" [11] conducted by the HSE Department of Sociology provides the following criteria for social entrepreneurship:

- The priority of social over the commercial factors, the social effect being a major driver of the enterprise;
- Commercial efficiency and self-sufficiency of the enterprise, in which most of the income is generated through operating activities and not through charitable donations;
- The use of innovative approaches in achieving the primary goal of solving specific social problems.

Scientific research mainly focuses on the fact that social entrepreneurship is also an activity aimed at solving environmental problems [14,15,17].

Due to the growing relevance of the environmental agenda, such movement as environmental entrepreneurship is being formed even in the field of social entrepreneurship. Eco-entrepreneurs specialize in protecting the environment through such business projects as the organization of separate waste collection at an enterprise or in a business center, the opening of bulk package-free stores, and others. There are also examples of large projects, such as the construction of power plants operating based on renewable sources (wind farms and solar energy), the creation of waste processing complexes, and the organization of waste-free production clusters.

In accordance with the Federal law "On amendments to the Federal law 'On the development of small and medium-sized businesses in the Russian Federation'" (July 26, 2019, No. 245-FZ) [3], social entrepreneurship was officially institutionalized in the regulatory framework. It should be recognized that the content of the "social entrepreneurship" and "social enterprise" concepts is sufficiently elaborated theoretically in this Federal law. In our opinion, the ground for it is the stakeholder concept. Thus, when listing the conditions for classifying SMEs as those operating in the field of social entrepreneurship, four interested parties were identified:

(1) A certain category of workers (socially vulnerable groups);
(2) An entrepreneur selling goods (works or services) produced by a certain category of workers;
(3) A certain category of consumers of a socially vulnerable group;
(4) Society.

As a result, four types of SMEs are formed, which the law classifies as social enterprises (Fig. 5.1).

The Federal law "On amendments to the Federal law 'On the development of small and medium-sized businesses in the Russian Federation'" (July 26, 2019, No. 245-FZ) provides a specific list of activities that, according to the legislator's intention, are aimed at achieving socially useful goals and contribute to solving social problems of society [3]. Their correlation with the types of economic activity according to the OKVED-2 classifier is shown in Fig. 5.2.

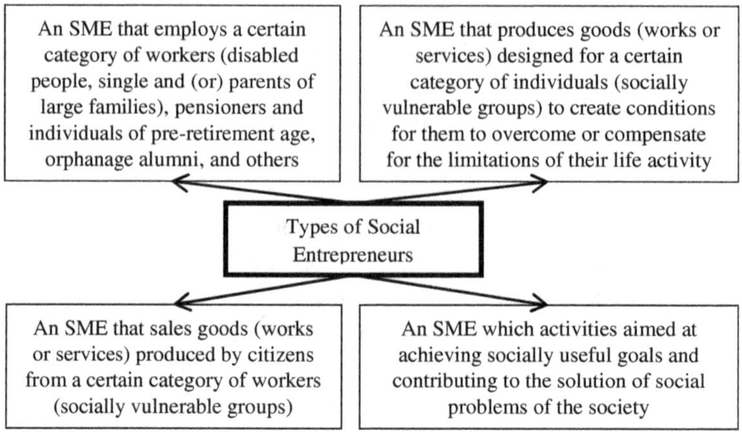

Fig. 5.1. Types of social entrepreneurship entities in accordance with Federal Law No. 245 of July 26, 2019.

Source: Compiled by the authors based on [3].

As a shortcoming of the federal law, we would note that the goals and problems of environmental orientation were not mentioned among "socially useful goals and goals contributing to the solution of social problems of society." This results in the situation when environmental entrepreneurs need to fulfill one or more of the above conditions in the scheme to formally obtain the status of a social enterprise. However, the Federal law "On amendments to the Federal law 'On the development of small and medium-sized businesses in the Russian Federation'" (July 26, 2019, No. 245-FZ) states that the constituent entities of the Russian Federation have the right to establish additional types to those listed in the law to recognize SMEs as social enterprises [3].

It should be noted that, in recent years, the sectoral and technological structure of entrepreneurship (including social entrepreneurship) has been influenced by the special socio-economic aspects in the context of the COVID-19 pandemic affecting the country and the world. A significant part of the business, including its industry and technological structure, has objectively "reconfigured" to much more active use of digital and "green" technologies. Judging by numerous estimates, such a trend will continue for long "COVID" and "post-COVID" periods [8].

Despite a significant number of studies on the conceptual content and theoretical justification of social entrepreneurship models and on

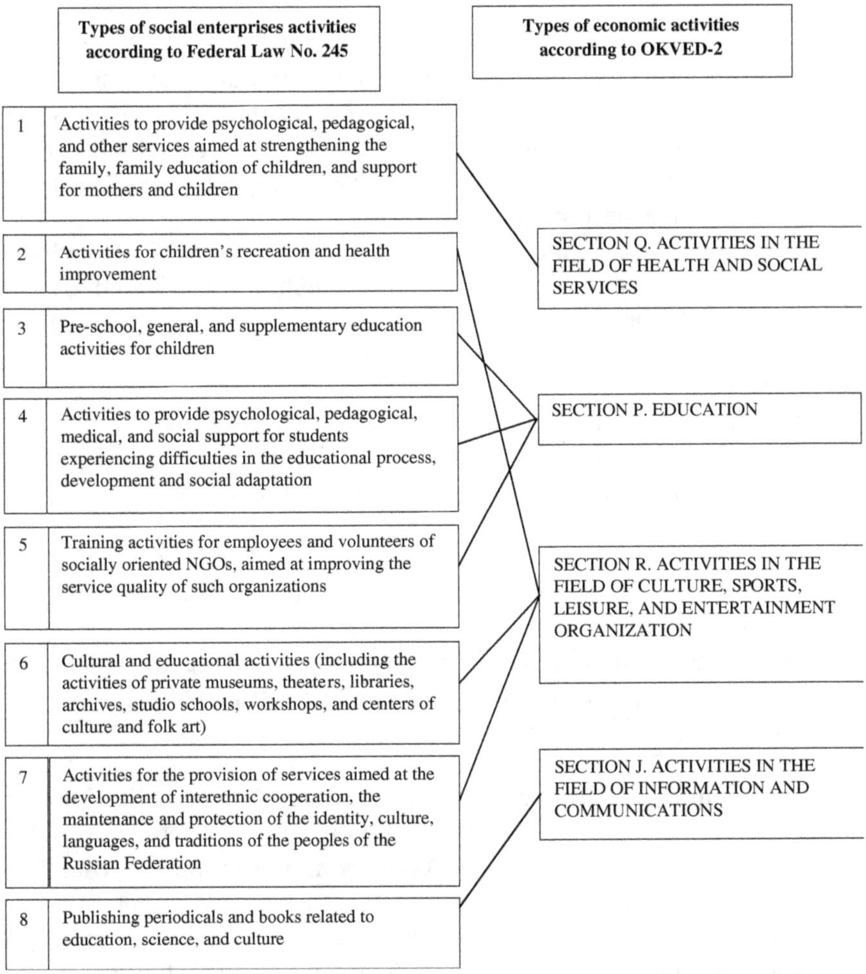

Fig. 5.2. Economic activities related to social entrepreneurship.

unleashing the social entrepreneurship potential at the national level, insufficient attention is paid to diagnosing the status and role of social entrepreneurship within specific regional socio-economic systems.

The chapter aims to study the state of social entrepreneurship and the potential for its involvement in solving the problems of sustainable development of the Rostov Region and diagnose the institutional conditions for implementing socially-oriented and environmental business projects.

5.2. Methods

To achieve the goal, the authors carried out a structural analysis of the share and contribution of social entrepreneurship in the regional economy, specifically in the context of SMEs. The dynamics of social enterprises relative to the entire SME sector will indicate competitive positions and potential for its further growth.

Considering the compliance of the types of economic activity with the federal list, the sector of social entrepreneurship was singled out. It includes the following:

(1) "Education;"
(2) "Activities in the field of healthcare and social services;"
(3) "Activities in the field of culture, sports, leisure, and entertainment;"
(4) "Activities in the field of information and communication."

In this research, we assumed that the dynamics of business activity in these types of activities largely characterize the potential for the development of social entrepreneurship.

The second group of industries closely related to eco-entrepreneurship and environmental protection was also identified. It includes the following activities:

(1) "Water supply; water disposal, organization of waste collection and disposal, activities to eliminate pollution" (as it keeps records of enterprises specializing in waste collection, processing, disposal, and recycling, as well as eliminating the consequences of pollution);
(2) "Professional, scientific, and technical activities" (because it keeps records of companies specializing in environmental consulting and testing and calculating environmental indicators: air pollution, water pollution).

On the other hand, to understand the level of the business climate and the comfort of the environment in which social enterprises operate, this research analyzes the institutional conditions, trends, and types of their support. Namely, a structural and meaningful analysis of projects supported by "Our Future" Foundation was carried out, which allows us to draw a conclusion regarding the regional specifics of social enterprises and assess the level of entrepreneurs' desire for such a status. A set of regional measures to support social enterprises has also been studied.

5.3. Results

Industry analysis of the number of SMEs dynamics (Table 5.1) indicates multidirectional trends in opening and liquidating activities. If the total number of SMEs is decreasing (a drop of 5.7% in 2020 compared to 2017) in the region, then the activities conditionally classified as referring to

Table 5.1. Industry dynamics of the number of SMEs in 2017–2020 in the Rostov Region, units.

No.	Type of economic activity	2017	2018	2019	2020	Growth rate 2020 to 2017
Total for all SMEs		177409	177454	174209	167268	94.3
A group of activities conditionally related to the social sector, including:		8596	9107	9571	9598	111.7
(1)	Education	989	1087	1243	1206	121.9
(2)	Health and social services activities	1954	1975	1943	1859	95.1
(3)	Culture, sports, leisure, and entertainment activities	1524	1602	1641	1626	106.7
(4)	Information and communication activities	4129	4443	4744	4907	118.8
A group of activities conditionally related to the environmental sector, including:		11153	11424	11731	11377	102.0
(5)	Water supply; water disposal, waste collection and disposal, elimination of pollution	516	509	528	535	103.7
(6)	Professional, scientific, and technical activities	10637	10915	11203	10842	101.9

Source: Compiled by the authors based on Ref. [9].

social and environmental areas, on the contrary, are growing: by 11.7% and 2.0%, respectively. The growth leaders are "education" (+21.9%) and "information and communication activities" (+18.8%).

Sectoral analysis of the dynamics of the total turnover of micro, small, and medium-sized enterprises (excluding individual entrepreneurs) (Table 5.2) indicates the outstripping nature of the growth of the sector of

Table 5.2. Industry dynamics of the total turnover of micro, small, and medium-sized enterprises in 2017–2020 in the Rostov Region, million rubles.

No. Type of economic activity	2017	2018	2019	2020	Growth rate 2020 to 2017
Total for all SMEs	1,215,994.9	1,308,756.6	1,363,284.8	1,332,603.6	109.6
A group of activities conditionally related to the social sector, including:	19,491.3	21,072.8	26,998.5	31,093.2	159.5
(1) Education	354.3	192.4	208.8	630.4	177.9
(2) Health and social services activities	7,133.9	7,815.9	9,608.7	11,308.7	158.5
(3) Culture, sports, leisure, and entertainment activities	962.3	1,862.1	3,431.5	4,733.9	491.9
(4) Information and communication activities	11,040.8	11,202.4	13,749.6	14,420.2	130.6
A group of activities conditionally related to the environmental sector, including:	29,614.2	32,800.2	43,026.6	3,5418.7	119.6
(5) Water supply; water disposal, waste collection and disposal, elimination of pollution	5,209.9	5,445.1	5,377.5	4,530.8	87.0
(6) Professional, scientific and technical activities	24,404.4	27,355.0	37,649.0	30,887.9	126.6

Source: Compiled by the authors based on Ref. [9].

socially-oriented and environmentally oriented enterprises. If the total turnover of micro, small, and medium-sized enterprises (excluding individual entrepreneurs) increased in the region by 9.6% in 2020 compared to 2017, then the types of activities conditionally classified as social and environmental are growing more actively: by 59.5% and 19.6%, respectively. Growth leaders are "culture, sports, leisure, and entertainment activities" (growth by 4.9 times) and "education" (growth by 1.8 times).

Industry analysis of the dynamics of the average number of employees of micro, small, and medium-sized enterprises (Table 5.3) indicates a more stable situation in the context of maintaining employment in the sector of socially-oriented and environmentally oriented enterprises.

Table 5.3. Industry dynamics of the average number of employees of micro, small, and medium-sized enterprises in 2017–2020 in the Rostov Region.

No. Type of economic activity	2017	2018	2019	2020	Growth rate 2020 to 2017
Total for all SMEs	332,421	327,651	310,398	307,349	92,5
A group of activities conditionally related to the social sector, including:	16,928	16,774	16,851	17,719	104.7
(1) Education	378	372	310	319	84.4
(2) Health and social services activities	7,578	7,396	7,464	7,948	104.9
(3) Culture, sports, leisure, and entertainment activities	1,203	1,270	1,212	1,445	120.1
(4) Information and communication activities	7,770	7,735	7,865	8,007	103.1
A group of activities conditionally related to the environmental sector, including:	21,684	21,501	20,717	20,897	96.4
(5) Water supply; water disposal, waste collection and disposal, elimination of pollution	3,202	2,753	2,718	3,011	94.0
(6) Professional, scientific and technical activities	18,482	18,749	17,999	17,886	96.8

Source: Compiled by the authors based on Ref. [9].

The average number of employees of micro, small, and medium-sized enterprises in the region decreased by 7.5% in 2020 compared to 2017, and activities conditionally classified as social increased by 4.7%; there is a milder decrease of 3.6% in the group of activities conditionally referred to the environmental sector. Growth leaders in the number of employees are "culture, sports, leisure, and entertainment activities (growth by 20.1%) and "health and social services activities" (growth by 4.9%).

One of the institutions for the development of social enterprises is the "Our Future" Foundation for Regional Social Programs. This foundation aims to promote qualitative social changes by investing resources and knowledge in the development of social entrepreneurship. From 2007 to 2021, the fund supported 354 projects from 59 regions of Russia for a total of 880.9 million rubles. Six projects from the Rostov Region were supported (the share in the country is 1.7%), the projects that meet the principles of social entrepreneurship. The summary of these projects is presented in Table 5.4.

Table 5.4. List of social enterprises of the Rostov Region supported by the "Our Future" Foundation on a competitive basis.

No.	Social enterprise	Specialization	Type of support	Financing from the fund, rub.
1	"Bobrenok" Children's Clinic	General pediatric medical institution with a flexible system of discounts for socially vulnerable citizens	Interest-free loan for 7 years	5,500,000
2	"Razumeyka" Family Center	Private kindergarten	Interest-free loan for 5 years	2,35,0000
3	"Blagodareniye" Social Shop	Social shop: retail trade at the lowest possible prices	Interest-free loan for 5 years	500,000
4	"Steps" Private primary school	Full-day school for children aged 6 to 10	Interest-free loan	500,000
5	Academy of Fairy Tale Sciences	Private kindergarten	Interest-free loan for 3 years	1,200,000
6	Specialized department on the basis of the "Bobrenok" children's dental clinic	Dental clinic providing the service of treating children under anesthesia	Interest-free loan for 3 years	500,000

Source: Compiled by the authors based on Ref. [13].

All projects supported by the "Our Future" Foundation were implemented within three sectors: healthcare, education, and retail trade. The small number of participants from the Rostov Region indicates a low demand for social enterprise status and an untapped potential to promote such status if it corresponds to the real content of the enterprise activities. Thus, for the regional authorities, the task of involving SMEs in socially-oriented projects and informing socially-oriented businesses about all existing and possible types of support is being updated.

Currently, great attention is paid to social entrepreneurship in the region. Thus, the advanced development of SMEs in the social sector is a structural goal of the "Strategy for the social and economic development of the Rostov Region for the period up to 2030" [2].

The document mentions the following parameters important for the possibility of increasing the business activity of social enterprises. These parameters are as follows:

- Formation of an ecosystem of social investment in the region;
- Development of educational programs in the area of social entrepreneurship on the basis of regional educational institutions of higher education and existing support institutions;
- Improving the image of social entrepreneurship;
- Development of fundraising and crowdfunding mechanisms;
- Development of a social impact contract tool to finance the implementation of projects of social entrepreneurs and other activities.

As a result of implementing the strategic project initiative at social enterprises, it is expected that the number of employees will increase by three times, and the turnover of investments in fixed capital will grow up to 600 million rubles.

Currently, the infrastructure to support social entrepreneurs in the Rostov Region includes the following:

- A network of "My Business" and "Tochka kipeniya" [Boiling Points] centers that provide consulting services;
- ANO MFC "Rostov Regional Agency for Entrepreneurship Support," which provides preferential microfinance loans and educational products, including those within the framework of acceleration programs;
- NGO "Guarantee Fund of RR" that provides preferential guarantees.

A preferential microloan "Social" was launched for social entrepreneurs on June 1, 2021. The amount of preferential microloan is from 100,000 to 5 million rubles for up to two years, with a rate of 2.75%. Additionally, grant support has been established for SMEs included in the register of social entrepreneurs in the amount of 100,000–500,000 rubles [1]. The grant is provided on the condition that the social enterprise co-finances at least 50% of the costs associated with the implementation of the project.

This set of measures resulted in a significantly increased interest in social entrepreneurship. Thus, 177 participants participated in the accelerator of social entrepreneurs launched by the network of "My Business" centers in 2021.

5.4. Discussion

The following main trends characterizing the role of social entrepreneurship in the sustainable development of the regional economy of the Rostov Region can be distinguished:

(1) The chapter concludes that by facilitating the creation and development of the social entrepreneurship institution, the country obtains a double advantage: employment of the population and the growth of the middle class through the creation of financially successful socially-oriented enterprises, as well as attracting targeted capital and resources to the implementation of socially significant projects and solving social problems.

(2) The sector of social entrepreneurship, taking into account the compliance of the types of economic activity with the federal list of the Federal law "On amendments to the Federal law 'On the development of small and medium-sized businesses in the Russian Federation'" (July 26, 2019, No. 245-FZ) [3], was studied as a part of: (1) "education," (2) "healthcare and social services activities," (3) "culture, sports, leisure and entertainment activities," and (4) "information and communication activities." The second group of industries closely related to eco-entrepreneurship and environmental protection includes: (1) "water supply; water disposal, waste collection and disposal, elimination of pollution" and (2) "professional, scientific and technical activities."

(3) Industry analysis of the dynamics of the number of SMEs, the total turnover of micro, small, and medium-sized enterprises (excluding individual entrepreneurs), as well as the average number of employees of micro, small, and medium-sized enterprises, indicates either the outstripping dynamics of activities conventionally classified as social and environmental sectors or their significantly more stable status compared with the general dynamics of the SME sector in the Rostov Region.

(4) Currently, there is a low demand for obtaining the status of social enterprises in the region and untapped potential for promoting such a status by enterprises in the region if it corresponds to the real content of their activities. However, since the start of the national project in 2018, the situation has been changing, and the interest of entrepreneurs is growing due to the launch of a complex support package for socially-oriented businesses.

(5) Links (interaction mechanisms) between the state and private business are needed to form a pool of efficient, financially successful, and self-sufficient socially-oriented enterprises. It is important to develop a multi-profile support infrastructure and create effective forms of public–private partnership.

5.5. Conclusion

For a number of proven reasons, the sector of social entrepreneurship is a promising, significant, and priority area of socio-economic development of the region. The strategic task is to develop new tools and mechanisms for interaction between authorities, private business, and society, aiming at the formation of effective socially-oriented business models, which will help attract new intellectual, labor, and financial resources to solve the most pressing problems facing the society and for the sake of future generations.

References

1. Government of the Rostov Region. Decree No. 655 "On the procedure for providing grants to small and medium-sized businesses included in the register of social entrepreneurs for financial support for the costs of providing comprehensive services and (or) providing financial support." Rostov, Russia; 2021 Aug 21.

2. Government of the Rostov Region. Decree No. 864, "On approval of the strategy for the social and economic development of the Rostov Region for the period up to 2030." Rostov, Russia; 2018 Dec 26.
3. Russian Federation. Federal Law No. 245-FZ, "On amendments to the Federal law 'On the development of small and medium-sized businesses in the Russian Federation' in terms of enshrining the concepts of 'social entrepreneurship,' 'social enterprise'." Moscow, Russia; 2019 July 26.
4. Aray YN, Burmistrova TA. Specifics of business models in social entrepreneurship. *Russian Management Journal*, 2014; 12(4): 55–78.
5. Bagdasaryan IS, Sochneva EN. Social entrepreneurship: The place and role in the regional economy innovative development. *Fundamental Research*, 2016; 9-2: 321–324.
6. Buyanova AV. Social business in Russia. Business in Law. *Economic and Legal Journal*, 2015; 4: 80–82.
7. Chernikova MS. Social entrepreneurship as one of the priorities for the strategic development of regions. In Akhmetov IG, Osyanina EI, Veisa LN (Eds.) *Economic Science and Practice: Materials of the V International Scientific Conference*, Chita, Russia: Molodoy ucheny; 2017. pp. 99–101.
8. Dzhukha VM, Sedykh YA, Aleshukin AA. Digital technologies in entrepreneurship and social life during the COVID-19 pandemic: EU experience. *Accounting and Statistics*, 2021; 1(61): 82–86.
9. Federal State Statistics Service of the Russian Federation. [n.d.]. Available from: https://eng.rosstat.gov.ru/
10. Karibov AP. Formation and development of the social entrepreneurship institution in Russia. *Economics: Yesterday, Today, Tomorrow*, 2020; 10(10A): 403–412. DOI: 10.34670/AR.2021.13.71.039
11. Moskovskaya AA (Ed.) *Social Entrepreneurship in Russia and in the World: Practice and Research*. Moscow, Russia: Publishing House of the HSE University; 2011.
12. Nikulina IY. The role of social entrepreneurship in socio-economic development of the territory. *Bulletin of the Expert Council*, 2018; 4(15): 36–43.
13. "Our Future" Foundation for Regional Social Programs. [n.d.]. Available from: http://www.nb-fund.ru
14. Patrakeeva OY. Social entrepreneurship in Russia: Opportunities and development prospects. *Social Entrepreneurship and Corporate Social Responsibility*, 2021; 2(3). DOI: 10.18334/social.2.3.113670
15. Ryabova OA, Meshchankin AV. Social entrepreneurship in environmental projects. *The World of the New Economy*, 2015; 2: 86–94.

16. Safarov SM. Social entrepreneurship as an instrument of regional economy development (socio-cultural approach). *Multilevel Social Reproduction: Theory and Practice*, 2017; 12(28): 133–145.
17. Voronina AA. Social entrepreneurship in the field of "green" economy: Main development trends. *Scientific and Methodological Electronic Journal "Koncept"*. 2016; 41: 60–64. Available from: http://e-koncept.ru/2016/56919.htm

https://doi.org/10.1142/9789811264252_0006

Chapter 6

Innovation for Sustainable Livestock Development to Meet Food Quality Challenges

Inna A. Chekunkova[*,†,¶], **Valery E. Gvindjiliya**[‡,‖] **and Maxim N. Yakovlev**[§,**]

[†]*Rostov State University of Economics, Rostov on Don, Russia*
[‡]*Don State Technical University, Rostov-on-Don, Russia*
[§]*Scientific and Production Association "Nation Health", Moscow, Russia*
[¶]*iakolesnik@mail.ru*
[‖]*inedden@yandex.ru*
[**]*m.yakovlev@npozn.ru*

Abstract: One of the fundamental ESG (Environmental, Social, Corporate Governance) principles is the distribution of technological innovations in the production processes, which will allow carefully and rationally using the available natural resources. This chapter discusses the problem of quality deterioration and quantity of the main component of life on the planet — water. The quality of water also determines the quality of natural products consumed by a person because the high

[*] Corresponding author.

level of veterinary and sanitary conditions of livestock farms primarily depends on the purity of water. Nowadays, the quality of drinking water used by animals for slaughter plays an important role because it is one of the foundations of their health and productivity. The chapter aims to study innovation in livestock farms for the purpose of quality input of drinking water for animals and to investigate the compliance of such farms with the vector of sustainable development in the ecological economy. In particular, the device of plasma cleaning and disinfection of the water, which does not require regular maintenance or modernization of filtration devices, is considered. The positive effects of the introduced innovative device in the livestock complex, corresponding to the provisions of the UN Sustainable Development Program, are given.

Keywords: Oxygenation; Water sterilization; Cattle breeding; Water purification system; Plasmafiltration.

6.1. Introduction

Sewage waters of industrial enterprises and agriculture contribute to the increasing pollution of groundwater [7]. Wastewater pollution inevitably leads to a shortage of freshwater, which may be felt by the population as early as this century because no decisions are being made today to help preserve natural water sources. Every industrial or agricultural enterprise, including livestock complexes, having in its arsenal of water treatment facilities, must provide technological cycles of wastewater treatment because the existing water treatment systems use many chemical solutions to treat large volumes of freshwater. After treatment, these chemical solutions, together with chemical impurities from the treated water, enter the sewage system. The main method of neutralizing the hazard of wastewater before it is released into the sewer system is its chemical treatment (oxidation–reduction reactions) to obtain technical water, which can be subjected to conventional biological treatment already in the external environment. Improving measures to neutralize hazardous wastewater pollution is possible with the use of more environment-oriented water treatment systems [13]. This tells us that it is necessary to manifest entrepreneurial initiatives related to introducing innovations in this area.

A. N. Norkina and A. S. Dvoretsky [9] call the attention that innovation is a means of solving socio-economic problems and a tool for increasing the competitiveness of the national economy.

Kuzmenko *et al.* [8] emphasize the role of innovations in improving the sustainability of enterprise development. According to the authors, if the company does not set itself the goal of introducing new technologies and producing high-quality products at the lowest cost, its market position will weaken over time.

The relevance of the issue of introducing innovations for sustainable livestock development is evidenced by the report of the Food and Agriculture Organization of the United Nations "World livestock: transforming the livestock sector within the framework of the sustainable development goals" [6]. The report shows that the main question in the development of the sector is how to produce more to meet the growing demand for animal products and feed the growing global population while minimizing the negative impact on the environment. One of the goals of the state policy in the field of sustainable development of beef cattle breeding for the period up to 2030 will be a steady increase in the stock of beef cattle breeding, increasing the volume and quality of beef production [1]. Ergashev, Fayzieva, and Beglaev [4] note that innovative activity in animal husbandry is the multiplicity of consistent actions to improve livestock products based on the use of the results of scientific research and development. Elenshleger [3] recognizes that one of the goals of introducing innovations in animal husbandry is the increase in the productivity of animals and its duration under retaining animal health.

One of the determining directions of increasing the efficiency of agricultural production based on the use of innovative technologies is to increase the production and technical potential of livestock complexes and introduce high-tech and resource-saving technologies [11].

Under these circumstances, this research discusses the introduction of an environmentally cleaner way of treating water with the help of cold plasma. The potential for water disinfection by cold plasma treatment is enormous. It lies in the absence of the need to use chemical reagents while maintaining the high efficiency of the destruction of pathogenic organisms and even improving the biological properties of water through the release of reactive oxygen species [2]. The implementation and discovery of alternative solutions among various sectors of the economy, including livestock, will definitely positively affect the ecological state of random water sources.

6.2. Methods

The relevance of the proposed initiative to introduce an innovative device into the activities of animal breeding complexes was assessed based on the analysis of current data on existing water purification technologies and relevant data on the statistics of the livestock sector in Russian agriculture. For a comparative analysis and the demonstration of the technical level of existing solutions in the field of water treatment of water in animal production, we used technical and economic data on the water treatment system for the water bottling lines of the company "Alt Group" and the water treatment plant "ARGUMENT DF" of the company "Vodresurs." To estimate the volume of demand for the proposed initiative to implement our innovation, we used data on cattle production in Russia obtained from the official statistics of the major players in the livestock market. The effect of using the developed devices is analyzed based on the experience of introducing the device into the private fish farming ownership "Podilskyi Rybokombinat." The required number of innovative installations for implementation is calculated based on information on the average consumption of drinking water by animals on large farms.

6.3. Results

The study on the effectiveness of the introduction of nature-saving and human-oriented technical innovations into the activities of the livestock farm and the compliance of such complexes with the vector of sustainable development in the ecological economy showed the following:

- The achievement of Sustainable Development Goal 2 ("End hunger, achieve food security and improved nutrition, and promote sustainable agriculture") requires the solution to the problem of ensuring that everyone has access to safe and nutritious food. It is estimated by the indicator "Food security among the population, measured on the scale of perception of food insecurity." The introduction of technologies that improve the quality of products is inextricably linked with the solution to this problem. As a result, the quality of drinking water does not always meet the standards of hygiene of animals. This fact is due to several reasons: the remoteness of animal farms from the central water supply, the non-compliance of local water sources with sanitary and epidemiological rules and standards, and outdated water treatment systems that have reached the end of their service life. Animals consuming low-quality water reduce productivity and develop various diseases, including infectious diseases that are detrimental to a large number of animals on the farm.

- The achievement of Sustainable Development Goal 6 ("Ensure availability and sustainable management of water and sanitation for all") requires the solution to the problem of universal and equitable access to safe and affordable drinking water. This involves, among other things, the local application of effective water management technologies. Actually, the changing environment requires adaptive water treatment solutions, while existing technologies, namely filter modules, cannot provide them without significant innovative changes.
- The analysis of water treatment systems revealed several shortcomings of existing solutions. First, most systems are a set of separate, various modules of filtration that require labor-intensive design at the facility and are difficult to modernize in the event of a change in the environmental situation on the territory of the livestock complex, which, unfortunately, is a contemporary problem. A second shortcoming is a large number of consumables used for water purification, from all kinds of filters to chemical reagents. Third, the use of chemical reagents requires their neutralization in sewage effluents, which entails material costs for livestock farms.

As mentioned above, the research considers the introduction of a device for oxygenation and disinfection of drinking water for livestock complexes based on innovative technology for the use of low-temperature plasma treatment. Using a cold plasma generator, the liquid is treated, which produces active oxygen particles at the periphery of the plasma jet, which is then mixed in the ejector with the flow of treated water, due to which it is saturated with oxygen to the limit of oxygen solubility in water. A vapor–gas mixture (steam of water and oxygen) is used as a plasma-forming gas. Ozone, formed in the electrical discharge of the plasma torch, provides disinfection of water from dangerous viruses, bacteria, and metals; unlike ozonation systems, the problem of ozone leakage is leveled in the developed technical version. No additional chemicals are added to the water, and the only consumable material is the electric current.

It is planned to introduce the device in the livestock complex. In livestock complexes, we include not only farms of cattle and pigs but also fish farms. The device can be used as an autonomous device for water purification and, as part of complexes of existing water treatment systems, for additional treatment of heavily polluted water sources. The declared functionality is provided by treating the flow of the water-ozonohydroxyl mixture and cold plasma treatment of the flash coronal electric discharge. Due to the good mixing of water with gas, it is saturated with oxygen to the limit of oxygen solubility in water at a given temperature and partial pressure of oxygen. The ozone produced in the electric discharge is not all consumed in contact with water; the rest of it goes back to the ejector. Concurrently, ozone accumulates, and its concentration gradually increases to a stationary value, determined by the ratio of generation and consumption rates.

We carried out a competitive analysis (Table 6.1). To implement this analysis, we selected characteristics significant for the purpose of

Table 6.1. Competitive analysis of water treatment systems.

Analysis parameter / **Product name**	**Gide O_2**	**"Alt group"**	**"ARGUMENT DF"**
In a package (1 set = purification of water from toxic impurities and metals and disinfection of water from pathogenic microorganisms)	available	not available	not available
Quantity of expendable supplies (filter separators), pcs.	1	>4	>4
Oxygen function	available	not available	not available
Displacement, l/hour	250	225	>25000
Iron content in source water (iron content in water treatment plant), mg/l	to 0.64 (0.07)	<3.2 (0.3)	<15 (0.3)
Oxidizability of source water (oxidizability of water treatment plant), mg/l	<8 (2.24)	<5.1 (3)	<8 (5)
Turbidity of source water (turbidity of water treatment plant), mg/l	<10.44 (0.2)	<4.79 (1)	<6 (<3.5)
pH of source water (pH of water treatment plant)	6–9	6.7–7.8 (6.5–8.5)	6.5 (6.75–8.5)

operation, ensuring the ease of use of the device by the end-user and the safety and usefulness of the product (water) obtained with its help.

It should be noted that the market is represented by other companies offering integrated water treatment solutions for agricultural needs, including, for example, the Complex Solutions Company, the SOYUZ-MASTER companies, NPO Aquatech LLC, etc. However, it offers constructive systems of interconnected various filter modules, each of which provides only one of the functions inherent in the innovative device. In aggregate, the obtained characteristics of such systems differ slightly from the characteristics of the analyzed solutions given by us. The incontrovertible advantage of our project is the complexity of all necessary functions in one device, the minimum possible number of consumables during operation, and the production of oxygenated water.

6.4. Discussion

The analysis of the current environmental situation and competitiveness of the proposed entrepreneurial initiative to introduce an innovative device showed the objective need for its implementation. Therefore, it is necessary to assess the demand for the device in the frame of Russia. To this end, a market analysis was conducted for the proposed initiative. In Russia, the production of cattle in agricultural organizations increased by 1.4% (1 million tons) in 2019 and by 2.3% (1.03 million tons) in 2020. The production of pigs in agricultural organizations also tends to increase: in 2019, the growth was 7.2% to 4.36 million tons, and in 2020, 10.9% to 1.45 million tons. Simultaneously, according to experts [12], the annual increase in the pig-breeding industry will remain at the level of 3–5%; by 2025, production will increase to 5.8 million tons (in live weight). The growth of this area of the agricultural sector was facilitated by an increase in investments in fixed assets in animal husbandry (from 2015 to 2018, they grew by 7.5%).

The Ministry of Agriculture of the Russian Federation includes the following key factors determining the positive dynamics in Russian animal husbandry: (1) the active use of state support measures by farmers; (2) the formation of a breeding stock-rearing farm base; and (3) strengthening veterinary protection. The last of the mentioned factors is key to our project because it aims to provide livestock farms with disinfecting drinking water for animals while maintaining the necessary properties and oxygen.

According to the Rusagro Group [10], against the increase in the production of cattle and pigs in Russia, the indicators of peasant farms and personal subsidiary plots are declining. In 2020, they produced 5% fewer products than in 2019 — 0.5 million tons. In this connection, our market analysis pays more attention to large companies in agriculture. The statistics on livestock production of the largest players in the industry are as follows:

(1) Agrocomplex: In 2020, more than 104,000 heads of cattle and 325.7 thousand heads of pigs were produced. Currently, the company owns 74 cattle-breeding farms and 24 pig-breeding farms.
(2) Concern Pokrovsky: The average number of cattle is 15,900 heads, distributed among 40 livestock farms and 18 dairy farms. The number of pigs is estimated at 240,000 heads (four farms with a maximum load of 60,000 heads).
(3) EkoNiva-AIC: For this group of companies, statistics are disclosed separately for dairy and beef breeding. The total number of cattle in dairy farming is 207,500 heads per 40 high-tech dairy complexes. The herd has 7,315 heads.
(4) RusAgro: The group manages 19 commercial pig-breeding complexes and five breeding stock-rearing farms to reproduce the herd. In 2020, the size of the average annual number of productive sows was 104,000 heads.
(5) "Rodina" (Agroholding "Step") has five dairy farms, including 12300 heads of cattle.
(6) Agrofirms of Agrosila Holding have five dairy production complexes with total livestock of 35.1 thousand heads. Also, the structure of the agricultural holding includes eight dairy complexes, each of which is designed to contain 1,000 cows.
(7) JSC "Krasny Vostok Agro" includes the 13 largest megafarms in Europe, each for 4,000–8,000 heads of cattle. Nowadays, the total number of livestock in the agricultural holding is about 72,000 heads and eight breeding farms.
(8) Cherkizovo Group slaughtered 302,000 tons of pork in 2020.
(9) Miratorg has 94 cattle farms with a total capacity of 108,000 tons in slaughter weight of cattle. Pig breeding includes 28 automated pig complexes with a capacity of 3.4 million heads per year.

Using data from the Unified Interagency Information and Statistical System on livestock statistics in Russia in the context of cattle and pigs, we can calculate the potential market volume for the implementation of the device under development. Thus, the number of cattle in farms of all categories amounted to more than 18 million heads in 2020. The average daily norms of water consumption (watering of animals) per head of cattle on average by species (dairy/meat cows, gobies, and young animals) equaled 30 liters. In total, water consumption can be at least 541 million liters. The number of pigs in farms of all categories amounted to about 26 million heads. The average daily norm of water consumption (watering animals) per head is 10 liters. Considering the capacity of plasma cleaners (no more than 250 l/h), the required number of devices in Russia is currently at least 191,000 pieces. As for the leading players in the industry, based on their production capacities in the aggregate, the industry currently requires at least 26,000 devices to ensure the purification of water with useful properties. Based on open data from the websites of large organizations whose business includes the production of cattle and pigs, the most significant demand is provided by "Miratorg" (about 14,000 units), the smallest number of devices is required by "Rodina" — no more than 100 units.

The technical instrument is also interesting to companies engaged in fishing activities. According to the UN, by 2030, the consumption of artificially grown fish will exceed the catch of wild fish for the first time. Aquaculture is developing by leaps and bounds in many countries of the world because the possibilities of increasing the catch are almost completely exhausted. The analysis of the data of the Federal State Statistics Service in the section "Fishing and fish farming" [5] allows us to draw the following conclusions on this segment of agriculture.

In 2019, there were 7,400 organizations in Russia by type of economic activity "Fishing and fish farming," which is 400 more than in the same period of 2018. In 2018, the volume of investments in fixed assets in the fishing and fish farming industries increased by two times compared to 2017. In 2018, more than 25 billion rubles were invested in the industry. In 2020, the cost of artificial reproduction of aquatic biological resources amounted to 7,220.9 million rubles, which is 9% more than in 2019. In 2020, the release of aquatic biological resources into water bodies of fishery importance amounted to 9,013.2 million pcs. According to the operational information of the Federal Agency for Fisheries, in 2019, the volume of production of commercial aquaculture products amounted to 286.8 thousand tons, which is 20% higher than in 2018. In February 2021, the volume of organizations with the main type of activity "Fishing and fish farming" amounted to 25.4 billion rubles. The actualized strategy for developing the fishing industry complex by 2030 established an indicator of aquaculture production in the amount of at least 700 thousand tons.

6.5. Conclusion

Thus, the entrepreneurial initiative to introduce the device for oxygenation and disinfection of drinking water in the activities of leading meat producers and fish farms in the Russian market, as well as in the work of medium-sized livestock and fish farms, is promising and justified. This will allow this industry to develop according to the vector of sustainable development and within the framework of the principles of ecological economics because the implementation initiative involves the following:

- Purification of toxic impurities and metals from toxic impurities and metals without the use of chemical reagents;
- Disinfection of water from pathogenic microorganisms in a way that is safe for the immunity of living organisms;
- Independent production of water saturated with oxygen, farm territory;
- Improving the immune system of cattle and pigs through the consumption of clean water without antibiotics;
- Minimizing the incidence of extinction of cattle and pigs on farms;
- Intensification of growth and development of young pigs on farms;
- Improving the meat quality of livestock and fish.

References

1. Amerkhanov KhA, Miroshnikov SA, Kostyuk RV, Dunin IM, Legoshin GP. Draft Concept for the Sustainable Development of Beef Cattle Breeding in the Russian Federation for the period up to 2030. *Herald of Beef Cattle Breeding*, 2017; 1(97): 7–12.
2. Berkova MD, Bykov AA, Velikodny VY, Vorotilin VP, Grishin VG, Dobrynetc YV, *et al*. Plasma technologies in ecological problems. *Proceedings of the ICCF 2007: 13*th *International Conference on Condensed Matter Nuclear Science*, Sochi, Russia; 2007. pp. 409–419.
3. Elenshleger AA. Innovative technologies — New livestock development path for food security Russian. *Innovations and Food Safety*, 2016; 2: 15–18. DOI: 10.31677/2311-0651-2016-0-2-15-18

4. Ergashev RK, Khamraeva SN, Fayzieva ShSh. Innovative development of infrastructure: Problems and ways of agriculture achievements. In: Yagarov YS, Kuznetsova EL (Eds.). *Market Economy Phenomenon: From the Sources to the Present Days*. Partnership Under Risk and Uncertainty: *Proceedings of 8th International Scientific-Practical Conference on Economics*, Maykop, Russia; 2020. pp. 310–319.
5. Federal State Statistics Service of the Russian Federation (n.d.). Fishing and fish farming. Available from: https://rosstat.gov.ru/folder/14305
6. Food and Agriculture Organization (FAO). Transforming the livestock sector through the Sustainable Development Goals — In brief. Rome, Italy: FAO; 2018. Available from: https://www.fao.org/3/CA1177EN/ca1177en.pdf
7. Kireycheva LV, Lentyaeva EA. The influence of agricultural production on pollution of water bodies. *Prirodoobustrojstvo* [*Nature Management*], 2020; 5: 18–26.
8. Kuzmenko OV, Saitov VV, Dyachenko VM. Technological innovations as a factor of sustainable development of an agricultural enterprise in the context of its strategic management. *International Research Journal*, 2021; 11-3: 174–177. DOI: 10.23670/IRJ.2021.113.11.109
9. Norkina AN, Dvoretsky AS. Strategy of Europe Union in research and innovation sphere as the main factor of solving climate and environmental problems. *Modern Science: Actual Problems of Theory and Practice. Series: Economics and Law*, 2017; 1: 28–32.
10. Rusagro Group. Annual report 2020: Meat market overview. 2021. Available from: https://ar2020.rusagrogroup.ru/en/companys-business/meat/market-overview
11. Stepanova EV. Organization of cooperation between educational institutions and business structures. *Era of Science*, 2020; 24: 263–267. DOI: 10.24411/2409-3203-2020-12454
12. TAdviser. Livestock in Russia. 2021. Available from: https://www.tadviser.ru/index.php/%D0%A1%D1%82%D0%B0%D1%82%D1%8C%D1%8F:%D0%96%D0%B8%D0%B2%D0%BE%D1%82%D0%BD%D0%BE%D0%B2%D0%BE%D0%B4%D1%81%D1%82%D0%B2%D0%BE_%D0%B2_%D0%A0%D0%BE%D1%81%D1%81%D0%B8%D0%B8
13. Vertinsky AP. Physical and chemical methods of wastewater treatment: Problems, current state and possible ways of improvement. *Innovation and Investment*, 2019; 11: 257–261.

Part 2

Institutional Provision and Financial Support of Social Entrepreneurship for the Sustainable Development of the Ecological Economy

https://doi.org/10.1142/9789811264252_0007

Chapter 7

The Role of the Global Stock Market in the Transition to the Green Economy in the Context of the Climate Risks

Elena N. Alifanova[†], Yulia S. Evlakhova[*,‡] and Elena I. Brichka[§]

Rostov State University of Economics, Rostov-on-Don, Russia
[†]*alifanovaen@mail.ru*
[‡]*evlahova@yandex.ru*
[§]*ktyxbr@inbox.ru*

Abstract: The chapter focuses on the identification of the role of the global stock market in the transition to the green economy in the context of climate changes and risks. Three hypotheses were formulated and confirmed in the research: (1) the influence of the "green" bond global market on the sector of the investment class corporate bond in the developed countries; (2) the influence of the "green" bond global market on the sector of the sovereign debt of the developed countries; (3) the influence of the "green" bond global market on the dynamics of the capitalization of the biggest public companies. The involvement of the stock exchanges in the ESG (Environmental, Social, Governance) transformation processes was measured with qualitative

[*]Corresponding author.

and quantitative tools. To achieve to goals of the research, the authors applied the regression analysis methods and the comparative analysis of the empirical data. It was concluded that "green" bond index change contributed to the dynamics of the global indices of the corporate and sovereign bonds of the countries with developed markets. A close connection of the index S&P Green Bond Index with the S&P 500 was established. It was revealed that, despite the global support of sustainable development and measures to adapt to climate changes, the world's stock exchanges manifest different levels of involvement in the ESG transformation.

Keywords: Global stock market; Green economy; Green bond index; Sustainable development; Climate risks; Climate change; ESG factors.

7.1 Introduction

The accumulated ecological problems are of the planetary scale, which implies the search for global solutions, including the search for funding sources for projects related to environmental protection and adaptation to climate changes. The world financial market is an intermediary ensuring the capital movement connected with the environment support (so-called "green" capital) and climate change risk reduction.

The role of the financial market in the transition to sustainable development in the context of climate risks primarily means the redistribution of the capital flows in favor of the sectors and brunches of the environmentally friendly economy, as well as the provision of the enterprises and organizations of the real sector, which readjust their technological and business processes to the requirements of ESG paradigm, with the financial resources.

Recent researches related to sustainable development show the following main trends:

(1) The analysis of the main aspects of the sustainable development concept
Initially, the sustainable development concept was considered an ecological one [1,9]. After the 2008–2009 financial and economic crisis, the notions of green economy and green growth appeared in the UN and the OECD documents; the socio-ecological and economic aspect of the sustainable development concept came to the fore; and clearly

defined objectives, tasks, and indicators appeared [12,21]. The sustainable finances concept has been actively developing during the last four years. Defining sustainable development as an integrated concept with three aspects (economic, social, and ecological), the authors of the sustainable finances concept see its essence in the laws of interaction of the financing processes with economic, social, and ecological issues [20].

(2) The analysis of the mechanisms of financing the transition to sustainable development
The issues of financing the expenses on the environment pollution abatement and the corresponding sustainable development objectives started to be solved at the first stages of adoption and implementation of the international programs in the area of climate change [22]. The problem of moving towards sustainable development of the society depends on the availability of the sufficient volume of the financial resources to implement necessary measures and on the efficiency of the distribution of funds among trends, subjects, and objects to finance the programs for combating negative climate changes [26]. In 2011, the German government proposed a strategic approach that engages the financial sector in the transition to a low-carbon and resource-efficient economy in the context of climatic changes [19]. In 2015, the People's Bank of China proposed political and institutional mechanisms to attract private investments in the "green" sectors such as environmental protection and energy-saving, green energy production through financial services, including credit, direct investments funds, bonds, shares, and insurance [14]. The possibility to apply financial mechanisms proposed in the frames of the Kyoto Protocol and the United Nations Framework Convention on Climate Change was quite limited due to the lack of adequate national and international institutions regulating processes of accumulation and distribution of the financial resources [8]. Bouwer and Aerts [4] described the low activity of the developed and developing countries while implementing the goals of sustainable development and financing events to combat climate changes.

(3) The development of the sustainable development indicators
A significant number of foreign researchers [2,3,6,7,10,11,13,21] review and compare indices developed to measure sustainable development. However, there is still no consensus on a single index most applicable to the scientific and political community [27], who

presented a comprehensive review and comparative assessments of six types of the sustainability indices and concluded that at the "global level, there is no clear understanding of how best to approach the sustainable development." There is an indication that ecological goals and sustainable development indicators are more agreed upon than social ones [23].

The literature review showed that there is currently no complex indicator of sustainable economic development, which would allow revealing macroeconomic variables for further analysis and building a mechanism to transfer the impulses from the green economy development to economic growth and global financial security.

As a hypothesis, our research puts forward the assumption that the stock market, which is the segment of the financial market that reflects the state of the national economy and acts as a leading indicator of its dynamics, becomes part of the mechanism of impulses transfer from the green economy to the financial and economic development.

The research aims to identify the role of the global stock market in the transition to the green economy in the context of climate changes and risks. Three tasks were set up to achieve this goal:

(i) To identify current conceptual approaches to researching the role of the stock market in the green economy and approaches to its ESG transformation processes;
(ii) Due to the lack of the complex indicator, it is necessary to study the impact of green debt financing on the global macroeconomic indicators, namely: sovereign and corporate debt and the capitalization of the largest developed stock market;
(iii) To analyze the degree of the national stock exchanges' involvement in the ESG transformation.

7.2. Methods

The basic theoretical constructions and conclusions of the work are gained in the frames of the conceptual basis of the sustainable development theory, green economy concept, and capital market theory. The application of the regression analysis methods and comparative analysis of empirical data allowed solving problems and achieving the research goal.

The research information basis was the company Standard and Poor's data on values of global stock indices: S&P Green Bond Index, S&P Global Developed Sovereign Bond Index, S&P 500 (2,606 and 2,524 daily observations for 2011–2021), and S&P Global Developed Corporate Bond Index (491 units daily observations for 2020–2021). The authors also used a database developed by Sustainable Stock Exchanges Initiative and a database ESG Score from global company CDP (Carbon Disclosure Project).

7.3. Results and Discussion

The accumulation and distribution of green capital affect the global debt market and the capitalization of the world's largest companies. It is manifested in the stock market through the dependence of the dynamics of the different stock indices on the financial market indices with an ecological component. In our research, it is S&P Green Bond Index and the assessment of its impact on the dynamics of global stock indexes of debt financing and the US stock market index as the largest developed stock market (40% of the world capitalization) and countries with the high ecological footprint.

In the frame of the research, we verify the following hypotheses:

- Responsiveness of the corporate bonds sector of the investment class of the developed countries to the changes of the global market of the "green" bonds;
- Responsiveness of the sovereign debt sector of the developed countries to the changes of the global market of the "green" bonds;
- Responsiveness of the dynamics of the largest public companies' capitalization to the changes of the global market of the "green" bonds.

Table 7.1. Paired correlation coefficients.

	S&P Green Bond Index
S&P Green Bond Index	1.000
S&P Global Developed Corporate Bond Index	0.969
S&P Global Developed Sovereign Bond Index	0.8999
S&P 500	0.763

Source: Calculated by the authors based on Standard and Poor's [15–18].

The authors calculated the paired correlation coefficients (Table 7.1) according to the daily empirical data and built three regression models. Each model was tested for Student's *t*-test, standard error, and Fisher's *F*-test. The reliability and accuracy of all models are proved with statistical characteristics of parameters.

The constructed matrix of the paired correlation coefficients allows concluding that there is the closest connection between S&P Global Developed Corporate Bond Index (USD) (Y) and S&P Green Bond Index (X) – 0.969. Simultaneously, the global market of the "green" bonds demonstrates the significant positive connection with sovereign debt bonds of the developed countries and the global market of the "green" bonds with the capitalization of the largest companies of the best-developed stock market — the US market.

In the first regression model, the S&P Global Developed Corporate Bond Index (Y) value was taken as an effective indicator, and the S&P Green Bond Index value (X) was taken as an independent variable.

The resulting regression equation is as follows:

$$Y = 11.36 + 0.63X \tag{7.1}$$

The determination coefficient indicates that 93.8% of the variation in the effective trait (Y) is due to the influence of the factor (X) included in the model.

The S&P Global Developed Sovereign Bond Index (Y) value was taken as an effective indicator; an independent variable (X), the S&P Green Bond Index indicator, was determined.

The resulting regression equation is as follows:

$$Y = 42.3 + 1.11X \tag{7.2}$$

The determination coefficient indicates that 80.9% of the variation in the effective trait (Y) is due to the influence of the factor (X) included in the model.

In the third model, the S&P 500 (Y) value was taken as an effective indicator, and the S&P Green Bond Index was determined as an independent variable (X).

The resulting regression equation is as follows:

$$Y = -7525.3 + 73X \tag{7.3}$$

The determination coefficient indicates that 58.2% of the variation in the effective trait (Y) is due to the influence of the factor (X) included in the model.

Having combined the results of the conducted analysis, it is possible to argue that the original hypotheses are confirmed: Global market significantly impacts the corporate debt sector of the developed countries, sovereign debt sector, and capitalization of the largest public companies of the most developed stock market (the US).

Sustainable Stock Exchanges Initiative (SSE) was formed in 2009 to form a global approach to the ESG transformation in the area of financial markets. This partnership program was organized by the UNCTAD, the UN Global Compact, UNEP FI, and the PRI. In the frame of the SSE Initiative, the stock exchanges-participants are classified according to different features such as: (1) Exchanges with SME listing platform; (2) Exchanges providing written guidance on ESG reporting; (3) Exchanges training on ESG topics; (4) Exchanges with sustainability reports; (5) Exchanges whose markets are covered by an ESG index; (6) Exchanges with ESG bond segments; and (7) Exchanges with mandatory ESG listing requirements.

We have proposed to group these features into three generalized criteria that reflect a different degree of the involvement of the stock exchange in the ESG transformation in key directions of the stock exchange's activity in this context. Thus, providing guidance to the issuers on ESG reporting, conducting trainings for the issuers and the investors on the ESG topics, and having obligatory ESG requirements to the securities listing can be combined into the criterion "including ESG factors in the assessment of the projects and interaction with the issuers and investors," because this range of issues in the diverse activity of the stock exchange is connected with sustainable development and climate finance. The presence of the stock exchange segments covered by the ESG index and separate ESG bond stock exchange segments can be referred to the criterion "development and circulation of the financial products related to the sustainable development." Finally, the fact that stock exchanges provide their reports on sustainable development characterizes the integration of ESG factors into the business processes, strategies, and tactics of the stock exchanges; correspondingly, it can be related to the criterion with a similar name.

The analysis of the distribution of the stock exchanges participating in the SSE initiative according to generalized criteria proposed by the authors showed the following. While comparing the number of the stock exchanges meeting different criteria separately, it is turned out that most of them correspond to the criterion of the integration of the ESG factors in the business processes, strategy, and tactic of the stock exchanges (58 units or 52.7% of the total) and the least (13 units or 11.8% of the total) — to the criterion "including ESG factors in the project assessment and interaction with the issuers and the investors." Additionally, 32 stock exchanges (29%) carry out the development and circulation of financial products related to sustainable development. It is also interesting that there are currently stock exchanges that are the partners of the SSE Initiative but correspond to none of the mentioned criteria. The number of such stock exchanges is 26 units (23.6% of the total). Mostly, these are frontier markets which are probably the potential of the qualitative development of the SSE Initiative itself.

Table 7.2 presents the distribution of the stock exchanges participating in the SSE Initiative by a summation of criteria.

While comparing the number of stock exchanges corresponding to the summation of the criteria, it turns out that the biggest number of stock exchanges follows the criteria "development and circulation of the financial products associated with the sustainable development" and "integration of the ESG factors in the business processes, strategy, and tactic" (29 stock exchanges or 26% of the total). It is interesting that the stock exchanges corresponding to all three criteria coincide in quantity and composition with stock exchanges corresponding to the summation of two criteria: "the inclusion of ESG factors in the assessment of projects and interaction with the issuers and the investors" and "the development and circulation of the financial products related to the sustainable development." These are six stock exchanges, including Hong Kong Exchanges and Clearing Limited, Bombay Stock Exchange, Indonesia Stock Exchange, Bourse de

Table 7.2 Matrix of the distribution of stock exchanges participating in the SSE Initiative by a summation of criteria reflecting a different degree of involvement in the ESG transformation (as of December 15, 2021).

Criteria	1 criterion	2 criterion	3 criterion
1 criterion		6	12
2 criterion	6		29
3 criterion	12	29	

Source: Calculated by the authors based on the Stock Exchange Database [24].

Luxembourg, Peru – Grupo BVL, and Singapore Exchange. Thus, only six stock exchanges in the world implement the ESG transformation in all identified directions. It is possible to suggest that the inclusion of the ESG factors in the project assessment and interaction with issuers and investors is a rather new and prospective development zone for many stock exchanges, unlike, for example, from the widespread reporting of its sustainable development measures.

The level of the integration of the ESG factors in the stock exchange's business processes can be measured not only according to the available reporting in the sustainable development area but also quantitatively with ESG ratings. In our research, we used data of the global company "Carbon Disclosure Project" that analyzes open data of the ecological indicators of the cities, regions, and companies, including stock exchanges. CDP ESG score reflects the company's progress towards the environment.

Comparing data on the number of the stock exchanges presenting sustainability development reporting with CDP ESG score allowed identifying that 6 out of 58 stock exchanges providing the ESG transformation reporting have ESG rating (Table 7.3).

Thus, the use of the ESG rating, in addition to the criterion "presenting sustainability development reporting," allows presenting a clearer

Table 7.3. World stock exchanges providing sustainability development reporting and having CDP ESG score 2021 rating.

Score band (Level)	Stock exchanges
A (Leadership)	(Empty)
A- (Leadership)	London Stock Exchange
B (Management)	Brazil – B3 Deutsche Börse
B- (Management)	Hong Kong Exchanges and Clearing Limited
C (Awareness)	Japan Exchange Group
C- (Awareness)	(Empty)
D (Disclosure)	Euronext NV
D- (Disclosure)	(Empty)

Notes: Not all companies requested to respond to CDP do so. Companies who are requested to disclose their data and fail to do so or fail to provide sufficient information to CDP to be evaluated will receive an *F*. An *F* does not indicate a failure in environmental stewardship.

Source: Compiled by the authors based on Stock Exchange Database [24] and Search and view past CDP responses [5].

picture of the degree of the ESG factor integration in the business processes, strategy, and tactic of the stock exchanges. Singling out the levels in the ESG-scoring allows identifying the integration degree.

At the same time, it is impossible to qualitatively assess the integration degree for those stock exchanges in group F because, according to the CDP methodology, this rating is obtained by those companies providing insufficient information for scoring or due to some other reasons not having the possibility to be assessed. Bolsa Mexicana de Valores (Mexican Stock Exchange), Moscow Exchange, Singapore Exchange, and Dubai Financial Market are among them.

Thus, in 2021, only London Stock Exchange fixed the leading positions that suggest almost maximum integration of the ESG factors in the stock exchange activity. It means that its achievements in sustainable development are the best practice in the sense because it is formulated by the organizations such as WWF, CEO Water Mandate. In 2021, a significant level of integration of the ESG factor into the stock exchange's activity, which suggests good environmental management, was reached by the three exchanges: Brazil – B3, Deutsche Börse, and Hong Kong Exchanges and Clearing Limited. The Japan Exchange Group has the average level of the integration of the ESG factors in the stock exchange activity, reflecting the company's awareness about how environmental issues intersect with its business. Nevertheless, it does not mean that the company took measures to solve environmental problems beyond the frames of the initial checks or assessments. The Euronext NV has an even lower level of the ESG factors integration in the stock exchange activity, suggesting only information disclosure.

Let us note that lists of the stock exchanges which, as it was revealed, implement comprehensive ESG transformation and have CDP ESG Score, intersect only in the Hong Kong Exchanges and Clearing Limited. We suppose that such a gap is due to the different approaches to the assessment: SSE pays attention to all three components, whereas CDP emphasizes the environment (climate changes, water resources, and forests conservation). Moreover, the CDP scoring methodology is based on respondents' answers; their approach is deeper (in terms of involvement analysis) and is also more subjective than SSE.

7.4. Conclusion

Such a high contribution of changes in the green bond index in the dynamics of the global corporate debt index of the countries with the developed markets testifies that the mechanism to transfer impulses from the "green" financing development to financial development and economic growth is formed. In the second regression model, the regression coefficient is more than 1 (1.11). This means that when the "green" bonds index changes by 1%, the global sovereign bond index of the developed markets increases by more than 1%, i.e., contribution to the "green" financing multiplies the sovereign debt assessment level. The revealed close connection of the S&P Green Bond Index with S&P 500 turned out to be less close than with global indices of corporate and sovereign bonds of the countries with the developed markets.

This is due to the indirect intermarket connection of the stock and bond market through the real activity of the companies, the growing share of the "green" financing in its provision, and, as a consequence, the growth of business value (capitalization) and market capitalization in general.

The analysis showed that, despite global support of sustainable development and measures to adapt to climate changes, the stock exchanges of the world demonstrate different levels of involvement of ESG transformation processes. We showed that the level of involvement of exchanges could be measured with different qualitative (in the form of the aggregated indicators, reflecting the presence or absence of the different ESG transformation attributes) and quantitative tools (in the form of ESG score). The fact that only 5% of the exchanges implement the transition to sustainable development comprehensively and the fact that 96% of all existing exchanges adhere to the initiative to transit to sustainable development and adapt to climate changes indicate a significant gap between intention and action needs and opportunities.

In this connection, we suppose it is important to extend the list of criteria for classifying exchanges according to their participation in sustainable development to cover a larger number of areas of their activities in this context. Thus, the list of the financial products connected with sustainable development is constantly growing, and, for example, the green IPO segment can be included in the exchanges. Over time, the only feature of "the presence of the exchange segments, where the tools connected with the sustainable development, are traded" can turn out to be insufficient. More complex criteria can be used for these purposes, for example, the share of the issued green bonds in the total volume of the issued bonds and others. Moreover, the level of integration of ESG factors in business processes, strategy, and tactic of exchanges can be analyzed and identified through sustainable development reporting and by revealing the presence of the corresponding development strategies and ESG ratings. Finally, it is very useful to present the assessments of the aggregated ESG factors sum, singing out each component (E-ecological, environmental, S-social, G-governance) separately. The foreign research in the banking sector proves that the nature of the impact of ESG factors on the firm's activity can differ while analyzing the aggregated factor or its individual component.

In terms of strengthening the role of the stock market in the transition to a green economy and adaptation to climate change, promising areas of research on the issues discussed in the article could be as follows.

First, the presented hypotheses can be verified for the markets of other assets, not only for the fixed income instruments but also for the wider range of the analyzed indices (including through indices of other investment agencies and international consulting organizations).

Second, reaching the global consensus on the taxonomy of green projects and standard approaches to measure climate finances will allow clarifying the stock exchange classification according to their qualitative and quantitative features.

Third, the methods and databases used in work can be scaled for other financial market participants (e.g., credit and non-credit financial institutions). The presented analysis can be periodically or regularly implemented, which will allow monitoring the stock exchanges' involvement in the transition to the green economy and adapting to the climate changes at different time horizons.

References

1. UNEP. Declaration of the United Nations Conference on the Human Environment. Stockholm, Sweden; 1972. Available from: https://wedocs.unep.org/bitstream/handle/20.500.11822/29567/ELGP1StockD.pdf?sequence=1&isAllowed=y
2. Bilbao-Ubillos J. The limits of Human Development Index: The complementary role of economic and social cohesion, development strategies and sustainability. *Sustainable Development*, 2013; 21(6): 400–412. DOI: 10.1002/sd.525
3. Böhringer C, Jochem PEP. Measuring the immeasurable: A survey of sustainability indices. *Ecological Economics*, 2007; 63(1): 1–8.
4. Bouwer LM, Aerts JC. Financing climate change adaptation. *Disasters*, 2006; 30(SI1): 49–63. DOI: 10.1111/j.1467-9523.2006.00306.x

5. CDP Worldwide. Search and view past CDP responses. Available from: https://www.cdp.net/en/responses
6. Estoque RC, Murayama Y. Social-ecological status index: A preliminary study of its structural composition and application. *Ecological Indicators*, 2014; 43: 183–194. DOI: 10.1016/j.ecolind.2014.02.031
7. Evans A, Strezov V, Evans T. Measuring tools for quantifying sustainable development. *European Journal of Sustainable Development*, 2015; 4(2): 291–300. DOI: 10.14207/ejsd.2015.v4n2p291
8. Flåm KH, Skjærseth JB. Does adequate financing exist for adaptation in developing countries? *Climate Policy*, 2009; 9(1): 109–114. DOI: 10.3763/cpol.2008.0568
9. Meadows DH, Meadows DL, Randers J. *The Limits to Growth: A Report to the Club of Rome*. New York, NY: Universe Book; 1972.
10. Moran DD, Wackernagel M, Kitzes JA, Goldfinger SH, Boutaud A. Measuring sustainable development — Nation by nation. *Ecological Economics*, 2008; 64(3): 470–474.
11. Nourry M. Measuring sustainable development: Some empirical evidence for France from eight alternative indicators. *Ecological Economics*, 2008; 67(3): 441–456.
12. OECD. Declaration on green growth. Adopted at the Meeting of the Council at Ministerial Level. Paris, France; 2009. Available from: https://www.oecd.org/env/44077822.pdf
13. Pillarisetti JR, van den Bergh JCJM. Aggregate indices for identifying environmentally responsible nations: An empirical analysis and comparison. *International Journal of Environmental Studies*, 2013; 70(1): 140–150.
14. Research Bureau of the People's Bank of China, UNEP, Inquiry. Establishing China's green financial system. Report of the green finance task force. Beijing, China; 2015. Available from: https://www.cbd.int/financial/privatesector/china-Green%20Task%20Force%20Report.pdf
15. S&P Dow Jones Indices (n.d.). S&P 500. Available from: https://www.spglobal.com/spdji/en/indices/equity/sp-500/#overview
16. S&P Dow Jones Indices (n.d.). S&P Global Developed Corporate Bond Index. Available from: https://www.spglobal.com/spdji/en/indices/fixed-income/sp-global-developed-corporate-bond-index/#overview
17. S&P Dow Jones Indices (n.d.). S&P Global Developed Sovereign Bond Index. Available from: https://www.spglobal.com/spdji/en/indices/fixed-income/sp-global-developed-sovereign-bond-index/#overview
18. S&P Dow Jones Indices (n.d.). S&P Green Bond Index. Available from: https://www.spglobal.com/spdji/en/indices/esg/sp-green-bond-index/#overview
19. Schaefer J. Green finance: An innovative approach to fostering sustainable economic development and adaption to climate change. Bonn, Germany: GIZ, GmbH; 2011.

20. Schoenmaker D, Schramade W. *Principles of Sustainable Finance*. Oxford, UK: Oxford University Press; 2018.
21. Siche JR, Agostinho F, Ortega E, Romeiro A. Sustainability of nations by indices: Comparative study between environmental sustainability index, ecological footprint and the energy performance indices. *Ecological Economics*, 2008; 66(4): 628–637.
22. Smit B, Burton I, Klein RJT, Wandel J. The science of adaptation: A framework for assessment. *Mitigation and Adaptation Strategies for Global Change*, 1999; 4: 199–213.
23. Steuer R, Hametner M. Objectives and indicators in sustainable development strategies: Similarities and variances across Europe. *Sustainable Development*, 2013; 21(4): 224–241.
24. Sustainable Stock Exchanges (SSE) (n.d.). Stock Exchange Database. Available from: https://sseinitiative.org/exchanges-filter-search/
25. UN Conference on Sustainable Development. The future we want. Rio de Janeiro, Brazil, 2012. Available from: https://sustainabledevelopment.un.org/content/documents/733FutureWeWant.pdf
26. Weiler F, Klöck C, Dornan M. Vulnerability, good governance, or donor interests? The allocation of aid for climate change adaptation. *World Development*, 2018; 104: 65–77. DOI: 10.1016/j.worlddev.2017.11.001
27. Wilson J, Tyedmers P, Pelot R. Contrasting and comparing sustainable development indicator metrics. *Ecological Indicators*, 2007; 7(2): 299–314. DOI: 10.1016/j.ecolind.2006.02.009

https://doi.org/10.1142/9789811264252_0008

Chapter 8

Eurasian Economic Union under the Economic Uncertainty and Geopolitical Transformation

Elima A. Israilova[†,¶], Dmitry K. Remizov[†,‖], Natalia N. Reshetnikova[*,†,‡,] and Zhanna V. Gornostaeva[§,††]**

[†]*Rostov State University of Economics, Rostov-on-Don, Russia*
[‡]*Don State Technical University, Rostov-on-Don, Russia*
[§]*Institute of Service and Entrepreneurship (Branch), Don State Technical University, Shakhty, Rostov-on-Don, Russia*
[¶]*elima84@mail.ru*
[‖]*Rdk.7777@mail.ru*
[**]*nata.dstu@yandex.ru*
[††]*mypochta-09@mail.ru*

Abstract: The chapter analyzes the consequences of the COVID-19 crisis, which affected the development of the world economy and integration processes, specifically on the integration of the Eurasian Economic Union (EAEU). We used the data presented in the analytical report of the International Monetary Fund Prospects for the development

[*] Corresponding author.

of the world economy (WEO). During the research, we applied empirical (observation and comparison) and theoretical (analysis and synthesis), and formal-logical research methods (induction). The authors formulated the tasks and objectives of the research. The authors concluded that the development and achievement of sustainable development goals in the EAEU space proceed under economic uncertainty and geopolitical transformation conditions. Nevertheless, its further strengthening and prosperity are facilitated by the aspiration, common goals, values, and guidelines of the heads of state and observers, which influence the effective development of the Union.

Keywords: Eurasian Economic Union (EAEU); Economic uncertainty; Geopolitical transformation; Integration; Digitalization of the economy; COVID-19 crisis; COVID-19 pandemic.

8.1. Introduction

Under economic uncertainty, the development of the world economy is characterized by an increase in the degree of uncertainty in international economic relations and structural changes in the world economy and politics. This situation leads to the occurrence of complex, versatile global processes and profound socio-economic transformations. Market mechanisms and international institutions that seemed extremely stable and reliable are malfunctioning. The period from 2008 to early 2020 was marked by several events of various scales: the global economic crisis, the fall and subsequent partial recovery of energy prices, the shale revolution, the development of military and political conflicts, and a slowdown in the growth of the world economy.

In the context of the COVID-19 pandemic, several economic and technological processes have intensified. Thus, the current course of restrictions in connection with the COVID-19 crisis has become a catalyst for economic development, despite the unprecedented drop in the level of indicators of the world economy. First of all, this activation was manifested in an increase in the share of the use and growth of the digitalization process and the widespread introduction of the latest information technologies in the Russian Federation and in the countries of the Western world and East Asia, as well as the transition to a new technological order.

The consequences faced by the whole world during the COVID-19 pandemic, including the millions of people left without work, have led to social and economic tension in the world community.

The current global economic situation demonstrates several interdependent negative phenomena, leading to an increase in inflation. So far, no one has even predicted what mark inflation will reach because there is no understanding of how long the current situation will last. The only example is China, which coped with the pandemic in a little over two months. However, the economy of this country has always been special, and it is quite problematic to predict the economic situation in the rest of the world on its basis.

Simultaneously, the priority area is an international cooperation between countries and the formation of common markets.

The Eurasian Economic Union (EAEU) was created by Russia, Belarus, Kazakhstan, Armenia, and Kyrgyzstan in 2015 as a strong and significant integration union on a global scale. This union can give a new impetus to the processes of international economic integration in the Eurasian space.

We believe that assessing its role, significance, economic indicators, results, and further development is an urgent topic in the scientific community, especially in terms of its interaction with its strategic partner China in the Asian direction.

8.2. Methods

The evolution of economic integration is widely covered in foreign and Russian scientific literature.

B. Balassa [4] was one of the first to define the concept of integration and give the forms of development of integration processes. The author defines international economic integration as "a process of economic interaction between countries, leading to the convergence of economic mechanisms, taking the form of interstate agreements and coordinately regulated by interstate bodies." In turn, Wile [27] defines economic integration as "two countries are integrated if their economies are similar to each other. This means that people occupying the same positions receive the same income, the qualification system of taxes, etc. are the same. In other words, economies are similar."

The Russian scientific school, which considers the theoretical analysis of international and regional economic integration, is represented by many scientists and their works, such as Osadchaya [10], Perskaya [13], Sopilko [21], Vartanova *et al.* [25].

These respectable researches and their works [9,15–20,22], are among the scientists of the Rostov research school, who have accumulated significant scientific experience in studying the global competitiveness of the economy and ensuring national economic interests in the system of world economic relations.

Let us overview the most significant studies on the topic of our research.

First, it is necessary to pay attention to the work covering the issues of the formation, development, and security of the EAEU.

Thus, Ushachev [24] concluded that it is necessary to ensure the national and collective food security of the countries of the Eurasian Economic Union (EAEU) and propose particular measures aimed at solving these problems.

In turn, Vinokurov and Tsukarev [26] examine the evolution of Eurasian integration, the history of the creation and functions of the EAEU institutions, and the prospects for developing this integration association. The authors examine in detail what needs to be done to maximize the positive effect of the EAEU. They also outline the most important items on the union' "agenda" for the coming years. The author of the work concludes that the EAEU can become one of the poles of the global economy and find its unique mission, which other existing international integration groupings will not be able to fulfill. Such a function could be an interaction between the old industrial world (West, the US) and new developing industrial powers (China, Asia, the BRICS countries, and Latin America). The author concludes that the EAEU can and should become the spokesman for the interests of the majority of the post-Soviet world, a bridge between the European integration project — the EU and booming China.

In our previous works [8], we analyzed the main aspects of trade and economic relations between Russia and the EU and highlighted the consequences of Brexit for the stability of the EU and the Eurozone. This research analyzes the trade and economic relations between the EU member states and Russia under the influence of sanctions against certain Russian companies and citizens, as well as the response of the Russian Federation concerning the import of certain types of products from

European countries. According to the authors, due to territorial, historical, and geopolitical factors, Russia and the EU are foreign economic partners with a long history of relations that constantly change under the influence of several reasons and events.

In addition to the work mentioned above, in the earlier work of Israilova [7], the author concludes that technological cooperation within the EAEU will increase the degree of localization in industries, enable the EAEU countries to reasonably allocate resources and promote their products on the domestic (within the EAEU) and the world markets. The author argues that this orientation will contribute to the development and commercialization of R&D results, technological improvement, and increased competitiveness of the EU member countries in the world market.

We have identified another important area — the interaction of the EAEU and the Chinese project "The Silk Road Economic Belt."

Thus, according to Syroezhkin [22], there are problems with this cooperation. "The Silk Road Economic Belt" project and the EAEU have some specific areas of conjugation; the combination of their potential can be beneficial to all participating countries. Simultaneously, the author argues that several positions of "The Silk Road Economic Belt" project act as a competitor to the EAEU.

Perskaya [11–13] analyzed large-scale projects of mutual interest of the EAEU countries within the framework of the Shanghai Cooperation Organization (SCO) — "The Silk Road Economic Belt." The author concludes that such infrastructure projects can act as a fundamental factor in developing EAEU integration and increasing its competitiveness. Moreover, when combined with the potential of the SCO, they can turn into an alliance of organizations that can withstand the current challenges and opponents of the transition to multipolarity.

The book by Alekseev and his co-authors [3] analyzes the interaction of the EAEU countries and China in forming transport infrastructure as a factor of spatial and territorial economic development. Additionally, the study analyzes the foreign economic policy of China in connection with the Chinese initiative of "The Silk Road Economic Belt," its metamorphosis over the past period, the impact on investment processes, and the economy of countries cooperating with China in the framework of the updated "The Silk Road Economic Belt."

The conducted review of sources allows us to conclude on the prospects for the development of the EAEU and its effective direction of cooperation with China in the framework of the SCO — “The Silk Road Economic Belt” project.

8.3. Results

8.3.1. *Macroeconomic Shocks and the Place and the Role of Russia and China in It*

The global economy is on a more solid footing only with diverging recovery trajectories amid high uncertainty.

The growing humanitarian impact worldwide and the millions of people left without work are grim evidence of the extreme social and economic tensions that are still felt by the global community (Figure 8.1).

Employment and participation in labor markets are still below their pre-pandemic levels, with emerging market and developing economies hit harder than advanced economies. Developments have been highly unequal across worker groups, with youth and lower-skilled workers still more impacted.

Thus, we believe that the world economy and international trade are in a state of slow and progressive recovery, and we will see growth in real GDP, trade turnover by country and region, and the world economy as a whole by the end of 2021.

However, the way out of this crisis, even with high uncertainty about the dynamics of the COVID-19 pandemic in the healthcare and economic sectors, is looking better.

The extraordinary ability of the scientific community provided us with many vaccines that can reduce the severity and frequency of the disease.

Simultaneously, adapting to life in the face of the COVID-19 pandemic has allowed the global economy to perform well, despite an overall decline in mobility, which led, on average, to stronger-than-expected recovery in various regions. In addition to the already unprecedented fiscal responses last year and ongoing monetary settlement, some countries have additional fiscal support (especially the US).

The outlook for emerging markets and emerging economies for 2021 was projected to be lower, especially for developing Asia. On the contrary, the forecast for advanced economies was revised upwards. These changes reflect the evolution of the COVID-19 pandemic and changes in policy support. A 0.5% increase for 2022 is largely due to

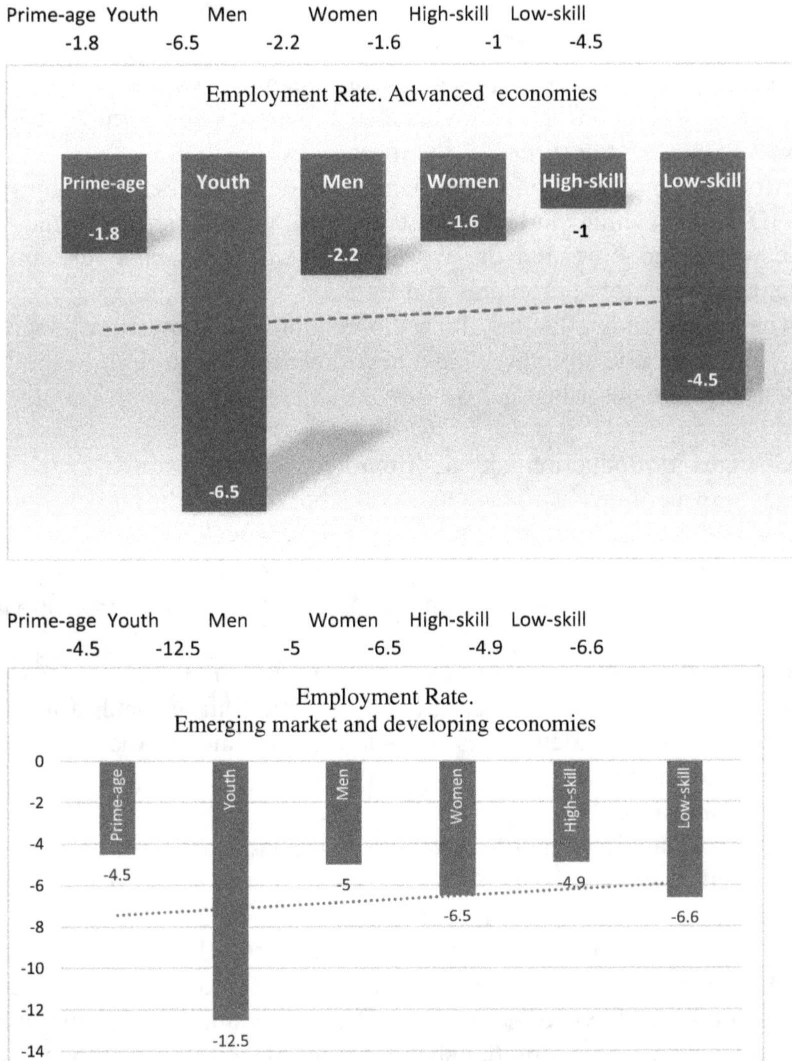

Fig. 8.1. Labor markets, by economy and worker groups (Average percent difference from 2019:Q4 to 2021:Q1).

Sources: Compiled by authors based on Ref. [6].

higher projections for advanced economies, especially the US, reflecting anticipated additional fiscal support legislation in the second half of 2021 and improved health outcomes for the group as a whole.

Unprecedented economic policy measures have already averted much worse consequences. The deep recession in 2020 could have been at least three times more severe if not for the widespread vaccination and government measures applied in most advanced economies and some emerging markets to combat the spread of the disease.

Along with the global challenges and threats caused by the COVID-19 pandemic and its consequences, which have affected the entire world economy and the world community, it seems relevant to reflect common global problems and trends.

The main trends affecting the socio-economic component of society, state, and economic structures have been identified according to the [5]. These trends are described below.

(1) Changes in production and labor markets
    The impact of production changes on labor markets through outsourcing and automation (introduction of digital technologies), and job cuts, especially in manufacturing sectors. Moreover, income inequality has increased in most countries. As a result, we see the following trends:
    - Growing migration flows (not labor migration);
    - The tightening of international borders during and after the COVID-19 pandemic has impacted the decline in labor migration across the board;
    - Urbanization;
    - Demographic aging of the city and population;
    - A city overpopulated by pensioners requires separate infrastructural and socio-economic solutions.

    However, the labor market continues to feel the effects of the shock caused by the COVID-19 pandemic. The most severely affected are youth and low-skilled workers. Previously dominant employment trends, characterized by the abandonment of jobs vulnerable to automation, have accelerated. Economic support measures aimed at retaining workers are very important in reducing the effects of "scars" and mitigating the uneven impact of acute shock in the COVID-19 pandemic. As the pandemic recedes and recovery normalizes, shifting to support for worker redeployment could help reduce unemployment faster and soften the adaptation to the lasting labor market impacts of the COVID-19 shock.

(2) The rapid development of technology and promotion of new technologies (information, AI, etc.)

Digital technologies in the agro-industrial complex have become very important, especially in the context of the growing world population.

The growing world population and changing dietary patterns increase the demand for food. Crop yields are declining in many parts of the world, oceans are deteriorating, and natural resources, including soil, water, and biodiversity, are becoming dangerously small. According to the UN Food and Agriculture Organization 2020 Report, 690 million people (8.9% of the world's population) are starving [28].

The problem is compounded by the extreme vulnerability of agriculture to climate change. The negative impacts of climate change are already being felt in the form of lower yields and an increase in extreme weather events that affect both crops and livestock. Substantial investment in adaptation will be required to maintain current yields and achieve the required increases in production.

It is necessary to form an IT cluster to develop end-to-end digital solutions and technologies and "smart agriculture"; decisions to increase yields based on the analysis and prediction of weather, temperature, humidity, soil condition, and other critical factors for agricultural producers; city farming; and vertical farming technologies. Moreover, it is necessary to strengthen local food supply chains and reduce dependence on manual labor.

We came to the following conclusions by taking into account the above.

We see the following prospects for the development of the world economy, characterized by high uncertainty.

The future course of events will depend on the trajectory of the health crisis, including whether new strains of COVID-19 prove to be susceptible to vaccines or extend the duration of the pandemic. The economy's ability to adapt to effective policies of limiting long-term economic damage, financial conditions, and commodity prices change.

The strengthening and weakening of these factors, as well as their combination with the characteristics of countries, will determine the pace of economic recovery and the scale of medium-term damage in different countries.

The priority should be given to the tasks of economic policy.

The factors that determine the optimal direction of economic policy depend on the country, especially its progress in normalizing the situation.

In this research, we aim to address the topical issue of international cooperation between the EAEU and the People's Republic of China (PRC) in the context of the COVID-19 crisis.

Let us cite general economic indicators of the EAEU. Thus, in 2020, the GDP of the EAEU amounted to $1738.3 billion, which is 3.2% of the structure of the world GDP. In 2020, industrial production reached 97.6% by 2019 and accounted for 2.2% of global industrial production. According to Eurasian Economic Commission, the volume of foreign trade in goods of the EAEU with third countries in 2020 amounted to $731.1 billion, which amounted to 2.4% of world exports [14].

The consequences of the COVID-19 crisis and its impact on the global and national economies have played a special role in the further development of cooperation between the EAEU and the PRC. In this regard, the measures applied to strengthen bilateral international trade are fundamental.

In the context of the COVID-19 pandemic, the intensification of several economic and technological processes has intensified. Thus, the current restrictions related to the COVID-19 crisis have become a catalyst for economic development, despite the unprecedented drop in the level of indicators of the world economy. This was primarily manifested in an increase in the share of use and growth of the digitalization process and the widespread introduction of digital technologies in Russia and in the Western and East Asian countries, as well as the transition to a new technological order.

The consequences faced by the world during the COVID-19 crisis, namely the millions of people left without jobs, are indicative of the social and economic tensions in the global community.

8.4. Discussion

It is challenging to predict how the situation will change. The next period is characterized by high uncertainty, associated primarily with the consequences of the COVID-19 crisis caused by the outbreak of COVID-19 around the world, starting from the end of 2019.

Thus, we believe that the world economy and international trade are in a state of slow and progressive recovery.

According to the International Monetary Fund Forecast, the world economy will grow by 6.0% percent in 2021 and 4.9% in 2022. The global outlook for 2021 is unchanged from the IMF in April 2021 World Economic Outlook (WEO) report.

Nowadays, the world requires the coordination of efforts of all participants in international relations. In this way, it will be possible to respond to the global challenges and threats caused by the COVID-19 pandemic.

It should be noted that integration between the EAEU and the PRC is not a process of one day or a year; it is a historically established process that has been formed over a long time. This fact further confirms the need and importance of strengthening trade relations between China and the EAEU countries, especially towards reducing barriers between countries, encouraging mutual exports, and creating joint ventures, which will lead to the further implementation of the planned projects in the field of trade.

As First Deputy Minister of Foreign Affairs of the Republic of Belarus Alexander Guryanov notes, "Cooperation between the EAEU and China is seen as a way out of the current difficult situation in the world."

The following infrastructure projects may become beneficial cooperation between the EAEU and China within the Agreement on trade and economic management between the EAEU and its member states:

- Industrial Park "Great Stone," which opened for the participation of investors from Belarus, China, and all EAEU countries.
- Development of another special economic zone in the East of Belarus "Bremino-Orsha," where the aviation component of the transport and logistics route is being worked out.

Partnership relations between Russia and China, especially within the framework of interaction with the EAEU, can become the key to economic cooperation in the "One Belt One Road" program. We see that the interaction between China and the EAEU can lead to a way out of the crisis global economy for all participants.

As statistics show, the volume of foreign trade turnover between the EU and the PRC is steadily growing. According to Eurostat [14], in 2020, the volume of foreign trade between the EU and China amounted to

586 billion euros. Even considering the consequences faced by the global economy during the COVID-19 pandemic, trade between the EU and China rose again in 2020. Thus, the volume of European exports to China increased by 2.2% to 202.5 billion euros, and imports from China increased by 5.6% to 383.5 billion euros. Simultaneously, the main cargo traffic is directed from China to the EU. In this regard, the presence of the developing transport network of the EAEU allows for providing transit cargo flows and communications between the West and the East.

Under its peculiarity, sea transport prevails in traffic between Asia and Europe. Nevertheless, current factors push the differentiation of communication routes and the turn of the vector towards land transportation between Asia and Europe:

(1) Growth of mutual trade between the PRC and the EAEU countries, while three out of five countries are landlocked.
(2) With a sharp rise in the cost of sea rates from December 2020 to January 2021, the freight rates of sea lines almost doubled.

In terms of the development of logistics infrastructure, it is necessary to use the well-established rail and road communications of the International Center for Cross-Border Cooperation "Khorgos," consisting of the Kazakh and Chinese parts, located on the border adjacent territories of the two states, to impart a Eurasian history to this physical infrastructure.

COVID-19 has changed the strategic battle to create commercial transport corridors from Europe to Africa across the Mediterranean Basin. Ahead of the COVID-19 pandemic outbreak, the EU already faces an urgent strategic challenge to formulate coherent and effective policies in North Africa in response to the increasingly significant role played by China, Russia, Turkey, and the Gulf States in developing trans-Mediterranean communications.

It is necessary to pay special attention to the further development of international cooperation between the EAEU and the PRC in response to measures to restrain negative consequences caused by the COVID-19 pandemic in the world.

Despite the atmosphere of cautious optimism in relations between Europe and Asia in the context of COVID-19, the relevance of the continuation and intensification of trade and economic cooperation within the EAEU and between the Union and China to ensure the stability of the economies and the possibility of joint implementation of ambitious infrastructure projects, programs in the field of digital solutions and technologies, the development of digital platforms, in particular the development of e-commerce.

8.5. Conclusion

According to the report of the Deputy Prime Minister of the Russian Federation, A. L. Overchuk, on the prospects for integration processes within the Eurasian Economic Union, the Federation Council of the Federal Assembly of the Russian Federation noted the following trends [2]:

(1) The EAEU is an international organization for regional economic integration, which is at the stage of unlocking its integration potential in the interests of creating a common economic space and sustainable economic development of the EAEU member states.
(2) The foundations of integration construction are laid down by the Treaty on the Eurasian Economic Union of May 29, 2014. These foundations are consistently strengthened. The member states are pursuing a single, agreed, and coordinated policy in key areas of interaction: macroeconomic issues, foreign trade, customs and technical regulation, the monetary and financial, transport, and energy sectors, and the agro-industrial complex.
(3) The external relations of the EAEU are expanding based on the agreements on a free trade zone signed with Vietnam, Serbia, Singapore, and Iran. Negotiations are also underway to conclude such agreements with Israel and Egypt, and preliminary consultations have been held with India. Working groups have been established and are operating with several states to study the prospects for preferential trade. Contacts of the EAEU with states that are interested in studying the experience of its activities are developing, the status of an observer state in the EAEU was granted to Moldova, Uzbekistan, and Cuba.
(4) The further advancement of integration processes in the Eurasian space is facilitated by the development of mutually beneficial cooperation with third countries and integration associations, primarily the Shanghai Cooperation Organization and the Association of Southeast Asian Nations.
(5) This initiative will allow the states of "Greater Eurasia" from the Atlantic to the Pacific Oceans to mutually build relations in the trade and economic sectors. Moreover, it will contribute to the formation of

> infrastructural connectivity in the Eurasian space, the growth and stability of the world economy, and the development of a meaningful positive agenda for solving urgent international problems. An important role in implementing the initiative of a large Eurasian partnership can and should be played by the parliaments of the states of "Greater Eurasia."

Thus, we can talk about the development and achievement of sustainable development goals in the territories of the EAEU countries. This cooperation occurs in the context of economic and geopolitical world transformation. However, its further strengthening and prosperity are facilitated by the aspiration, common goals, values, and guidelines of the heads of state and observers, which can positively influence the development of the EAEU.

References

1. Eurasian Economic Commission. Coupling EAEU with China and Europe is key idea of Great Eurasian partnership. 2020. Available from: http://www.eurasiancommission.org/en/nae/news/Pages/27-10-2020-4.aspx
2. Federation Council of the Federal Assembly of the Russian Federation. Resolution No. 427-SF "On the prospects for integration processes within the Eurasian Economic Union". Moscow, Russia; 2021. Available from: http://council.gov.ru/activity/documents/128320/
3. Alekseev P, Ginoyan A, Dakhnenko S, Krasavina L, Perskaya V, Revenko N, *et al.* Eurasian vector of the Chinese "The Belt and Road" initiative: Territorial, economic and legal aspects. Moscow, Russia; 2021.
4. Balassa B. *The Theory of Economic Integration.* London, UK: Allen and Unwin Press; 1962.
5. Global Trends: Challenges and Opportunities in the Implementation of the SDGs. March 2017. Available from: https://www.undp.org/library/global-trends-challenges-and-opportunities-implementation-sdgs
6. International Monetary Fund (IMF). World economic outlook: Managing divergent recoveries, 2021. Available from: https://www.imf.org/en/Publications/WEO/Issues/2021/03/23/world-economic-outlook-april-2021
7. Israilova E. Priority areas of Eurasian integration. In: Gerasimov VI (Ed.) *Greater Eurasia: Development, Security, Cooperation: Yearbook of RAS INION.* Moscow, Russia: RAS INION; 2021, pp. 225–226.
8. Israilova E. Trade and economic relations of the Russian Federation and the European Union. *Economic Sciences*, 2021; 201: 197–200.

9. Meskhi B, Bondarenko V, Efremenko I, Romanishina T, Rudoy D, Olshevskaya A. Impact of globalization and digitalization on the efficiency of environmental development of territories. *E3S Web of Conferences*, 2020; 217: 06012. DOI: 10.1051/e3sconf/202021706012
10. Osadchaya GI, Vartanova ML, Kireev EY, Seleznev IA, Chernikova AA. Assessing the sustainable growth potential of the Eurasian Economic Union member states' economies. *Journal of Tourism Studies & Practices*, 2020; 3(Caderno Suplementar): 1–9. Available from: http://geplat.com/rtep/index.php/tourism/article/view/545/520
11. Perskaya VV. Formation of sustainable competitive advantages for the EAEU member states based on the implementation of the Silk Road Economic Belt. *Eurasian Union: Issues of International Relations*, 2016; 3(17): 16–20.
12. Perskaya VV. The comparison of the energy markets of the EAEU and the Scandinavian countries: Best practices for the energy integration. *International Journal of Energy Economics and Policy*, 2020; 10: 81.
13. Perskaya VV. The integration process in the Eurasian Economic Union (EAEU): Interstate relations instead of supranational under the conditions of multipolarity. *Revista Espacios*, 2017; 39. Available from: https://www.revistaespacios.com/a18v39n11/a18v39n11p11.pdf
14. R&D expenditure in the EU at 2.3% of GDP in 2020. Available from: https://ec.europa.eu/eurostat/web/products-eurostat-news/-/ddn-20211129-2
15. Reshetnikova N, Magomedov M, Buklanov D, Zakharchenko E. The international business cooperation and its influence on enterprise financial security under globalization. In: Popkova EG (Ed.) *The Future of the Global Financial System: Downfall or Harmony*. Cham, Switzerland: Springer; 2019, pp. 294–308. DOI: 10.1007/978-3-030-00102-5_31
16. Reshetnikova N, Magomedov M, Buklanov D. Digital finance technologies: Threats and challenges to the global and national financial security. *IOP Conference Series: Earth and Environmental Science*, 2021; 666: 062139. DOI: 10.1088/1755-1315/666/6/062139
17. Reshetnikova N, Magomedov M, Zmiyak S, Chernysheva Y. Digital technologies adoption in the agro-industrial complex as a priority of regional development in the conditions of global macroeconomic changes. In: Beskopylny A, Shamtsyan M (Eds.) *XIV International Scientific Conference "INTERAGROMASH 2021"*. Cham, Switzerland: Springer; 2021, pp. 3–12. DOI: 10.1007/978-3-030-81619-3_1
18. Reshetnikova N. Digital society and the information age: Challenges and threats for man, business and the state. *Reality of Politics. Estimates-Comments-Forecasts*, 2021; 17(3): 145–154. DOI: 10.15804/rop2021308

19. Reshetnikova NN, Magomedov MG. Influence strategic competitive advantage international business cooperation in the frame of the financial crisis. In: Solovev D (Ed.) *Smart Technologies and Innovations in Design for Control of Technological Processes and Objects: Economy and Production*, Cham, Switzerland: Springer 2018. pp. 399–408. DOI: 10.1007/978-3-030-15577-3_39
20. Shatkovskaya TV, Epifanova TV, Vovchenko NG, Maslova IS. Goals and interests in the law of the digital age. In: *Institute of Scientific Communications Conference*, 2019; pp. 899–907.
21. Sopilko NY, Navrotskaia NA, Myasnikova OY, Bondarchuk NVE. Potential and development prospects assessment of electric power integration of the Eurasian economic union countries. *International Journal of Energy Economics and Policy*, 2020; 10, 37.
22. Syroezhkin K. Joining of Eurasian Economic Union and Silk Road Economic Belt. *Russia and New States of Eurasia*, 2016; 2: 37–55.
23. Taranov PV, Israilova EA, Roshchina LN, Basenko AM, Samygin SI. Five key trends in the global architecture of the world economy in the conditions of reducing consequences of the global economic crisis. In: Popkova EG, Sergi B (Ed.) *Artificial Intelligence: Anthropogenic Nature vs. Social Origin.* Cham, Switzerland: Springer; 2020 March; pp. 565–573. DOI: 10.1007/978-3-030-39319-9_63
24. Ushachev IG. Problems of ensuring national and collective food security in the EAEU. *AIC: Economics, Management*, 2014; 10: 3–15.
25. Vartanova ML. Study of integration processes in the EAEU countries: Socio-economic trends and development prospects. *Bulletin of the Academy of Knowledge*, 2020; 5(4): 80–91.
26. Vinokurov E, Tsukarev T. Agenda for the EAEU economy. *Journal of Eurasian Economic Integration*, 2015; 4(29): 7–21.
27. Wile PJD. *Communist International Economics*. Oxford, UK: Basil Blackwell; 1968.
28. World Bank. Agriculture and food: Overview. 2021. Available from: https://www.worldbank.org/en/topic/agriculture/overview#1

https://doi.org/10.1142/9789811264252_0009

Chapter 9

Issues of State Regulation of Beekeeping in the Context of the COVID-19 Pandemic

Tatyana A. Skvortsova[*,†,‡,¶], **Tatiana V. Epifanova**[†,‖], **Gennady S. Pratsko**[‡,§,**] **and Denis B. Ilasov**[§,††]

[†]*Rostov State University of Economics, Rostov-on-Don, Russia*
[‡]*Rostov State Transport University, Rostov-on-Don, Russia*
[§]*Don State Technical University, Rostov-on-Don, Russia*
[¶]*tas242@yandex.ru*
[‖]*rostovshell@mail.ru*
[**]*dasha_sam94@mail.ru*
[††]*dilyasov1977@mail.ru*

Abstract: The chapter aims to study issues of state regulation of beekeeping in the context of the COVID-19 pandemic. To achieve the research objectives, the authors studied the issues of state regulation of the quality and safety of beekeeping products and investigated the patterns of combining beekeepers and beekeeping farms into clusters. The research methodology includes general scientific and private

[*]Corresponding author.

scientific methods of studying economic and legal relations, including the method of analysis and synthesis, the comparative-legal method, and others. Based on the scientific analysis carried out in the work, the authors conclude on the need to improve the system of legal regulation of the quality and safety of beekeeping products, particularly by establishing requirements for its authenticity (naturalness). The authors also proposed a cluster model for uniting beekeepers and beekeeping farms, which allowed overcoming the crisis phenomena caused by the COVID-19 pandemic and substantiated the need for state support of individual subjects of beekeeping activities and cluster associations of beekeepers. An effective state policy in the field of regulation of beekeeping and beekeeping activities is indeed a factor in the development of beekeeping and the agricultural industry in general and in overcoming the crisis in the economy caused by the negative impact of the COVID-19 pandemic. In this regard, the authors consider the proposed measures as directions of state policy in the field of beekeeping in the context of the COVID-19 pandemic.

Keywords: Beekeeping; Beekeeping products; Entrepreneurship; State Regulation; COVID-19 pandemic.

9.1. Introduction

Nowadays, beekeeping is one of the areas of entrepreneurship supported by governments worldwide. This is primarily because food security in various countries is still very acute.

According to the Food and Agriculture Organization of the United Nations (FAO), between 720 and 811 million people went hungry in 2020. Simultaneously, the number of hungry people on the planet has increased as a result of the adverse effects of various restrictions caused by the COVID-19 pandemic [13]. For the period of the negative impact of the COVID-19 pandemic, the Prevalence of Undernourishment (PoU) indicator rose to 9.9% in 2020, up from 8.4% in 2019, highlighting a significant increase in the number of people experiencing food shortages.

Beekeeping involves the production of organic food — honey and other beekeeping products, as well as the breeding of bees, which are natural pollinators of agricultural plants [15]. The number of pollinators directly impacts the state of crop production — the most important branch of agriculture. Accordingly, the development of the beekeeping industry directly contributes to the normal functioning of crop production in the country.

According to FAO, one billion people are currently employed in agro-industrial production, which is higher than in any other sector of the economy. However, food production could negatively affect the environment, contributing to a decrease in biodiversity. Nonetheless, three billion people cannot afford healthy diets as being overweight and obesity continue to rise globally [14]. Therefore, along with pollination, it is currently important to obtain high-quality natural beekeeping products, forming the basis of proper nutrition for the population.

The development of beekeeping in Russia and around the world helps solve the problem of preserving biological diversity on the planet and providing the population with environmentally friendly food [17,18].

As a branch of agriculture, beekeeping is widespread on all continents, while the production volume differs. Asia leads in honey production (about 830 tons). Europe produces about half as much (Fig. 9.1).

In the context of the COVID-19 pandemic, due to the closure of borders and the introduction of various restrictions by countries, the situation with the production of beekeeping products has worsened. The

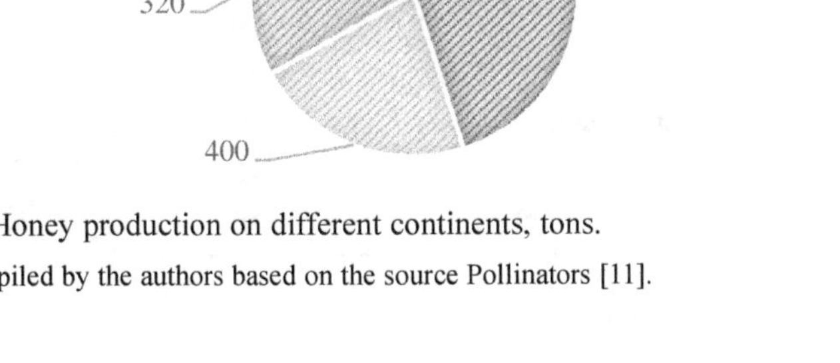

Fig. 9.1. Honey production on different continents, tons.

Source: Compiled by the authors based on the source Pollinators [11].

COVID-19 pandemic has led to the bankruptcy of enterprises in various sectors of the economy, including agricultural producers [19].

Therefore, it becomes necessary to properly regulate beekeeping activities by the state and take the necessary support measures in relation to organizations carrying out this activity.

9.2. Methodology

The research methodology includes general scientific and private scientific research methods of economic and legal relations. The methodology used in the work is based on the dialectical method of cognition as a system of general and particular scientific methods, particularly the logical method, methods of induction, deduction, synthesis, and analysis, the systemic method, and the comparative method.

9.3. Results

9.3.1. *State Regulation of the Quality and Safety of Beekeeping Products*

The important role of bees in the ecosystem is beyond doubt. The primary function of bees at the present stage of the development of human civilization is pollination. The disappearance of pollinators can mean the loss of some of the nutritious food needed for a healthy diet. FAO estimates that

Table 9.1. Dependence of major crops on pollination.

Crops	Dependence on pollination, %
Bulb onion	90–100
Pumpkin	90–100
Apple	80–100
Watermelon	70–100
Sunflower	50–100
Rape plant	50–100

Source: Compiled by the authors based on the source Pollinators [11].

if pollinator insects decrease, they threaten 75% of the world's crops requiring pollination [11]. Table 9.1 presents the dependence of major crops on pollination.

Therefore, the development of beekeeping and, consequently, the increase in the number of pollinators contribute to an increase in the yield and quality of crops.

Pollinators also play a critical role in maintaining and enhancing biodiversity. Bees are the dominant link providing biological diversity, which is the key parameter characterizing the ecosystem's state. This parameter serves as the basis for the environmental policy of states that seek to ensure the safety of their biological resources, thus guaranteeing sustainable economic development.

According to paragraph 1 of the Rome Declaration of November 13, 1996, "On world food security" and the Action Plan of the states participating in the World Food Summit [12], the need for urgent action to combat the erosion of biological diversity was identified. Determining the goals of countries' activities to ensure food security, paragraph 33 of the Rome Declaration consolidated the need to combat the destruction of biological diversity.

In 2000, the UN Environment Program approved an international initiative for the conservation and sustainable use of pollinators, the most important of which are bees. Similar initiatives have been approved for Europe, North America, Africa, Oceania, and Brazil, establishing the international scientific committees on pollinators.

The UN General Assembly has declared May 20 as World Bee Day, which has been celebrated since 2018. This contributes to educating the population about the important role that bees play in the planet's ecosystem. In 2021, this was celebrated amid the global community's struggle with the consequences of the COVID-19 pandemic. In this regard, on this day, the FAO platform actively discussed the need to support beekeeping throughout the crisis period.

The Russian Federation also makes certain efforts to regulate beekeeping. Thus, the norms of the Federal law of the Russian Federation "On beekeeping in the Russian Federation" (December 30, 2020, No. 490-FZ) [8] contain certain mechanisms aimed at legal regulation of relations for developing beekeeping and preserving bees. This legal act contains six chapters devoted to the definition of general provisions for the regulation of beekeeping, the regulation of economic foundations of the implementation of beekeeping activities, the basics of management in the field of beekeeping, the procedure for carrying out beekeeping activities, as well as issues of preserving bees.

Similar laws have been adopted in other CIS countries. Thus, in the Republic of Kazakhstan, the Law “On beekeeping” (March 12, 2002, No. 303-II) [4], with subsequent amendments and additions, is currently adopted. The law includes five chapters regulating the basics of beekeeping in the Republic of Kazakhstan. Along with the regulation of general provisions (consolidation of basic concepts, sources of legal regulation, the subject of legal regulation, and legal consolidation of the foundations of activities in the field of beekeeping), the law regulates the protection of bees, starting from the protection of bees in their natural habitat during forestry work, breeding conditions, places of migrations, and migration routes of bees. Moreover, the law consolidates the protection of bees when using plant protection products, mineral fertilizers, and other preparations. State regulation in the field of beekeeping, the regulation of which is enshrined in Chapter 4, is complicated by numerous changes and additions to almost all articles of this chapter, which complicates law enforcement practice [4].

The law “On beekeeping” is currently in force in the Republic of Armenia, adopted on March 19, 2009 [3], and signed by the President of the Republic of Armenia on April 8, 2009. Unlike the legal acts on beekeeping in force in other CIS countries, the law “On beekeeping” of the Republic of Armenia includes norms regulating the implementation of ecological beekeeping (Article 9). Along with the consolidation of the general requirements for the implementation of ecological beekeeping, Article 9 contains norms establishing requirements for beekeeping products as environmentally friendly. The law “On beekeeping” regulates relations in the state administration of the beekeeping sector and consolidates the powers of the Government of the Republic of Armenia in the field of beekeeping. The law of the Republic of Armenia allows creating a Council for the Development of Beekeeping in the Republic of Armenia along with the authorized body. The interaction of the Council for the Development of Beekeeping with the authorized body is carried out following the law in the manner established by the head of the authorized body [3].

In our opinion, this experience of legal regulation of beekeeping in Armenia should be adopted in Russia. The Russian law “On beekeeping in the Russian Federation” (December 30, 2020, No. 490-FZ) does not establish requirements to ensure the quality and safety of beekeeping products. Article 14 of this normative act contains only a reference norm of the following content: "Safety requirements for beekeeping products (including sanitary, epidemiological, hygienic, and veterinary requirements) and the processes of production (manufacturing), storage, transportation, sale, and disposal are established in accordance with the legislation of the Russian Federation on technical regulation or technical regulations of the Eurasian Economic Union" [8].

The fundamental normative acts in the formation of the Russian legislative framework in the field of ensuring the quality and safety of any product, including beekeeping products, are the Federal laws of the Russian Federation "On technical regulation" (December 27, 2002, No. 184-FZ) [6], "On standardization in the Russian Federation" (June 29, 2015, No. 162-FZ) [5], and "On the quality and safety of food products" (January 2, 2000, No. 29-FZ) [7]. Nevertheless, these documents do not and cannot contain requirements for beekeeping products as natural (genuine) and environmentally friendly products. At the level of the Customs Union, there is also no special technical regulation for honey and other beekeeping products. There is only fragmentary regulation in paragraph 11 of part 5 of Article 7 of the technical regulation of the Customs Union "On safety of food products," adopted by the Decision of the Commission of the Customs Union of December 9, 2011, No. 880 [1]. It establishes that natural honey and beekeeping products containing the veterinary medicinal products listed in this article or other preparations established by the acts of the bodies of the EAEU and used for the treatment of bees are not allowed for the circulation and production (manufacture) of food products, the presence of residual quantities of which are not allowed. Requirements for the authenticity (naturalness) of beekeeping products at the level of the Eurasian Economic Union are not established. In this regard, producers of honey and other beekeeping products can be held liable only in case of violation of these requirements (e.g., Determination of the Supreme Court of the Russian Federation dated June 26, 2019, No. 307-ES19-9225 in case No. A44-10859/2017 [9]) but not in the case of the manufacture of counterfeit beekeeping products under the guise of natural.

Currently, the Order of the Ministry of Agriculture of the Russian Federation "On approval of the veterinary rules for keeping honey bees for the purpose of their reproduction, breeding, sale, and use for pollination of agricultural entomophilous plants and obtaining beekeeping products" (September 23, 2021, No. 645) has been adopted and has entered into force on January 3, 2022 [2]. However, this subordinate legal act also does not define the methods and rules for establishing the authenticity (naturalness) of beekeeping products.

It seems that such requirements could be established in the Federal law of the Russian Federation "On beekeeping in the Russian Federation" (December 30, 2020, No. 490-FZ) [8]. For this purpose, we consider it expedient to make the appropriate additions to Article 14 of this law. It is also advisable to adopt the Technical Regulations of the European Economic Union "On safety of beekeeping products," which should provide for special requirements to ensure the safety of beekeeping products.

9.4. Beekeeping Associations and State Support

In the Russian Federation, as in most CIS and Western European countries, beekeeping is mainly carried out by small entrepreneurs — amateur beekeepers with small apiaries, personal subsidiary plots, and farms.

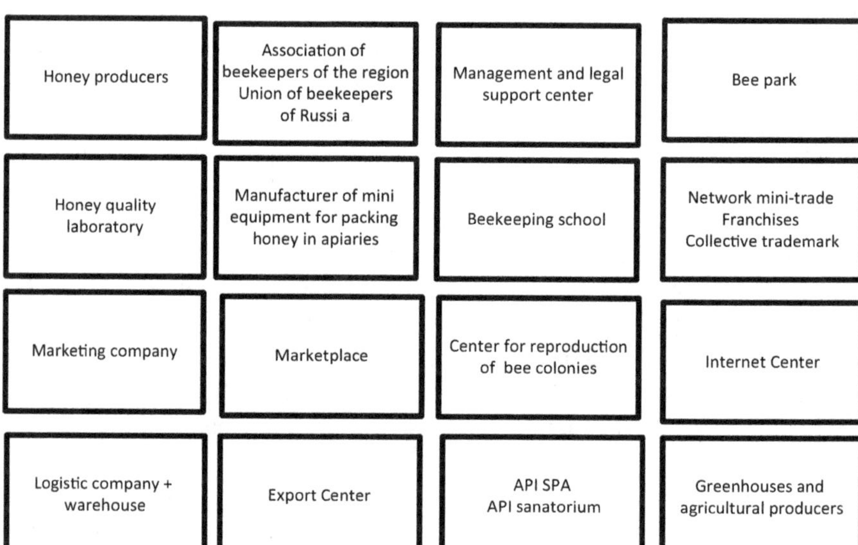

Fig. 9.2. Recommended beekeeping cluster model.

One of the most efficient forms of association of beekeeping farms is the beekeeping cluster [10,16]. In our opinion, such an association appears as an ecosystem for the development of entrepreneurship in the field of beekeeping, which includes legally and financially independent participants united by a common idea of preserving the bee population, insect biodiversity in Russia, aimed at producing high-quality beekeeping products and interested in the joint promotion of beekeeping products on the world market. The recommended model of the beekeeping cluster is presented in Fig. 9.2.

The Association of Beekeepers of the region administers and coordinates the cluster members. The Union of Beekeepers of Russia provides the protection of beekeepers of Russia and assistance in obtaining government support.

The Center for Management and Legal Support provides legal support to cluster members and assistance in preparing legal documents for the effective functioning of the cluster.

Internet Center provides Internet support for the cluster, promoting the products online. Moreover, it provides access to databases of experts, beekeepers, laboratories, and treatment regimens with beekeeping products.

The beekeeping school acts as an educational center for training beekeepers, preparing educational courses for beekeepers on the production of beekeeping products that meet European standards and the promotion of beekeeping products to foreign markets, helps form a range of products, and conducts open seminars for agricultural producers on the benefits of pollination of crops by bees to increase yields.

A marketing company is responsible for the formation of a long-term policy of pricing and promotion of honey as a quality food and beekeeping products as environmentally friendly medicines, as well as the promotion of the brand on the world market. It organizes advertising companies, exhibitions, fairs, and honey holidays; prepares colorful booklets describing beekeeping products and indicating useful properties; gives recommendations for use to prevent various diseases; provides assistance in promoting beekeeping products via the Internet; develops souvenir containers and packaging; creates souvenir and promo samples of beekeeping products; develops a label; and directs tourist routes through apiaries.

Honey producers are members of the cluster: agricultural cooperatives, peasant farms, personal subsidiary plots, and amateur beekeepers.

The manufacturer of mini-equipment for packing honey in apiaries is a manufacturing enterprise that produces equipment for packing honey, beehives, and other products for honey.

Bee Park is an ecological park stylized as a beehive, where honey plants grow, and masterclasses and fairs are held. It is a place for family recreation and apitherapy.

Honey quality laboratory proves the quality of beekeeping products for sale in the domestic and foreign markets.

The marketplace is a trading platform that sells goods and services of cluster members via the Internet. One either can create own platforms for beekeepers or can use existing ones, such as Ozon, Sber, and Wildberries.

Greenhouses and agricultural producers provide fields and greenhouses on mutually beneficial terms for beekeepers, increasing yields and producing quality food.

The reproduction center for bee colonies and other pollinators is a place where bee colonies are bred and sold.

Mini-trade refers to the concept of a mini-store of beekeeping products implemented under a franchise.

The collective trademark will help protect the cluster's products from counterfeiting.

Logistics companies and storage facilities are intended for carrying out the transportation of beekeeping products. They may be outsourced without being part of the cluster.

Export Center helps to export beekeeping products produced in the cluster.

API-SPA is a spa center that offers unique spa treatments (vaping, wraps, masks, and massages) using the cluster's beekeeping products.

API-sanatorium is a health center using beekeeping products produced in the cluster.

Such a cluster beekeeping association framework will fully realize the capacity of honey production and other beekeeping products, provide support to small producers, and ensure the marketing and other widespread use of beekeeping products. In the context of overcoming the negative consequences of the COVID-19 pandemic, such a cluster will eliminate the consequences of the economic downturn and lead to the growth of the beekeeping sector of the economy.

Unfortunately, at the state level in Russia, there are no effective mechanisms to support beekeepers and beekeeping associations, including in the conditions of the COVID-19 pandemic. It seems necessary to provide such support to individual manufacturers of beekeeping products and various beekeeping associations, including cluster ones. This requires the development and adoption of a state program to support beekeeping in Russia.

9.5. Conclusion and Recommendations

Beekeeping requires a special approach to the implementation of government regulation and support in the context of the COVID-19 pandemic. Bees play an important role in pollinating plants, including agricultural ones, and sustaining the biodiversity of the planet. Therefore, beekeeping, along with providing the population with environmentally friendly and healthy food, contributes to the development of crop production and maintenance of the ecological balance.

Thus, the government should create conditions for producing genuine (natural) beekeeping products. Currently, Russia has no proper legal regulation of the requirements for the quality and safety of beekeeping products, including in terms of ensuring their ecological purity and naturalness. In this regard, it is proposed to make the appropriate additions to Article 14 of the Federal law of the Russian Federation "On beekeeping in the Russian Federation" (December 30, 2020, No. 490-FZ) and also to develop and adopt the Technical Regulations of the European Economic Union "On the safety of beekeeping products," which establishes special requirements for the safety of beekeeping products.

In Russia and several other countries, beekeeping is mainly carried out by individual amateur beekeepers and small beekeeping farms, which makes them highly vulnerable to external factors, including the adverse effects of the COVID-19 pandemic. In this regard, it is recommended to create and develop beekeeping clusters with a higher degree of economic sustainability. Mechanisms of state support for beekeepers and their cluster associations should be created to help overcome the negative factors of the COVID-19 pandemic.

References

1. Commission of the Customs Union. Decision No. 880 "On adoption of technical regulations of the Customs Union 'On food safety'" Internet. Moscow, Russia; December 9, 2011 [cited January 5, 2022]. Available from: https://www.alta.ru/tamdoc/11sr0880/

2. Ministry of Agriculture of the Russian Federation. Order No. 645 "On approval of the veterinary rules for keeping honey bees for the purpose of their reproduction, breeding, sale, and use for pollination of agricultural entomophilous plants and obtaining beekeeping products." Moscow, Russia; 2021.
3. Republic of Armenia. The law "On beekeeping." Yerevan, Armenia; 2009.
4. Republic of Kazakhstan. The Law No. 303-II "On beekeeping." Nur-Sultan, Kazakhstan; 2002.
5. Russian Federation. Federal law No. 162-FZ "On standardization in the Russian Federation." Moscow, Russia; 2015.
6. Russian Federation. Federal law No. 184-FZ "On technical regulation." Moscow, Russia; 2002.
7. Russian Federation. Federal law No. 29-FZ "On the quality and safety of food products." Moscow, Russia; 2000.
8. Russian Federation. Federal law No. 490-FZ "On beekeeping in the Russian Federation." Moscow, Russia; 2020.
9. Supreme Court of the Russian Federation. Determination No. 307-ES19-9225 in case No. A44-10859/2017. Moscow, Russia; 2019. Available from: https://legalacts.ru/sud/opredelenie-verkhovnogo-suda-rf-ot-26062019-n-307-es19-9225-po-delu-n-a44-108592017/
10. Borisova O, Abramova L, Zageeva L, Popkova EG, Morozova, I, Litvinova T. Role of agricultural clusters in provision of food security. *European Research Studies Journal*, 2015; XVIII(3): 287–298. DOI: 10.35808/ersj/472
11. FAO and IZSLT. Pollinators. Rome, Italy; 2019. Available from: https://www.fao.org/documents/card/en/c/ca4656en
12. Food and Agriculture Organization (FAO). Rome Declaration on World Food Security and World Food Summit Plan of Action. Rome, Italy: FAO; 1996. Available from: https://www.fao.org/3/w3613e/w3613e00.htm
13. Food and Agriculture Organization (FAO). State of food security and nutrition in the world, 2021. Available from: https://www.fao.org/3/cb4474en/online/cb4474en.html
14. Food and Agriculture Organization (FAO). World food day. 2021. Available from: https://www.fao.org/world-food-day/about/en/
15. Gül A, Şahinler N, Onal AG, Hopkins BK, Sheppard WS. Effects of diluents and plasma on honeybee (*Apis mellifera* L.) drone frozen-thawed semen fertility. *Review Theriogenology*, 2017; 101: 109–113. DOI: 10.1016/j.theriogenology.2017.06.020
16. Popkova EG, Litvinova T, Saveleva N, Sarakhmanova V, Popova T, Mayer S. Problems and perspectives of formation of agricultural clusters for increasing food security of developing countries. *European Research Studies Journal*, 2015; XVIII(3): 177–186. DOI: 10.35808/ersj/464

17. Romanenko NG, Epifanova TV. Convergence of food standards in the beekeeping industry: Legal aspect. *Forestry Journal*, 2017; 2(26), 7(2): 97–105. DOI: 10.12737/article_5967ea119610c7.87163497
18. Skvortsova TA, Shatveryan NG, Alimova OV. Organizational basis of the formation and activity of Beekeeping Associations in Russia. *Advances in Economics, Business and Management Research*, 2020; 147: 333–337. DOI: 10.2991/aebmr.k.200729.063
19. Skvortsova TA., Pasikova, TA, Vereshchagina LN, Pozdnishov AN, Sukhovenko AV. The problem of bankruptcy of business entities as a consequence of the COVID-19 pandemic. *International Journal of Economics and Business Administration*, 2020; VIII(4): 828–837. DOI: 10.35808/ijeba/632

https://doi.org/10.1142/9789811264252_0010

Chapter 10

Legal Regime of Specially Protected Natural Territories as a Factor in the Development of Ecological Economy: Theoretical and Legal Aspects

Ruslan G. Nepranov[*,†], Irina V. Abdurakhmanova[‡], Natalya E. Orlova[§] and Galina V. Mezhenskaya[¶]

Rostov State University of Economics, Rostov-on-Don, Russia
[†]teorii.kafedra@yandex.ru
[‡]ira_rd@rambler.ru
[§]kin1997@mail.ru
[¶]meghen@list.ru

Abstract: The chapter contains the results of a theoretical and legal analysis of the problem of ecological economics and the legal status of specially protected natural territories as a factor in its implementation. The authors prove that the need to implement the ecological economy model is due to the national priorities fixed in the regulations, affecting the area of national security and sustainable socio-economic development. The formation of such territories has become an important direction of the state's implementation of its environmental functions, which requires

[*] Corresponding author.

the effective legal regulation of legal relations, considering the specifics of these objects. This scientific research allowed the authors to classify the lands of specially protected natural areas and determine their place in the system of objects of civil rights. The authors identify directions for improving civil regulation of these objects, considering the proposed classification.

Keywords: Ecological economy; Specially protected natural territories; Legal regime of specially protected natural territories; Environmental legislation; Environmental safety; Lands of specially protected natural territories.

10.1. Introduction

At each stage of the development of human civilization, the new realities of its existence created the need to develop new conceptual approaches to the economy. It has always been the most important area of vital activity of the society on the one hand and a condition for its survival and progress on the other. The concept of the ecological economy has become the result of awareness and scientific understanding of current challenges and global threats. The very formulation of the question of the need to introduce a new economic model was the result of awareness at the domestic and international levels of the objectively determined interconnection and interdependence of economic, social, and environmental problems. Without considering these interrelations, it is impossible to further economic development. Moreover, the very survival of human civilization is impossible because we are talking about creating an effective mechanism for minimizing global risks and countering global threats. The priority is to overcome the consumer attitude to the ecosystem, which can threaten the survival of humanity. Thus, the most significant aspects of the relevance of the problems of ecological economics are universal or, in other words, global.

We emphasize that an equally significant aspect of the conditionality of the theoretical and legal development of this problem is the domestic aspect because the implementation of the ecological economy model is determined by the implementation of national priorities in economic, social, environmental, technological, and other sectors. The documents of the long-term development of the Russian Federation emphasized the need to ensure environmental safety during the modernization of the economy and innovative development. Ecology is firmly integrated into the national security system [6].

The strategy of ecological safety of the Russian Federation also directly links challenges and threats in this area with the introduction of a new economic model, namely, with the development of innovative and environmentally friendly technologies and environmentally friendly industries. Natural objects, of which the lands of specially protected natural territories are a variety, should become the subject of close attention of scientists specializing in the problems of eco-economics. The complexity and specificity of their study, in our opinion, lie in their integrative nature. It is necessary to use economic, historical, legal, and geographical data for their comprehensive research. The aspect of legal regulation of the use and protection of these lands is essential.

The legal regulation of specially protected natural areas in Russia has a long historical tradition. However, the current legal literature has not developed a unified approach to the concept and classification of specially protected natural areas, which adversely affects the prospects for improving the legal regulation of these objects.

The research hypothesis is that the lands of specially protected areas constitute an independent object of the civil regulation, which requires the development of the objective criteria for their classification to improve the effectiveness of the legal regulation and legal protection. The development of a methodology for classifying lands of specially protected natural areas should be the expected result of the scientific analysis of the current legislation and the main conceptual approaches.

The chapter aims to analyze the lands of specially protected natural areas as specific objects of civil rights.

The research tasks are as follows:

- To identify the essential features of the lands of specially protected natural areas as objects of civil rights;
- To identify the criteria for the classification of lands of specially protected natural areas;
- To classify the lands of specially protected natural areas as objects of civil rights.

10.2. Materials and Methods

The conceptual basis is scientific articles on the research topic.

The empirical base of the research includes the data of the Federal State Statistics Service of the Russian Federation (Rosstat) [10], the normative-legal acts of the Russian Federation, and international acts [1–4].

The research presents a comprehensive and systemic analysis of the lands of specially protected natural areas as objects of the civil law regulation, which used formal-legal, comparative-legal, logical, and functional methods.

The analysis allows the authors to prove the lack of knowledge about the lands of specially protected natural areas as objects of civil rights and the legislative regulation of these objects.

10.3. Results

Ecological economics should be understood as a practical model of economic development and a new integrative branch of scientific knowledge. Being in the process of its formation, it needs conceptual understanding and development of theoretical and methodological aspects. It is apparent that the understanding of ecological economics has gone beyond its interpretation as the economics of environmental management. In this case, the object will be correctly defined as a set of relations arising in the process of economic life between natural resources and socio-economic processes. The task of ecological economics is to optimize these relationships. Only in this case will it be possible to reproduce the habitat.

The official definition of specially protected natural territories is contained in the Federal law "On specially protected natural territories of the Russian Federation" (March 14, 1995, No. 33-FL) [1]. The essence of the legislative norm is to consolidate the regime of special protection and conservation, which contributes to the implementation of the environmental policy of the country. This also corresponds to the needs of the ecological economy in its long-term perspective. We emphasize that the effectiveness of the country's environmental policy at each stage of historical development can be assessed only after a certain time.

The very name of specially protected natural territories emphasizes their uniqueness and significance, which go far beyond the ecological economy. They are of exceptional importance for the conservation and reproduction of biological diversity [5]. Cultural and natural landscapes have ecological, scientific, ethical, and cultural values.

The land is an important component of all categories of protected areas without exception. The International Union for Conservation of Nature has introduced the following classification of specially protected objects of natural areas [11]:

- Strictly protected nature reservation and wildlife area;
- National park;
- Natural monument;
- Territory of species habitat regulation;
- Protected landscape;
- Protected area with the regular use of resources.

In accordance with international standards and considering the peculiarities of the regime of specially protected natural areas, the Russian legislation classifies specially protected natural areas into state nature reserves, national parks, natural parks, state nature reserves, natural monuments, dendrological parks, and botanical gardens. According to official data, in 2018, the Russian Federation had 290 specially protected natural areas of federal importance, 12 of which were created in 2018 [10]. In the territories of subjects, there are, for example, a biological station, a swamp complex, a city park, a historical and landscape complex, a historical and natural museum, a forest park, an ecological corridor, a territory of recreational importance, etc.

This classification also previously included lands of therapeutic areas and resorts and territories of traditional nature management of indigenous and small peoples of the North, Siberia, and the Far East, but from January 1, 2014, they are subject to separate legal regulation. The disadvantage of this classification, contained in the Russian legislation, is the lack of the legislative consolidation of the status of such a category as wetlands of international importance. However, on February 2, 1971, Russia ratified the Ramsar Convention on Wetlands of International Importance [4]. Despite its recommendatory nature, its main provisions should be reflected in domestic law.

The lands of specially protected natural areas of regional importance include the lands of state nature reserves, natural monuments, dendrological parks and botanical gardens, and natural parks [9]. Another classification of lands of specially protected natural areas is based on the sign of conservation. Accordingly, it is possible to determine land that is subject to the regime of the absolute commandment, relative commandment, and mixed regime. The regime of absolute protection applies to state reserves and natural monuments. It completely excludes economic activity in this territory. The mixed regime combines protected areas with areas used for recreation and tourism, such as national parks and nature parks.

The cadaster plays an important role in implementing the state policy on the protection and use of specially protected natural territories. Its management allows developing and scientifically substantiating the prospects for developing specially protected natural territories, including as objects of civil rights.

The very term "objects of civil rights" is debatable in civil law. We can name three main approaches developed to date in domestic civil law. The first one is monistic; its proponents consider only one component as an object, for example, action or abstinence from action. In this case, according to scientists, the object and content of the legal relationship will coincide, which is the main drawback of this approach. Things are also considered a monistic object of civil rights in the scientific literature. This is the material theory of the object, which refers to such objects of the material world, the products of spiritual creativity. Another type of the monistic approach is the recognition of the legal regime as the sole object, which is criticized by the majority of authors. The pluralistic theory recognizes the diversity of objects, including tangible and intangible benefits in this structure. A peculiar combination of monistic and pluralistic conceptions was embodied in a comprehensive approach [8].

The concept of land as an object of civil rights is not enshrined in the law. According to Articles 6 and 11 of the Land Code of the Russian Federation, it is correct to speak about it as the object of land relations. Paragraph 3 of Article 6 of the Land Code of the Russian Federation defines the parcel of land as the object of the property right and other rights provided by the Land Code of the Russian Federation [3]. The characteristics of the land plot of specially protected natural territories as objects of civil rights include the ability to meet the needs of the subjects of legal relations, discreteness, legal binding, consistency, and the civil law regime. As an object of civil rights, the land plot of specially protected natural areas is considered as an immovable thing capable of satisfying recreational, sports, cultural, scientific, aesthetic, health, and other needs of participants in legal relations [8]. Their economic use is prohibited or restricted by the environmental protection system.

The system of objects of civil rights has a multilevel character and hierarchy. The main elements of this system are tangible and intangible benefits. The system of objects of civil rights consists of subsystems or types of objects fixed by Article 128 of the Civil Code of the Russian Federation [2]. In the system of objects, depending on their commodity expression, scientists distinguish objects of civil rights that do not have the economic form of goods (personal non-property benefits) and objects of civil rights that have the economic form of goods. The well-known Russian scientist Lapach proposes to divide the objects of civil law into three main groups: property and property benefits, non-property benefits related to the person, and property and non-property benefits [7].

Central to the system of objects of civil rights are those that relate to things. In the legal sense, things are "objects of the material world of interest to the subjects of civil turnover" [8]. The scientific literature highlights the different classifications of things based on different criteria: things allowed for circulation, limited in circulation, and withdrawn from circulation. Another classification proposes to distinguish the following:

- Movable and immovable things;
- Individually defined things and objects, characterized by patrimonial signs;
- Divisible and indivisible things;
- The main things and accessories.

Land plots, subsoil plots, and everything firmly connected with the land (i.e., objects that cannot be moved without incommensurate damage to their purpose) are considered immovable things. Additionally, these are conditional real estate objects, including air and sea vessels, inland navigation vessels, and space objects. That is, real estate acts as a legal condition or legal characteristic of movable things in the physical understanding. Land, including land in specially protected natural territories and other real estate objects, is non-consumable.

Since ecological economics is an intersectoral problem, it needs a comprehensive study by environmentalists, economists, lawyers, financiers, and sociologists, which will allow combining theoretical, methodological, and sectoral aspects. Another area of scientific understanding of the ecological economy and its prospects is connected with constitutional law and with the implementation by the rule of law of the rights and freedoms of citizens enshrined at the constitutional level and their duties (e.g., to take care of the environment).

The current geopolitical realities and the sanctions regime against the Russian Federation have caused global economic consequences that have yet to be comprehended from the perspective of the prospects of the financial market, international trade, and the global economy. In this regard, the problem of ecological economics needs to be understood, taking into account the new realities that give rise to its new aspects. The emerging new world order will certainly affect global and domestic economic processes. An equally significant direction should be the study of this issue in the context of the national security doctrine because the ecological economy is inextricably linked with the country's environmental policy, and ensuring environmental safety is an element of national security in general.

Even though this research directly focuses on the legal aspect of forming an eco-friendly economy model, it seems necessary to emphasize the importance of the mental aspect. Along with the economic, regulatory, technological, and financial components of this problem, the appropriate level of environmental awareness and culture of citizens is also a condition for its successful implementation and effective functioning from a historical perspective. The formation of the necessary level of environmental awareness should become the state's task. It involves the development of a long-term, scientifically based environmental education program aimed at all social and age categories of the population.

Environmental education should presuppose the formation of ecological ideas based on socio-cultural, historical, and economic ones. The developed eco-consciousness of society, which will create an ecological economy, should be based on the developed eco-consciousness of an individual citizen. We emphasize that the constitutional basis of this process is the norms of the Constitution of the Russian Federation on the duty of citizens to take care of the environment. The formation of the mental prerequisites of the ecological economy should presuppose the rejection of the model of the consumer society, its values and priorities incompatible with the developed ecological consciousness. Additionally, ecological consciousness should also include ideas about natural-climatic and ecological identity, which is an integral part of national-historical identity as a whole.

10.4. Conclusion

The ecological economy is a theoretical and legal framework in need of scientific justification and development, as well as a new model of economic development. The objective need for the practical implementation of this model is due to new realities and threats of a global nature. The relevance of studying this issue is also due to domestic factors, namely, the need to implement national priorities for long-term strategic development. In this context, it is important to analyze the issues of ecological economics. Another aspect of its theoretical and legal study should be the interdependence of environmental, economic, social, and technological development issues. One of the factors in implementing the ecological economy in Russia is the legal regulation of the status of specially protected natural areas.

The ecological economy model should be integrated into the political and economic system of the country, enshrined in the Constitution of the Russian Federation. The totality of citizens' rights and freedoms includes a citizen's right to a healthy environment. The position of the land plot of specially protected natural territories, among other objects of civil rights, is determined by the norms of civil, land, and environmental law, which enshrine public prohibitions and obligations. Land as an element in the system of objects of civil rights refers to material goods, namely to real estate. This object is endowed with all features of other objects of civil rights. Simultaneously, it has specific features.

Thus, on the one hand, the land is an integral part of specially protected natural areas and, therefore, the subject to protection. On the other, it is a subject to civil rights and a subject to civil law regulations. This is the peculiarity of this object and its legal regulation. Given that the ecological economy proceeds primarily from the need to conserve nature, we emphasize that the object of conservation should be all natural resources, including all lands, in particular, the lands of specially protected natural territories.

Considering the complex geopolitical realities caused by the COVID-19 pandemic and the sanctions regime against the Russian Federation, we believe that a new legal regulation of their use for tourism purposes should become a promising direction for the use of lands of specially protected natural territories. This, of course, will be quite consistent with the ecological economy and the implementation of certain economic tasks of replenishing the federal and regional budgets. This will also contribute to the solution of several social tasks, which corresponds to the national priorities set out in the documents of the long-term strategic development of the country. It is necessary to revise the existing legal regime of the lands of protected natural territories in the direction of lifting restrictions on their use, which will correspond to the environmental and economic policy of the country.

At the present stage of the development of civilization, the legal regulation of the use and protection of lands of specially protected natural territories should reflect a new conceptual understanding of the problems of ecological economics and its practical implementation to overcome economic, social, and environmental problems effectively.

The importance of legal regulation of the lands of specially protected natural territories in the context of ecological economics is due to its understanding as a qualitatively new type of interaction between public authorities, society, and the environment.

The trend of theoretical understanding of the ecological economy model is universal. However, in our opinion, it should be implemented considering the national-state historically formed features. We are convinced that there is and cannot be any universal model of ecological economy common to all countries. Each country existing on the political map of the world is unique in terms of the natural resources that it possesses and uses. Consequently, the legal regime for using, protecting, and reproducing natural resources is also unique. We emphasize that the legal regulation of the protection and use of natural resources, including land, is historically determined.

We are talking, first of all, about the raw materials economy inherent in Russia, which largely actualizes this problem. As recent events show, the interdependence of the world and regional economies with Russian raw materials has turned out to be much more significant than was commonly believed. It turns out that the indicator "share in the world economy" has lost its significance because it no longer reflects the real dependencies and conditionalities of the world economy.

The problems of the ecological economy and the potential opportunities for its implementation in Russia should take a central place in integrative scientific research and regulatory acts, including long-term ones. The issues of building a model of the ecological economy at the global level, considering current geopolitical realities, are questionable, and its creation within the framework of regional cooperation seems to be quite a promising direction.

References

1. Russian Federation. Federal law No. 33-FL "On specially protected natural territories of the Russian Federation." 1995, Moscow, Russia. Available from: http://ivo.garant.ru/#/document/10107990/paragraph/73179:1

2. Russian Federation. The Civil Code of the Russian Federation (Part one). Moscow, Russia. Available from: https://base.garant.ru/10164072/
3. Russian Federation. The Land Code of the Russian Federation. Moscow, Russia. Available from: https://base.garant.ru/12124624/
4. UNESCO. Convention on Wetlands of International Importance, Mainly as Waterfowl Habitat. 1971; Ramsar, Iran. Available from: https://base.garant.ru/2540816/
5. Dubovik IE, Sharipova MY, Zakirova ZR. Blue-green algae in soils of specially protected natural territories in the Cis-Ural and Southern Ural Regions. *Eurasian Soil Science*, 2007; 40(2): 163–167.
6. Krotik AS. Legal problems of organization and functioning of specially protected natural territories of federal significance (Synopsis of Dis. ... Candidate of Legal Sciences). Moscow, Russia: Lomonosov Moscow State University; 2003.
7. Lapach VA. (2002). *The System of Objects of Civil Rights: Theory and Judicial Practice*. St. Petersburg, Russia: Press Law Center.
8. Luneva EV. Land plots in specially protected natural territories as objects of civil rights (Synopsis of Dis. ... Candidate of Legal Sciences). Kazan, Russia: Kazan Federal University; 2014.
9. Skibin SS. Features of the legal regulation of the subsoil use in limited economic activity within specially protected natural areas (Synopsis of Dis. ... Candidate of Legal Sciences). Moscow, Russia: Institute of Legislation and Comparative Law under the Russian Federation; 2015.
10. Stishov MS, Dudley N. Protected natural areas of the Russian Federation and their categories. Moscow, Russia: WWF; 2019. Available from: https://wwf.ru/en/resources/publications/booklets/okhranyaemye-prirodnye-territorii-rossiyskoy-federatsii-i-ikh-kategorii/
11. Tishkov AA. Development of Russia's network of nature reserves and academic science of the 20th century. *Bulletin of the RAS*, 2017; 87(4): 385–395. DOI: 10.7868/S0869587317080072

https://doi.org/10.1142/9789811264252_0011

Chapter 11

Global Threats and Challenges to the National Financial Security under the COVID-19 Pandemic

Natalia N. Reshetnikova[*,†,‡,¶], **Magomedgabib G. Magomedov**[‡,||], **Sergey S. Zmiyak**[‡,**] **and Yulia S. Chernysheva**[§,††]

[†]*Rostov State University of Economics, Rostov-on-Don, Russia*
[‡]*Don State Technical University, Rostov-on-Don, Russia*
[§]*Institute of Service and Entrepreneurship (Branch), Don State Technical University, Shakhty, Rostov-on-Don, Russia*
[¶]*nata.dstu@yandex.ru*
[||]*srasto@mail.ru*
[**]*sergey_zm@list.ru*
[††]*julia_chern@mail.ru*

Abstract: The chapter focuses on global challenges and threats to national financial security in the context of geopolitical tensions and the COVID-19 pandemic. An urgent methodological task is to form a study of national financial security through its global dimension, namely,

[*]Corresponding author.

through the prism of analyzing the structural transformation of the global financial market into national financial security and the integration of countries with emerging markets into global financial security based on market instruments. The chapter provides a comprehensive review of financial flows. It allocates financial flows in the following areas: (1) analysis of the dynamics of the central bank in relation to financial risks and the onset of global financial crises and (2) the development of indicators of financial shocks (stresses) calculated to assess the instability of the financial system. The authors used analytical materials from the International Monetary Fund, the World Bank, the Central Bank of Russia, the Federal Financial Monitoring Service, other international organizations, and interdepartmental and intergovernmental organizations of the Russian Federation. Additionally, the research provides an overview of Guidelines for the Advancement of Information Security in the Financial Sector for 2019–2021 by the Central Bank of the Russian Federation.

Keywords: Financial Safety; Financial Globalization; Global Financial Market; Global Stock Market; Global Financial Safety Net; GFSN; Emerging Market Countries; Global Dimension; Threats and Challenges; Digital Economy; Structural Transformation; Corona crisis; COVID-19 pandemic.

11.1. Introduction

It is particularly important to strengthen national financial security in the face of new challenges and threats, such as the post-crisis stagnation of the global economy, the emergence of financial innovations, the introduction of digital and management technologies in the financial business, geopolitical tensions, and the COVID-19 pandemic.

These challenges and threats bring a structural transformation of the global financial market, including the tasks of identifying shifts in the structure of the global market and determining the nature and directions of their impact on the financial security indicators of the country.

The use of market tools is a new, unexplored, and unexpected direction for developing a global financial security network. In today's conditions, the fundamental scientific problem is to counter the new external and internal threats to national financial security. This problem requires new scientific solutions.

This research is devoted to these scientific decisions. The relevance of solving this problem is determined by emerging new challenges and threats of a global nature: the COVID-19 pandemic, increased volatility in commodity and financial markets, a recession in the global economy, and others. After all, the development of the Russian economy, the preservation of its economic sovereignty, and stable financial development are currently accompanied by unprecedented external, economic, political, and information pressure.

In world science, financial security at the macro level is interpreted as financial stability. Recent foreign research in the field of ensuring and assessing financial stability has two directions:

(1) Analysis of the role of the central bank in ensuring financial stability and the onset of global financial crises. A description of this direction is given in the works of Bordo [13], Bordo and Meissner [12], Woodford [69], and others;
(2) Development of indicators of financial shocks (stresses) designed to assess the instability of the country's financial system. A description of this direction is given in the works of Giglio *et al.* [27], Sandahl *et al.* [56], and others.

The second line of research is of the most significant interest and is considered in the context of this application.

Financial stability indicators must be used to assess financial security (in particular, in the works of Bertay *et al.* [10] and Kim [39]).

Additionally, we should note the "financial secrecy index" — an indicator developed and calculated by the international organization, The Tax Justice Network. Based on this index, described in the sections "What is the Financial Secrecy Index" [66] and "Method and Concepts" [65], countries are ranked according to their level of security and the scale of their offshore financial activity.

In the framework of this research, we consider it essential to refer to publications covering this topical aspect.

The Global Financial Safety Net (GFSN) was created after the global financial crisis of 2008–2009 to prevent and resolve crises effectively.

The research studies by Scheubel and Stracca [58], Denbee, Jung, and Paternò [18] describe the issues of the functioning of the Global Financial Safety Net and its role, fragmentation, and management in a multipolar system in the global financial architecture.

In particular, U. Volz [68] explores the prospects for the development of the GFSN, its structure (including the International Monetary Fund [IMF]), regional financial agreements (RFAs), and bilateral or multilateral central bank swap agreements and the relationship between them. Additionally, the author emphasizes the heterogeneity of the GFSN and the lack of much reason to expect significant progress in improving cooperation between the RFAs and the IMF unless the latter's governance structure undergoes significant changes. The author concludes that the GFSN will become even more fragmented with the further development of the European Stability Mechanism and the advent of the BRICS Contingent Reserve Agreement. This requires significant reform of the IMF's governance.

The activities of the IMF mainly focus on relatively short-term macroeconomic crises to promote the development of international cooperation in the monetary and financial sectors and are given a special place in the world and native literature, for example, in the IMF policy paper "Adequacy of the Global Financial Safety Net" [33].

Reshetnikova *et al.* [49–53] are among the scientists of the Rostov research school who have accumulated significant scientific experience in studying the global competitiveness of the economy and ensuring national economic interests in the system of the world economic relations.

According to the IMF report [33] on the adequacy of the GFSN, questions were raised on reforming the Fund's lending tools to strengthen the GFSN further. In this context, a proposal was considered for a new mechanism for maintaining liquidity and improving the existing tools of the Fund to prevent crises. The reforms emerging from these discussions are part of the Fund's broader program to strengthen the Global Network by introducing new policy coordination tools and an expanded framework for cooperation with regional funding mechanisms.

For example, Forster *et al.* [23] highlight the structural adjustment programs of the IMF. In accordance with the authors, it is an important but internationally understudied determinant of inequality in the developing world.

For example, Stubbs, Kentikelenis, and King [36] explore the relationship between IMF programs and aid commitments ("aid catalysis"). The authors conclude that the IMF's influence on the global development agenda is multidimensional — a factor previously ignored in aid distribution studies — while refuting the supposed positive impact of IMF programs on social policy assistance.

The trigger for global changes that actualize the problem of ensuring global and national financial security in 2020–2021 was the COVID-19 pandemic.

Mühlich *et al.* [47], Gelpern, Hagan, and Mazarei [26], Stubbs *et al.* [62], and Gallagher *et al.* [25] focus on expanding the GFSN in response to COVID-19.

The works of A. Hawkins *et al.* [31] consider the formation of elements of the global financial safety net and the impact of the financial crisis on the global financial architecture.

The works of Yeyati [71], Bellas *et al.* [9], Aizenman, *et al.* [3], Maltritz [43], Dominguez, Hashimoto, and Ito [19], Csonto and Ivaschenko [17], Grabel [30], Kilp *et al.* [38], Berzon and Erofeeva [11] focus on the influence of different levels of the GFSN on the cost of sovereign borrowing in emerging market economies (identifying the factors that determine sovereign bond spreads in foreign currency in emerging market economies).

The works of Alfaro *et al.* [4], Chari *et al.* [15], Asis *et al.* [8], and Chari [16] are devoted to market exposure capital in emerging markets.

Scheubel, *et al.* [57] consider the role of the global financial cycle (GFC) in stimulating international capital flows in emerging market economies.

Thus, in world science, the main focus is on the prevention of financial crises and macroeconomic shocks using indicators of financial security (stability) as well as on cross-country comparisons of financial security levels and the formation of a global financial security network and the contradictions of its development.

In the native literature, the problem of an indicative assessment of national financial security is being developed in a slightly different direction; the main issues are as follows:

- Selection of socio-economic indicators that are optimal for displaying the level of national financial security;
- Determination of threshold values of financial security indicators to monitor their level;
- A timely and effective response to changes in the level of financial security.

Rubtsov [54] devotes his works to the development of financial and economic systems in the two latest decades, paying special attention to the consequences of the global financial crisis that erupted in 2007–2008 and the measures to overcome it.

Rubtsov [54] also considers changes in the institutional architecture of financial markets after the global economic crisis and assesses the role of the financial sector in the economies of leading countries, using the statistics of the Financial Stability Board as an empirical base.

Works of native authoritative scientists such as Sylvestrov [63,64] and Zvonova *et al.* [73] focus on the problems of assessing and monitoring the state of economic security of the Russian Federation, as well as the development of approaches to strategic planning in the field of economic security. The works of Senchagov [59,60] present a comprehensive approach to studying the impact of global risks on the Russian economy and the level of its economic security.

The works of a team of scientists led by Gorshkova [29], Dykhova [20], Loktionova [42], Krivorotova *et al.* [40], Karanina [34], Alifanova and Evlakhova [5] explore the problems of assessing and monitoring national financial security.

The works by Ershov [21], Glazyev [28], Rubtsov [54], Mirkin [46], and Krupnov [41] focus on the functioning of the global financial market in the face of structural changes in the global economy. The authors analyze the market and its changes as a result of the global financial crisis in terms of the systemic stagnation of the current economy, geopolitical risks, and monitoring and assessing the state of economic security.

Mirkin [45] focuses on the key long-term trends in global finance, structural changes in the global economy and global finance, including those caused by the coronavirus pandemic.

The study of Abramova *et al.* [1] considers the development of the financial market of the Russian Federation for 2019–2021 under the current macroeconomic and financial instability in order to assess the depth and balance of the main directions of its development in terms of achieving the task of accelerating growth and increasing the efficiency of the economy.

The works of Teplova and Stolyarov [67], Berzon and Erofeeva [11] are devoted to the analysis of the determinants of the nominal yield of sovereign bonds in large emerging markets (BRICS countries).

The works of Karminsky and Stolbov [35], Andryushina and Karminsky [6] are devoted to the issues of systemic risk.

The analysis of the risks associated with this process is of particular importance in the study of the digital transformation of the financial market in Russia. The impact of digitalization on the risks of the financial sector and the levels and goals of managing these risks are presented in the works of Maramygin *et al.* [44] and Silvestrov *et al.* [61]. Khalin and Chernova [37] analyze the risks of digitalization for society and the Russian economy.

Since the research covers the problems of employment and income of the population, it is advisable to note the current state of research on this problem.

Hines [32] investigates long-term perspectives of the transformation of labor as a source of livelihood in the so-called post-work world, the key drivers of which are the development of artificial intelligence and automation, shifts in the value system (from traditional to postmodern), and a decrease in the role of work as a separate measurable type of activity due to its combination with other aspects of people's daily life.

Fossen and Sorgner discussed medium- and short-term effects of digitalization on the labor market and employment structure, their subdivision into destructive and transformational ones, and a model for mapping professions according to the degree of exposure to the effects of digitalization [24].

The analysis of the impact of digitalization on the Russian labor market is presented in studies of international organizations (such as McKinsey [7], Boston Consulting Group, etc.), as well as in the works of Russian scientists, including Zemtsov [72], Osipov [48], Sadovaya [55], and others. Noteworthy is the project "Atlas of Emerging Jobs" [2], which incorporates the results of the Foresight Competency 2030 study organized by the Moscow School of Management SKOLKOVO and the Agency for Strategic Initiatives.

The presented studies on the transformation of the Russian labor market in the context of digitalization emphasize the potential threat of an increase in social and economic inequality, as well as the risks of large-scale technological unemployment under certain conditions. However, it does not touch upon the corresponding consequences for the welfare of the population and its participation in the activities of the Russian financial market. Actually, these consequences and aspects are supposed to be investigated within the framework of the proposed project.

A review of the above works has led us to the conclusion that the global perspective of the issues raised in the research requires reflection and the formation of a new approach to solving these scientific and methodological problems through the prism of a global dimension.

11.2. Methods

The methodological basis for conducting large-scale research on the global dimension of financial security is created by the following stages:

(1) Development of a methodology for global measurement of national financial security and its approbation in the study of the impact of the structural transformation of the world stock market on the national financial security of countries with emerging markets;
(2) Development of the concept of their integration into the global financial safety net based on the use of new tools — market instruments.

The study of the GFSN through the prism of the transformation of the entire global financial market, the network of its elements, and the global financial architecture will help solve the problems mentioned above.

This will help predict transformational shifts and their impact on national and global financial security, as well as on the development of the GFSN.

The research will allow us to develop a strategy for ensuring financial security and its monitoring based on a new methodology, i.e., its global dimension, which corresponds to one of the Priority Directions for the Development of Science, Technology, and Engineering in the Russian Federation — Security and Countering Terrorism.

11.3. Results

The post-crisis stagnation of the global economy, the emergence of financial innovations, the introduction of digital and management technologies in the financial business, geopolitical tensions, global financial disintegration, and the COVID-19 pandemic are the triggers for global changes that actualize the problem of ensuring national financial security.

Nowadays, the fundamental scientific problem — countering new external and internal threats to national financial security — has its solutions. At the theoretical and methodological level, this is the formation and development of a methodology for indicative assessment of national financial security. At the practical level, this is the adoption of a set of strategies for national, economic, and other types of security; the implementation of the measures enshrined in them; and monitoring of the national security level. However, these solutions only partially meet the new challenges and threats. Thus, the experience of past world crises shows that the global financial market retains the leading role in generating shocks, which, in a certain sense, outstrips other triggers in terms of the likelihood of crises and the potential for negative impact. Simultaneously, the "mirror" of the state of the national economy, the leading indicator of its dynamics, is precisely the stock market, which is closely integrated with other segments of the global financial market. Thus, the stock market can be considered a central link in a network of vulnerabilities to ensure national financial security in the face of threats generated by the global financial market. The level of threats to national financial security associated with the global financial market is intensified by its structural transformation in the context of digitalization and "radical uncertainty." In this regard, it is of particular importance to strengthen national financial security, considering the challenges and threats that the structural transformation of the global financial market brings with it, including the tasks of identifying shifts in the structure of the global market and determining the nature and directions of their impact on the national financial security indicators. During the COVID-19 pandemic, several contradictions in the development of financial markets were exposed and aggravated, which is manifested in the multidirectional trends, structural shifts in the economic and institutional structure of the global financial market and its sectors, changes in monetary policy, and the manifestation of negative secondary effects of these processes.

The vulnerability of the global economic system is exacerbated by two interrelated trends in monetary policy.

The first is the transition to zero interest rates as a long-term benchmark that forms expectations regarding the development parameters not only of national economies and their financial markets but also of the global economy and its markets, which means a qualitative transformation of monetary policy. The second is a bias in regulatory methods in favor of the repurchase of assets in financial markets by central banks, i.e., in favor of non-traditional methods of regulation, which, in the post-crisis period since 2008, have changed from temporary to permanent, dominant, and long term.

The range of secondary effects (including negative ones) of these methodological distortions of regulation is extremely wide and varied in strength and levels of manifestation.

Let us note some of them:

- Deformed recovery of stock markets due to inflating and maintaining market bubbles in developed markets, which means a stable distortion in the pricing of financial assets and increases the fragility of the financial system, negatively affecting the structure of the economy;
- An increase in the share of central bank assets in national and global GDP affects the structure of the financial market and the economy as a whole through the ownership structure.

Structural shifts in the financial market:

- Hypertrophied growth of the risk redistribution market — derivative financial instruments, the volume of which is already many times greater than the volume of global GDP and the market of major financial assets;
- The growth of the market of digital assets, including cryptocurrencies, occurs due to the inversion of the expectations of market participants. The contradiction between the high-risk economic nature of cryptocurrencies, where the main component of pricing is expectations rather than real security, on the one hand, and the need for protective assets during the COVID-19 pandemic, on the other hand, have led to a paradoxical modification: bitcoin has turned into a protective asset in the expectations of investors, and its high-risk nature has been distorted into its opposite.

As a result, the flow of funds from the stock market to the cryptocurrency market in anticipation of reducing risks due to such redistribution has led to a new structural deformation of the financial market.

The market of the riskiest asset has turned into the most growing segment of the market during the crisis, which reached its historical high in terms of capitalization and price (bitcoin).

This paradox means another line of distortion in the formation of prices of financial assets. Thus, as a fundamental factor, the inversion of expectations can change the market structure and distort the implementation of the market function. In this case, risk reduction is possible due to risk redistribution among market participants.

There is also a mechanism for maintaining these distortions: after the rise in prices, prominent players (e.g., public companies such as Tesla) come to the market, demand increases due to significant investments, which leads to an even more significant speculative rise in prices, their volatility, and risk.

The digital transformation of the financial market has accelerated, proceeding unevenly in various market segments.

There has been a large-scale trend in developing projects by the central banks of more than 70 countries to launch digital currencies (digital yuan, ruble, euro, etc.). The role of the American stock market in generating and maintaining the systematic risk of the global market is growing.

The trend toward concentration of assets in management companies of institutional investors becomes increasingly pronounced, which can also influence the mechanism of formation of prices for financial assets.

The networked nature of relationships in financial markets increases the likelihood of "domino" and "contagion" effects in the event of systemic risks that grow in the face of these trends, contradictions, and distortions of the market pricing mechanism, as well as long-term monetary policy in countries with developed financial markets.

These contradictions and adverse effects require theoretical understanding in the context of global and national financial security and the consequences for economic growth.

The following logical questions arise:

- What are the spillovers and implications for emerging markets?
- What are the mechanisms for expanding the GFSN?

These issues remain among the topical areas of research and require the formation of a methodology for studying financial security through its global dimension.

Countering these threats and the destructive potential of their consequences is possible through multilateral cooperation within the GFSN.

In accordance with the Eurasian Economic Commission [22], the experience of the Russian Federation in creating regional development funds in the EAEC (The Eurasian Economic Community, EurAsEC) space (by analogy with regional agreements on IMF financing) can be assessed positively because it represents the formation of a regional component of the GFSN, which allows overcoming the fragmentation of the latter.

Given the variety of financing instruments and their characteristics, a separate issue is the choice of financial support mechanisms: market instruments vs. administrative ones.

The use of market instruments is a new, unexplored, and undeveloped direction in the development of the GFSN. Thus, in today's conditions, the fundamental scientific problem — countering new external and internal threats to national financial security — requires new scientific solutions, which will certainly become the basis for future research by the team of authors.

Digital transformation creates multiple benefits for the consumers of financial services and inherently increases the quality and speed of the opportunities for interaction between the consumers of financial services and financial institutions while causing additional risks. The rise in cybercrime, primarily in the credit and financial sector, is a global trend that requires coordinated efforts by regulators, law enforcement agencies, credit and financial institutions, and financial service consumers. Large-scale cyberattacks inflict material economic damage, affect geopolitical relations, and decrease the level of confidence on the Internet. Cyberattacks on digital financial systems can provoke a financial crisis. The Global Risks Report 2018 by World Economic Forum [70] defines cyberattacks as a type of global technological risk. As a global trend, there has been an increase in financial losses from cyberattacks and a disruption of the integrity and continuity of operations in the financial market (17% of all cyberattacks occur in the financial sector). The elaborate methods, techniques, and instruments used to commit cyberattacks demand that regulators take flexible and prompt action and use innovative digital technologies and work methods. The US, Canada, Singapore, Australia, Malaysia, New Zealand, Japan, the UK, and Austria are the countries best prepared to counter cyberattacks, making them the most attractive to the consumers of financial services and accelerating their economic development. The key risks in the credit and financial area are as follows:

- Financial losses of clients (financial service consumers) undermining confidence in advanced financial technologies;

- Financial losses of individual financial institutions that may have a negative (critical) material impact on their financial standing;
- Disruption of the operational reliability and continuity of financial services causing reputational damage and growing social tension;
- A potential systemic crisis in the case of information security incidents in institutions that are critical to the financial market.

The International Organization of Securities Commissions (IOSCO) set the following criteria for the proper functioning of critical financial market infrastructure:

- The capability to restore operations within two hours after disruption;
- The capability to perform settlements on due dates and ensure completeness of transactions. According to the Bank of Russia's Financial Sector Computer Emergency Response Team (Bank of Russia's FinCERT) [14], unauthorized transactions in corporate accounts amounted to 1.469 billion rubles in 2018 (vs. nearly 1.57 billion rubles in 2017, nearly 1.89 billion rubles in 2016, and nearly 3.7 billion rubles in 2015).

In 2018, unauthorized transactions with the use of payment cards (settlement, credit, and prepaid cards) issued by Russian credit institutions carried out in Russia and abroad totaled 1.384 billion rubles (vs. 0.961 billion rubles in 2017, 1.08 billion rubles in 2016, and 1.14 billion rubles in 2015) [14]. In 2018, such transactions accounted for 0.0018% of the total amount of transactions using payment cards issued by Russian credit institutions (0.018 rubles per 1,000 rubles transferred) [14]. Meanwhile, the maximum allowable percentage of unauthorized money transfers stipulated by the European Banking Authority (EBA) equals 0.005% (€0.05 per €1,000 transferred). No incidents leading to critical damage in systemically important credit and financial institutions have been registered in the Russian Federation. However, there were several incidents disrupting the continuity of financial services and, consequently, causing growth in social tension. Information security incidents in small and medium-sized financial institutions may result in the termination of their business. According to the findings of the analysis of attempted thefts of credit institutions' funds, the amount of funds exposed to the risk of theft is comparable to the average daily balance of a credit institution's correspondent account opened with the Bank of Russia, plus the average daily receipts into the given correspondent account. For small and medium-sized financial institutions, this amount of funds is often comparable to their equity (capital).

11.4. Discussion

The scientific novelty of the research is substantiated by the following:

(1) The formation of a new methodological approach to studying national financial security, reflecting its global dimension through the prism of the impact of the structural transformation of the global financial market on national financial security and the integration of countries with emerging markets into the global financial security network based on market instruments.
(2) The integrity of the study of the structural transformation of the global stock market is based on a new (for this research object) network approach in conjunction with the institutional approach, considering the following:
   - Analysis of the levels of structural transformation (sectoral, intersectoral, and institutional);
   - The study of the channels for transferring the systemic risk of the global stock market and the consequences of its structural transformation to the level of the national economy and its financial security;
   - The formation of a system of indicators for assessing structural changes in the global stock market (according to the levels of its transformation);
   - Determination of the character and direction of the structural transformation impact of the world stock market on the national financial security.
(3) Developing a concept for integrating emerging market countries into the GFSN based on market-based instruments, which are a new financing mechanism within this network, in contrast to credit, regional, and central bank swaps.

The scientific novelty of the research forms the heuristic significance of the expected results, namely the planned methodological approach to the study of national financial security, reflecting its global dimension, can also be used to analyze other research objects of economic science, such as economic growth, socio-economic inequality, digital transformation economy, and sustainable development.

The rationale for the direction of the research is as follows:

(1) The impact of shifts in the global stock market on national financial security;
(2) Determining the positions and prospects of countries with emerging markets (including Russia) and developing countries in the global financial safety net;
(3) Determining financial interconnectedness and the level of integration of segments of the global financial market based on the adaptation of the IMF methodology to a new research subject;
(4) Network analysis to identify structural shifts in the transformation of the global stock market.

11.5. Conclusion

We will present the Guidelines for the Advancement of Information Security in the Financial Sector for 2019–2021 (the Guidelines).

The Guidelines describe the prerequisites and trends in the development of information security in the Russian financial sector, the Bank of Russia's objectives and priority activities in the area of information security and cyber resilience, as well as measures to be taken in this area. The measures stipulated in the Guidelines were developed, among other things, to implement a range of particular objectives as part of the federal projects of the National program "Digital Economy of the Russian Federation," approved by Minutes No. 8 (May 6, 2019) of the meeting of the presidium of the Governmental Commission for Digital Development and Using Information Technology for Improving the Quality of Life and Conditions of Doing Business.

The key digital technology-based infrastructure projects for which the Bank of Russia sets information security requirements in the first place are as follows:

- Remote identification platform (Unified Biometric System);
- Faster Payments System;
- Marketplace platform;
- Digital customer profile.

In the future, the digital transformation will cause major alterations in financial service technologies. Therefore, guided by the global development trends, the Bank of Russia should elaborate new approaches to ensuring information security and cyber resilience of the financial ecosystem in the following conditions:

- Changes in the system architecture (the use of distributed ledger technology);
- Remote access to financial services and wide application of mobile technologies;
- Application of new advanced technologies for information security and cyber resilience purposes (big data, artificial intelligence);
- The Internet of Things as an element of the payment space.

To ensure control for the absence of software vulnerabilities, including those associated with programming bugs that may enable successful cyberattacks, it is critical to create organizational and technical conditions for financial institutions to analyze vulnerabilities in the software they use to transfer funds (or conduct other financial transactions) and identify the software that should be analyzed.

The Guidelines stipulate the following objectives in the information security and cyber resilience area:

(1) Cyber resilience;
(2) Protecting the rights of consumers of financial services by monitoring indicators of financial losses;
(3) Promoting the development of innovative financial technologies by controlling the levels of risk of information security incidents and ensuring adequate information security;
(4) Supervision over the information security risk (cyber risk) level in credit and non-bank financial institutions and national payment system participants;
(5) Countering the dissemination in the credit and financial sector of information on illegal operations and services of market players; and
(6) Building an environment for promoting a culture of information security and cyber hygiene in credit and finance.

We attach great importance to international cooperation for the development. Global cybersecurity threats require nations to join their efforts as long as these threats are cross-border, disrupt existing business models, and cause new challenges in international economic relations. The Bank of Russia stipulates its competent participation in developing an up-to-date agenda that meets Russia's interests as a key goal within the international cooperation in the area of information security and cyber resilience. The main objectives comprise cyberthreat data exchange, assistance in the implementation of uniform standardized approaches to ensuring cybersecurity, as well as sharing the experience in the regulation and deployment of financial technologies.

A comprehensive study of the current threats, challenges, and vulnerabilities put forward by national financial security in this work substantiated the situation caused by real problems: the COVID-19 pandemic, increased volatility in commodity and financial markets, a recession in the global economy, and others.

References

1. Abramova MA, Lavrushin OI, Pishchik VY, Rubtsov BB, Solyannikova SP. The draft guidelines for the development of the Russian financial market in 2019–2021 prepared by the Bank of Russia: Expert opinion of Financial University. *Economics. Taxes. Right*, 2019; 12(3): 17–24. DOI: 10.26794/1999-849X-2019-12-3-17-24
2. Agency for Strategic Initiatives and SKOLKOVO School of Management. Atlas of Emerging Jobs. 2014. Available from: https://skolkovo.ru/public/media/documents/research/sedec/SKOLKOVO_SEDeC_Atlas.pdf
3. Aizenman J, Jinjarak Y, Park D. International reserves and swap lines: Substitutes or complements? *International Review of Economics & Finance*, 2011; 20(1): 5–18.
4. Alfaro L, Asis G, Chari A, Panizza U. Corporate debt, firm size and financial fragility in emerging markets. *Journal of International Economics*, 2019; 118: 1–19. DOI: 10.1016/j.jinteco.2019.01.002
5. Alifanova EN, Evlakhova YS. The comparative analysis of methodological approaches to indicative assessment of the national financial security. *Financial Research*, 2016; 3(52): 8–16.
6. Andryushin SA, Karminsky AM. Modern financial institutions and markets, their regulation in crisis conditions: international experience and Russian practice (Review of the speeches of the participants of the thematic conference "banks and financial markets" of the fourth Russian economic congress). *Bulletin of the Institute of Economics RAS*, 2021; 2: 182–198. DOI: 10.52180/2073-6487_2021_2_182_198
7. Aptekman A, Kalabin V, Klincov V, Kuznecova E, Kulagin V, Yasenovec I. Digital Russia: a new reality. Report of McKinsey. 2017. Available from: http://www.mckinsey.com/~/media/McKinsey/Locations/Europe%20and%20Middle%20East/Russia/Our%20Insights/Digital%20Russia/Digital-Russia-report.ashx

8. Asis G, Chari A, Haas A. In search of distress risk in emerging markets. Cambridge, MA: National Bureau of Economic Research; 2020. Available from: http://www.nber.org/papers/w27213
9. Bellas D, Papaioannou MG, Petrova I. Determinants of emerging market sovereign bond spreads. In: Braga AP, Vincolette C (Eds.). *Sovereign Debt and the Financial Crisis: Will This Time be Different?* Washington DC: World Bank; 2010. pp. 77–101.
10. Bertay AC, Demirgüç-Kunt A, Huizinga H. Should cross-border banking benefit from the financial safety net? *Journal of Financial Intermediation*, 2016; 27: 51–67. DOI: 10.1016/j.jfi.2016.05.005
11. Berzon NI, Erofeeva TM. Russian corporate bond market: history of development, current trends, problems and prospects. *Tomsk State University Journal of Economics*, 2018; 44: 150–165.
12. Bordo MD, Meissner CM. Fiscal and financial crises. In *Handbook of Macroeconomics*. Elsevier; 2016. Vol. 2, pp. 355–412. DOI: 10.1016/bs.hesmac.2016.04.001
13. Bordo MD. An historical perspective on the quest for financial stability and the monetary policy regime. *The Journal of Economic History*, 2018; 78(2): 319–357. DOI: 10.1017/S0022050718000281
14. Central Bank of the Russian Federation. Guidelines for the advancement of information security in the financial sector for 2019–2021. Moscow, Russia; 2019. Available from: https://www.cbr.ru/Content/Document/File/103460/onrib_2021_e.pdf
15. Chari A, Stedman KD, Lundblad C. Taper tantrums: QE, its aftermath and emerging market capital flows. Cambridge, MA: National Bureau of Economic Research; 2017. Available from: https://www.nber.org/system/files/working_papers/w23474/w23474.pdf
16. Chari A. Capital market risks in emerging markets. The Reporter. 2020; 3. Available from: https://www.nber.org/reporter/2020number3/capital-market-risks-emerging-markets
17. Csonto B, Ivaschenko IV. Determinants of sovereign bond spreads in emerging markets: Local fundamentals and global factors vs. ever-changing misalignments. IMF Working Paper. 2013; 13/164. Available from: https://www.imf.org/en/Publications/WP/Issues/2016/12/31/Determinants-of-Sovereign-Bond-Spreads-in-Emerging-Markets-Local-Fundamentals-and-Global-40770
18. Denbee E, Jung C, Paternò F. Stitching together the global financial safety net. Bank of Italy Occasional Paper. 2016; 322. DOI: 10.2139/ssrn.2772513
19. Dominguez KM, Hashimoto Y, Ito T. International reserves and the global financial crisis. Journal of International Economics. 2012; 88(2): 388–406. DOI: 10.1016/j.jinteco.2012.03.003

20. Dykhova AL. Criteria for the effectiveness of financial policy in the context of ensuring Russia's financial security. *Journal of Economy and Entrepreneurship*, 2020; 1(114): 500–503.
21. Ershov MV. Ten years after the global crisis: Risks and prospects. *Voprosy Ekonomiki*, 2019; 1: 37–53. DOI: 10.32609/0042-8736-2019-1-37-53
22. Eurasian Economic Commission. Economy and financial policy. [date unknown; cited 2022 Jan 10]. Available from: http://www.eurasiancommission.org/en/act/finpol/dofp/finance/Pages/default.aspx
23. Forster T, Kentikelenis AE, Reinsberg B, Stubbsc TH, King LP. How structural adjustment programs affect inequality: A disaggregated analysis of IMF conditionality, 1980–2014. *Social Science Research*, 2019; 80: 83–113. DOI: 10.1016/j.ssresearch.2019.01.001
24. Fossen F, Sorgner A. Mapping the future of occupations: transformative and destructive effects of new digital technologies on jobs. Foresight and STI Governance. 2019; 13(2): 10–18. DOI: 10.17323/2500-2597.2019.2.10.18
25. Gallagher KP, Gao H, Kring WN, Ocampo JA, Volz U. Safety first: Expanding the global financial safety net in response to COVID-19. *Global Policy*, 2021; 12(1), 140–148.
26. Gelpern A, Hagan S, Mazarei A. Debt standstills can help vulnerable governments manage the COVID-19 crisis. In: Obstfeld M, Pozen A (Eds.) *How the G20 Can Hasten Recovery from COVID-19*. Washington, DC: Peterson International Institute for International Economics; 2020. Available from: https://www.piie.com/sites/default/files/documents/piieb20-1.pdf
27. Giglio S. Kelly B, Pruitt S. Systemic risk and the macroeconomy: an empirical evaluation. *Journal of Financial Economics*, 2016; 119(3): 457–471. DOI: 10.1016/j.jfineco.2016.01.010
28. Glazyev SY. Problems and prospects of the Russian financial market in the context of structural changes in the world economy. *Finance: Theory and Practice*, 2020; 24(3): 6–29. DOI: 10.26794/2587-5671-2020-24-3-6-29
29. Gorshkova NV. (Ed.) *Scientific and Practical Aspects of Financial Security (at the level of the state, region, organization and individual)*. Kursk, Russia: Publishing house Universitetskaya kniga; 2018.
30. Grabel, I. Continuity, discontinuity and incoherence in the Bretton Woods Order: A Hirschmanian reading. *Development and Change*, 2019; 50(1), 46–71. DOI: 10.1111/dech.12469
31. Hawkins A, Rahman J, Williamson T. Is the global financial safety net at a tipping point to fragmentation? *Economic Roundup*, 2014; 1: 1–20. Available from: https://treasury.gov.au/publication/economic-roundup-issue-1-2014/economic-roundup-issue-1/is-the-global-financial-safety-net-at-a-tipping-point-to-fragmentation
32. Hines A. Getting ready for a post-work future. *Foresight and STI Governance*, 2019; 13(1): 9–30. DOI: 10.17323/2500-2597.2019.1.19.30

33. International Monetary Fund (IMF). IMF executive board discusses proposals for toolkit reform, concludes review of the flexible credit line and precautionary and liquidity line. 2017. Washington, DC: IMF. Available from: https://www.imf.org/en/News/Articles/2017/12/19/pr17507-imf-executive-board-discusses-proposals-for-toolkit-reform
34. Karanina EV. *Financial Security* (at the level of the state, region, organization, individual). Kirov, Russia: VyatSU; 2016.
35. Karminsky AM, Stolbov MI. Assessing the link between financial soundness and systemic risk for key Russian banks. *Journal of Corporate Finance Research*, 2016; 10(1): 77–87. DOI: 10.17323/j.jcfr.2073-0438.10.1.2016.77-87
36. Kentikelenis AE, Stubbs TH, King LP. IMF conditionality and development policy space, 1985–2014. *Review of International Political Economy*, 2016; 23(4), 543–582. DOI: 10.1080/09692290.2016.1174953
37. Khalin VG, Chernova GV. Digitalization and its impact on the Russian economy and society: advantages, challenges, threats and risks. *Management Consulting*, 2018; 10(118): 46–62. DOI: 10.22394/1726-1139-2018-10-46-63
38. Kilp J, Anvari V, Springfield S, Roberts C. The impact of the global financial safety net on emerging market bond spreads. *Russian Journal of Money and Finance*, 2019; 78(2): 43–66. DOI: 10.31477/rjmf.201902.43
39. Kim C. Strengthening the global financial safety net: Challenges and prospects. *Emerging Markets Finance and Trade*, 2016; 52(10): 2212–2220. DOI: 10.1080/1540496X.2016.1174854
40. Krivorotov VV, Kalina AV, Belik IS. Threshold values of indicative indicators for diagnosing the economic security of the Russian Federation at the present stage. Vestnik UrFU. *Series: Economics and Management*, 2019; 18(6): 892–910.
41. Krupnov YA. Crisis vaccine: Analysis and forecast of post-crisis geoeconomic conditions for the development of the world and domestic economy. *Proceedings of the Southwest State University. Series: Economics, Sociology and Management*, 2020; 10(3): 10–22.
42. Loktionova EA. Developing the methodology to assess the Russian financial market security in current conditions. *Finance and Credit*, 2018; 24(6): 1469–1481. DOI: 10.24891/fc.24.6.1469
43. Maltritz, D. Determinants of sovereign yield spreads in the Eurozone: A Bayesian approach. *Journal of International Money and Finance*, 2012; 31(3): 657–672. DOI: 10.1016/j.jimonfin.2011.10.010
44. Maramygin MS, Chernova GV, Reshetnikova LG. Digital transformation of the financial services market in Russia: Trends and specificity. *Upravlenets* [*The Manager*], 2019; 10(3): 70–82. DOI: 10.29141/2218-5003-2019-10-3-7

45. Mirkin YM. New realities of the global economy and their impact on Russia. *Scientific Works of the Free Economic Society of Russia*, 2020; 223(3): 106–110. DOI: 10.38197/2072-2060-2020-223-3-106-110
46. Mirkin YM. Transformation of the economic and financial structures of the world: the impact of growing shocks of catastrophes. *Outlines of Global Transformations: Politics, Economics, Law*, 2020; 13(4): 97–116. DOI: 10.23932/2542-0240-2020-13-4-5
47. Mühlich L, Fritz B, Kring WN, Gallagher K. The global financial safety net tracker: Lessons for the COVID-19 crisis from a new interactive dataset. Boston, MA: Boston University, Global Development Policy Center; 2020. Available from: https://www.bu.edu/gdp/files/2020/04/GEGI-GDP_Policy Brief_FInal.pdf
48. Osipov VS. Gap of the employment in the digital economy. *CITISE*, 2019; 1(18): 35.
49. Reshetnikova N, Magomedov M, Buklanov D, Zakharchenko E. The international business cooperation and its influence on enterprise financial security under globalization. In: Popkova EG (Ed.). *The Future of the Global Financial System: Downfall or Harmony*. Cham, Switzerland: Springer; 2019. pp. 294–308. DOI: 10.1007/978-3-030-00102-5_31
50. Reshetnikova N, Magomedov M, Buklanov D. Digital finance technologies: Threats and challenges to the global and national financial security. *IOP Conference Series: Earth and Environmental Science*, 2021; 666: 062139. DOI: 10.1088/1755-1315/666/6/062139
51. Reshetnikova N, Magomedov M, Zmiyak S, Chernysheva Y. Digital technologies adoption in the agro-industrial complex as a priority of regional development in the conditions of global macroeconomic changes. In: Beskopylny A, Shamtsyan M (Eds.) *XIV International Scientific Conference "INTERAGROMASH 2021."* Cham, Switzerland: Springer; 2021, pp. 3–12. DOI: 10.1007/978-3-030-81619-3_1
52. Reshetnikova N. Digital society and the information age: Challenges and threats for man, business and the state. *Reality of Politics. Estimates-Comments-Forecasts*, 2021; 17, 145–154.
53. Reshetnikova NN, Magomedov MG. Influence strategic competitive advantage international business cooperation in the frame of the financial crisis. In: Solovev D (Ed.) *Smart Technologies and Innovations in Design for Control of Technological Processes and Objects: Economy and Production*. Cham, Switzerland: Springer; 2018, pp. 399–408. DOI: 10.1007/978-3-030-15577-3_39
54. Rubtsov BB. The shifts in the financial markets architecture after the global economic crisis of 2007–2009. *Banking Services*, 2020; 10: 9–21. DOI: 10.36992/2075-1915_2020_10_9

55. Sadovaya E. Digital Economy and a new paradigm of the labor market. *World Economy and International Relations*, 2018; 62(12): 35–45. DOI: 10.20542/0131-2227-2018-62-12-35-45
56. Sandahl JF, Holmfeldt M, Rydén A, Strömqvist M. An index of financial stress for Sweden. *Sveriges Riksbank Economic Review*, 2011; 2. http://archive.riksbank.se/Upload/Rapporter/2011/POV_2/er_2011_2_forsssandahl_holmfeldt_ryden_stromqvist.pdf
57. Scheubel B, Stracca L, Tille C. Taming the global financial cycle: What role for the global financial safety net? *Journal of International Money and Finance*, 2019; 94: 160–182. DOI: 10.1016/j.jimonfin.2019.01.015
58. Scheubel B, Stracca L. What do we know about the global financial safety net? Rationale, data and possible evolution. *ECB Occasional Paper*. 2016; 177. Available from SSRN: https://ssrn.com/abstract=2843608
59. Senchagov VK, Lev MY, Gelvanovsky MI, Rubin BV, Ivanov EA, Karavaeva IV, *et al*. Optimization of indicators and threshold levels in the development of financial, banking and consumer indicators in the system of economic security of the Russian Federation. Moscow, Russia: Maska; 2017.
60. Senchagov VK, Pobyvaev SA, Solovev AI. Assessment of the global risks impact as a tool for devising the economic strategy of Russia: Indicative approach. *Economic Strategies*, 2016; 18(8): 24–31.
61. Silvestrov SN, Krupnov YA, Starovoitov VG. Determination and implementation of national development goals in Russian strategic planning. *Russian Economic Journal*, 2021; 1: 32–44. DOI: 10.33983/0130-9757-2021-1-32-44
62. Stubbs T, Kring W, Laskaridis C, Kentikelenis A, Gallagher K. Whatever it takes? The global financial safety net, Covid-19, and developing countries. *World Development*, 2021; 137: 105171. DOI: 10.1016/j.worlddev.2020.105171
63. Sylvestrov SN, Starovoitov VG, Larionov AV. Developing the system for monitoring the implementation of the economic security strategy of the Russian Federation. *National Interests: Priorities and Security*, 2020; 16(12): 2202–2217. DOI: 10.24891/ni.16.12.2202
64. Sylvestrov SN. Countering development challenges of the international monetary and financial system. Development and Security. 2019; 2: 4–12.
65. Tax Justice Network. Method and concepts. Available from: https://fsi.taxjustice.net/en/methodology/method-and-concepts
66. Tax Justice Network. What is the Financial Secrecy Index? 2020. Available from: https://fsi.taxjustice.net/en/faq
67. Teplova TV, Stolyarov AI. The features of the main segments of stock market development in the Russian federation (bonds and stocks) at the present stage. *Bulletin of the Institute of Economics of the RAS*, 2017; 6: 31–48.
68. Volz, U. Toward the development of a global financial safety net or a segmentation of the global financial architecture? *Emerging Markets Finance*

and Trade, 2016 Aug 02; 52(10): 2221–2237. DOI: 10.1080/1540496X.2016.1186011

69. Woodford M. Quantitative easing and financial stability. *Journal Economía Chilena* (*The Chilean Economy*). 2016; 19(2): 4–77.
70. World Economic Forum. The Global Risks Report 2018. Geneva, Switzerland; 2018. Available from: https://www.weforum.org/reports/the-global-risks-report-2018
71. Yeyati EL. The cost of reserves. *Economics Letters*, 2008; 100(1): 39–42.
72. Zemtsov S. Robots and potential technological unemployment in the Russian regions: review and preliminary results. *Voprosy Ekonomiki*, 2017; 7: 142–157. DOI: 10.32609/0042-8736-2017-7-142-157
73. Zvonova EA, Kuznetsov AV, Pishchik VY, Silvestrov SN. Features and prospects of building a two-contour monetary and financial system at the national and regional level. *The World of New Economy*, 2020; 14(1): 26–33. https://doi.org/10.26794/2220-6469-2020-14-1-26-33

https://doi.org/10.1142/9789811264252_0012

Chapter 12

Metamorphoses of the System of Sectoral and Institutional Principles of Administrative Law Through the Prism of Ecological Economics: Problems and Prospects of Their Solution in the Context of the COVID-19 Pandemic

Alexey N. Pozdnyshov[†,§], Victoria A. Teselkina[*,†,¶], Alexey A. Shchetinin[†,‖] and Ilya E. Shvachkin[‡,]**

[†]*Rostov State University of Economics, Rostov-on-Don, Russia*
[‡]*Russian State University of Justice, Rostov-on-Don, Russia*
[§]*rsue2017@yandex.ru*
[¶]*eva.tes@yandex.ru*
[‖]*kfiap@yandex.ru*
[**]*ilya5.shvachkin@gmail.com*

The legal community is far from understanding all functional possibilities of applying the principles of law.

Scott Shapiro [11]

[*]Corresponding author.

Abstract: The chapter focuses on the problems of administrative liability of legal entities in cases of administrative offenses in the field of transport. The authors explore the trend of increasing the number of principles of administrative responsibility and its individual institutions in the context of globalization and convergence of administrative law. The principles that are not fixed by law but exist due to doctrine and judicial practice are studied. The issue of the implementation of state policy in the field of passenger transportation in the context of the spread of coronavirus infection (COVID-19) is revealed. In this chapter, the constitutional right to judicial protection is considered through the prism of cases of administrative offenses. The aspect of providing high-quality passenger transportation services and fully meeting the population's needs in this direction is investigated.

Keywords: Administrative law; Ecology; Responsibility; Principles of law; Administrative responsibility; Transport; Entrepreneurship.

12.1. Introduction

In the era of globalization, countries may face various extraordinary problems and circumstances when there is an urgent need to introduce restrictive legal measures.

In 2019–2020 and up to the present, humanity has faced a new threat of an unknown scale — a new type of coronavirus infection (COVID-19). In its report, the World Health Organization (WHO) noted that the COVID-19 outbreak is an emergency in the field of public health and the well-being of the world's population of international importance [15].

The spread of COVID-19 has put a complex of interrelated, interdependent problems before the world community, including medical, legal, and socio-economic problems. The reaction of the world community to a new global problem has become apparent. To ensure the survival of humankind, it is necessary to introduce new specialized legal regimes of a temporary nature. One of the main tasks of such regimes has become the consideration of state governments to reduce the spread of the transmission rate of a new type of coronavirus infection from person to person.

A set of measures that is associated with the restriction of the legal personality and legal capacity of the population, as well as partial restriction of freedom of movement, resulted in the isolation of citizens at their place of residence (stay) and registration, which in the current agenda is called a lockdown from April 2020 to the present.

Thus, in the context of the spread of COVID-19, the law-making, law enforcement, and doctrinal aspects of relevance are becoming issues of monitoring the observance of human rights and freedoms and their associations in emergency situations, as well as their implementation, particularly the implementation of the right to judicial protection.

In this chapter, the constitutional right to judicial protection is considered through the prism of cases of administrative offenses. In particular, we are interested in controversial theoretical and practical issues of administrative liability of legal entities in cases of administrative offenses in the field of transport through the prism of judicial interpretation and application of atypical principles of administrative responsibility, which directly or indirectly affect the sanction against a legal entity.

These judgments served as starting points in rethinking the purpose and practical application of the principles of administrative responsibility in relation to the activities of legal entities in the field of transport relations through the prism of Russian legislation of the COVID-19 period and administrative doctrine. Correlation and a similar, atypical formulation of the problem of the influence of the principles of administrative responsibility on the activities of legal entities through the prism of atypical principles of administrative responsibility raise practically-oriented questions in the field of administrative law and economic turnover.

Foreign science theoretically stated the urgent need to rethink the problems of this study [14]. The Russian doctrine of administrative law pays review attention to the discussed problems [12], which does not allow either theoretically or practically approaching the resolution of such a problem. It should be noted that the review component is associated with the convergence of administrative law and the dynamics of public relations, which are included in the subject of regulation of administrative law. Thus, even the legal community represented by scientists does not have time to navigate such a rapidly changing agenda.

Despite the popularity of the application of the principles of administrative responsibility for the qualification of an offense committed by a legal entity in the field of transport relations and the impact of such acts on the system of economic turnover and environmental economics, theoretical and practical understanding of their essence is practically absent in current legal science of Russia.

In today's realities, the administrative responsibility of legal entities, in addition to law enforcement, has received a clearly expressed fiscal nature. Most of the administrative offenses are of a formal nature and do not lead to damage. However, an administrative penalty is most often imposed on a legal entity in the form of a fine for the offense committed.

In various branches of law, the liability of legal entities has its own specifics. Additionally, there are many concepts regarding the essence of a legal entity as a collective subject of law, which complicates the issue of the guilt of a legal entity. A unified approach to the concept of the guilt of a legal entity has not yet been developed, which determines the relevance of this research topic in the theory of law and branch sciences.

The research problems are of interest because the practical application of the principles of administrative responsibility in the proceedings on administrative offenses, as well as industry research on these issues, reveals serious disputes and mutual misunderstandings of representatives of science and practice about the impact of the principles of administrative responsibility on the size and content of the sanction, which confirms the scientific and applied relevance in the study of this phenomenon in the Russian legal order [10].

The materials used in this research allow us to trace the evolution and transformation of the nature of the principles of administrative responsibility. In its entirety, the research material shows the absence of a comprehensive analysis: general and special in the qualification of atypical principles of administrative responsibility in national administrative law.

Thus, this research is undertaken to comprehend the rethinking of the theoretical essence of atypical principles of administrative responsibility and suggest ways to unify and differentiate the application of the principles of administrative responsibility in cases of administrative offenses against legal entities in the field of legal transport relations in the conditions of convergence of administrative law.

Achieving this goal required solving the following interrelated research tasks:

(1) To characterize the essence and content of atypical principles of administrative responsibility and identify their correlation with the principle of administrative responsibility.
(2) To analyze the implementation of atypical principles of administrative responsibility in cases of administrative offenses against legal entities

in the field of legal transport relations based on the materials of judicial and law enforcement practice.

(3) To identify problematic aspects of the implementation of atypical principles of administrative responsibility through various technologies of judicial enforcement in cases of administrative offenses against legal entities in the field of legal transport relations.

12.2. Methodology

The methodological aspect of this research is presented by the following list of basic methods: historical, comparative, dialectical, and complex analysis. In addition to these methods, the work embodies synthesis, abstraction, deduction, induction, and generalization. The methods of interpretation of legal concepts, logical methods of study, and lexical techniques were used as research tools.

12.3. Results

A retrospective approach to the study of the essence of judicial interpretation of normative acts included in the system of sources (forms) of administrative law suggests that the interpretation of the norms of administrative law by the courts and the generalization of the principles of law, in general, and the principles of administrative law, in particular, is the story of finding the right and stable balance in the relationship of the individual, society, and countries.

The most significant legal positions of the national higher authorities in administrative cases are an attempt to find a balance between private and public, and between the rights of individuals, their associations, and the needs of society. Such judgments allow us to conclude that humanity lives in an era of proportionality; this term can characterize the current legal matter [6].

The correlation of the principles of administrative responsibility in relation to the norms of administrative law, in particular, to the Code of the Russian Federation on Administrative Offenses (December 30, 2001, No. 195-FZ) [4] is expressed not only in the generalization function of the principles as the initial prerequisites for the existence of legal matter; the primary purpose of the principles is the interpretation of ordinary norms of administrative law.

Simultaneously, in the context of globalization and convergence of administrative law, there is a tendency to increase the number of principles of administrative law and its individual institutions, which are not fixed by law but are induced by doctrine and judicial practice.

An illustrative example is the principle of proportionality, which generally expresses the criteria of proportionality of the legal means used, balance of legal interests, and adequacy of response to the circumstances that give rise to certain legal consequences. In procedural law, in relation to cases of administrative offenses, the principle of proportionality is expressed in assessing the balance of procedures and the proportionality of the procedural capabilities of participants in legal relations [13].

Summarizing the provisions of the scientific literature on the topic of this research, we note that the core problem in applying the principle of proportionality in cases of administrative offenses against legal entities in legal transport relations is the issue of compliance with the structural stages (elements) of the proportionality test (proportionality) of the restriction of rights, namely in the narrow sense — weighing the affected interests of legal entities, particularly legal entities (balancing test).

The principle of proportionality was "invented" by the Prussian lawyer Carl Gottlieb Svarez, the spiritual father of the Prussian General Land Code (*Preussiches Allgemeines Landrecht*) in 1794 [9], and concretized by the Supreme Administrative Court in its decisions in the Kreuzberg case in 1880 and 1882 [5].

If we turn to the legal system established in the Russian Federation, we can see that the principle of proportionality is observed in the legal positions of the Constitutional Court of Russia. Thus, it can be seen that one of the ways to restrict rights and freedoms is to establish liability measures for the misuse of norms. The Constitutional Court of the Russian Federation has deduced a general rule according to which the measures of legal responsibility must necessarily be proportionate to the degree of the offense committed, and the level of interests protected [3].

At the end of the 20th century, the Constitutional Court of the Russian Federation laid the foundation for applying the principle of proportionality in cases of administrative offenses by the courts of the Russian Federation.

The practical application of the principle of proportionality can be found in the process of "simplification of administrative procedures."

The examples of procedural "simplification" are often found in the materials of judicial practice in cases of administrative offenses. Thus, the

Administrative Code of the Russian Federation does not oblige judges to keep a record when considering a case. However, in some situations, this possibility is allowed [2].

The consideration of supervisory complaints and protests against resolutions or decisions on administrative offenses that have entered into force does not require a court session because this is not provided for by the Administrative Code of the Russian Federation [7].

Additionally, courts of general jurisdiction, considering cases on bringing persons to administrative responsibility, using the provisions of part 1 of Article 29.11 of the Administrative Code of the Russian Federation, often build their practice based on the possibility of a ruling on an administrative offense by a judge immediately after the end of the case without removal to the advisory room. By themselves, these provisions of the Administrative Code of the Russian Federation do not prevent a decision from being made in the conference room but only develop the principles of continuity and immediacy of the trial.

Therefore, the principle of proportionality has become a part of every section and every norm of the Administrative Code of the Russian Federation. Therefore, nowadays, it can and should claim the status of an institutional, intersectoral, and industry principle of administrative law.

Concerning the proceedings on administrative offenses in the field of legal transport relations, an ambiguous situation is emerging, as indicated by the materials of law enforcement practice in the regions of the Russian Federation.

Road transport has a significant impact on the economy of Kuban, and the development of the region as a whole depends on its sustainable functioning.

In 2020, the industry enterprises in Kuban received support for more than 340 million rubles at the expense of the regional budget.

It should be noted that passenger transportation on urban and suburban routes tends to a more stable recovery of the previous level, in contrast to intercity communication, where there is a decrease in transport performance.

Simultaneously, the state policy in the field of passenger transportation by road will aim to provide high-quality passenger transportation services and fully meet the needs of the population in this direction.

The problem of illegal transportation using the resources of the Internet continues to be relevant with their increase.

It is important to note that not only the driver is involved in such illegal transportation. In addition to the driver's seat, vehicles have eight or more seats, which allows moving people regularly on paid terms. Buses weighing up to five tons also participate in transportation.

A significant number of persons illegally carry out passenger transportation activities using vehicles utilized as passenger taxis.

There is a threat of a complete transition of this type of business activity from the category of official to illegal, which will lead to a decrease in the safety and quality of transportation by passenger taxis.

If a person is engaged in entrepreneurial activity without the necessary state registration as an individual entrepreneur or without the formation of a company, as well as if there is no special permit, then a violation of the law occurs, and such a person is subject to liability under part 1 and part 2 of Article 14.1 of the Administrative Code of the Russian Federation.

The internal affairs bodies check all documents, identify such offenses, and draw up protocols.

For example, according to the Ministry of Transport of the Krasnodar Territory, in 2021, 2,245 events were organized and conducted by working groups, 3,672 protocols on administrative offenses were drawn up (including 1,009 protocols under part 1 of Article 14.1 of the Administrative Code of the Russian Federation and 1,050 protocols under part 2 of Article 14.1 of the Administrative Code of the Russian Federation). As part of the administrative proceedings under part 2 of Article 14.1 of the Administrative Code of the Russian Federation, 590 vehicles were seized by police officers [8].

Additionally, on the territory of many regions of Russia, there is also a negative trend towards an increase in the number of persons carrying out illegal regular passenger transportation by buses under the guise of registered carriers, and their number increases many times during the holiday season.

Illegal transportation of passengers and baggage leads to a deterioration of the existing road traffic situation and forms a negative opinion about the provision of passenger transportation on the territory of the subjects of Russia.

The actions of persons carrying out these regular passenger transportations under the guise of registered ones completely duplicate the routes of regular transportation, reduce passenger traffic, and cause damage to existing road transport enterprises.

Transportation is carried out with an indication of daily trips to medical institutions. However, in reality, illegal carriers have developed routes within which any passengers are picked up and disembarked. The systemic departure of buses according to a fixed schedule and movement along established routes (streets, highways) qualifies passenger transportation exclusively as regular.

Nowadays, passenger transportation organized in this way is not isolated. In the city, buses of illegal carriers are dispatched to the municipalities of the regions from territories adjacent to regional medical institutions, bus stations, train stations, and the airport. Information about these carriers is placed in the form of ads in municipalities in crowded areas, in printed publications, on advertising business cards and banners, as well as using the Internet.

12.4. Conclusion

The formulation of the problem outlined in the research in terms of the methodology of applying the principle of proportionality requires clarification because it shows that the authors of theoretical arguments about its essence are aiming at a deductive way of thought movement. Moreover, they are little focused on a full-fledged comparison of individual ways of applying the principle of proportionality in proceedings on administrative offenses.

Principles are the basic guiding foundations of every branch of law. Many scientists have investigated the content of the principles through the prism of their relationship with each other. However, many aspects remain unresolved. Thus, there was no consensus in the legal doctrine on the question of what principles are exactly enshrined in administrative procedural legislation, which constitutes a system of principles of administrative law.

It seems theoretically correct and practically productive to conclude that the essence of the principle of proportionality in the field of administrative law in the contemporary realities of the COVID-19 pandemic remains largely unclear. Opinions about its functional and dynamic role in the mechanism of legal regulation are polar, as evidenced by various decisions of the Constitutional Court of Russia. Additionally, there is a pluralism of opinions in the reporting of the ministries of the regions that are engaged in the analysis.

Simultaneously, scientists and practitioners agree that the value nature of the principle of proportionality is aimed at considering the causal relationship between the decisions and actions of the authorities and the goals achieved.

In the situations considered, the purpose of the principle of proportionality was manifested in focus on ensuring a balance of interests and proportionality of goals and consequences in the implementation of legal regulation on cases of administrative offenses and law enforcement, as the tendency to apply the principle of proportionality in administrative law inclined to a teleological interpretation of legislation, expanding the purpose and nature of the applicable law.

In conclusion, we note that the principle of proportionality accumulates not only the axiological (evaluative) nature of the norms of applicable law but also expresses their summary and generalizing nature. Under the influence of the Constitutional Court of Russia and its legal positions, the principle of proportionality as a doctrine of judicial protection and a principle of administrative law will find preferential support in proceedings on administrative offenses during the COVID-19 pandemic, which will allow us to approach the unification of the process, and, consequently, harmonize the administrative and legal landscape and judicial practice and develop relations in the field of economics.

References

1. Constitutional Court of the Russian Federation. Ruling No. 4-O "On the complaint of the citizen Iraida Petrova Valerianovna a breach of her constitutional rights, the second part of article 100 of the Federal constitutional law 'On the constitutional Court of the Russian Federation.'" 1999. Available from: http://www.consultant.ru/document/cons_doc_LAW_24098/
2. Constitutional Court of the Russian Federation. Ruling No. 598-O "On refusal to accept for consideration the complaint of the limited Liability Company "Management Company 'Housing and Maintenance Site-15' of the city of Stavropol" for violation of constitutional rights and freedoms by Article 30.15 of the Code of Administrative Offences of the Russian Federation." St. Petersburg, Russia; 2012. Available from: https://www.garant.ru/products/ipo/prime/doc/70068096/
3. Plenum of the Supreme Court of the Russian Federation. Resolution No. 5 "On some issues arising from courts when Applying the Code of Administrative Offences of the Russian Federation." 2005. Available from: http://www.consultant.ru/document/cons_doc_LAW_52681/
4. Russian Federation. Code of the Russian Federation on Administrative Offenses. Moscow, Russia. Available from: http://www.consultant.ru/document/cons_doc_LAW_34661/

5. Supreme Administrative Court of Prussia. The decisions of the case of Kreuzberg (Kreuzberg-Urteile) from 1880 June 10 and 1882 June 14. DVBl. 1985. pp. 216–226.
6. Barak A. *Proportionality: Constitutional Rights and Their Limitations*. Cambridge, UK: Cambridge University Press; 2012. DOI: 10.1017/CBO9781139035293
7. Main Directorate of the Ministry of Internal Affairs of Russia in the Krasnodar Territory. Information and analytical note on the results of the activities of the police of the Main Directorate of the Ministry of Internal Affairs of Russia in the Krasnodar Territory in 2020 to the report of Police Lieutenant General V. L. Andreev before the Legislative Assembly of the Krasnodar Territory. 2020. Available from: https://23.xn--b1aew.xn--p1ai/folder/23106937
8. Ministry of Transport and Road Management of the Krasnodar Territory of the Russian Federation. Statistical materials of the on cases of administrative offenses for 2021. 2021. Available from: http://stat.gibdd.ru/
9. Peters A. Proportionality as a global constitutional principle. Max Planck Institute for Comparative Public Law & International Law (MPIL) Research Paper. 2016 May 3; 2016-10. Available from SSRN: https://ssrn.com/abstract=2773733
10. Serkov PP. *Administrative Responsibility in Russian Law: Modern Understanding and New Approaches*. Moscow, Russia: INFRA-M; 2012. pp. 387–389.
11. Shapiro SJ. Legality (Koval S, Transl. from English; Pavlov A (Ed.)). Moscow, Russia: Publishing House of the Gaidar Institute; 2021.
12. Soldatov AP. On the issue of administrative responsibility of legal entities. *Society and Law*, 2012; 5(42): 220–225.
13. Umnova-Konyukhova IA, Kotyleva ED. Constitutional restrictions of rights and freedoms: A comparative legal study of the decisions of the Constitutional Court of the Russian Federation, the Supreme Court of the Russian Federation and the ECHR. Moscow, Russia: Russian State University of Justice; 2021.
14. Winter H. *Issues in Law and Economics* (Shishkina T, Transl. from English; Odintsova M (Ed.)). Moscow, Russia: Publishing House of the Gaidar Institute; 2019.
15. World Health Organization (WHO). WHO-convened global study of the origins of SARS-CoV-2 (including annexes). 2021. Available from: https://www.who.int/emergencies/diseases/novel-coronavirus-2019/origins-of-the-virus

Part 3

Climate-Smart Innovations in Production for Resource Efficiency of Social Entrepreneurship

https://doi.org/10.1142/9789811264252_0013

Chapter 13

Water Resource Management for Sustainable Development in the South of Russia in Low Water Conditions: Economic Evidence

Natalia G. Vovchenko[†,§], **Olga V. Andreeva**[†,¶], **Valeria D. Dmitrieva**[*,†,‖] and **Marusya I. Lyubcheva**[‡,**]

[†]*Rostov State University of Economics, Rostov-on-Don, Russia*
[‡]*University "Prof. d-r Assen Zlatarov", Bourgas, Bulgaria*
[§]*nat.vovchenko@gmail.com*
[¶]*olvandr@yandex.ru*
[‖]*riyachan2807@gmail.com*
[**]*milyubcheff@gmail.com*

Abstract: The chapter aims to analyze the current state of water resources in Southern Russia in the context of achieving sustainable development goals. Recent climatic changes lead to abnormal and irreversible transformations of territories. In particular, the South of Russia is characterized by excessive aridization and desertification. Methodologically, this chapter has an applied analytical nature, relying on comprehensive statistical sources. The authors of this chapter

[*]Corresponding author.

conclude that social motivation and fiscal instruments are not working. In this case, the attention of researchers and policy-makers should be paid to other mechanisms that allow determining the ways of rational, balanced environmental management.

Keywords: Sustainable development; Safe water; Water scarcity; Water resources management; Water crisis; Water stress; Water risks; Agenda 2030; Water Action Decade.

13.1. Introduction

Water is the most abundant and the scarcest resource on the planet: 97% of all water resources are unusable saltwater. Simultaneously, although water is a renewable resource and a public good, access to it is often limited. The UN estimates that about 40% of the world's population suffers from a lack of clean water [13]. The availability of clean water and hygiene products is a fundamental requirement in the fight against infectious diseases, particularly the COVID-19 pandemic.

The years 2018–2028 have been declared the Water Action Decade, which involves mobilizing economic and administrative resources, promoting scientific thought and public initiatives to tackle "water-related challenges, including limited access to safe water and sanitation, increasing pressure on water resources and ecosystems, and an exacerbated risk of droughts and floods" [15].

Global climate change (primarily the long-term trend of an increase in the average annual temperature and an increase in extreme weather events), generated by irrational human activities, can change the landscape of the planet beyond recognition: the level of the ocean is already rising due to the melting of ice, the zones of forests, tundra, permafrost, and drought zones are expanding. The total number and intensity of dangerous hydrometeorological phenomena (hurricanes, tornadoes, showers, snowstorms, surge floods, etc.) have significantly increased globally over the past 20 years, by some estimates, by two to three times. The collateral economic and social damage is also growing.

Despite the general improvement in the quality of life, the development of the digitalization of the economy, and the active attention of various foundations and organizations to human rights issues, the problem remains open: hundreds of millions of inhabitants of the planet do not have access to safe water (every ninth person on the planet) and sanitary conditions (three out of ten) [14].

The water crisis negatively affects people's health (physical and mental) and their way of life. The problem of inequality, including gender inequality, is increasing because the burden of water extraction often falls on the shoulders of women and girls.

This gives rise to another aspect of inequality, generated in part by the water crisis — access to education. Children engaged in household chores, including water extraction, do not have the opportunity to go to school. The lack of proper sanitation makes such a lifestyle even more hazardous to health.

One gets the impression that, on a planetary scale, the water problem has the level of a humanitarian catastrophe. For several regions of the world, it is a humanitarian catastrophe: the most challenging situation in the field of water resources management has developed in most of the countries of South America, Africa, and Central and South Asia. Water sources are often contaminated, unsafe, or inaccessible for use due to their remote location or private property. As a result, the stress of the water use system only increases, which is facilitated by the climatic characteristics of the regions, an increase in the size and density of the population, high levels of poverty, and armed conflicts in the Arab region and Africa. The situation is especially acute in terms of ensuring access to safe water for refugees [7].

These problems are unusual for Russia. Nevertheless, this does not mean that water is available to everyone in the country. Statistics show that only 87.5% of the population has access to clean and safe water [1]. Simultaneously, natural and climatic changes lead to the degradation of water and land resources, which causes irreparable damage to the economy of certain regions.

13.2. Methodology

This research aims to analyze the current state of water resources in Southern Russia in the context of achieving sustainable development goals. Recent climatic changes lead to abnormal and irreversible transformations of territories. In particular, the South of Russia is characterized by excessive aridization and desertification.

This problem is complex and interdisciplinary. Its solution requires the joint efforts of ecologists, geographers, geologists, biologists, botanists, economists, and representatives of government authorities, public organizations, and technological companies.

This study has an applied analytical nature. The definition of effective economic instruments of the water management system is critical for the theoretical understanding of the studied problem.

Statistical sources of the research are presented by official open reports of the UN, Water Risk Atlas project [4], the Analytical Center for the Government of the Russian Federation [3], the Ministry of Natural Resources and Environment of the Russian Federation [8], and passports of the National program "Ecology" [2] and the state program "Environmental Protection" [1].

13.3. Results

13.3.1. *Some Trends in Climate Change in the Southern Macro-Region of Russia*

According to experts, over the past 40 years, climate warming in Russia has occurred faster and more extensively than on average on the planet. According to the Hydrometeorological Center of the Russian Federation, in 2019, it became the warmest in the history of meteorological observations in Russia [9].

Climate modeling indicates the long-time trend towards an increase in the average annual temperature in the country (and on the planet) and an increase in the frequency of dangerous hydrometeorological phenomena (hard rainfall and flood, drought, storms, etc.). These trends significantly impact the life and health of people and cause direct damage to economic activity.

On the territory of the regions of Southern Russia, the following changes are noted [6]:

- An increase in the average annual temperature of air and water for all seasons;
- An increase in precipitation in any form;
- More frequent negative meteorological phenomena;
- Change in wind activity, etc.

In such conditions, the problem of aridization is most acute. The southern macro-region is distinguished by a significant array of arid territories, which significantly affects the spatial development of regions and contributes to the strengthening of socio-economic inequality.

Climate change leads to the fact that in some regions (in particular, the Volgograd Region, the Rostov Region, and the Republic of Kalmykia), anomalous values of the aridization index are observed and long periods of droughts are noted. The number of periods with different conditions of annual moisture differs by region: for example, in the above regions, there are four periods (wet, dry, wet, and dry); in the Astrakhan Region and the Krasnodar Territory, there are only two periods (dry and wet); in the Stavropol Territory, there are five periods (dry, wet, dry, wet, and dry) [17].

These changes lead to negative consequences, including environmental, social, and, last but not least, economic consequences. It is essential to mention the problem of spatial inequality of regions. Under the new conditions, the conditions and prospects for agriculture are changing, and, consequently, the entire sectoral structure of the region's economy should be transformed. On the other hand, living conditions in the region are changing, which impacts the level of development of the quality of life, leading to migration of the population, which again returns to the question of the transformation of industries.

13.3.2. *The State of Water Resources of the Southern Macro-region of Russia*

The water resources of the southern macro-region are represented by rivers belonging to the basins of the Azov and Black Seas of the Atlantic Ocean and the closed area of the Caspian Sea, lakes, other artificial reservoirs, swamps and wetlands, glacial deposits (in the Caucasus).

The Southern and North-Caucasian Federal Districts, the subjects of which make up the territory of the southern macro-region, are distinguished by low quantitative characteristics of the state of water resources. Thus, the Southern Federal District ranks last in terms of the density of the river network, the area of swamps and wetlands, and the North Caucasian District is the last in terms of the length of the river network, lakes, area of bogs and wetlands (Fig. 13.1).

Simultaneously, in the context of climatic changes and active industrial activity, the state of water resources continues to deteriorate.

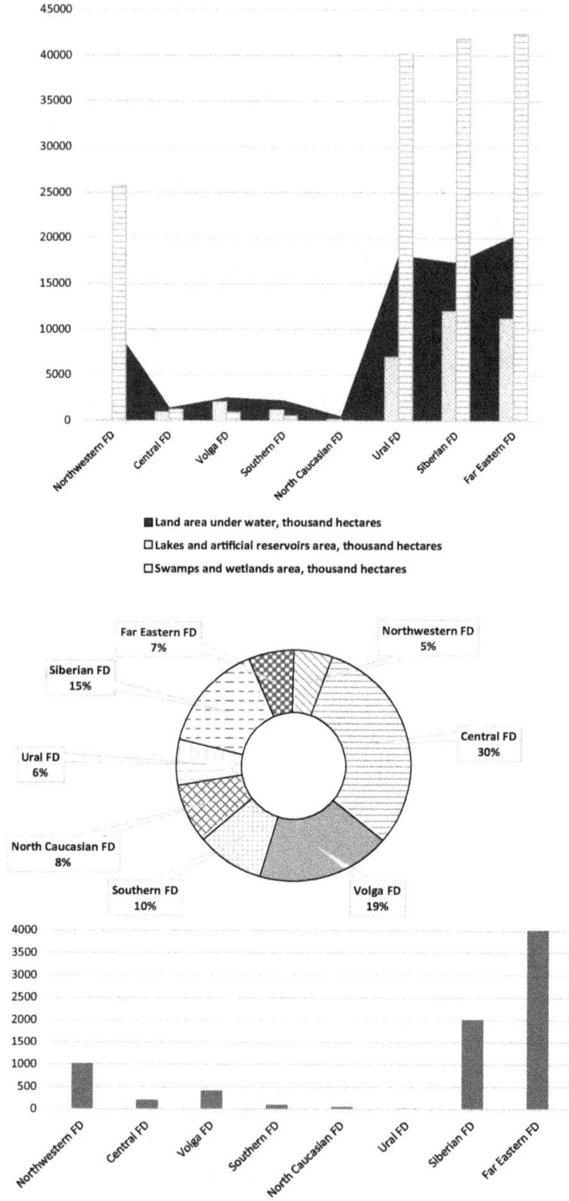

Fig. 13.1. Water fund by federal districts of the Russian Federation, 2018.

Notes: 1 – Water fund areas, thousand hectares; 2 – Groundwater reserves, m³/km; 3 – River network, thousand km.

Source: Compiled by authors based on Ref. [8].

Prolonged droughts and vast areas of arid territories are typical for all regions of Southern Russia. The Krasnodar Territory and Stavropol Territory, the Republic of Crimea, and the Rostov and Volgograd Regions stand out, especially against the general background. According to the Hydrometeorological Center of the Russian Federation, in 2020, droughts in the South of Russia began in the spring and lasted for more than 14 months [8]. In addition, abnormal temperatures were recorded even in the winter months (January and February) of 2020.

13.3.3. *Challenges of Water Resources Management in the Context of the Agenda 2030*

The irrational use of water resources threatens human existence: 70% of the planet's freshwater is used for irrigation remaining inaccessible for personal consumption, and 80% of industrial wastewater is not treated [14]. Simultaneously, we note that pollution of the environment (particularly water) contributes to a decrease in the quality of life, which is especially true for the population living in extreme poverty or in vulnerable conditions (including at the epicenter of hostilities). With this approach, the situation of inequality seems even more unfair because water is a gift of nature and a free public good, but access to it is limited [7].

In 2016, the United Nations General Assembly adopted the resolution declaring 2018–2028 as the International Decade for Action "Water for Sustainable Development." According to the resolution, the main tasks are as follows [15]:

- Sustainable development and integrated water resources management to achieve social, economic, and environmental goals;
- Implementation and promotion of related programs and projects;
- Promoting cooperation and partnership at all levels to achieve internationally agreed water goals and targets, including those set under the 2030 Agenda for Sustainable Development.

Thus, there is a need for integrated water resources management, which includes three levels of interaction between the state, society, and business [16]:

- Water in its various dimensions (surface and ground), which implies a systematic examination of its quality and quantity;

- Water as an ecosystem interacting with other resource systems;
- Water as one of the components of each of the elements of sustainable development — the economy, society, and the environment.

In practice, only about 80% of the world's countries have created a solid foundation for achieving the goals of the policy of introducing integrated water resources management. Simultaneously, in Russia, within the SDG6 "Clean water and sanitation" sub-goal "The degree of implementation of integrated water resources management," according to the Analytical Center for the Government of the Russian Federation, state management of water resources is carried out in accordance with the basic principles of sustainable development; developments are underway to create digital water resources management (through digital twin models). Simultaneously, the tasks in the field of sanitation and provision of the population with accessible drinking water are solved by implementing the National project "Ecology" [3].

At the regional level, monitoring of the achievement of sustainable development goals is carried out by branches of the Federal State Statistics Service (Rosstat). In particular, the Rostov Region regularly publishes the statistical collection "Rostov Region — Moving Towards Sustainable Development Goals," prepared in cooperation with regional ministries and departments and with the support of the Center-Invest Bank [12].

13.3.4. *Economic Aspects of Water Resources Management in the Southern Macro-region of Russia*

The supply of freshwater is decreasing everywhere. In the Don and Kuban basins, the stage of low water level continues. It began in 2007, with a sharp decrease in runoff observed in 2019–2020. A similar situation is observed in the Terek basin [8]. It is important to note that this situation is observed in general for freshwater resources in 11 subjects of the southern macro-region, with the exception of the Republic of Kalmykia, the Astrakhan Region, and the Volgograd Region (Fig. 13.2). The most significant deviations from the average long-term value are observed in the Rostov Region (57.2%), the Republic of Adygea (46.1%), and the Stavropol Territory (43.3%).

The deteriorating state of freshwater resources in the region indicates the need for a more rational approach to water use. In practice, the principles of rational water use are not followed: water intake is almost twice

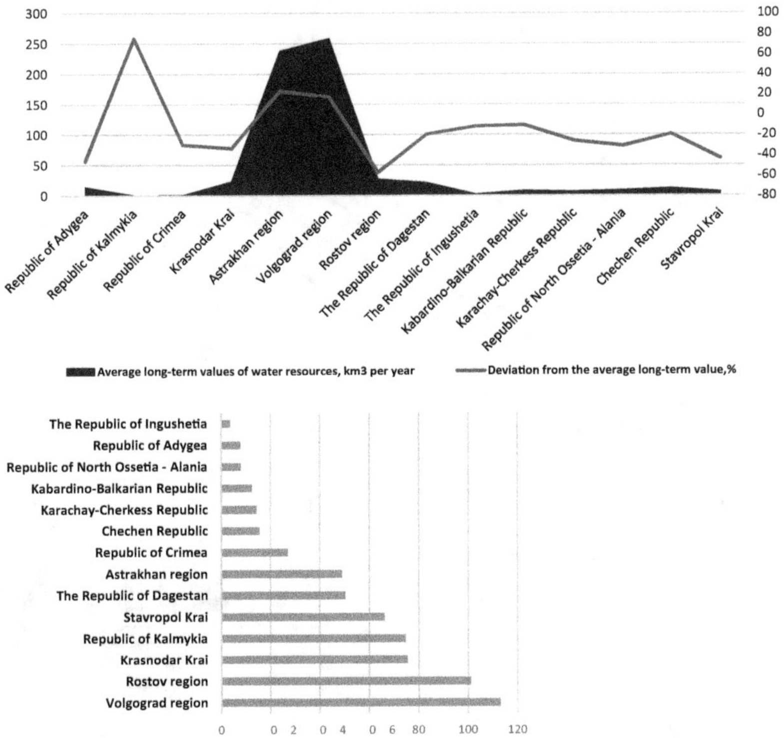

Fig. 13.2. Resources of river flow by subjects of the southern macro-region of Russia, 2020.

Source: Compiled by authors based on Ref. [8].

the volume used for various needs. Simultaneously, the largest share of freshwater used is consumed in agriculture (particularly for irrigation) (Fig. 13.3).

The dynamics of the reduction in the volume of polluted water discharges in the regions of the Southern Federal District are also virtually insignificant. The greatest damage to the region's water resources is caused by enterprises and organizations of the Krasnodar Territory and the Rostov Region, while the discharge of polluted wastewater was not recorded in 2020 in the Republic of Adygea, the Republic of Ingushetia, the Chechen Republics, and the Astrakhan Region (Table 13.1).

Economic instruments for water resources management are designed to create incentives for rational water use and reduction of polluting emissions. Primarily, these include payments for water use and payments for ecosystem services.

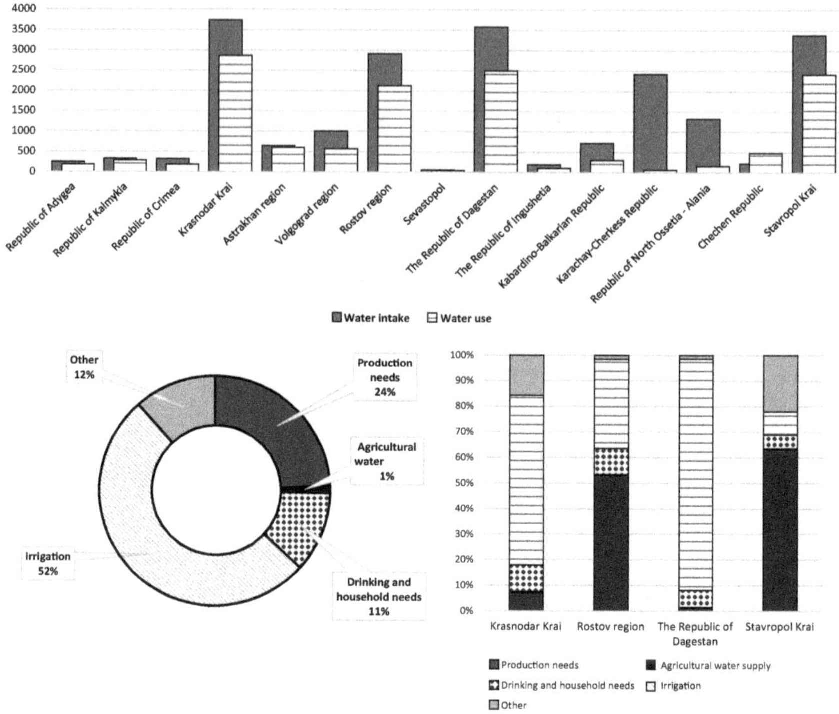

Fig. 13.3. The structure of water use by subjects of the southern macro-region of Russia, 2020.

Notes: 1 – Water intake and water use; 2 – Water use structure, total, all subjects of the South of Russia; 3 – Water use structure, the main users among subjects of the South of Russia.
Source: Compiled by authors based on Ref. [8].

The following types of economic instruments for water resources management can be distinguished [11]:

- Taxes for the withdrawal of mineral resources,
- Water taxes, fees for the abstraction (withdrawal) of groundwater,
- Payment for water use,
- Fines for the use of water area facilities,
- Fines for water pollution, etc.

In Russia, direct budgetary financing should be added to economic instruments, in which a programmed-target budgeting method is applied.

Table 13.1. Water disposal and discharge of polluted wastewater by subjects of the southern macro-region of Russia, 2020, million cubic meters.

Subjects of the federal district	Discharge of contaminated wastewater without treatment	Discharge of contaminated wastewater with insufficient treatment	Water disposal
Southern Federal District			
Republic of Adygea	—	23.50	155.46
Republic of Kalmykia	13.70	1.00	17.50
Republic of Crimea	6.70	90.20	113.05
Krasnodar Territory	384.60	133.90	2420.77
Astrakhan Region	—	30.30	142.84
Volgograd Region	9.70	82.00	128.18
Rostov Region	29.50	158.40	1116.24
Sevastopol	3.70	21.00	29.37
North Caucasian Federal District			
The Republic of Dagestan	15.80	58.97	537.84
The Republic of Ingushetia	—	0.92	3.12
Kabardino-Balkarian Republic	0.42	28.39	32.65
Karachayevo-Chirkassian Republic	7.16	35.48	43.80
Republic of North Ossetia - Alania	3.79	87.46	145.45
Chechen Republic	—	—	14.69
Stavropol Territory	16.90	148.00	986.83
Total	491.97	871.13	5887.79

Source: Compiled by authors based on Ref. [8].

Thus, the national project "Ecology" mentioned above includes four federal projects directly related to water [2]:

- "Clean Water" (2018–2024) — project financing within the framework of the national project "Housing and urban environment" [2];
- "Improving the Volga" (2018–2024);
- Lake Baikal Conservation (2019–2024);
- "Conservation of unique water bodies" (2019–2024).

Only these four federal projects are planned to be financed in the amount of 1585.7 billion rubles, which is 42.2% of the total financial support of the national project allocated for the entire implementation period.

Separately, it is worth highlighting the state program “Environmental protection” (2012–2024) [8] and improving the ecological state of the Volga and Lake Baikal.

It is important to note the lack of consistency of documents among themselves: there is inconsistent priority assigned to goals and duplication of tasks, which means double funding. Until now, when using target program budgeting in Russia, an adequate system for assessing the effectiveness of the implementation of measures and spending of budgetary funds has not been built, which is a significant drawback of this regulatory tool.

The undoubted advantage of economic instruments is that, despite their limitations, they allow promoting methods of efficient water use by households and industry, including through the introduction of best practices and the development of economic technologies for water use and protection of water resources.

Note that for Russia, at different stages of its development, a situation is typical when economic instruments are more effective than exhortations (the same social motivation).

Thus, the question of rationalizing water use in Russian regions remains open. Despite the imposed material sanctions, the level of water pollution in several regions of the country is not decreasing. It is easier for businesses to pay a fine than to treat wastewater. The development of other more effective tools is required. In particular, the following tools are required:

- Setting a water withdrawal limit, especially in conditions where the water withdrawal is actually twice the amount required for use;
- Development of an integrated reservoir management system;
- Creation of a large-scale unified system for managing the country’s water resources [5];
- Development of models of digital twins of territories.

Despite the complexity of the solution and the high cost of implementation, models of digital twins of territories are of particular interest. The federal project of integrated water resources management “Digital Ob-Irtysh basin,” which has no analogs in the world, has already been developed, which is a complex of mathematical and simulation models of Siberian river ecosystems based on big data. This project is very large scale, created with the participation of the largest research institutes and large technology companies. Public discussions are currently underway. The digital twin project is a powerful tool for making managerial decisions at various levels based on identifying the main factors that critically affect the level of technogenic pressure on the water resources of the Ob-Irtysh basin [10].

We believe that such digital twins are necessary for water basins and land areas through which waterways pass. The analysis of the state of groundwater, rivers, and other water sources in a specific territory is extremely important for the development of managerial decisions by state and local authorities, water users, and public associations. In the conditions of climate aridization and desertification of the territories of Southern Russia, such a project will optimize agricultural processes based on forecasts of degradation of water resources and soil, as well as to conduct an examination of design measures for irrigation of territories.

13.4. Conclusion

The authors of this chapter emphasize that the problem of aridization and desertification of the territories of Southern Russia is large scale and in the context of regional development and on a global scale. The ongoing degradation of water resources is long-term and is explained by natural-climatic and anthropogenic factors: long-term droughts, reduced runoff, wastewater pollution, excessive water intake, etc.

To solve this problem, it is necessary to develop effective tools for water resources management: social motivation, fines, and taxes no longer create incentives for rational water use because enterprises consider them seen as a fair price for constant pollution.

Activities within the framework of project-target budgeting give tangible results. Nevertheless, they also have drawbacks; in particular, we are talking about duplication of goals and items of spending budget funds within the framework of various program documents.

The authors seek to substantiate that in conditions when fiscal instruments stop working, attention should be paid to other mechanisms that allow determining the ways of rational balanced environmental management. These primarily include the formation of a large-scale unified water management system (including digital) and the development of models of digital twins of territories.

The conclusions obtained in the framework of this study can contribute to rethinking and adjusting the current economic policy in the field of water use in the southern macro-region.

References

1. Government of the Russian Federation. Resolution No. 326 "On approval of the state program of the Russian Federation 'Environmental Protection.'" Moscow, Russia; 2014. Available from: https://base.garant.ru/70643488/
2. Ministry of Natural Resources and Environment of the Russian Federation. National project "Ecology." Moscow, Russia; 2019. Available from: https://www.mnr.gov.ru/upload/medialibrary/0bd/NP_EkologiyaPasport.pdf
3. Analytical Center for the Government of the Russian Federation. Voluntary national review of the implementation of the agenda 2030 for Sustainable Development: report. 2020. Available from: https://ac.gov.ru/uploads/2-Publications/analitika/DNO.pdf
4. Aqueduct Water Risk Atlas (n.d.). Available from: https://www.wri.org/aqueduct
5. Bogomolov YuG, Golubev SM. On the creation of a centralized system for managing water resources in Russia. In: Karlov GA (Ed.) *Management of Water Resources in Russia. Legislative Regulation and Prospects*. Moscow, Russia: Publication of the State Duma; 2014. pp. 77–81.
6. Dashkevich LV. Long-term trends in changes in meteorological parameters of the Sea of Azov region. *Ecology Economics Informatics,* 2020; 5: 130–137. DOI: 10.23885/2500-395X-2020-1-5-130-137
7. Matishova, GG, Albekov AU, edited. Water resources of the southern macroregion in the context of sustainable development. Rostov-on-Don, Russia: RSUE; 2021.
8. Ministry of Natural Resources and Environment of the Russian Federation. State report "On the state and protection of the environment in Russia in 2020". Moscow, Russia; 2021. Available from: https://www.mnr.gov.ru/docs/gosudarstvennye_doklady/gosudarstvennyy_doklad_o_sostoyanii_i_ob_okhrane_okruzhayushchey_sredy_rossiyskoy_federatsii_v_2020/
9. Moscow School of Management SKOLKOVO. The global climate threat and the Russian economy: in search of a special path. 2020 May. Available from: https://energy.skolkovo.ru/downloads/documents/SEneC/Research/SKOLKOVO_EneC_Climate_Primer_RU.pdf

10. NTI Competence Center Peter the Great St. Petersburg Polytechnic University. Federal project "Digital Ob-Irtysh basin project." St. Petersburg, Russia. Available from: https://nticenter.spbstu.ru/nti_projects/43
11. OECD. Economic instruments for water resources management in the Russian Federation. Paris, France; 2013. Available from: https://www.oecd.org/env/outreach/EIs%20for%20WRM%20in%20Russia_English_Final%20web.pdf
12. Rosstat Regional Office of Rostov Region. Rostov region — Movement towards sustainable development goals: 2016–2020. Rostov-on-Don, Russia: Rostovstat; 2020. Available from: https://rostov.gks.ru/storage/mediabank/7DwI4Sd7/%D0%A6%D1%83%D1%80_2021_%D1%81%D0%B0%D0%B9%D1%82.pdf
13. United Nations. Global issues: water [date unknown; cited 2021 Nov 17]. Available from: https://www.un.org/en/global-issues/water.
14. United Nations (n.d.). Sustainable Development Goals: Goal 6. Available from: https://www.un.org/sustainabledevelopment/water-and-sanitation/
15. Water Action Decade. United Nations Secretary-General's plan: Water Action Decade 2018–2028; 2018. Available from: https://wateractiondecade.org/wp-content/uploads/2018/03/UN-SG-Action-Plan_Water-Action-Decade-web.pdf
16. World Meteorological Organization (WMO). The guide to hydrological practices. Volume II: Management of water resources and application of hydrological practices. 6th ed. Geneva, Switzerland: WMO; 2009. Available from: http://www.whycos.org/chy/guide/168_Vol_II_en.pdf
17. Zolotokrylin AN, Titkova TB, Cherenkova EA. Spring-summer dry characteristics in dry and wet periods in the South of European Russia. *Arid Ecosystems*, 2020; 4(85):76–83. DOI: 10.24411/1993-3916-2020-10121

https://doi.org/10.1142/9789811264252_0014

Chapter 14

The Global Energy Transition as the Basis for the Formation of Green Economy

Natalia N. Gavrilko[†], **Anastasia V. Khodochenko**[*,‡], **Luiza A. Seferyan**[¶] and **Marina O. Otrishko**[‖]

Rostov State University of Economics, Rostov-on-Don, Russia
[†]*nata_nik@mail.ru*
[‡]*anastasia.kh61@mail.ru*
[¶]*luiza.seferyan@mail.ru*
[‖]*starka13@mail.ru*

Abstract: The chapter focuses on the energy transition as a necessary prerequisite for developing a green economy. The features of the new energy transition are based on the introduction and use of clean technologies, such as renewable energy and hydrogen. The urgency of taking drastic measures to transition to green energy is connected with the speedy solution to climate problems on the planet. The countries are actively taking measures to decarbonize economic processes; businesses are adopting business strategies that include reducing the negative impact on the environment and introducing green technologies.

[*]Corresponding author.

The paper analyzes current trends in the energy sector to identify the readiness of a new energy transition to the principles of a green economy.

Keywords: Sustainable development; Energy transition; Green economy; Climate problems; Environment; Decarbonization; Energy; Renewable energy; Oil exporters; World economy; Business strategy.

14.1. Introduction

Every year, the planet is experiencing rapid population growth and the expansion of production capacity and energy consumption. These processes will inevitably lead to significant environmental losses in the near future. Thus, there is a need to move to an effective economic model that can overcome the current environmental crisis and prevent its consequences in the future. One of the most pressing problems of our time is the creation of an effective economic model aimed at improving the welfare of the population of any state and, at the same time, ensuring the energy and environmental security of the country. The traditional economic growth model has led to significant environmental degradation and increased social inequality. The transition to a green economy in countries should be accompanied by improvements in current socio-economic development strategies and regulatory frameworks.

In 2015, 196 countries adopted the Paris Agreement in accordance with the UN Framework Convention on Climate Change. The Agreement contains measures to reduce carbon dioxide emissions into the atmosphere. The countries have set themselves ambitious goals for the transition to green energy. These goals have become part of national strategies that consider the Paris Agreement to achieve zero carbon emissions by 2030. The energy transition will contribute to the process of replacing the coal economy with renewable energy and reducing other carbon energy resources. Despite the COVID-19 pandemic and the economic crisis, many countries and companies continue to actively implement decarbonization plans.

The countries are actively involved in the climate agenda. They strengthen their competitive position in the international green energy market. Countries use cross-border carbon regulation and related measures to regulate international trade. The creation of sustainable conditions for the development of a green economy is a priority task for ensuring global climate security. The need for a large-scale transformation of the world economy and its sectors, although not completely new, has acquired a pronounced relevance and urgency.

The key sector of the green economy is energy. The energy sector is the basis on which the economy of any country functions. The energy transition should be based on the targets and technological potential of countries and their energy opportunities. Due to the development and complexity of the technological structure and the growth of human needs on the planet, the pace of energy transfer is accelerating. In the new reality, there is a need to use low-carbon energy. The question arises about the ability of the world economy to adapt to the global energy transition quickly.

14.2. Methodology

The research is based on the works of Russian and foreign scientists in the field of green economy, sustainable development, decarbonization, and renewable sources such as Andrea *et al.*, Georgeson *et al.*, and others [1,8]. The research methodology includes the generalization and systematization of various research information sources. The methods of analysis used include the logical-dialectical method of cognition of phenomena and processes in the world economy, the method of logical and historical approach for the study of international experience in the formation of green energy, methods of induction and deduction for the study of the green economy, the method of system analysis and generalization for the study of the implementation of renewable energy, and methods of synthesis and comparative analysis for the study of the directions of development of current business in the energy sector. The research is based on official sources and materials of international organizations, including statistical data and materials from periodicals in this field of research.

14.3. Results

Current global problems have consequences related to climate change for future generations. According to forecasts, more than 1.5 billion people on the planet will additionally be exposed to climate hazards at a warming temperature of 2.0°C (Fig. 14.1), compared to a warming of 1.5°C by 2030 [2]. Thus, "almost half of the world's population could be exposed

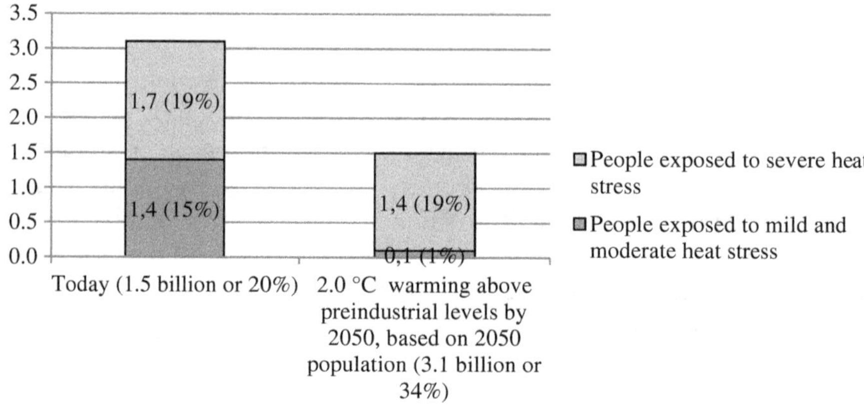

Fig. 14.1. A 2.0°C warming scenario, number of people.

Source: Compiled by the authors based on Ref. [2].

to a climate hazard related to heat stress, drought, flood, or water stress in the next decade, up from 43% (3.3 billion people) today" [2]. If urgent measures are not taken, about 1.4 billion people will be exposed to climate problems that affect their health and ability to work.

Current global environmental problems require radical changes in all sectors of society, including the energy sector. An increasing number of countries support the abandonment of fossil fuels. According to the forecasts of the International Energy Agency (IEA), "the volume of global oil consumption in 2040 in the hypothetical scenario of sustainable development, assuming the achievement of climate goals, is 32% lower than in the inertial scenario, gas — 36% lower, and coal — 61% lower" [17]. In the scenario of the stated policy (Stated Policies Scenario), after 2030, aggregate demand for fossil fuels will slow down and continue to decline by 2050.

For example, a growing number of countries in the world are ready to completely abandon fossil fuels such as coal. In 2017, the "Alliance against Coal" (Powering Past Coal Alliance) was created in Germany and today includes 41 national governments, 41 regions and cities, and 55 companies. All participants support the abandonment of coal generation. However, one feature is that the participating countries play an insignificant role in the installed coal generation capacity in the world — about 5% [17].

Another example is the Lofoten Declaration, signed in 2017 at a meeting on the Lofoten Islands in Norway. All participants of the declaration recognize that there is a possibility of reducing the production of oil and gas resources, therefore, reducing demand [12]. Assessing the gap between the achievement of the goals of the Paris Agreement and the plans of the countries for the extraction of coal, oil, and gas in 2020, "the Production Gap Report" showed that this gap remains significant: to reach the trajectory of 1.5°C in 2020–2030, the world should annually reduce the extraction of fossil fuels by about 6%, whereas in reality it is planned to grow by 2% per year" [17].

The energy transition has become a necessary part of many national strategies for environmental conservation and the subject of global competition for new energy markets. After the COVID-19 pandemic in 2020, the leading countries set goals for the early decarbonization of their economies. "We have taken measures to limit the growth of global temperature within 1.5°C. Last year, 20 countries (including the EU and China) set ambitious goals to achieve carbon neutrality by the middle of the century" [14]. Nowadays, these countries account for about 70% of the world economy and 63% of all greenhouse gas emissions. Such a transformation can become a starting point for developing a green economy (Fig. 14.2).

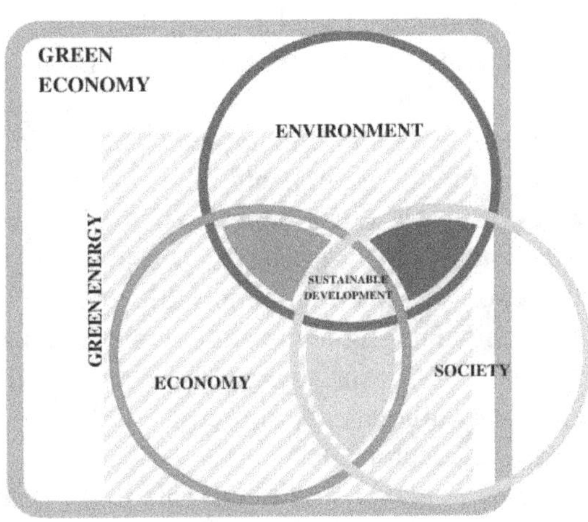

Fig. 14.2. The interrelation of elements of sustainable development and the green economy with energy.

The green economy can be interpreted as a suitable means of refocusing sustainable development on the most important means of achieving it and on the internal links between the economy and the environment [8]. Thus, the green economy includes the economy, the environment, and society, which confirms the entry into the concept of sustainable development. Since the green economy includes green energy, then energy covers most of the elements. The illustrated elements are examples of many statements about the need to achieve the country's sustainable development. There is an interaction between all elements. In total, green economy strategies can contribute to the energy transition.

The green economy acts as a tool for achieving Sustainable Development Goals for most national strategies. For many countries, the green economy has become the answer to the most important global problems of sustainability. Business issues, reduction of traditional fuel consumption, and financial and economic crisis influenced the development of a new direction in the economic system. One or another set of mechanisms and tools should be adapted to the specific features of the country: socio-economic development, availability of certain natural resources, environmental situation, etc. The choice of tools should consider national priorities and development strategies, as well as various costs, risks, benefits, and opportunities. As a result, there is no single way of the energy transition for all countries that seek to reduce the anthropogenic impact on the environment. The energy transition is a global process that requires the activation of all countries.

The energy sector plays a crucial role in delivering global climate goals and decarbonization of the economy. Nationally Determined Contributions (NDCs) are the action plan of each country within the framework of the Paris Agreement on Climate Change aimed at reducing emissions and adapting to climate impacts. The energy sector contributed almost three-quarters of global GHG emissions. All 194 parties of NDCs presented include the energy sector in climate action plans (Fig. 14.3) [11].

To achieve the energy transition, renewable energy sources are an effective option for achieving climate change goals. The parties to NDCs aim to reduce harmful emissions in the energy sector to mitigate the consequences based on renewable energy sources. Much remains to be done to decarbonize the energy sector.

Renewable energy can play a significant role in the energy transition. According to the IRENA scenario, with the growth of global temperature within 1.5°C, "electricity would be the main energy carrier by 2050, with more than a 50% direct share of total final energy consumption — up

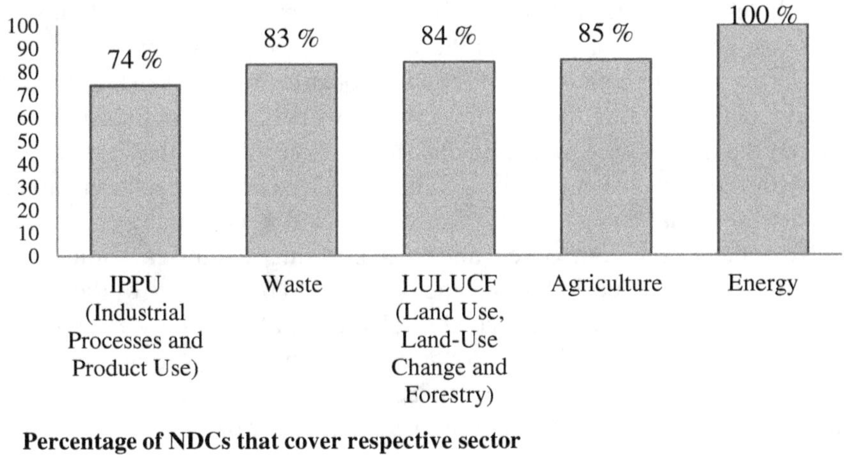

Fig. 14.3. Sectors covered in the updated NDCs.
Source: Compiled by the authors based on Ref. [11].

from 21% in 2018" [11]. Thus, the added power must come from clean sources, which requires ambitious renewable energy targets to achieve a share of 90% in the structure of electricity production by 2050 [11].

Climate change is the main driving force for introducing renewable energy sources in all sectors of the economy. Additionally, the use of renewable energy is conditioned by energy security and other socio-economic benefits. This requires international support in the form of investment, technology exchange, and expert support.

14.4. Discussion

One of the factors of the energy transition is the impact on demand. The changes in the supply market naturally affect demand. Thus, new energy sources contribute to developing new sources of energy demand. New energy sources are accelerating on a global scale. For example, coal was first used as fuel for heating, and then it was actively used in other areas of industry. For half a century, the global energy demand has increased faster than the world's population [6]. As a result, coal has become the main fuel for generating electricity. Nowadays, the whole world is rapidly introducing clean technologies that have less impact on the environment.

Nevertheless, it is difficult to talk about the full effectiveness of their use; this is just a transitional stage on the way to a green economy.

More and more countries actively promote the principles of sustainable development, including the transition to green energy. The main difference between the new energy transition and the previous ones is that it is associated with the prevention of climate change. The energy transition should consider the social and economic consequences for each country.

Nowadays, oil companies and oil-exporting countries should not ignore the transition period in the energy sector. The subjects of the world economy should consider the speed of changes in technology, despite the long-term impact of oil demand. Additionally, it is challenging to determine which technology will be successful and what the final energy transition will look like. The energy transition will be different for each country. The study raises the question of how countries for which carbon resources are the primary income of the budget will develop. Apparently, oil-exporting countries have risks of losing substantial foreign exchange earnings from exports. This fact will lead to a violation of their socio-economic well-being. The risk of their budget dependence on oil revenues impacts energy consumption and economic growth in general.

One of the ways out is to invest part of the revenues from the export of hydrocarbons in the development of green energy. If we look at the existing practices, then traditional energy functions together with green energy. For example, the United Arab Emirates (UAE), where there were no renewable energy installations until quite recently, plans to increase energy production from alternative sources.

In 2020, the installed capacity of renewable energy sources in the UAE amounted to 2.3 GW, about 91% of which is accounted for by solar photovoltaic projects. By 2025, the country plans to increase solar photovoltaic energy to 9 GW [16]. Renewable energy is the mechanism that will significantly contribute to the diversification of the country's energy sector. "The share of renewable energy in the UAE's power generation mix is set to increase from 7% in 2020 to 21% in 2030, and to 44% by 2050" [16].

The National Renewable Energy Program of Saudi Arabia provides for the construction of 9.5 GW of solar and wind energy capacity by 2023 as an "initial goal." This value is almost twice the planned volume of commissioning of renewable energy capacities in Russia by 2024. Saudi Arabia plans to provide its solar power plants with local components, form a complete value chain in the renewable energy sector, and create a "regional hub" for exporting solar industry products to neighboring regions and Europe.

In the future, the diversification of the energy sector in these countries will contribute to a complete energy transition. There is no denying that traditional resources will play a key role for a long time to come. However, for oil-exporting countries and oil-importing countries, traditional resources have a significant impact on the speed of the global energy transition and the transition to green energy.

To completely get rid of carbon dioxide emissions, it is necessary to abandon the burning of fossil fuels everywhere. There are alternatives in the form of nuclear power. However, there is a problem with operational safety due to past accidents (e.g., Japan).

Natural gas is singled out among green energy sources. According to the forecasts of the IEA, its global consumption may grow up to 25% by 2040.

Another type of green energy is hydrogen. Hydrogen can be used as energy, a source of heating, and in the chemical industry. Nevertheless, there are difficulties in use: loss of energy during electrolysis, leakage during operation, etc. Within the framework of the Sustainable Development Goals, green hydrogen can contribute to achieving results in the fight against climate change.

At the UN Climate Conference COP 26, green hydrogen was included in several commitments to reduce emissions of harmful substances as a way to decarbonize industry, transport, shipping, and aviation. Governments and businesses have recognized green hydrogen as an important pillar for a green economy with zero emissions.

The demand for green hydrogen as an environmentally friendly energy carrier is growing, despite the high cost of production. According to EY-Parthenon, "by 2030, the installed capacity for its production should reach almost 140 GW, which implies an astronomical growth rate, since in 2020 the figure did not reach even 1 GW" [5] (Fig. 14.4). Green hydrogen will be a key element of the energy transition based entirely on renewable energy in the long term.

According to IRENA experts, the hydrogen business will be more competitive and less profitable than the oil and gas business. However, hydrogen has the potential for competitive production in many sectors of the economy. "This will limit the possibilities of capturing economic rents akin to those generated by fossil fuels, which today account for some 2% of global GDP. Moreover, as the costs of green hydrogen fall, new and

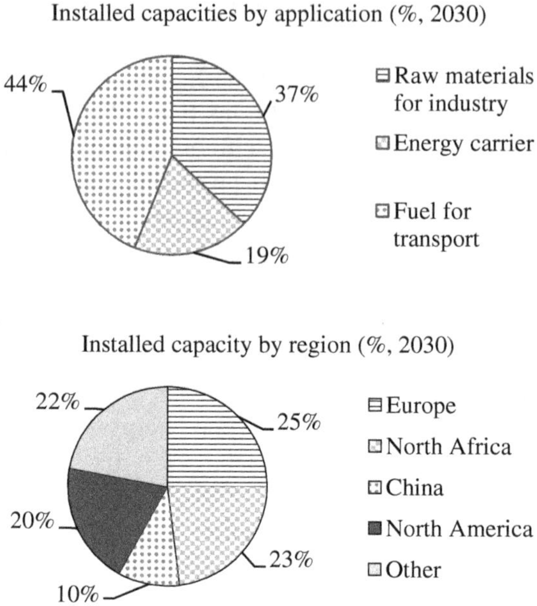

Fig. 14.4. Installed capacity by 2030 by application and region.
Source: Compiled by the authors based on Ref. [5].

diverse participants will enter the market, making hydrogen even more competitive" [10]. In fact, hydrogen acts as a new stage in the energy transition. Nowadays, the growing number of transactions indicates that international relations in the energy sector are changing. More attention is paid to green energy than to hydrocarbon energy. With changing trends in the energy sector, countries are changing their national strategies. "More than 30 countries and regions have hydrogen strategies that include import or export plans, indicating that cross-border hydrogen trade is set to grow considerably" [10].

The efficiency of using renewable energy sources is being actively discussed worldwide. Currently, the use of renewable energy in some countries is very limited. However, with the adoption of the green agenda, investment flows in clean energy began to increase actively. Renewable energy sources are becoming affordable and increasingly cost-competitive with traditional energy sources.

Each country can implement renewable energy. Thus, it is understood that the potential of renewable energy leads directly to energy security and energy availability for the population. Renewable energy has an advantage: energy is generated without the emission of carbon dioxide into the atmosphere, which is the cause of current environmental problems. Consequently, the tasks of the green economy on a national scale will be successfully solved.

Moreover, the lack of use of clean energy sources may soon lead to additional costs in the business. The EU member states have already discussed the prospects of introducing a special carbon tax on products coming from countries that do not pay enough attention to the development of green energy.

Yet, renewable energy, namely the process of creating equipment, does not guarantee the transition to sustainable energy development. Another problem is the instability of energy sources, depending on the weather and time of day, which causes the need to accumulate and store generated energy.

In fact, renewable energy acts as a transitional stage in the decarbonization of energy because there are still problems with the production, operation, and disposal of equipment, placement in natural areas (landscape change), etc. For example, in Europe, wind power faces difficulties in recycling turbine blades, consisting of composite materials unsuitable for recycling. "First-generation wind turbines become obsolete, and they need to be replaced with more advanced and efficient ones. This process, called capacity renewal, has started at different rates across Europe" [13]. The real problem is the formation of landfills for the burial of non-decomposing parts of wind turbines. Thus, humanity is only at the initial stage of the green energy transition.

European countries strive for green energy. European politicians persuade their business people to switch to renewable energy, thereby trying to make fossil fuels too expensive. However, an abrupt transition can cause an energy crisis. The EU has presented its 2030 Strategy, which sets mandatory targets for emissions and renewable energy sources on the path to sustainable development. However, measures to achieve sustainable development are often perceived as costly and potentially slowing down the economy. There is an assumption that there is a relationship between wealth and sustainability. Less affluent EU countries have made less progress in meeting their renewable energy targets. On the contrary, more prosperous EU countries have made significant progress in achieving their renewable energy goals [1].

Thus, the energy transition cannot be ignored. However, renewable energy currently cannot fully meet the population's needs. In the near future, traditional energy will continue to occupy a dominant position in the global energy sector. The main function of energy is to provide people with affordable and reliable energy resources without interruption.

Another tool is the tax on emissions of harmful substances into the atmosphere, which forces European businesses to switch to green energy, including importing countries. The carbon pricing system is one of the most radical measures in terms of achieving the goals of reducing harmful emissions into the atmosphere. The EU initiative to introduce cross-border carbon regulation may change the terms of international trade due to climate restrictions and, therefore, will cause discrimination, for example, against Russian products because Russia is the EU's largest trading partner. "If the most negative scenario for Russia is realized, the losses of Russian exporters to the EU until 2030 only for oil, petroleum products, gas, liquified natural gas, and polyolefins, according to the authors of the report, can amount to 1.4–2.4 billion euros per year, depending on the scenario, and from 0.2 to 0.5 billion euros per year for fertilizers" [7].

At the corporate level, large oil companies publicly declare their intention to achieve carbon neutrality in production processes. However, oil companies face difficulties mainly due to abrupt changes in their business models and in finding ways to integrate low-carbon assets. The companies should gradually expand their portfolio of assets in which green technologies are present.

Are oil companies ready to invest in renewable sources? Oil companies traditionally invest in highly profitable mining projects. The companies are often not ready to invest in renewable energy. Companies are not ready to take risks by investing in unstable technologies. Another factor is the regulation of the renewable energy market (at the level of large companies), so companies usually compete for efficiency in the traditional market. "BP invested $8.3 billion in wind and renewable assets in 2005–2013. It failed to find a buyer for its 1.6 GW of US wind capacity in 2013. The replacement cost at today's wind prices is estimated at around $2.3 billion" [6].

Regardless of the energy transition, global oil consumption will decrease. Over the next 30 years, it may decrease from about 100 million barrels per day to 50 million [4]. All oil corporations will have to change their policies if they want to cooperate with investors who are gradually abandoning investments in fossil fuels. Most large oil companies are diversifying their business and increasing spending in the field of renewable energy and other green technologies.

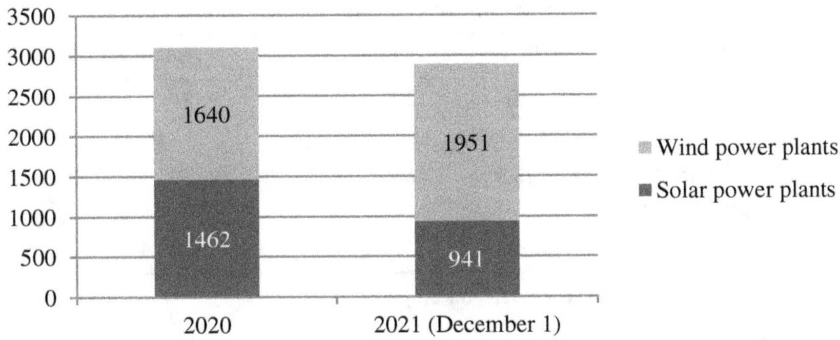

Fig. 14.5. The total installed capacity of renewable energy power plants in Russia, MW.
Source: Compiled by the authors based on Ref. [15].

The energy transition is a major challenge for the Russian economy because the country still depends on oil exports. The alternatives are gas, hydrogen, and renewable energy (especially hydropower). For example, "the Russian government has announced its intentions to conquer 20% of the global hydrogen market. A roadmap and a concept for the development of hydrogen energy have been approved, and work is underway on a program for the development of low-carbon hydrogen energy" [4]. According to the strategy of low-carbon development of the Russian Federation until 2050, the country should achieve carbon neutrality by 2060. The main objective is to reduce greenhouse gas emissions by 79% by 2050.

In 2021, Russia actively developed the renewable energy industry (Fig. 14.5). It was decided to extend the renewable energy support program until 2035, which will provide additional commissioning of about 9 GW of renewable energy generation facilities. As part of the competitive selection of renewable energy investment projects, the minimum values for the final price of solar electricity and wind energy have been achieved: the declared prices have decreased almost three times relative to the limit values. Wind energy has become the cheapest resource in the Russian energy market [15].

The renewable energy industry is one of the youngest and most promising in the Russian economy. In the last few years, the growth rate of renewable energy has been steadily growing. Renewable energy sources allow ensuring the formation of sustainable competitive advantages for the Russian industry and the economy as a whole in the long term.

Table 14.1. Gross emissions into the atmosphere (Thousand tons).

	2016	2017	2018	2019	2020
NOX	19.2	22.1	25.6	26.7	28.6
SO_2	128.4	69.0	74.8	38.9	18.4
Volatile organic compounds (VOCs)	128.3	120.3	96.7	102.1	90.7
Total	600.8	474.3	508.3	529.4	452.6

Source: Compiled by the authors based on Ref. [7].

Russian oil companies have started paying increasing attention to environmental issues because this will become the main indicator of the country's investment attractiveness in the near future. Rosneft plans to reduce greenhouse gas emissions by 20 million tons in CO_2 equivalent by 2035. LUKOIL has planned about 60 measures to reduce greenhouse gas emissions by 2030 [4].

For example, Gazprom Neft treats the environment responsibly. In 2020, the company allocated 8.1 billion rubles of investments for environmental protection. The company's strategic objectives are the refusal to burn associated petroleum gas, the use of solar energy in infrastructure (administrative buildings, gas stations, etc.), objective assessment, and the desire to minimize environmental risks from its activities [7]. In 2020, Gazprom Neft reduced gross emissions by 14.5% due to a large-scale program of modernization and reconstruction of the company's refining assets (Table 14.1) [7].

Gazprom Neft is among the leaders of the Carbon Disclosure Project (CDP) international rating. CDP examines companies on climate responsibility indicators. In 2020, Gazprom Neft received the highest rating of category "B" among Russian oil and gas companies [3].

As part of decarbonization, Gazprom Neft is working on a direction for producing hydrogen fuel from natural gas. Gazprom Neft, together with other international fuel and energy companies, implements projects in the field of the development of production, transportation, storage, and use of hydrogen. Thanks to the exchange of experience, companies will be able to reduce their carbon footprint.

If we compare Russia with other oil countries, it will be much easier for the Russian economy to adapt to current trends due to the availability of natural gas exports. According to experts, the demand for gas will be relatively stable; perhaps it may even grow in the next 10–15 years [4].

At the legislative level, projects are being introduced to require companies to disclose information about their environmental risks and climate action plans. The companies will need to conduct more thorough monitoring of all their processes (supply chains and others). Nowadays, the largest transnational companies have experience in the field of sustainable development. Reducing emissions is one of the most difficult problems throughout the entire business process cycle.

The task of the business is to prepare reports, calculate the carbon intensity of products, and compare this indicator with European companies. This analysis shows the potential of reducing the carbon footprint to implement future energy efficiency projects. On the part of the states, European colleagues should recognize the results of these projects. In fact, the energy transition will contribute to improving the competitiveness of companies and ensuring the stability of their business.

14.5. Conclusion

In the current world, scientific and technological progress has generated clean technologies. In the 21st century, it has helped the development of green energy. More and more often, we hear about the rejection of the use of traditional energy resources and the transition to alternative energy. Phasing out the use of traditional fuels will increase the country's energy efficiency. The global trend towards decarbonization will only gain momentum, which will affect European countries and many other countries and international institutions. Unfortunately, existing mechanisms are not enough to keep the global temperature rise within two degrees.

The transition to green energy is not being carried out as quickly as we would like to save humanity from an ecological catastrophe. Nevertheless, it is impossible to deny attempts to transition to a behavior model that can stop environmental degradation and provide energy to all segments of the country's population. Energy transfer is an extremely difficult task for forming a green economy because no country can completely abandon traditional energy today. To do this, it is necessary to build the appropriate infrastructure, which requires the joint work of all international organizations, supranational institutions, countries, business representatives, and citizens.

The countries have yet to fully integrate into the new energy transition based on green energy. Oil exporting countries still have a lot to do to develop and implement measures to exit the energy-intensive, carbon-intensive, and resource-dependent economy. The process of diversification of oil companies' assets has begun. To reduce the carbon footprint of its products, it is necessary to modernize existing technologies and ensure the transition to a green economy in the country.

At the corporate level, in conditions of restrictions due to COVID-19, many companies achieve better results. They are more financially stable due to the effective consideration of environmental, social, and corporate risks in their activities. As a result, the company should pay much more attention to implementing strategies in the field of sustainable development, moving from the traditional business model to the green model, which aims to minimize negative consequences to the environment. As for the green economy, it can also open up new opportunities for the development of green energy (renewable energy sources, hydrogen, and others), green cities, decarbonization, and the implementation of environmental initiatives. This will allow forming more effective sources of economic growth for the countries of today's world economy.

References

1. Andrea JJ, Burns C, Touza J. Renewable energy as a luxury? A qualitative comparative analysis of the role of the economy in the EU's renewable energy transitions during the "Double crisis." *Ecological Economics*, 2017; 142: 81–90. DOI: 10.1016/j.ecolecon.2017.06.011
2. Bowcott H, Fomenko L, Hamilton A, Krishnan M, Mysore M, Trittipo A, *et al*. Protecting people from a changing climate: The case for resilience. McKinsey. 2021 November 2008. Available from: https://www.mckinsey.com/business-functions/sustainability/our-insights/protecting-people-from-a-changing-climate-the-case-for-resilience
3. CDP. Companies scores. 2021. Available from: https://www.cdp.net/en/companies/companies-scores
4. Drebentsov V. The challenges of energy transition for the Russian economy. *ECONS*. 2021. Available from: https://econs.online/articles/opinions/vyzovy-energoperekhoda-dlya-rossiyskoy-ekonomiki/
5. EY Global. How hydrogen can help dramatically reduce emissions. 2021. Available from: https://www.ey.com/ru_ru/strategy/how-hydrogen-can-spark-the-next-zero-emissions-revolution
6. Fattouh B, Poudineh R, West R. (2018). The rise of renewables and energy transition: What adaptation strategy for oil companies and oil-exporting countries? Oxford, UK: Oxford Institute for Energy Studies. 2018. Available from: https://www.oxfordenergy.org/wpcms/wp-content/uploads/2018/05/

The-rise-of-renewables-and-energy-transition-what-adaptation-strategy-for-oil-companies-and-oil-exporting-countries-MEP-19.pdf
7. Gazprom Neft. Sustainable development report – 2020. St. Petersburg, Russia; 2020. Available from: https://ir.gazprom-neft.ru/upload/iblock/3ba/Sustainable_Development_Report_2020_RUS.pdf
8. Georgeson L, Maslin M, Poessinouw M. The global green economy: A review of concepts, definitions, measurement methodologies and their interactions. *Geo: Geography and Environment*, 2017. DOI: 10.1002/geo2.36
9. IEA. World Energy Outlook. 2021. Available from: https://iea.blob.core.windows.net/assets/888004cf-1a38-4716-9e0c-3b0e3fdbf609/WorldEnergyOutlook2021.pdf
10. International Renewable Energy Agency (IRENA). Geopolitics of the energy transformation: the hydrogen factor. Abu Dhabi, UAE; 2022. Available from: https://www.irena.org/-/media/Files/IRENA/Agency/Publication/2022/Jan/IRENA_Geopolitics_Hydrogen_2022.pdf
11. International Renewable Energy Agency (IRENA). NDCs and renewable energy targets in 2021. 2022. Available from: https://www.irena.org/publications/2022/Jan/NDCs-and-Renewable-Energy-Targets-in-2021
12. Lofoten Declaration: A global call for climate leadership. 2017. Available from: http://www.lofotendeclaration.org
13. Pinna M. Utilization of turbine blades: The Achilles heel of wind power. *Euronews*, 2021. Available from: https://ru.euronews.com/2021/06/25/ru-unreported-europe-wind-blades-recycling
14. Poryadin A, Beloglazova O. Global decarbonization: Evolution of approaches of oil and gas companies. EY. 2021. Available from: https://www.ey.com/ru_ru/oil-gas/global-decarbonization-evolution-of-oil-and-gas-companies-approaches
15. Russia Renewable Energy Development Association (RREDA). The future of renewable energy in Russia. 2021. Available from: https://rreda.ru/information-booklet-december-2021
16. Smith S. Rystad Energy: UAE set for solar growth. *Energy Global*. 2021. Available from: https://www.energyglobal.com/solar/10022021/rystad-energy-uae-set-for-solar-growth
17. The CSR Foundation and the Analytical Center of the Fuel and Energy Complex of the Ministry of Energy of Russia and the Situational Center LLC (2021). The climate agenda of Russia: Responding to international challenges. Available from: https://www.csr.ru/upload/iblock/521/521091011093dc8b5ece74cdd8552680.pdf

https://doi.org/10.1142/9789811264252_0015

Chapter 15

Environmental Performance of Countries in Dynamics of Economic Growth

Denis S. Ushakov[*,†,§] and Khodor Shatila[‡,¶]

[†]*Rostov State University of Economics, Rostov-on-Don, Russia*
[‡]*Sagesse University, Furn El Chebbak Baabda, Lebanon*
[§]*fintaliano@yandex.ru*
[¶]*info1@iprocares.com*

Abstract: The global ecology and the global economy are inseparable. The natural environment is basically the source and proto-resource of the global economy, while environmental conditions are the factors of purely economic consumption or production, investment attractiveness, or innovative capacity. On the other hand, the enormous possibilities of the global economy increasingly "dilute" the concept of environmental and economic feasibility, thus mainstreaming the issue of ensuring future environmental sustainability and security of current resources and sources of boosting economic growth these days. Based on statistics, the chapter analyzes trends of national economic growth facilitated through predatory and unreasonable consumption of natural resources. The chapter offers conclusions on effective tools to ensure long-term economic

[*]Corresponding author.

progress with a priority on greening manufacturing and commercialization processes.

Keywords: Environmental Performance Index; Economic growth; Green economy.

15.1. Introduction

The current world is virtually a unified, bounded, and ultimate ecological system, diverse but interrelated, despite the factor of geographic localization. The same global, interacting, bounded, and ultimate pattern is currently attributed to the global economic system, which, within the second half of the 20th century, rapidly transformed from a fragmented space of nation-states into a complex set of multinational corporations, supranational economic regulation systems, global markets (including those totally autonomous in their operation), cross-border production and distribution systems, etc.

We have seen an increase in environmental problems worldwide for several decades. International summits at the highest level, international and domestic documents regulating the environmental impact, and multi-billion-dollar costs of ensuring environmental well-being do not remove the acuteness of the problem. Moreover, this problem is becoming more acute every year.

There is an understanding that environmental problems are directly related to the development of the economy and the solution of socio-economic problems, that they can lead to tragic consequences for humanity. There is a desire and significant real infusion of funds in solving environmental problems. Some local successes have already been achieved, but the overall result is negative.

In our opinion, in the system of contemporary economic paradigms, environmental problems cannot be solved and will grow. As we see it, the point here is not bad environmental legislation or the unwillingness of the authorities to solve environmental problems.

Environmental problems have always accompanied humanity. Nevertheless, with the development of scientific and technical potential, these problems began to acquire a global character, becoming a real threat to human safety.

Scientific and technological progress was accompanied by rapid economic growth and the replacement of the classical economic formula "commodity–money–commodity" with the formula "money–commodity–money." In this formula, money itself acts as a commodity. As has already been noted many times [10, 16], a new formula contributing to the creation of global economic space and the globalization of the economy, primarily in the form of a unified banking system, does not in any way contribute to the preservation of nature and the solution of environmental problems.

Based on statistical data analysis and international expert groups' indicators, the research aims to reveal the global trends of facilitating the national economic growth through predatory and unreasonable consumption of natural resources and draw conclusions on suggesting effective tools to ensure long-term economic progress of the world nations.

Research hypotheses are as follows:

- Asynchronous dynamics of economic growth in world countries, inherent in today's globalized world economy, are expressed among others in the diversity of instruments for responsible use of natural resources and proper environmental management;
- The economic growth of world countries in different ways depends on the degree and scope of the environment and potential ecological exploitation by the national and transnational businesses;
- The most rapid economic growth is often associated with the predatory overexploitation of the country's natural resources;
- A reduction in economic growth in world countries does not necessarily lead to environmental quality improvement or its maintenance at the acceptable level within the country;
- The level of dependence of economic growth on the degree of exploitation of national environmental potential is reduced (in most cases) upon the increasing of material welfare of the local population.

15.2. Literature Review

The ancient Greeks referred to economics as "natural sciences" and opposed to chrematistics — a branch of human activity associated with the extraction of benefits. In today's sense, economics is viewed as a science that studies the system of social relations from the standpoint of the concept of price and value.

The main function of the economy is to constantly create such benefits that are necessary for people's lives, without which society cannot develop. However, as we can see, by creating benefits, the current economy creates serious global and regional environmental problems.

The world's ecological predicament, which can be described as a state of ecological crisis, as well as the worsening of global socio-economic and political difficulties, necessitates reversing dangerous tendencies and altering the trajectory of contemporary civilization's development. The conflict between economic expansion and the desire to conserve natural resources is one of the most significant conflicts.

To overcome this most difficult problem, a combination of political efforts, and a shift in economic paradigm involving the transition from the civilization-based economic system to the ecological-economic system, is required. When we talk about the clash of economic goals with environmental standards, we talk about the material, "physical" influence of people on nature, such as natural resource consumption and pollution. As a result, it may appear that in an ecological environment, one should only speak about material production rather than the economy as a system of production commodity-money linkages between people.

However, this is correct only partially.

Production, distribution, consumption, and exchange are involved in the relationship between society and the technosphere with their natural environment, at least to the extent that money, goods, and services are required for the use and reproduction of natural resources, the conservation of valuable natural objects, and the conditioning of the human habitat. However, because the examination of interactions leads to the inclusion of macroeconomics, macroecology encompasses the entire field of macroeconomics.

Their subordination and interdependence are becoming more apparent.

This is something that economists and ecologists will have to get used to. The foundation of macroeconomics is formed by the following essential facts:

(1) Material needs of individuals and the entire human civilization are endless and insatiable;
(2) Material resources — i.e., methods of meeting requirements — are scarce or non-existent.

These facts apply to the entire economic problem and represent the optimality economic criterion, defined as the maximum possible fulfillment of requirements with finite resources.

However, the development of civilization, particularly the economy, has determined a large volume of supra-biological consumption, and most technosphere resources — i.e., nonbiotic resources — are unsuitable for natural assimilation in the biosphere before and after human processing. This foundation of macroeconomics has become the central problem of macroecology. These elements, combined with the enormous population, which is partly driven by the economy, have become the primary causes of the natural equilibrium being disrupted and the environment's quality deteriorating. Most economic growth attributable to a single person is almost entirely caused by greater usage of supra-biological resources and secondary consumer goods manufacturing sources.

This is due to the massive expansion of subsoil resources and technical energy exploitation. The technosphere has grown on this foundation. This provided the idea that the economy was unaffected by biosphere resources.

Indeed, the businesses that meet people's basic needs — agriculture, food, light industry, and utilities — make up a minor part of the economy in most industrialized countries, accounting for 32% of global GDP.

However, as thousands of years ago, the most basic human requirements — food, oxygen, clothes, and, to a lesser extent, water and housing — are met primarily through the products of living nature. The fact that many of these items now come from fields and farms rather than woods and steppes implies a redistribution of human labor rather than a reduction in reliance on natural biological processes.

Agriculture, forestry, fishing, lighting, food, and microbiological industries rely on the ecosphere's biological resources. For a long time, the provision of natural resources to the economy was not seen as reliance on ecological laws.

What causes economic development to come to such a halt? The answer can be found in the principles. The economy has always been focused on providing society's tangible requirements. Social demands have grown as evolution has progressed, demanding technological advancement.

As a result, economic development in the 21st century is impossible without scientific and technological advancement, which ensures and maintains consistent rates of output growth, implying an ever-increasing reliance on natural resources.

The conditions for the operation of the economy are determined by the available natural and human resources, the amount of technical expertise, and the system of institutions. Natural resources have always been important to society. The difficulty is that this dependence is not reflected in the economy.

Humanity is more interested in consuming than in preserving. Thus, the primary contradiction between economic and environmental development is that, on the one hand, the economy must advance and, on the other hand, this development has adverse environmental effects.

The issues of economic growth and the state of the environment have been a focus of research by economists throughout the history of economic thought: the classical theories were based on the fundamental character of the land and natural resources as the factors and primary sources of economic growth [6,8,14], and, consequently, on the dependence of dynamics and prospects of economic development on the quality of the natural environment.

An American scientist, Kuznets [11], was one of the first to assume the relationship between the dynamics of economic growth and the level of environmental pollution, having analyzed the statistics of atmospheric emissions in major American cities and other countries around the world. It should be noted that the Kuznets model — i.e., an environmental Kuznets curve (EKC) — still serves as the theoretical rationale for the whole range of studies. In 1999, Perman and Stern [15] estimated the EKC for sulfur emissions using a panel data set for 74 countries over 30 years.

Contemporary economic theory is based on the so-called monetarist concept.

Monetarism is a theory according to which the money supply in circulation plays a decisive role in stabilizing and developing the market economy. According to the monetarist theory, money is the main factor that determines the movement and development of production. The demand for money has a constant upward trend; to ensure a correspondence between the demand for money and its supply, it is necessary to pursue a course toward a constant increase volume of money in circulation.

It is apparent that money, unsecured by produced goods but already included in the economic turnover by the state, stimulates production, primarily by lending to entrepreneurs at the expense of future (not yet produced) goods and services. Simultaneously, the presence of money, unsecured by goods and services, stimulates the increasing involvement of natural resources in economic activity because, in such an economic paradigm, the only way for entrepreneurs to pay off loans is to increase the production of goods and services, their sale, and profit. At the same time, the faster and more goods and services are sold, the more profit, naturally, the faster the money supply, not provided with real goods, grows, and the faster natural resources are involved in economic activity.

The likelihood of maintaining the value of goods and services at a high level also increases (up to the destruction of what has already been produced to obtain maximum profit). The likelihood that a manufacturer will make a profit by producing products that are not too necessary but which increase the cost of the main product or service (packaging that goes almost entirely to waste, minor design changes, unnecessary options, etc.) also increases.

On the other hand, the country forms the so-called state debt, which is legally defined by the budget code as the sum of the country's debt obligations to legal entities and individuals, foreign states, international organizations, and other subjects of international law. State debt does stimulate economic growth, but it also raises unsolvable environmental problems.

According to the IMF, in 2011, the total public debt of the largest economies in the world (USA, China, Japan, Brazil, Russia, India, and 18 leading EU countries) averaged about 80% of GDP. In 2013, the total public debt of these countries increased to 90% of the total GDP of these countries. Thus, for nine months of 2011 and almost a year ahead in 2013, these states have planned an increase in the consumption of natural resources, environmental pollution, and an increase in the number and consequences of environmental problems. The total debt of the world economy, operating in the paradigm of monetarism, inevitably grows over time. Nowadays, only three countries with tiny GDPs (Brunei, Macau, and the Republic of Palau) have no external debt. With the growth of public debt, the world GDP is growing, along with it is the production of waste, which now amounts to about 20 tons per year for each inhabitant of the Earth, or more than 35 kg of waste for every dollar of world GDP.

Environmental issues and economic growth have moved to the forefront of global science since the early 2000s, when sustainable development has been recognized as a single universal concept that envisages not only the state of the environment but views it as a key success factor driving economic progress of a country or corporation. A large body of research on ensuring economic growth in the era of environmental globalization (including ineffective natural resources management) was conducted in an industry context [9] and in regional settings [1] to justify the feasibility of purely economic [2] and political [5] changes and reforms.

Back in 2005, environmental issues were included in the fundamental monograph — a *Handbook of Economic Growth* — as the lead paragraph in which the authors [3] originally posited that the relationship between economic growth and the environment is, and will always remain, controversial. It was an attempt to find answers to the following questions:

(1) What is the relationship between economic growth and the environment?
(2) How can we escape the limits to growth imposed by environmental constraints?
(3) Where should future research focus its efforts?

Later on, the contradictory nature of the relationship between economic growth, economic development, and the natural environment was grounded by Buşan [4], who analyzed the economic consequences of environmental disasters and concluded that the adaptation of growth in volume and quality of natural resources at a time and use of natural resources and environmental conditions in a rational manner is required.

Halkos and Paizanos [7] examined the effects of economic growth and government spending on the environment using a panel of 71 countries from 1970 to 2008. In particular, they tested a hypothesis on the existence of an inverted U-shaped relationship between economic performance and pollution, along with the hypothesis of a negative direct relationship between fiscal spending and pollution.

Of special interest are the attempts of scientists to identify the interdependence between the environmental dynamics and the individual economic indicators of a country or territory. Thus, in 2011, López *et al.* [12] published a study that suggested a model predicting that a reallocation of government spending composition towards social and public goods reduces pollution. Mesagan [13], as well as Ushakov and Kharchenko [17], focused on the role played by foreign direct investment in the relationship between quality environment and economic growth and recommended that a country should adjust its environmental policies to attract proper and appropriate technology to boost its economic progress as suggested by the interaction terms in the model.

This study is based on the Yale University expert group data offering a methodology for calculating the Environmental Performance Index published annually since 2008. The World Bank Statistics (macroeconomic global development indicators from 2010 to 2019) have also been used.

15.3. Research Methodology

To test the proposed hypotheses, we have conducted a five-step statistical data analysis on the dynamics of the Environmental Performance Index (Yale University data) and macroeconomic indicators (the World Bank data) for 143 countries in the period from 2010 to 2019.

Stage 1. Identification of a correlation between the dynamics of the indicators of the national GDP and Environmental Performance Index in 143 world countries over the period from 2010 to 2019.
Stage 2. Determination of the correlation between the dynamics of the indicators of the national GDP and Environmental Performance Index subject to the global economic growth dynamics in the period 2010–2019.
Stage 3. Analysis of the correlation between the dynamics of the indicators of the national GDP and Environmental Performance Index only for the countries whose GDP for the period 2010–2019 increased in its absolute value (103 countries divided into nine geographic groups: Africa, Latin America, English speaking countries of the APEC, Asia-Pacific, former Soviet Union, EU countries, Middle East countries, the countries of Central and South Asia, and Eastern Europe).
Stage 4. Analysis of the correlation between the dynamics of the indicators of the national GDP and Environmental Performance Index only for the countries whose GDP for the period 2010–2019 increased in its absolute value (103 countries divided into ten dozens by the size of individual GDP per capita).

15.4. Research Findings

The data in Table 15.1 evidence that the maximum negative correlation between the dynamic indicators of the national GDP and Environmental Performance Index is observed in the countries of Africa and the Middle East, where economic development (particularly in the agricultural and industrial sectors) is still based on the active exploitation of natural resources, and the authorities are deliberately holding environmental business standards at a low level to attract foreign investors and entrepreneurs (the absence of other advantages of doing business, such as ownership rights protection, availability of transport and financial infrastructure, availability of credit, receptive local markets, etc. are quite common for these states). Japan's presence at the top of the list of negative ratings is surprising.

This could be explained by the fact that in the studied period, Japan demonstrated a certain decline in GDP against the growth of the country's environmental indicators, which led to a high negative correlation (further on, under deeper investigation, this fact will become more apparent).

Demonstrating the highest correlation to the GDP dynamics and environmental conditions, leaders of the rating are the developed countries of Europe which, over the last decades, have implemented a strategy of sustainable economic development, spending their national GDP growth potential on environmental quality assurance, along with translating a high level of quality of the national ecological environment into the source of economic growth. The leading position of Bosnia and Herzegovina in the rating refers not to the success of a national strategy for greening economic progress, rather, it is due to the fact that the country has reduced its gross national product along with slightly putting down ecological status estimates.

Moreover, Table 15.1 also reveals that the economic growth of China, which is considered to be the most aggressive nature-exploiting market system, in fact, is less dependent on environmental degradation than, for example, Thailand, Argentina, or India. The leading oil- and gas-exporting countries (Middle East monarchies and Russia) demonstrate a withdrawal from the rapacious consumption of resources, along with a positive correlation between their economic growth and environmental quality within the country. The UAE and Kuwait have achieved particular success.

In the second stage of the study, we will group the countries subject to their economic growth dynamics (GDP) from 2010 to 2019 (Table 15.2).

Table 15.2 demonstrates that the most rapid growth in the world so far, unfortunately, is ensured at the expense of environmental quality to a greater (Ethiopia and Papua New Guinea) or a lesser extent (China and Nigeria). For the record, in Panama, the GDP growth has not led to a significant deterioration in the environmental quality. Apparently, the third

Table 15.1. Correlation between economic growth and Environmental Performance Index dynamics in world countries, 2010–2019.

Lowest correlation						Highest correlation		
No.	**Country**	**Correlation index**	**No.**	**Country**	**Correlation index**	**No.**	**Country**	**Correlation index**
1	Ghana	–0.88327	21	Argentina	–0.58722	135	Iceland	0.891451
2	Japan	–0.88233	41	Thailand	–0.45552	136	France	0.921416
3	Eritrea	–0.87728	50	China	–0.35237	137	Latvia	0.931599
4	Nepal	–0.87049	56	Indonesia	–0.32641	138	Austria	0.937936
5	Egypt	–0.86272	91	Russia	0.106552	139	Poland	0.957137
6	Madagascar	–0.81239	108	USA	0.386275	140	Finland	0.961463
7	Ethiopia	–0.77474	117	Australia	0.57868	141	Belgium	0.964021
8	Iran	–0.75147	118	Italy	0.592782	142	Estonia	0.978809
9	Congo, Rep.	–0.73266	129	UAE	0.82849	143	UK	0.980789
10	Papua NG	–0.73004	130	Germany	0.839425	144	Bosnia and Herzegovina	0.985764

Table 15.2. Correlation between Global Economic Growth and Environmental Performance Index dynamics which ranks world countries by their economic growth dynamics, 2010–2019.

The fastest growing economies			Reference countries			The biggest decline in GDP		
1	Zimbabwe	−0.57	24	India	−0.39	135	Slovenia	0.68
2	China	−0.35	29	Indonesia	−0.32	136	Italy	0.59
3	Nigeria	−0.19	38	Pakistan	−0.66	137	Portugal	0.24
4	Ethiopia	−0.77	49	Kazakhstan	−0.21	138	Latvia	0.93
5	Lao PDR	−0.66	74	United States	0.38	139	Spain	0.05
6	Uzbekistan	−0.32	94	Brazil	−0.4	140	Congo, Rep.	−0.73
7	Bangladesh	−0.49	103	Canada	0.19	141	Cyprus	0.08
8	Panama	0.11	122	Lithuania	0.65	142	Croatia	0.4
9	Papua NG	−0.73	124	Denmark	0.84	143	Greece	−0.18
10	Mongolia	−0.68	134	Kuwait	0.87	144	Ukraine	0.4

column shows that, in some European countries (Italy, Portugal, and Latvia), the decline in GDP prompted a decrease in environmental quality, which on the one hand, proves the insignificant role of nature as a factor in economic growth in these countries and, on the other hand, acknowledges the importance and effectiveness of public funding programs for environmental management, the reduction of which due to economic hazards has resulted in a drop in the environmental quality. Only Congo univocally demonstrates the critical need to maintain the environmental potential in ensuring the country's economic progress.

Stage 3 of our research covers the analysis of only 103 countries whose GDP increased in their absolute values from 2010 to 2019. The countries were classified into 11 groups according to their geographical location.

Out of 35 studied African countries, the most favorable situation in the area of environmental management was established in Sierra Leone, Angola, and Guinea, where dynamic economic growth has contributed to environmental quality enhancement. In contrast, the most deplorable situation is observed in Ghana, Eritrea, Madagascar, and Ethiopia.

In all Western European countries that demonstrated economic growth in 2010–2019 (a total of five countries were analyzed), the most favorable situation is observed everywhere, especially in Ireland, where a significant improvement in the quality of the environment has been revealed under low economic growth. In most countries of the Middle East and North Africa (nine countries were analyzed), a direct relationship between economic growth and environmental quality has not been detected. The exceptions are only Mauritania (negative correlation) and the UAE (high positive correlation, typical for Europe).

None of the 11 Asian-Pacific countries that have demonstrated economic growth over 2010–2019 positively correlate with GDP growth and environmental quality. The lowest negative correlation coefficients (close to zero) were observed in South Korea, Malaysia, and Cambodia; the highest coefficients were observed in Papua New Guinea, Mongolia, and Myanmar.

Among seven countries of the former Soviet Union covered by this research, neither a high negative nor positive correlation between the analyzed indicators has been registered.

In a special group of English-speaking countries of the Pacific region (USA, Canada, Australia, New Zealand, and some Islands of Oceania), all countries demonstrate a positive correlation between domestic GDP and the environmental quality (maximum values are held by Australia and the Solomon Islands, the lowest indices in the group are observed with New Zealand and Canada).

In the group of 21 countries of Latin America, a true leader is Mexico. Its economic growth from 2010 to 2019 was accompanied by a noticeable improvement in the environmental quality indicators. In all other countries of the group (except Panama), the correlation is negative, approaching the most negative values in Venezuela, Ecuador, and Haiti, which reflects the persistence of the predatory exploitation of the environment in these countries. Finally, in the last analyzed group of countries (the countries of Central and South Asia), the situation is also negative, revealing a high degree of dependence of economic growth on the exploitation of natural resources. This dependence reaches its maximum in Nepal and Pakistan (the correlation ranges within –0.7).

At the final stage of the study, the world countries which have demonstrated the growth of domestic GDP over the period 2010 to 2019 (103 countries) were grouped into 10 deciles (net of the three poorest countries of the world) by the volume indices of the national GDP per capita (Table 15.3).

Table 15.3. The number of countries with a negative correlation between the national GDP dynamics and environmental status in the groups of world countries.

	Countries in the decile under study	Number of countries with a negative correlation
Decile 1	South Korea, United Arab Emirates, Israel, New Zealand, Canada, Australia, Switzerland, Ireland, United States, Luxembourg	1
Decile 2	Uruguay, Mexico, Malaysia, South Africa, Chile, Botswana, Mauritius, Argentina, Oman, Saudi Arabia	7
Decile 3	China, Colombia, Namibia, Panama, Iran, Dominican Republic, Kazakhstan, Brazil, Thailand, Costa Rica	9
Decile 4	Philippines, El Salvador, Lebanon, Jordan, Fiji, Peru, Azerbaijan, Belize, Venezuela, Macedonia	8
Decile 5	Indonesia, Jamaica, Ecuador, Egypt, Cuba, Guatemala, Morocco, Paraguay, Sri Lanka, Swaziland	9
Decile 6	Ghana, Angola, Papua New Guinea, Bolivia, Cambodia, Vietnam, Honduras, Georgia, India, Nicaragua	9
Decile 7	Uzbekistan, Djibouti, Laos, Mongolia, Sudan, Cameroon, Guinea, Moldova, Mauritania, Pakistan	8
Decile 8	Nepal, Cote d'Ivoire, Haiti, Senegal, Zimbabwe, Kyrgyz Republic, Myanmar, Solomon Islands, Iraq, Bangladesh	7
Decile 9	Benin, Ethiopia, Rwanda, Kenya, Burkina Faso, Mozambique, Tajikistan, Togo, Uganda, Chad	10
Decile 10	Tanzania, Dem. Rep. Congo, Niger, Guinea-Bissau, Sierra Leone, Madagascar, Yemen, Mali, Eritrea, Zambia, Nigeria	10

Table 15.3 evidences that with the growth of material welfare, the state gradually moves toward more environmentally friendly factors and resources to ensure further economic enhancement through the use of increasing budgets.

15.5. Conclusions and Recommendations

(1) The analysis of the correlation between the national GDP and the environmental quality indicators in world countries demonstrates the

universality and globality of the trend of the need for environmental efficiency, differentiation approach to nature as a factor and the condition of global economic development subject to the economic progress dynamics, material well-being, and even environmental management practices. Thus, in several countries, the environment is commonly viewed as a resource for economic growth and a factor in the country's attractiveness for foreign business and capital. In other countries, the environment is an important characteristic of the internal market receptiveness (spurring the growth in the number of consumers and consumption quality). In some countries, the environment is not only the living environment but an area where innovations and new products are generated, opening and facilitating further prospects for economic growth. Consequently, as a critical attribute of today's country and local community, the environment perfectly fits in the global competitiveness pyramid along with such purely economic categories as capital capacity, workforce, innovation potential, etc.

(2) Global multi-mode patterns from the perspective of the perception of the environmental challenge logically contribute to the diversity of national environmental strategies, as well as to developing practical tactics aimed at conducting various environmental assessments, successful implementation of environmental legislation, funding nature-protection enterprises, etc. These strategies are realized asynchronously and with varying degrees of effectiveness. However, considering long-term prospects for the globalization of the economy, we could argue that the transition, e.g., of today's Ghana to environmental strategies, inherent to contemporary Portugal or UAE, will never occur. It is not the point of low efficiency or backwardness of Ghana; more important is that the specific nature of the current world economy (international financial markets, the system of international standards, and supranational infrastructure of government regulation) virtually will not allow Ghana to rise to a higher level in the global competitiveness pyramid (at which the factor of national competitiveness is not the natural resource anymore or the possibility of the predatory exploitation of the environment but the national consumption capacity), thus depriving Ghana of the mere economic feasibility of changing their national paradigm of natural resources management. This negates the economic capabilities of environmental control instruments, especially in developing countries and fast-growing economies. Based on the finiteness of natural resources, the

interrelated nature of the processes in the world environmental system, as well as the mutual integration of national markets and the production and distribution systems, there is no way to continue business strategies built upon the predatory and unwise environmental management (otherwise, the consequences of environmental disasters will affect the environmental quality even in rather effective and environmentally friendly economies). Apparently, economic prospects for many of the world's poorest countries are directly associated with the possibilities and conditions for predatory environmental management practices in them (this draws foreign capital investment, facilitates exports, contributes to the development of the local services market, etc.). The implementation of approaches to environmental management, typical, e.g., for the countries of Northern Europe (taxes, fines, standards, and regulations), would deprive the local production and agriculture of any chance to enter the world market, wind up the production costs (making impossible its sale in the domestic market), thus condemning the population of developing countries to starvation. From this perspective, the era of economic globalization triggers a basic environmental dilemma — either to perish due to the global ecological disaster or to allow the death of the economies which are, due to economic reasons and low government efficiency, unable to ensure the greening of national business strategy. Nowadays, the severity of this dilemma is being leveled by high raw materials costs along with the supra-profitability of financial and innovative sectors. However, the impending world transformation in favor of food markets, agricultural land, clean water, and tourism resources designates this dilemma to the agenda of all, without exception, international organizations and countries of the world.

(3) Avoiding extreme scenarios of the world economy development in light of tightening environmental security and stability maintenance instruments is possible under elaboration and implementation of barter trade tools between the resource-rich countries practicing predatory extraction and the countries actively consuming natural resources. In particular, Ghana can export its capacity as the world landfill of discarded home appliances and computers, not in exchange for money (which is plundered or transferred by government officials to their Swiss or American accounts) but in trade for new disposal technology and recycling, which is possessed, e.g., by Japan or

Sweden. Thus, instead of the notorious coast of death in Bangladesh, the Finns, e.g., might build up a ship breaking and recycling plant, or the Niger Delta could host scientific centers for oil wastewater treatment technology set up by the Shell company, etc. In this case, the country will not lose its own economic attractiveness as an exporter of natural raw materials or low-level processing products. Moreover, it will obtain new working places, new prospects for innovative industry growth, and more tax deductions. On the other hand, the importing country will only benefit from such schemes, gaining additional impetus for enhancing its own innovation-based production and the ability to redirect to it a part of imports costs.

Such externally promoted "fridge" to the world trade of inefficient environmental management results can and should facilitate the problem of environmental stability, offer greater opportunities for the poorest countries to catch up more quickly, and preserve their economic and population growth dynamics in the long-term perspective.

References

1. Ayesha A, Kashif M. Effect of economic growth, trade openness, urbanization, and technology on environment of selected Asian countries. *The B.E. Journal of Economic Analysis & Policy*, 2004; 3(2): 1–24.
2. Ayong Le Kama A, Schubert K. Growth, environment and uncertain future preferences. *Papiers d'Economie Mathematique et Applications*, 1999; 52: 28–39.
3. Brock W, Taylor S. Economic growth and the environment: A review of theory and empirics. In: Aghion P, Durlauf S (Eds.). *Handbook of Economic Growth*. 1st edn. Vol. 1A. Amsterdam, Netherlands: North Holland Publishing Co.; 2005. pp. 1749–1821.
4. Buşan G. Contradictory nature of the relationship between economic growth, economic development and the natural environment. *Anale. Seria Stiinte Economice. Timisoara*, 2012; XVIII: 337–341.
5. Ederington J, Levinson A, Minier J. *Trade Liberalization and Pollution Havens*. Lexington, KY: University of Kentucky; 2007.
6. Encyclopaedia Britannica. Physiocrat. 2005. Available from: https://www.britannica.com/topic/physiocrat
7. Halkos G, Paizanos E. Exploring the effect of economic growth and government expenditure on the environment. Pireaus, Greece: Pireaus University; 2005.

8. Kaplan SL. *Bread, Politics and Political Economy in the Reign of Louis XV*. Dordrecht, Netherlands: Springer; 1976; pp. 113–148.
9. Arrow K, Bolin B, Costanza R, Dasgupta P, Folke C, Holling C, *et al.* Economic growth, carrying capacity, and the environment. *Environment and Development Economics*, 1996 Feb; 1(1): 104–110. DOI: 10.1017/S1355770X00000413
10. Kosykh PG, Kutapo AA. *Ethics of Nature Management and Institutional Economics*. Moscow, Russia: Publishing House of State University of Management; 2007.
11. Kuznets S. *Modern Economic Growth: Rate, Structure, and Spread.* Washington, DC: The National Academy Press; 1966.
12. López R, Galinato, G, Islam A. Fiscal spending and the environment: Theory and empirics. *Journal of Environmental Economics and Management*, 2011; 62(2): 180–198. DOI: 10.1016/j.jeem.2011.03.001
13. Mesagan E. Economic growth and environment nexus: The role of foreign direct investment. *A Research Journal on Contemporary Issues and Development*, 2019; 4(3): 44–52.
14. Mill J. *Elements of Political Economy.* 1st edn. London, UK: Baldwin, Cradock, and Joy; 1821.
15. Perman R, Stern D. The environmental Kuznets Curve: Implications of non-stationarity. *Working Papers in Ecological Economics*, 9901, Canberra, Australia: Australian National University; 1999.
16. Smurov AV (2017). Year of Ecology. Why not reduce environmental problems? Opinion of the ecologist. *Zhizn Zemli*, 2017; 39(1): 5–11.
17. Ushakov D, Kharchenko L. Environmental factors of national competitiveness in modern MNCs' development. *International Journal of Ecological Economics and Statistics*, 2017; 38(2): 141–149.

https://doi.org/10.1142/9789811264252_0016

Chapter 16

Issues of Energy Saving and Energy Efficiency Policy: Foreign and Russian Experience

Olga Yu. Patrakeeva[*,†,¶], **Margarita Bogdanova**[‡,‖], **Tatyana V. Plotnikova**[§,**] and **Irina V. Lipchanskaya**[§,††]

[†]*Federal Research Centre The Southern Scientific Centre of the Russian Academy of Sciences (SSC RAS), Rostov-on-Don, Russia*

[‡]*Dimitar A. Tsenov Academy of Economics, Svishtov, Bulgaria*

[§]*Rostov State University of Economics, Rostov-on-Don, Russia*

[¶]*OlgaPatrakeyeva@yandex.ru*

[‖]*m.bogdanova@uni-svishtov.bg*

[**]*tatyana0918@mail.ru*

[††]*lipiv@list.ru*

Abstract: The development of measures and patterns to increase energy efficiency appears as one of the key objectives of the world economy and is aimed at solving environmental problems associated with energy consumption and climate change. The chapter focuses on the issue of the

[*] Corresponding author.

impact of economic growth and structural changes on the energy intensity of territories. Empirical studies highlight a significant influence of macroeconomic, demographic, and political factors on changes in the energy intensity of economies. Russia has significant capacity for improving energy efficiency, primarily in the electricity and housing sectors. The released volumes of fossil fuels can be exported, reduce emissions into the atmosphere, and, as a result, improve the quality of life. A consistent reduction in the consumption of fuel and energy resources due to the transition to a new technological order is demonstrated by the electric power industry, the manufacturing industry, and the transport sector. For Russia, the transition from a raw-material model of the economy to an innovative one is a priority for sustainable development. To overcome the causes of low energy efficiency and realize the existing potential, it is necessary to intensify the state policy at the regional and federal levels. Simultaneously, measures to save energy and increase energy efficiency will not be able to achieve the goal of reducing the energy intensity of GDP/GRP without high economic growth rates. The authors present the analysis of the influence of the structure of the gross regional product on energy consumption in the Rostov Region and characterize the structure of the economy and the electricity consumption of the region. It was noted that the development of the service sector and high-tech industries, as well as investment in environmental technologies, will allow the Rostov Region to move to an energy-efficient model of economic growth.

Keywords: Energy efficiency; Consumption; Sustainable development; Energy intensity; Economic growth; Structural changes.

16.1. Introduction

Energy is an inherent material basis for economic development and social progress. Industrial production is the primary sector supporting economic development and, at the same time, the largest energy consumer. In industrialized countries, a significant reduction in energy intensity (energy consumption per production unit) is spotted, driven by improvements in energy efficiency, as well as economic structural changes. However, CO_2 emissions are growing rapidly due to increasing energy demand and the carbon intensity of the energy sector [24].

Growing public demand for sustainable economic growth and knowledge of technological change is prompting governments to create appropriate conditions for the efficient use of resource growth and environmental protection, with particular attention to energy efficiency and energy conversion. However, there is very little empirical research on the role of environmental regulations and policies on energy demand [21].

Achieving environmental sustainability, energy efficiency, and green economic growth is in line with sustainable development goals. In today's environment, countries and regions consider energy efficiency as a vital component of energy and a strategic direction to address energy security and reduce CO_2 emissions targets.

16.2. Materials and Methods

Over the past decade, energy and climate issues have been of interest to politicians, industrialists, world leaders, and environmental scientists. However, few studies aimed to study factors that determine energy consumption and energy intensity. Additionally, there is a "gap" in studying the impact of environmental policies, regulations, and technologies on energy demand and the energy intensity of the economy [21].

Empirical findings [7,17] showed that for Organization for Economic Co-operation and Development (OECD) countries, there is a long-term relationship between real GDP, trade development, capital accumulation, and renewable energy consumption. Simultaneously, for the Mediterranean countries, the development of agriculture and tourism positively impacts the consumption of renewable energy sources [5]. Advanced environmental technologies contribute to energy saving and energy efficiency of buildings and structures. Researchers believe that energy efficiency is the primary driver of the observed decline in energy intensity in OECD countries [22].

Reducing carbon emissions and achieving greener growth are current research issues. In the scientific literature, special attention is paid to the relationship between energy intensity, energy efficiency, and structural changes in the economy, as well as the main factors affecting the dynamics of these indicators (world demand and energy prices, GDP index, per capita income, industrial production structure, R&D financing, etc.) [4,9,15].

The results reported in the research by Tenaw [26] highlight the need to improve energy efficiency in specific sectors (industry and households) to ensure economic growth and environmental sustainability. Additionally, the importance of encouraging activities that contribute to the transformation of clean energy and the improvement of the institutional structure is emphasized. Thus, empirical studies indicated the existence of a long-term relationship between real GDP and the consumption of renewable energy sources. In OECD countries, clean technologies reduce overall energy consumption and improve energy efficiency [21]. According to a number of scientists [14], the increase in energy efficiency could be identified with an increase in labor productivity in the industry.

The results of the study by Paramati *et al.* [21] indicate that economic progress and growth in prosperity lead to an increase in energy consumption per capita. For example, as incomes rise, the demand for household appliances (air conditioners, fans, heaters, etc.) increases. Simultaneously, income growth plays an important role in improving energy efficiency by encouraging the population to use energy-efficient electrical equipment.

Tajudeen [25] shows that in the development of energy policy, it is appropriate and informative to consider energy prices and asymmetric price effects in the analysis of energy efficiency factors. Periods of high energy prices could lead to improvements in energy efficiency due to changes in consumer behavior or the introduction of energy-saving technologies that continue to be applied after price reductions.

Due to the openness of the Chinese economy (Fig. 16.1), technological effects are manifested not only in the accumulation and exchange of advanced international technologies but also in an increase in environmental pollution.

China's extreme industrial development model, based on fossil energy sources as the main sources of carbon emissions, led to an unbalanced development between energy consumption and environmental pollution, which caused considerable damage to the ecological environment and questioned the limit of ecosystem sustainability. A study of the Chinese economy found that changes in energy prices, R&D spending, and business ownership reform were important in reducing energy intensity. Additionally, changes in the industry structure and the share of production by region also acted as the main determinants of changes in this indicator [13]. There is also a significant role of foreign direct

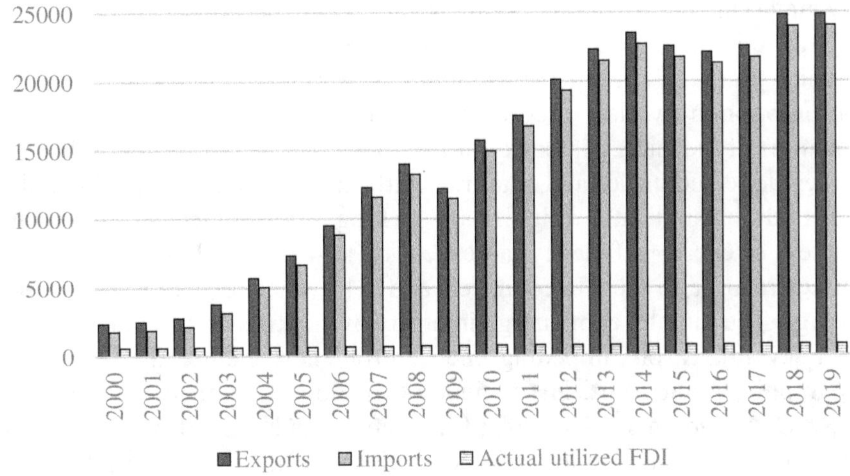

Fig. 16.1. The trends of exports, imports, and actual utilized foreign direct investment (FDI) ($, 100 million).

Source: Compiled by the authors based on Ref. [8].

investment in improving energy efficiency at the national and regional levels [8].

For energy-importing countries (e.g., Germany and Japan), the implementation of an energy efficiency policy involves the diversification of energy sources and the significant development of alternative and renewable energy sources to reduce dependence on imported fuel. Simultaneously, the priority of China, which ranks first in the world in terms of carbon dioxide emissions, in addition to the development of renewable energy, is the transition to a low-carbon economy and, as a result, the creation of environmentally friendly cities and the development of the automotive industry using new energy sources [19].

The problem of increasing energy efficiency is of particular relevance for Russia.

16.3. Results

The main goal of the state program of the Russian Federation "Energy development" is a reliable, high-quality, and economically justified provision of the needs of the domestic market for energy carriers, energy, and raw materials on the principles of energy saving and energy efficiency, as well as the fulfillment of obligations under foreign contracts [3]. In Russian practice, energy intensity indicators of GDP/GRP and energy consumption are widely used as energy indicators. A comparison of the dynamics of the energy intensity of Russia's GDP with a similar indicator for developed countries and countries with similar climatic and geographical conditions indicates a significant backlog of the domestic economy in the field of energy efficiency: an excess of 1.74 times relative to Canada, 3 times relative to the EU countries, and 2.19 times relative to the world average. The high level of energy intensity of the Russian economy results from several reasons impeding energy efficiency, including natural and geographical conditions, insufficient motivation of companies, low level of R&D development, lack of infrastructure, and lack of experience in financing and implementing relevant projects [19].

According to the Ministry of Economic Development of Russia, the largest contribution to the increase in the energy intensity of GDP in 2015–2018 was made by the manufacturing industry and the housing sector (+17.7 million tons of standard fuel), while the mining industry, power industry, and transport strived for reduction (saving 33.5 million tons of standard fuel). Simultaneously, the increase in production volumes, climatic factors, and structural shifts promoted the consumption of fuel and energy resources (+83 million tons of standard fuel), while technological factors associated with an increase in the energy efficiency of production allowed reducing energy consumption by 30 million tons of standard fuel (other factors — by 12 million tons of standard fuel) [20].

The technological factor is a key potential driver for reducing energy intensity in sectors such as manufacturing, transport, housing, and communal services through the introduction of innovative technologies (combined-cycle plants, combined electricity and heat generation plants, electrification and gasification of transport, energy-efficient building structures and thermal insulation materials, weather control systems, and resource consumption metering devices) [20].

The analysis of the Russian capacity for resource saving and the experience of implementing energy efficiency policies indicated that the Russian economy has a significant capacity for energy saving, primarily in the electric power industry and the housing sector. However, its implementation requires intensified government activities in this area, especially in terms of overcoming the reasons for the low efficiency of the national economy [19].

Due to the implementation of program measures in the field of energy efficiency and energy saving, 3,429 million tons of production and consumption waste were disposed of and neutralized. The increase in environmental costs (Fig. 16.2) is due to the growth of environmental costs in economically developed regions (Moscow and Moscow region), including industrial resource regions (Sverdlovsk Region, Krasnoyarsk Territory, and Khanty-Mansiysk Autonomous District) focused on heavy industry, mining, and manufacturing and requiring serious "environmental compensation" for the damage [12].

In the South of Russia, the problems of increasing energy efficiency are of particular relevance; the energy intensity of the economy in most southern regions is higher than the average Russian level.

For the Rostov Region, as an industrially developed region of the country, the introduction of energy-efficient technologies, equipment, and materials in the fuel and energy sector, as well as the development of leasing high-tech equipment, seems to be relevant and in demand. Energy efficiency measures are consistently funded at over 3% of GRP. The program "Energy efficiency and development of industry and energy" [1] sets

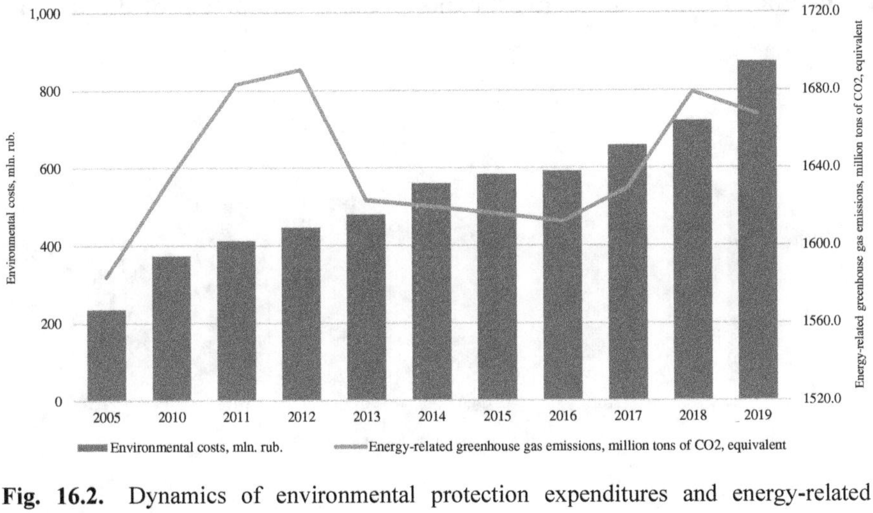

Fig. 16.2. Dynamics of environmental protection expenditures and energy-related greenhouse gas emissions in the Russian Federation.

Source: Compiled by the authors based on Ref. [11].

the goal of "creation of conditions for increasing energy production by generating facilities operating based on the use of renewable energy sources." Thus, by 2023, it is planned to launch three wind farms with a total capacity of 300 MW.

The production sector of the Rostov Region has a high capacity for energy saving. The region maintains a steady downward trend in the energy intensity of the GRP. Thus, in 2012, the energy intensity of the region's GRP exceeded the energy intensity of the country's GDP by 35.7%. However, by 2017, the figures were almost equal (Fig. 16.3). In the Rostov Region, the rate of reduction in energy intensity exceeded the rate of economic growth. However, this progress was driven by structural changes in the economy rather than investment in energy conservation and technological factors.

Relatively high energy consumption is due to the presence of energy-intensive industries in the region (heavy and agricultural engineering, metalworking, coal mining) — the industry forms 27.6% of GRP. The second place in the sectoral structure of the economy belongs to trade — 17.8%. Accordingly, the primary sources of economic growth in the Rostov Region are the manufacturing industry and trade.

According to the strategy for the socio-economic development of the Rostov Region, a significant decrease in the energy and material intensity of production is predicted [2]. A further reduction in the energy intensity of the GRP requires large investments in the re-equipment of production

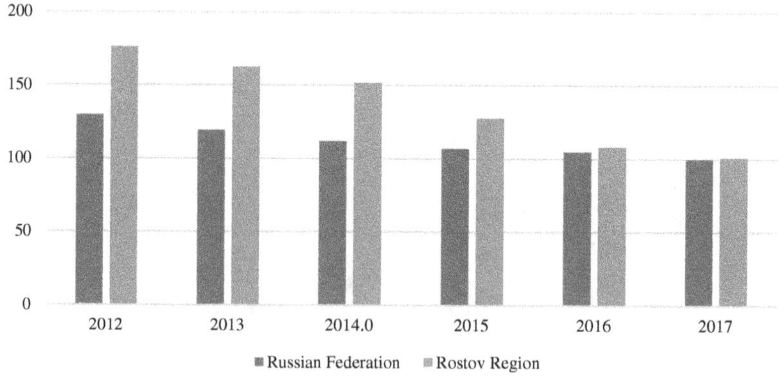

Fig. 16.3. Energy intensity of Russia's GDP and Rostov region's GRP, kg of standard fuel per 10 thousand rubles.

Source: Compiled by the authors based on Ref. [10].

facilities and the introduction of the latest energy-saving technologies. Tsybatov [27] notes that to assess the real prospects for reducing the energy intensity of GRP, it is necessary to correlate the goals of energy-efficient development with the goals of developing the region's economy. However, if the economy's structure changes over time from an energy-intensive industrial sector to an increasing share of the service sector, energy intensity could drop markedly without any change in energy efficiency.

Economic growth is the primary condition for reducing the energy intensity of GRP due to economies of scale, the rapid growth of "non-energy" sectors (changes in the structure of the economy), and lagging behind the volume of energy-consuming property of the population from the volume of GRP. The development of the service sector and high-tech industries, which, as a rule, use less energy-intensive technologies, as well as investment in environmental technologies, will allow the Rostov Region to move to an energy-efficient model of economic growth.

The government of the Rostov Region recognizes the apparent climate change in the region and notes the risks of natural and climatic anomalies as one of the key problems [2].

The outdoor temperature in the region affects the consumption of electricity. Over the past 120 years, the average air temperature in Rostov-on-Don has shown a steady upward trend: if in the first two decades of the last century, it fluctuated between 7.6–9.3°C, then over the past 20 years, it has been from 10 to 11.8°C. The most significant temperature increase is typical for June–October (Table 16.1).

Air conditioning systems and electric heaters are actively used during periods of high and low temperatures. Moreover, the population increasingly uses electrical devices (kettles, stoves, and microwave ovens) in everyday life. Thus, in 2012–2019, electricity consumption in the Rostov Region increased by 10%, while household consumption increased by 32% (Fig. 16.4).

Over the studied years, the average annual production-consumption of electricity increased by 5.4%, which indicates that the growth of the economy of the Rostov Region is due to the active development of production, the expansion of wholesale and retail trade (an increase in consumption by 24.7%), and construction (an increase in consumption by 64.7%).

With an increase in the duration of hot and dry periods, the need for water intake to feed the cooling pond for the Rostov NPP may increase.

Table 16.1. Average air temperatures in Rostov-on-Don, °C.

	Jan.	Feb.	Mar.	Apr.	May.	Jun.	Jul.	Aug.	Sep.	Oct.	Nov.	Dec.	Mean annual
1900	−8.1	−5.4	−1.4	7.7	15.9	18.3	23.1	23.1	13.5	11.8	−0.7	−1.0	8.1
1910	−2.8	−2.5	0.0	10.3	16.8	20.9	23.0	20.7	15.5	7.2	4.9	−2.1	9.3
1920	−4.8	−10.8	2.9	12.0	17.5	19.8	23.0	25.0	16.0	3.6	−4.7	−8.2	7.6
1930	−4.0	−5.5	3.8	10.3	17.1	17.6	22.8	24.8	14.8	10.0	4.7	−5.1	9.3
1940	−9.8	−6.7	−0.8	9.5	15.1	20.6	23.4	23.2	16.7	6.8	5.2	−3.0	8.4
1950	−16.1	−4.6	1.6	14.7	18.9	19.4	21.9	20.1	18.6	8.3	3.4	0.9	8.9
1960	−1.2	−3.0	−1.1	8.9	15.0	21.8	24.1	20.8	14.9	11.7	3.3	3.3	9.9
1970	−4.1	−0.3	2.9	13.6	17.2	19.4	25.5	20.9	16.2	8.7	4.6	−3.5	10.1
1980	−8.6	−5.1	−3.0	9.0	15.6	20.5	23.5	20.2	15.5	8.5	4.6	3.4	8.7
1990	−7.1	−8.4	4.1	10.6	16.7	18.7	25.6	24.7	16.8	8.8	1.1	−9.0	8.6
2000	−3.1	0.8	2.6	13.8	14.4	19.7	23.3	22.0	15.3	8.9	1.3	0.8	10.0
2010	−5.7	−2.4	2.3	10.7	18.1	24.1	26.6	27.5	19.1	8.1	8.9	2.5	11.7
2020	1.2	0.9	7.7	9.3	15.3	23.1	25.2	23.1	20.1	14.6	3.7	−2.9	11.8
2021*	−0.9	−2.0	2.1	10.1	18.1	21.9	26.5	24.8	15.8	9.3	—	—	—

Note: *No data for November–December 2021 was available at the moment of publication.
Source: Compiled by the authors based on Ref. [29].

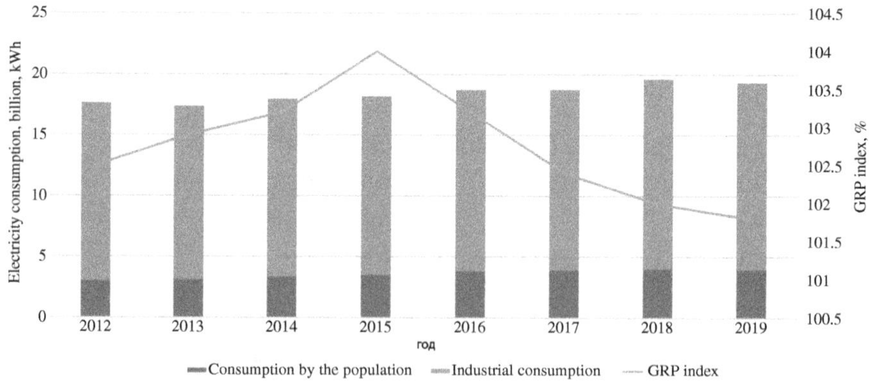

Fig. 16.4. Electricity consumption and GRP Index in the Rostov Region.
Source: Compiled by the authors based on Ref. [28].

Therefore, in the future, it is necessary to develop measures to ensure reliable backup cooling systems for power units. Since there is a long-term trend towards "electrification" of households and an increase in air temperatures, the load on high-voltage networks and equipment of transformer substations will increase. In this regard, the task of increasing the efficiency of the power grid complex is particularly relevant.

Thus, creating conditions for increasing energy production by generating facilities based on the use of renewable energy sources is one of the main tasks aimed at improving the energy efficiency of the region's economy.

16.4. Discussion

Energy efficiency is often used as a general term that refers to the use of less energy to produce the same volume of services or useful products; it is seen as a way to manage and contain growth in energy consumption. According to scientists, there is no single definition of energy efficiency because the use of energy efficiency concepts in engineering, environmental, economic, and other studies may include various methods and goals [6].

Energy intensity is one of the most commonly used indicators of integrated energy efficiency, which reflects the economic benefits of energy use. Reducing energy intensity is an important indicator for a green or circular economy [18].

According to Proskuryakova and Kovalev [23], state policy measures in the energy field, taken based on the priority of the energy intensity indicator are rather limited. First, this indicator, as an indicator of energy efficiency, indicates the general economic situation in the industry or the economy as a whole, which does not allow for forming specific and more targeted recommendations for improving energy efficiency. Second, energy intensity does not provide estimates of the extent to which energy efficiency can be improved within the framework of applied technologies. According to Kapusuzoglu and Karan [16], a direct result of the reduction in energy intensity is the decoupling of economic growth from energy consumption. Therefore, it is more appropriate to consider energy intensity as an indicator of consumption.

For an adequate energy efficiency assessment, Proskuryakova and Kovalev proposed creating publicly available clear thermodynamic indicators of the equipment used. The scorecard should promote the dissemination of energy-efficient solutions and the promotion of best technology practices at the level of corporate decision-makers and engineering managers responsible for the company's technology strategy. Simultaneously, it is possible to use energy intensity, economic, thermodynamic, and environmental indicators as energy consumption indicators.

16.5. Conclusion

The introduction of energy-saving technologies will reduce the negative effects of economic activity and encourage countries to reconsider their approach to energy consumption in various sectors through the efficient use of resources (e.g., through waste recycling and the introduction of environmentally friendly modes of transport). Regulators should pursue a consistent policy to promote innovation in clean and energy-efficient technologies by providing funding for related R&D. The COVID-19 pandemic impacted the development of the scientific and technological revolution. Strengthening the capacity for technological innovation is an important measure to cope with international changes and an important way to improve energy efficiency.

Energy-saving projects require long-term funding. The development of mechanisms and programs for long-term support for projects to create energy-efficient technologies, integrated strategies for introducing environmental technologies, and energy-efficient household appliances is a priority area of state policy. Since the problem of improving energy efficiency is extremely relevant for the Russian economy and its regions, the transition to a non-primary economic model is a priority for sustainable growth and sustainable development of the country.

Thus, innovations in clean and energy-saving technologies will reduce overall energy consumption and the impact on climate change by reducing greenhouse gas emissions.

Acknowledgments

The publication was prepared as part of the implementation of the state task of the Southern Scientific Center of the Russian Academy of

Sciences, project state registration number 122020100349-6 (Strategic vectors for the development of the socio-economic complex of the South of Russia, taking into account regional resilience (economic and demographic aspects)).

References

1. Government of the Rostov Region. Passport of the state program of the Rostov Region "Energy efficiency and development of industry and energy." Appendix No. 1 to Decree No. 760 . Rostov, Russia; 2018 November 29. Available from: https://www.donland.ru/documents/9887/ (accessed on 1/12/2021)
2. Government of the Rostov Region. Strategy for socio-economic development of the Rostov Region for the period up to 2030" (approved by Decree No. 864 dated December 26, 2018) . Rostov, Russia; 2018. Available from: https://www.donland.ru/activity/2158/
3. Government of the Russian Federation. Decree No. 321 "On approval of the state program of the Russian Federation 'Energy development.'" Moscow, Russia; 2014 April 15.
4. Aboagye S, Alagidede P. Energy consumption efficiency in Sub-Saharan Africa: Evidence and policies. *Ghanaian Journal of Economics*, 2016; 4(1): 116–138.
5. Alola AA, Alola UV. Agricultural land usage and tourism impact on renewable energy consumption among Coastline Mediterranean Countries. *Energy Environment*, 2018; 29: 1438–1454. DOI: 10.1177/0958305X18779577
6. Ang BW. Monitoring changes in economy-wide energy efficiency: From energy-GDP ratio to composite efficiency index. *Energy Policy*, 2006; 34(5): 574–582. DOI: 10.1016/j.enpol.2005.11.011
7. Apergis N, Payne J. Renewable energy consumption and economic growth: Evidence from a panel of OECD countries. *Energy Policy*, 38(1): 656–660. DOI: 10.1016/j.enpol.2009.09.002
8. Cheng M, Yang S, Wen Z. The effect of technological factors on industrial energy intensity in China: New evidence from the technological diversification. *Sustainable Production and Consumption*, 2021; 28: 775–785. DOI: 10.1016/j.spc.2021.06.032
9. Deichmann U, Reuter A, Vollmer S, Zhang F. Relationship between energy intensity and economic growth: New evidence from a multi-country multi-sector data set. World Bank Group. South Asian Region. Policy Research Working Paper. Available from: https://openknowledge.worldbank.org/bitstream/handle/10986/29288/WPS8322.pdf?sequence=5&isAllowed=y
10. Federal State Statistics Service of the Russian Federation (Rosstat). Energy intensity of GDP (GRP), 2012–2017 . Moscow, Russia; 2019. Available

from: http://www.gks.ru/free_doc/new_site/effect/energo.xls (accessed 26 October 2021)

11. Federal State Statistics Service of the Russian Federation (Rosstat). Environment. Available from: https://rosstat.gov.ru/folder/11194
12. Finexpertiza. Green money: Russian business increased environmental spending during the pandemic. 2021. Available from: https://finexpertiza.ru/press-service/researches/2021/zelenye-dengi/
13. Fisher-Vanden K, Jefferson GH, Liu H, Tao Q. What is driving China's decline in energy intensity? *Resource and Energy Economics*, 2004; 26(1): 77–97. DOI: 10.1016/j.reseneeco.2003.07.002
14. Geller H, Harrington P, Rosenfeld AH, Tanishima S, Unander F. Polices for increasing energy efficiency: Thirty years of experience in OECD countries. *Energy Policy*, 2006; 34(5): 556–573. DOI: 10.1016/j.enpol.2005.11.010
15. Jimenez R, Mercado J. (2013). Energy intensity: a decomposition and counterfactual exercise for Latin American countries. Working Paper Series, no. IDB-WP-441 (Inter-American Development Bank).
16. Kapusuzoglu A, Karan MB. The drivers of energy consumption in developing countries. In: Dorsman A, Simpson J, Westerman W (Eds.) *Energy Economics and Financial Markets*. Berlin; Heidelberg, Germany: Springer; 2013. DOI: 10.1007/978-3-642-30601-3_4
17. Koengkan, M. The positive impact of trade openness on consumption of energy: fresh evidence from Andean community countries. *Energy*, 2018; 158: 936–943. DOI: 10.1016/j.energy.2018.06.091
18. Luan BJ, Huang JB, Zou H, Huang C. Determining the factors driving China's industrial energy intensity: Evidence from technological innovation sources and structural change. *Science of the Total Environment*, 2021; 737: 139767. DOI: 10.1016/j.scitotenv.2020.139767
19. Matraeva L, Solodukha P, Erokhin S, Babenko M. Improvement of Russian energy efficiency strategy within the framework of "green economy" concept (based on the analysis of experience of foreign countries). *Energy Policy*, 2019; 125: 478–486. DOI: 10.1016/j.enpol.2018.10.049
20. Ministry of Economic Development of the Russian Federation. State report on the state of energy saving and energy efficiency in the Russian Federation. Moscow, Russia; 2020. Available from: https://www.economy.gov.ru/material/file/c3901dba442f8e361d68bc019d7ee83f/Energyefficiency2020.pdf
21. Paramati SR, Shahzad U, Dogan B. The role of environmental technology for energy demand and energy efficiency: Evidence from OECD countries. *Renewable and Sustainable Energy Reviews*, 2021; 153: 111735. DOI: 10.1016/j.rser.2021.111735
22. Parker S, Liddle B. Energy efficiency in the manufacturing sector of the OECD: analysis of price elasticities. *Energy Economics*, 2016; 58: 38–45. DOI: 10.1016/j.eneco.2016.06.003

23. Proskuryakova L, Kovalev A. Measuring energy efficiency: Is energy intensity a good evidence base? *Applied Energy*, 2015; 138: 450–459. http://dx.doi.org/10.1016/j.apenergy.2014.10.060
24. Shahiduzzamana M, Alam K. Changes in energy efficiency in Australia: A decomposition of aggregate energy intensity using logarithmic mean Divisia approach. *Energy Policy*, 2013; 56: 341–351. DOI: 10.1016/j.enpol.2012.12.069
25. Tajudeen IA. The underlying drivers of economy-wide energy efficiency and asymmetric energy price responses. *Energy Economics*, 2021; 98: 105222. DOI: 10.1016/j.eneco.2021.105222
26. Tenaw D. Decomposition and macroeconomic drivers of energy intensity: The case of Ethiopia. *Energy Strategy Reviews*, 2021; 35: 100641. DOI: 10.1016/j.esr.2021.100641
27. Tsybatov VA. Economic growth as the most important factor in reducing the energy intensity of the gross regional product. *Economy of the Region*, 2020; 16(3): 739–753. DOI: 10.17059/ekon.reg.2020-3-5
28. Unified Interdepartmental Information and Statistical System (UIISS). Moscow, Russia; 2021. Available from: fedstat.ru
29. Weather and climate. Average monthly and annual air temperatures in Rostov-on-Don. Available from: http://www.pogodaiklimat.ru/history/34730.htm

https://doi.org/10.1142/9789811264252_0017

Chapter 17

Green Mortgage as the Key to Energy-Efficient and Resource-Saving Real Estate

Svetlana A. Litvinova[†,¶], Olga B. Ivanova[‡,||], Oksana S. Chernobay[*,‡,] and Venera R. Zarubina[§,††]**

[†]South-Russian Institute of Management (Branch) of the Russian Presidential Academy of National Economy and Public Administration, Rostov-on-Don, Russia
[‡]Rostov State University of Economics, Rostov-on-Don, Russia
[§]Kostanay Engineering and Economic University named after M. Dulatov, Kostanay, Kazakhstan
[¶]sv-lit@mail.ru
[||]sovet2-1@rsue.ru
[**]oksana.chernobay1982@yandex.ru
[††]zarubina_v@mail.ru

Abstract: In recent years, sustainable development has become a global trend worldwide. Responsibility and environmental friendliness extend to many areas, including real estate construction. The research is based on the theoretical approaches of the concepts of sustainable development and the green economy, suggesting the need to justify the use of new

[*] Corresponding author.

financial instruments. The chapter discusses one of the tools of green financing — green mortgage, which contributes to the development of an effective tool for increasing the sustainability of the environment — green construction. During the research, the authors used data from open sources published on the official websites of Russian and foreign banks, the Ecology Building Society (UK), and others. The available scientific publications on the subject of green lending were analyzed. The experience of various countries (USA, UK, China, Russia, etc.) on the implementation of the green mortgage was studied. Moreover, the authors formulated a number of conditions that will contribute to the more active development of green mortgages.

Keywords: Green economy; Green construction; Green financial instruments; Green mortgage; Resource-saving technologies; Sustainable development.

17.1. Introduction

The relevance of sustainable development and interest in sustainable investments have formed new trends in the financial market, such as the disclosure of non-financial information, the assessment of ESG indicators, and the emergence of new financial instruments.

Russia's focus on sustainability should improve people's standard of living and implement plans to save the environment and minimize the impact on the climate [14].

Nowadays, the entire world has realized the need to move to a new economic model — i.e., a green economy. Such an economy aims to maintain and improve the quality of life of people while maintaining a healthy environment.

A significant number of countries worldwide began to pay close attention to energy saving; reduction of emissions of toxic substances into the atmosphere, water, and soil; and waste control. All kinds of measures are taken to develop the green economy, including green financial instruments.

Considerable environmental problems caused by a greater degree of irresponsible consumption and economic activities of people were the reason for this. There has come an understanding of the depletion and non-renewability of natural resources through their intensive and unsustainable use [6].

One of the key issues on the agenda of many international congresses and forums was the creation of an international financial system that would be very effective in terms of attracting green investments. The Russian economy requires new growth poles, and green financing can play a significant role here.

Simultaneously, the green sectors of the economy have the greatest potential compared with resource-intensive sectors that cause the most significant damage to the environment [12].

Additionally, green projects need investment flows, new highly competitive industries are created with new jobs, and new green innovative technologies are used that can save natural resources for our future generations; these will contribute to the development of human potential.

First, the stimulation of green investments in green projects gives Russian companies significant competitive advantages in the form of a reduction in unit costs for resource consumption. Second, it creates opportunities for obtaining additional income based on the use of available resources, for example, production waste. Third, it improves the quality of products and the demand for them due to their environmental friendliness and significantly strengthens the position of Russian companies in the markets.

The growing threat of global climate change, the reduction of natural resources, and the crisis of the global ecosystem have given rise to various measures to assist in the implementation of the concept of green financing. The implementation of the green concept requires the global mobilization of public and private sources of financing and the development of green financial instruments. Part of this concept is green lending, including mortgage lending, which significantly impacts the country's economy.

17.2. Methodology

The research methods include general (analysis, synthesis, generalization, and comparison) and special scientific methods (expert assessments and statistical data analysis). The research is based on the theoretical approaches of the concepts of sustainable development and the green economy, suggesting the need to justify the use of new financial instruments, such as green lending, including green mortgages. The research is based on the data from open sources published on the official websites of

Russian and foreign banks, the Ecology Building Society (UK), and others. The available scientific works on the subject of green lending were analyzed. The authors study the experience of various countries (USA, UK, China, Russia, etc.) on the implementation of the green mortgage.

17.3. Results

The Climate Bonds Initiative summed up the results of the global green finance market in 2020: a record volume of total emissions in the amount of $269.5 billion ($3 billion more than the previous year), in 2018 — $171.4 billion. A cumulative $1 trillion green milestone will be reached in 2020.

In 2020, green bonds, loans, and credits were placed in 53 countries. Another positive sign of product diversification is the increase of green lending: it more than doubled from 11 countries in 2019 to 23 in 2020. The USA is in the first place (Fig. 17.1). France is still holding onto the top three in 2017, 2018, and 2019, with Germany appearing in the top three for the first time [8].

In 2019, there were emissions of bonds and loans, which, according to the international classification, belong to the green category, for a total amount of $254.9 billion. This is a record value of the indicator, which is 49% higher than the level of 2018, and $171.1 billion have been raised

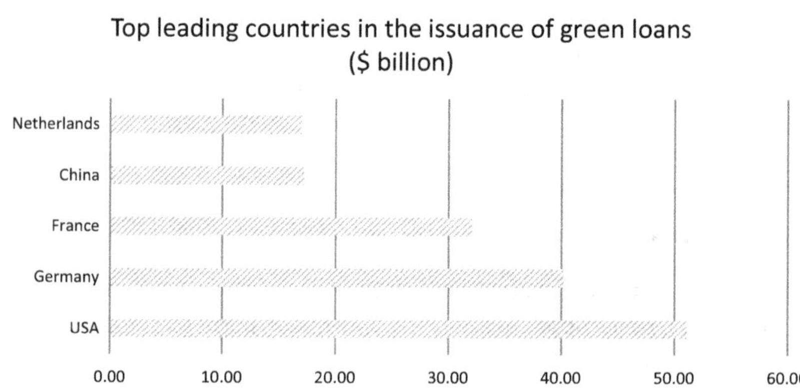

Fig. 17.1. Top five leading countries in issuing green loans.

Source: Compiled by the authors based on Ref. [8].

using green financial instruments. In 2019, the total sum of green loans accounted for only 2.6% ($6.8 billion) [18].

Currently, 117 banks in 37 countries are the financial industry's benchmark for identifying and assessing the management of social and environmental risks associated with the project financing process. European banks are leading the way. Banks that operate in the Asia-Pacific region (Japan and China) develop green lending [7].

Nowadays, the green credit products of banks for the construction of environmentally friendly housing, renewable energy facilities, green transport and car loans, climate credit cards, etc., have become widespread. Green loan products of foreign commercial banks include green loans for the purchase or construction of ecological housing (this product encourages people to buy or build green houses, banks provide borrowers with preferential green loans at below-market interest rates), green loans for development construction (designed for development companies building environmentally friendly real estate), etc.

As we can see from the table, a wide range of green loans is presented in foreign countries.

Starting in 2005, the two main US banks — Wells Fargo and Bank of America — began to allocate funds for sustainable entrepreneurship. This meant funding the construction of environmentally sustainable or safe knowledge and businesses. These were the first green loans for the construction of green houses.

Of particular interest is the strategy of the Green Homes (GH) or Green Mortgages (GM) program, developed by the Horizon 2020 funded project SMARTER Finance for Families. The potential impact of this project on the mainstream housing market has yet to be assessed to see if consistent green practices are possible on a large scale, throughout the value chain and with stakeholder participation [15].

When designing housing policy, it is important to understand whether higher incomes, lower mortgage rates, and environmental income tax credits affect housing prices [3].

The year 2007 is considered the beginning of green lending in China. Green lending in China was further developed in February 2012, when the main document that currently guides the country's banking institutions in the field of green lending, the Green Lending Guide, was prepared [22].

Green finance has become a priority for China's central bank. During the 14th Five-Year Plan (2021–2025), according to the Governor of the

People's Bank of China, efforts will be made to improve the standardization of the green finance system.

According to official data, by the end of 2020, China's green loans reached almost 12 trillion yuan (about $1.84 trillion), which is the highest globally.

To meet its commitment to reduce its carbon footprint to zero by 2050, the UK creates financial incentives for investment in a green (carbon-free) economy.

This is not only about large investors but also about retail consumers of financial services — a market that has just begun to develop.

Davidson [5], the author of "The big green money guide: How to make everything from your mortgage to bank account, savings, energy and broadband more environmentally friendly," published on *This is Money*, provided an impressive overview of the new green financial services sector. She says that the concern for climate change and the desire to help the planet makes many think about the "proper" use of their money and offers its readers several ideas on how to invest or spend money environmentally soundly.

Financial services companies were the first to take up the idea; in the wake of media-fueled interest in climate sustainability, mortgages, loans, savings accounts, and other green-labeled products began to be offered.

For example, in June–August 2020, green mortgage loans began to circulate, designed to financially reward borrowers for making their homes more energy-efficient.

Green mortgages in Europe are loans issued to purchase real estate with a high level of energy efficiency, and it is also possible to obtain such a loan if a person repairs old housing and increases its energy efficiency by at least 30%.

For example, in 2019, the volume of green loans issued by foreign banks amounted to $6.8 billion [7].

Meanwhile, Nest, the UK's national pension system set up to house and manage retirement savings, has announced plans to phase out carbon-intensive investments and funds that have failed to demonstrate progress toward a cleaner future.

The concept of a green mortgage is only developing all over the world and does not yet have clear provisions and rules. Green mortgages are designed to promote the sale of buildings with a high resource-saving level.

The rates for purchasing such eco-houses or eco-apartments will be less than usual. Also, citizens who plan to buy or refurbish an old building, thereby increasing its resource-saving, will be able to receive a discount.

In the UK, the nascent green mortgage market shows signs that it is ready to take off. Encouraged by the innovations of their peers in green lending, 11 banks and building communities have launched green mortgage products since early 2020. The opportunities for lenders in this space are enormous. The UK Climate Change Committee has shown that £250 billion should be invested in refurbishing UK housing by 2050, meaning that there is a potential for significant capital inflows in the form of green mortgages in the coming years.

Since many green mortgages target a small number of properties that are already energy efficient, more mortgage products and other green loans need to be used. The evolution of the green property market in the UK dates back to 2006 when the green building society became the first British lender to offer green mortgages. This product offered reduced mortgage rates to homeowners building or converting green homes or upgrading and improving energy efficiency. For sustainable homes and retrofits, the amount of rebates received by homeowners depended on the outcome after completing the project. For example, for mortgages discounted for retrofits to a standard variable rate, a discount of 0.25% was applied for each energy efficiency certificate class that improves the property. In total, the project brought in £39.3 million in 2020. In February 2021, a new Variable Rate Renovation Mortgage was introduced, offering broader discounts to homeowners renovating homes. As a result, already in the first three months of 2021, the same number of loans for repairs as in the whole of 2020 was allocated [11].

It should be noted that 89% of potential homeowners are interested in buying sustainable homes (prefer to have solar panels and energy-efficient boilers than a back garden). This conclusion is supported by an increasing number of green mortgage deals.

In August 2020, the UK Government unveiled a Green Home Grant, available to those who make energy-efficient improvements to their homes.

UK homeowners can apply for a voucher to cover the cost of installing energy-efficient and low-carbon heating systems in their homes, which can save up to £600 per year on electricity bills. The government will provide a voucher that covers up to two-thirds of the cost of qualifying home improvements. The maximum value of a voucher is £5,000 [21].

A green mortgage is one of the drivers of the global green finance market. According to a Climate Bonds report [9], Fannie Mae was the largest green bond issuer in 2020, with a total issuance of $13 billion.

The Multifamily Green MBS program is used to finance green mortgages backed by multifamily properties that have received green building certifications or demonstrate audited performance improvements.

Financial institutions can significantly reduce the risk of default on mortgages through the issuance of green mortgages and increase the asset valuation of the homes they finance. In our opinion, they can offer a lower cost of financing.

Lower costs provide the homebuyer with greater purchasing power to invest in building improvements because green mortgages help reduce energy, repair, and medical costs for those buying green homes. Green mortgages will also help the market better appreciate the positive value of prudent borrowing for proper investment early in the construction process. This initiative will create a consortium between banks, investors or developers, and buyers.

Energy savings and other benefits such as better health and lower and less frequent house renovation costs will significantly reduce mortgage risk, allowing the lender to lower the monthly interest rate while maintaining the rate of return.

This encourages the homeowner to invest in a more energy-efficient and environmentally friendly home while reducing the total monthly cost of ownership compared to a standard home.

Financial institutions may also offer other green finance products, such as loans to renovate small residential projects.

The introduction of a financial product such as the green mortgage is very timely in the context of current and upcoming directives, which require a move toward zero-energy buildings and a significant reduction in construction waste and toxicity of building materials, and will be mandatory for all new and existing residential buildings.

Growing energy security concerns and rising energy costs also require residential projects that require less costly and limited natural resources to build and operate.

There is a direct correlation between the energy efficiency and environmental friendliness of a house and the level of quality in the design, construction, and operation of this house.

Often, misunderstandings arise among property buyers, forcing homeowners to make suboptimal decisions. They underinvest in the process of designing and building real estate (often choosing homes at the lowest cost per square meter), resulting in homes that are more expensive to heat and cool and require expensive maintenance and more frequent repairs compared to green houses.

The most cost-effective time to invest in energy efficiency and other environmentally friendly features of a home is in the earliest moments of its initial design and construction. This is particularly important for building structures, roofs, windows, and walls, which significantly contribute to energy efficiency but are the most expensive and problematic to improve after the initial construction.

In 2013, some studies in Romania compared 71,000 homes by the level of risk of mortgage default. It turned out that in energy-efficient and environmentally friendly houses, green houses were found to have a 32% reduction in mortgage risk compared to standard houses [19].

The study found that homes that exceeded the minimum standard to be considered green for the study showed a higher reduction in default risk. Another comprehensive academic study found that mortgage defaults were as follows:

- 32% less likely if the apartment building is within 1.5 km of protected open space;
- 34% less likely if the building is located in an area with at least 16 retail stores;
- 58% less likely if located in an area where at least 30% of employees travel by subway or surface transport.

Another hypothesis was tested in the study by combining information on mortgages with preliminary building energy ratings in the Netherlands [1]. It was found that the default rate is lower for borrowers with lower disposable income. Energy performance ratings complement borrowers' credit information, and a lender, using information from both sources, can make better credit decisions than a lender using only traditional credit information.

A study of 1.6 million homes in North America published in 2014 concluded that the selling price of certified green houses already increased by 9% compared to standard ones.

All green houses that were included in the research, on average, provided energy savings of 20–30% compared to standard houses [19].

Such performance ensures that green building pioneers have financial instruments to build houses and bring them to market today or in the near future, which are strong business arguments for all stakeholders.

Currently, the entire global construction industry is at a new stage. The fact is that buildings around the world consume about 40% of all primary energy and about 67% of electricity. They produce 35% of all carbon dioxide emissions and almost half of all municipal solid waste and consume at least 14% of all drinking water supplies [20]. In this regard, in our opinion, compared with the construction of traditional buildings and structures, the priority is the construction of buildings (apartments, houses, offices, and other structures) using innovative eco-technologies. It is possible to create favorable conditions for human life and ensure the protection and rational use of natural resources while limiting the negative impact on nature from construction activities by using green standards in construction. The following global standards are currently distinguished: BREEAM, LEED, and GREN Globes [2,10].

Therefore, green construction is becoming an effective tool for increasing the sustainability of the environment. This is a construction with minimal environmental impact. Moreover, these green environmental principles are observed at all stages, from the construction of a building to its destruction.

On September 21, 2021, the Government of Russia adopted a resolution approving a package of documents that creates the regulatory framework for the market for sustainable financing, including green financing, in the Russian Federation (taxonomy) and the requirements for the verification system for such projects.

The taxonomy consists of two sections:

- Taxonomy of green projects, including a list of projects recognized as green in accordance with world practice;
- Taxonomy of adaptation projects, including a list of projects aimed at adapting the economy to climate change, which is not explicitly recognized as green in accordance with global practice.

A "green" project can be in the areas, such as waste management, energy, construction, industry, transport, water supply, agriculture, biodiversity, and environmental conservation. Specific qualitative and quantitative criteria have been developed for each area.

The requirements for the verification system for sustainable development projects establish the procedures necessary for the correct assessment of a particular project, the list of documents to be verified, and the requirements for companies (verifiers) preparing conclusions.

The adopted resolution will help establish common criteria for green and adaptation projects and create economic incentives for the transition to advanced environmental standards.

Many sustainable development projects are capital intensive and institutionally complex. Depending on the structure of a particular green project, its financing can be carried out in various forms.

The construction of eco-objects is a good project to attract significant investments and the engine of an innovative economy, which will improve the quality of human life and positively affect the state of the environment, forming a healthy society.

Such buildings and structures are built using advanced innovative technologies, thereby conserving and rationally using natural resources, significantly reducing the flow of toxic substances into the soil and water, reducing greenhouse gas emissions, and protecting the natural habitat.

The most important outcome of green construction is resource-saving. This is especially true for Russia, where the efficiency of energy use for home heating is relatively low. On the contrary, the energy-saving potential of Russia is high. This can be achieved through advanced insulation technologies with thermal insulation materials, the use of innovative (emission) glass units, water-saving aerators, and detailed consideration of the orientation and shape of the house. These measures will allow achieving significant savings from the initial costs.

First, it is necessary to say about the basic principles of green construction:

- The principle of environmental friendliness — reducing the negative impact on the environment and human health; the maximum preservation of the natural landscape of the site; the design considers many aspects (e.g., wind direction, the shape of the house, discharge of wastewater, etc.);
- The principle of efficiency — resource-saving technologies and equipment are used; environmentally friendly materials are used in the construction and disposal;
- The principle of safety — environmentally friendly materials are used in the construction; the ventilation and acoustics system is thought out;
- The principle of durability — materials and systems that last for a long time are used [13].

We consider it possible to supplement this list with the principle of recycling, which involves the use of "closed" cycle technologies and the transition from a linear to a circular production process, in our case, construction when waste is minimized during the construction process, and the object itself (real estate) is designed in such a way as to ensure the reuse of any waste (e.g., purified water for watering plants, etc.).

With all the many advantages of green construction, there is a significant disadvantage — expensive design and construction and a long payback period. It is necessary to clarify that green technologies, although effective, are quite expensive, but the effect that will be obtained in the future will cover the initial costs.

A green house or apartment is, first of all, a great contribution to the health and well-being of future generations. Russia is still far behind other developed countries in the transition to green rails.

In the Russian Federation, the promotion of the ideas of the concepts of sustainable development, green economy, and green finance began relatively recently.

The issues of sustainable development and changes in the economic model have reached the global level; the green economy has become a priority and is discussed in detail at international congresses and forums. To build such a model of the economy, a variety of green financial instruments are required [25].

We consider green mortgages to be one of such instruments.

The Central Bank of Russia defines a green mortgage as a bank loan product under which the borrower of the loan receives funds on favorable terms, provided that the real estate that he or she is going to buy with these funds meets the standards of environmental and energy efficiency or, by raising funds for the reconstruction of real estate, the borrower undertakes to ensure the modernization of real estate to environmental and energy efficiency standards [4].

The DOM.RF Bank believes that the implementation of a green mortgage is possible only after the approval of the general standards of green construction; the bank is developing a project for a green mortgage and is going to present its own version of the criteria for recognizing green houses and apartments. It is highly likely that the criteria will not differ significantly from international ones [17].

Another important condition for introducing green mortgages in Russia will be economic feasibility; state support for banks will be crucial. Nowadays, some Russian banks have already begun to develop ESG services and products for individuals. The most common service may be loans for the purchase of green housing built with eco-materials or technologies that reduce energy consumption, water, and the most comfortable for housing on many parameters.

VTB Bank became the first bank in Russia to launch preferential green mortgages in September 2021 with a discount of up to 1.6% to the base mortgage rate [16].

Rosselkhozbank specialists believe that already in 2023, green mortgages in the budget and medium segments will bring more than 2 trillion rubles to housing construction [23]. Simultaneously, representatives of the Ministry of Construction and Housing and Public Utilities suggested that Russia will have the first "safe for the planet" residential building that fully complies with environmental standards by 2024 [24]. However, these buildings are still being developed. In this case, the key criteria are environmentally friendly building materials, location, and energy-efficient engineering systems.

Sberbank and Gazprombank also plan to create and develop a green mortgage mechanism. Sberbank plans to launch green project financing in housing construction in early 2022. Rosbank believes that government support will be a key driver for the development of the project and a great incentive for the emergence of new facilities and the development of infrastructure. Alfa-Bank is also considering introducing green mortgages and other sustainable development products.

The expectation of demand for green mortgages is primarily aimed at young people because the demand for responsible consumption is much higher among the younger generation than among more mature people. However, it should not be denied that people of a more mature age will also focus on green, environmentally friendly consumption [16].

In our opinion, the active development of the green mortgage will be facilitated by certain conditions:

- Mobilization of the efforts of business structures (construction companies, realtors, banks), the scientific community, and the state to search for, develop, and disseminate the best practices of green lending in the real estate sector through forums, conferences, and other joint events;
- State support for the banks (stimulating policy, special subsidized mortgage programs) and citizens (e.g., through additional property tax deductions when purchasing green real estate);
- Preparation and popularization of the results of scientific research on the positive impact of the green mortgage on the quality of life of citizens, the environmental well-being of the planet;

- Implementation of financial literacy programs, including explanations about the principles of sustainable development, the green economy, the circular economy, and the ESG approach.

17.4. Conclusion

Such a financial instrument as a green mortgage in Russia is still under development due to the lack of eco-housing criteria for the provision of green financing. However, based on the experience of foreign countries where such a tool is already being implemented, in general, we can talk about some general trends. In order for the implementation of the green concept in Russia to be more active, it is necessary to create a single coordination center for coordinating various issues of green lending, in particular, green mortgages, which could, among other things, make proposals on the legal framework governing green finance.

It is necessary to involve state financial institutions as much as possible in the implementation of green financing programs by developing mechanisms to stimulate green mortgages. It is necessary to inform people about the eco-technologies used in the construction of green houses, showing all advantages of green construction.

Green houses should be beneficial not only to developers but also to customers. State incentives in the form of preferential lending terms and interest rates should be below market rates; it should be possible to use a differentiated repayment schedule. This and more will encourage people to buy and build sustainable homes. As a result, the high quality of the project (innovative technologies, eco-materials) and lower maintenance costs for such apartments or houses will attract people to buy eco-housing, which means that it will have a positive impact on human health and the environment. It is also necessary to implement one of the areas of green financing — to increase the green financial literacy of the population.

References

1. Billio M, Costola M, Pelizzon L, Riedel M. Buildings' energy efficiency and the probability of mortgage default: The Dutch case. *The Journal of Real Estate Finance and Economics*, 2021. DOI: 10.1007/s11146-021-09838-0
2. Bogdanova EO. "Green" construction in Russia. *Modern Scientific Research and Innovation*, 2016; 11(67): 156–160.

3. Brotman BA. Green federal tax credits impact on US housing prices. *International Journal of Housing Markets and Analysis*, 2020; 13(4): 553–564. DOI: 10.1108/IJHMA-10-2019-0104
4. Central Bank of the Russian Federation. Glossary of Sustainable Development Terms: "Green" mortgage. Available from: http://www.cbr.ru/develop/ur/faq /#highlight=зеленая%7Cипотека
5. Davidson S. The big green money guide: How to make everything from your mortgage, to bank account, savings, energy and broadband more environmentally friendly. 2020. Available from: https://www.thisismoney.co.uk/money/saving/article-8686003/Green-money-guide-make-finances-greener.html
6. Eco-region. Depletion of natural resources: Meaning, types, facts, causes, consequences and solutions. Available from: https://этна-регионы.рф/problemy/nehvatka-prirodnyh-resursov.html
7. Eremina OI, Morozova GV, Filichkina YY. International experience in the development of green loan as a tool for green financing. *Kontentus*, 2021; 1(102): 34–42.
8. Expert Agency "Open Communications." The volume of the green finance market in 2020 reached more than $260 billion. 2021. Available from: https://infragreen.ru/news/obem-rynka-zelenyx-finansov-v-2020-godu-dostig-bolee-260-mlrd.html
9. Fannie Mae. Green Bond Impact Report 2020. Washington, DC; 2020. Available from: https://www.fanniemae.com/media/40246/display
10. Gelmanova ZS, Amirkhanova MA, Georgiadi IV. "Green" construction as an effective tool for sustainable development of territories. Scientific Review. *Economic Sciences*, 2016; 1: 12–14.
11. Green Finance Institute. The way ahead for the UK's green mortgage market. Available from: https://www.greenfinanceinstitute.co.uk/wp-content/uploads/2021/05/GREEN-FINANCE-GREEN-MORTGAGES.pdf
12. InvestFuture. Industry: Top 10 major environmental pollutants. 2019. Available from: https://investfuture.ru/news/id/promyshlennost-top-10-glavnyh-zagryazniteley-okrujayushchey-sredy
13. Koshkina SY, Korchagina OA, Voronkova ES. "Green" construction as major factor of improving environmental quality and human health. *Problems of Contemporary Science and Practice*, 2013; 3(47): 150–158.
14. National PPP Center & VEB.RF. Sustainable development and infrastructure. Overview of trends in Russia and the world. Moscow, Russia; 2021. Available from: https://вэб.рф/downloads/spief_sd_short_final_02.05.2021_1.pdf#:~:text=Ориентация%20России%20на%20устойчивость%20позволит,уровнем%20качества%20и%20устойчивости%20объектов
15. Paez C, Gonzalez AG, Erten D, Cristoforetti S. Key indicators & assessment of sustainable buildings for (EU) market uptake through housing green mortgages. *IOP Conference Series: Earth and Environmental Science*, 2020; 588: 022074. DOI: 10.1088/1755-1315/588/2/022074

16. Pechatnikov A. VTB intends to launch “green” mortgage in September. 2021. Available from: https://www.interfax.ru/business/788090
17. Prime. The Central Bank told how the green mortgage will work. 2021. Available from: https://1prime.ru/banks/20210518/833690154.html
18. Regional Energy and Energy Saving. Green finance grew by 50% to over $250 billion in 2019. 2020. Available from: https://energy.s-kon.ru/obyomy-zelyonogo-finansirovaniya-vyrosli-na-50-i-prevysili-250-mlrd-v-2019-godu/
19. Romania Green Building Council. Green mortgages & renovation loans: A toolkit for financial institutions. 2017. Available from: https://green-council.org/publik/SMARTER_Finance_for_Financial_Institutions_Toolkit.pdf
20. Russian Green Building Council. Advantages of green building. 2014. Available from: https://ardexpert.ru/article/901
21. Russian News Agency. The UK is inflating the retail green finance bubble. 2020. Available from: http://новости-мира.ru-an.info/новости/великобритания-надувает-пузырь-розничных-зеленых-финансов/
22. Savinsky SP. Formation and development of “green” lending in China. *Economic Research*, 2019; 4: p. 1.
23. Tashevskaya N. Prospects for a new type of mortgage are named. 2021. Available from: https://lenta.ru/news/2021/11/19/green_mortgage
24. Tashevskaya N. The Russians were promised safe housing for the planet. 2021. Available from: https://lenta.ru/news/2021/10/07/eco_dom/
25. Vovchenko NG, Ivanova OB, Semenyuta OG, Khakhonova NN, Medvedkina EA, Bogataya IN. The financial contour of the “green” economy: From region to state. In: Albekov AU, Matishov GG (Eds.). *Green Economy. Modernization of the Socio-economic System of Southern Russia*. Rostov-on-Don, Russia: Rostov State University of Economics; 2017. pp. 174–236.

https://doi.org/10.1142/9789811264252_0018

Chapter 18

Sustainable Business Development in the Concept of its ESG Responsibility

Elena N. Makarenko[†], **Yulia G. Chernysheva**[*,‡], **Irina A. Polyakova**[§] **and Irina A. Kislaya**[¶]

Rostov State University of Economics, Rostov-on-Don, Russia
[†]*Makarenko.rsue@yandex.ru*
[‡]*julia282001@mail.ru*
[§]*mirgan15@mail.ru*
[¶]*kislaya_irina@mail.ru*

Abstract: The chapter discusses issues related to the sustainable development of business in the current VUCA (variability, uncertainty, complexity, ambiguity) world. Business causes social, environmental, and economic problems because companies focus primarily on short-term financial results, increasing profits, and ignoring key market needs and conditions with the most significant impact on long-term consequences, including widely understood social or environmental issues. Therefore, the long-term and sustainable development of a business depends on the success of solving problems in the social, environmental, and economic sectors, i.e., on its Environmental, Social, and Governance (ESG) responsibility. Hence, ESG issues of business responsibility are particularly important for its sustainable development. Despite the importance of having an ESG responsibility for entrepreneurs, many of them are still

[*]Corresponding author.

uneager to implement it. There is a certain contradiction: on the one hand, the development of ESG responsibility is an important task allowing the companies to obtain additional value (as a result of expanding their obligations to the society in general and their collective of employees) being an established global trend, and many companies realize this. On the other hand, many organizations still do not want to realize the need to move from "business as a means of generating income" to the category of "ESG responsible entrepreneurs." Based on this, the authors believe that to solve this problem, it is necessary to identify the root causes of low ESG responsibility of business, on the basis of which new methodological approaches should be sought that contribute to its improvement to ensure sustainable development of business. The research methodology should involve the study of the essence of social and environmental responsibility of business, the study of the essence and justification of the importance of ESG responsibility in its relationship with sustainable business development, identification of the reasons for the low level of ESG responsibility of business, and development of a set of measures to increase the ESG responsibility of the business based on meeting the needs of stakeholders.

Keywords: Sustainable business development; ESG responsibility; Social responsibility; Environmental responsibility.

18.1. Introduction

The influence of the rapidly changing and unstable VUCA world affects all its sectors, including the economy, ecology, resource security, politics, the food component, and many others. Climate change; the threat of resource depletion; and natural, economic, and political crises suggest a possible approaching catastrophe. The concept of sustainable growth could not allow us to overcome the problems of today's world. This led to the formation of a Planetary Project, which is a scientific theory and a practical program for creating a new economic base of a polycentric world. It is a scientific concept of the socio-economic development of today's society, involving the solution of global problems, improvement of the biosphere, and the formation of integral civilizational foundations. It forms a unity in the people's attitude to the planet and brings people together to make the right decisions based on reason, spirituality, and compromise. It assumes that each country will be able to take its place in the global division of labor and achieve a satisfactory standard of living while preserving cultural diversity.

The main idea of the Planetary Project is aimed at solving global problems of the world and minimizing global world contradictions, using new economic technologies, preserving the Earth's biosphere for present and future generations, stimulating global integration of humanity, and achieving social harmony and its relationship with the environment based on social justice, biocompatible ethics, and global spiritual synthesis. It allows taking a deeper look at the problems of sustainable development, considering contemporary facts, processes, and trends. Solving the global problems of today's world is difficult and requires high costs. However, it becomes possible if there is a sufficient resource base, material resources, precise planning of financial resources, and a properly chosen organizational scheme.

One of the problems addressed by the concept of the Planet Project is the problem of Environmental, Social, and Governance (ESG) business responsibility, which involves the integration of social, environmental (including climate), and governance responsibility. In the current world, the long-term and sustainable development of a business depends on the success of solving problems in the social, environmental, and economic sectors, i.e., on its ESG responsibility. Therefore, ESG issues of business responsibility are particularly important for its sustainable development.

18.2. Methods

Nowadays, ESG responsibility is one of the most pressing problems. Today's businesses have come to understand the need to move from creating current value for their owners to creating long-term value that is meaningful to a wider range of stakeholders, including owners, investors, employees, customers, suppliers, local communities, and government.

To increase the level of ESG responsibility of a business and, therefore, its sustainable development, it is necessary to comply with international and national goals, standards, and principles in the field of ESG and sustainable development, including the UN Sustainable Development Goals (SDGs), the Principles of the UN Global Compact, Principles of Responsible Banking (Principles for Responsible Banking UNEP FI), and other global initiatives.

In this regard, based on the identification of the reasons for the low ESG responsibility of business, it is necessary to look for new methodological approaches that contribute to its improvement to ensure sustainable business development. The research methodology should involve the following:

- The study of the essence of social and environmental responsibility of business;
- The study of the essence and justification of the importance of ESG responsibility in its relationship with sustainable business development;
- Identification of the reasons for the low level of ESG responsibility of business;
- Development of a set of measures to increase ESG business responsibility based on meeting the needs of stakeholders.

18.3. Results and Discussion

Sustainable development is a very broad concept that can be considered both at the macro level and the level of an individual enterprise. "Sustainable development allows achieving human development goals while maintaining the ability to save the ecosystem and carefully using natural resources the economy and society depend on. The desired result is a state of society in which living conditions and resources are used without undermining the integrity and stability of the natural system. Sustainable development can be defined as development that meets the needs of the present without compromising the ability of future generations to meet their own needs. The Sustainable Development Goals aim to solve global problems, including poverty, inequality, climate change, environmental degradation, peace, and justice" [6].

The concept of sustainable development systematized several ideas that appeared in the 18th and 20th centuries, which concerned the fate of humankind under the influence of the relationship "man–society–nature." The concept proposed an alternative economic growth model in the form of a noosphere-oriented civilization of a transitional type. The concept of sustainable development embodies an attempt to solve global problems by economic means using some integration processes. Hence, sustainable growth was first treated in the context of the interrelation of humans, society, and nature.

The term "sustainable development" came into use after publishing the report of the World Commission on Environment and Development created under the auspices of the United Nations "Our common future," prepared in 1987. Usually, the scientific literature uses the definition of "sustainable development," which is given in the report *Our Common Future*: Sustainable development is "a development that meets the needs of the present without compromising the ability of future generations to meet their own needs" [3].

The fundamental difference between the sustainable development concept and the industrial paradigm of economic growth is that it requires today's civilization with its production not to use nature expansively but to consider the laws of the biosphere, its prohibitions, and limitations.

The main goal of sustainable development is to prevent ecological catastrophe and complete the comprehensive greening of economic and social practices, as well as a public consciousness. National strategies for the transition to sustainable development should be based on relevant regional, infrastructural, and social features.

As already noted, the sustainable development concept was originally tied to the relationship between people, society, and nature. Sustainable development presupposes measures approved by global international institutions (e.g., the UN), such as regulatory and other mechanisms to curb human economic interference in nature, minimization of side effects of globalization, and some other principles. These measures based on the interrelation of economic and social development and environmental protection should contribute to the global objective of humanity — achieving a balance between people and the ecosystem, being significant for the living and development of future generations. Thus, the term "sustainable development" refers to a holistic approach that leads us to the endpoint of sustainability and will allow achieving a strategic balance of human activity and consumption, maintaining the regenerative capacity of the biosphere that can be considered the most important criterion for sustainable development on a global scale.

The transition to sustainable development presupposes the greening of all methods of production and consumption, as well as other cardinal transformations of human activity, attitude, and consciousness, which should proceed purposefully and systematically.

Managing the transition to sustainable development involves decisive actions in conditions of uncertainty and risk because neither a slowdown in socio-economic dynamics nor a halt in socio-economic growth will solve global problems and eliminate the threat of environmental catastrophe.

The concept of sustainable development is considered at the macro- and microeconomic level as the sustainable development of enterprises. The creation of a sustainable enterprise involves the transformation of the entire value chain from the supply of materials to product design, operations, sales, and marketing.

The concept of sustainable development is essentially depicted through three central goals concerning the future development of humankind: society, economy, and ecology (usually quoted as "triple bottom line: people–profit–planet"). This concept boils down to functioning based on the achievement of three main goals:

- Ecological — consisting in reducing the degradation of the environment and eliminating its threats;
- Economic — expressed in meeting the basic material needs of humanity using methods and technologies that do not harm the environment;
- Social — ensuring the provision of a subsistence level (eradication of hunger, poverty, and misery), health protection, development of the spiritual sphere of a person (culture), security, and education.

"Thus, considering ESG factors, the concept of ESG business responsibility is based on the same principle as the concept of sustainable development but with an emphasis on the company's activities" [5]. In addition to ensuring economic sustainability, ESG business responsibility is used by investors to evaluate companies in three aspects: environment, social development, and governance.

Until recently, much attention was paid only to the social responsibility of business. Current conditions of the market economy have made it necessary to search for new reserves that can improve business efficiency. For some time, the use of the social reserve has been considered by a completely new and progressive direction. The social responsibility of entrepreneurs is ultimately beneficial for themselves (because employees work in a socially comfortable climate, which has a positive effect on the results of their work) and for the employees with social security. Doing business assumes that an entrepreneur must constantly make decisions while striving to prevent the deterioration of the social situation of employees and improving own positions.

"The concept of 'the social responsibility of business' is a broad concept that can be considered from two positions: from the position of achieving socially useful goals and from the position of having various forms of responsibility for their employees, increasing their level of social security" [1].

The concept of social responsibility of entrepreneurship is accepted by all researchers of entrepreneurship. The analysis of the Russian and world practice of social responsibility of business shows how much they differ in the used models, principles, financial resources, and measures of state influence on these processes. The main conditions determining these specific differences, first of all, include the general level of development of the country, cultural communications, institutional norms, and economic culture of doing business.

In our opinion, a socially responsible entrepreneur is the one who has a high level of economic consciousness and carries out business in accordance with social and ethical norms, without infringing on the rights of employees, that is, being responsible for fulfilling social obligations to them: provides a social package and additional social bonuses and observes labor safety.

Social responsibility includes interaction between employees of the organization and the entrepreneur and the implementation of social projects aimed at solving social problems of society. Ensuring the social responsibility of entrepreneurs is important for the economy and a particular enterprise. This allows for solving the socio-economic problems of a market economy and thereby increasing economic stability. Simultaneously, as noted, most entrepreneurs are not fully aware of the benefits of increasing the level of their social responsibility.

In world practice, several types of corporate social responsibility are distinguished, which differ in their orientation and degree of state participation, without separating this concept and the concept of social responsibility. In today's world, corporate social responsibility is used by companies to grow their reputation in business circles and increase profitability.

This system currently includes economic, environmental, and social issues related to non-financial risks aimed at the sustainable development of the company, balanced relationships with customers, partners, employees, state, and local authorities, public organizations, and the media. For example, companies invest in employee training, conducting business seminars, programs to develop their regions, environmental protection, and scientific research on innovative developments.

Corporate social responsibility is developing most successfully in American and European businesses. The country is directly involved in this, although, in general, corporate social responsibility issues are supervised by non-governmental organizations.

At the end of the 20th century, the problem of environmental responsibility of business was added to the problem of social responsibility of business. Currently, the global environmental situation is one of the most relevant topics. The most significant environmental problems include the following:

- Pollution of the atmosphere as a result of an increase in the number of cars and emissions of enterprises, as a result of which the morbidity of the population of industrial centers and, above all, children has increased;
- Soil pollution, including the use of chemicals in agriculture. The substances included in their composition have a negative impact on the soil: the chemical composition of its components changes, the activity of microorganisms also changes, and entire micro-ecosystems die. The impact of household and industrial waste is also high. Over the past decades, their volume has grown several times. The issue is particularly acute in northern Europe;
- Water pollution occurs mainly due to wastewater from industrial plants and plastic waste, which clogs the water and leads to soil contamination and mass death of mammals, birds, and marine animals [2].

Simultaneously, it is impossible to completely exclude the entry of harmful substances into the external environment. Currently, it is only possible to reduce the negative impact of organizations on the environment. This can be achieved only if the level of social and environmental responsibility of business increases and enterprises comply with established environmental standards. This is relevant for large, medium, and small businesses. The preservation of natural living conditions is one of the most important tasks for all countries because it is directly related to maintaining the population's health and, therefore, contributes to the growth of labor productivity and, accordingly, their economic potential [4].

Abroad, concepts such as social activity and business responsibility began to form somewhat earlier than in Russia. In addition to social responsibility toward their employees, these concepts often included an environmental aspect. Socially responsible organizations also include organizations that adhere to high environmental standards in their activities, often higher than provided for by law. Observing environmental legislation, the organization seems to show respect for citizens without polluting the environment and, consequently, preserving their health. Currently, advanced organizations are increasingly taking a very active environmental position. They not only comply with the environmental legislation of their country but also take initiatives to strengthen environmental regulations within their organization, often more stringent than those specified in the legislation.

The concepts of social activity and business responsibility in developed countries arose from business practices related to social issues and standards on environmental protection. Organizations that comply with environmental standards receive additional competitive and economic advantages — the expansion of the partner base and the circle of consumers of their goods and services because the authorities, partner organizations, and buyers in developed countries prefer to deal with those enterprises that care about the protection of nature and produce environmentally friendly products [7].

Nowadays, in Russia and throughout the world, there is a transition to a socially and environmentally oriented economy, which is characterized by an improvement in the socio-economic conditions of activity for employees, which is confirmed by the appearance and increase in the number of socially responsible entrepreneurs and enterprises that comply with minimum environmental standards and strengthen their environmental responsibility. The issues of ESG responsibility of business have become relevant.

The socio-economic relations that develop between an entrepreneur and employees play an important role in the sustainable development of the enterprise. No less important are the issues of environmental responsibility of business. Foreign countries consider these issues in inseparable unity with social responsibility. In Russia, these issues are considered only from the position of compliance with environmental standards.

Therefore, in addition to environmental and social responsibility, it is important to focus on corporate governance of the company, including economic results, as well as on the evaluation of the performance of managers based on key performance indicators in conjunction with long-term goals and ESG risks, on which sustainable development depends. Additionally, independent audit, the openness of the company to shareholders, and assessment of the company's behavior (corporate ethics, transparency in the tax sphere, absence of corruption, and fair competition in the market) are also important for achieving the necessary economic results.

Simultaneously, the environmental situation in Russia and the level of social responsibility, not the rate of increase in ESG responsible business, are quite low due to the low interest of business in mandatory compliance with environmental standards (and, consequently, in the production of environmentally friendly and safe products) and in compliance with social guarantees for their employees, which is primarily characteristic of small businesses, which adversely affects economic results, reducing economic sustainability. As a result, there is a low ESG responsibility of the business.

The ecological aspect considers the impact of the company's activities on the environment. The social aspect includes the well-being of employees and local communities, and the management factor considers such components as corruption, business ethics, gender composition, and remuneration of top managers.

It is believed that business causes social, environmental, and economic problems, which is mainly based on the thesis that companies focused on short-term financial results and increasing profits ignore the key needs and market conditions that have the greatest impact on long-term consequences, including widely understood social or environmental problems.

ESG entrepreneurship responsibility is a decision-making process that considers possible negative consequences on social and environmental aspects. These decisions are based on respect for employees and consumers, concern for the environment, and the formation of correct management decisions regarding the economy of the enterprise without deteriorating the enumerated aspects. Thus, the reduction of ESG responsibility has an adverse impact on the organization from inside and outside. That is, the low level of staff satisfaction due to the low social responsibility of the business reduces the attractiveness of the organization to the employees themselves. They work with less impact. Additionally, an external factor of its negative impact affects the sustainability of the business as a whole.

18.4. Conclusion

Despite the importance of having an ESG responsibility for entrepreneurs, there is a problem with the transition to this status. Many organizations still do not want to realize the need to move from "business as a means of generating income" to the category of "ESG responsible entrepreneurs." The state can activate this process.

In accordance with the principles of the Planetary Project, approaches to solving problems are also changing. The search for a solution to any problem should begin with identifying the stakeholders involved in it and their interests (needs). Thus, to identify the causes of the aggravation of the contradiction between the high importance of ESG business responsibility and the low interest of entrepreneurs in it, it is necessary to identify the main stakeholders affected by it. In our opinion, these stakeholders are as follows:

(1) The country, because it must provide safe conditions for the life and health of the population, must ensure social stability in society, which is inextricably linked with the success of the development and existence of the country as a whole;
(2) The population, while its interest is also manifested twice because, on the one hand, it is interested in a safe environment, food, and goods, and, on the other, in social responsibility to them as employees, in terms of providing social guarantees;
(3) Organizations whose economic stability may deteriorate. Their interest is that under the condition of high ESG responsibility, they will receive additional competitive advantages and additional investments in the business.

The identified reasons for the low level of ESG business responsibility will affect all listed stakeholders, and the proposed measures to increase it should be aimed at meeting the needs of these stakeholders in increasing the level of ESG business responsibility. The effectiveness of measures should be determined by the degree of satisfaction of the needs of stakeholders in increasing the socio-environmental responsibility of the business. That is, the more the needs of stakeholders are met, the more effective certain measures can be considered.

Thus, one of the reasons for the low environmental responsibility can be called the Russian mentality of attitude to natural resources, which has been developing for many years. Russia has practically inexhaustible natural resources that do not have to be protected and are not necessarily used wisely.

In our opinion, another reason is the high level of costs for activities, equipment, and materials to ensure compliance with environmental standards when doing business. This is the most significant reason for small businesses, which, as a rule, do not have enough funds, e.g., to build sewage treatment plants or recycle garbage. Attracting loans for this purpose will also not be an option because there is a risk of their non-repayment. Small businesses have low viability, especially in Russia. Even without considering such additional costs, it is difficult for small businesses to conduct such activities and develop themselves.

The next reason, related to the previous one, is that it is often more "profitable" for enterprises to pay a small fine for violating the law than to spend significant funds on its compliance. Often, from year to year, this is done by large organizations, which consider fines not as a means of economic impact to remedy the situation but as payment for the opportunity to continue operating without complying with environmental standards provided for by law.

Additionally, the reasons for the low share of ESG responsible entrepreneurs include the situation in the labor market and violations of labor legislation by entrepreneurs. The unfavorable situation in the labor market is caused by a high level of unemployment, inflation, and legally illiterate workers. This gives an advantage to employers, as a result of which an "informal" relationship develops between employees and their employers. The settlement of conflict situations and the admission and dismissal of employees are currently practically not regulated by the government, lying in the field of private agreements between the employee and the employer.

It is possible to increase the level of ESG responsibility of business when conducting an active public policy in this area, as the main interested party that has significant powers in solving this issue and higher-level economic interest.

It seems that an increase in the level of ESG responsibility of business can be achieved by implementing the following types of measures at the federal level:

(1) Strengthening state control over compliance with environmental standards and increasing the amount of fines for their violation, including in terms of tightening the requirements for mandatory environmental audits. For example, one can set a "progressive" scale according to which, with each repeated detection of a violation, the amount of fines will increase significantly;
(2) Strengthening the promotion of the need to conduct business with a minimal negative impact on the environment (or without negative impact);
(3) State control of the price level for environmentally friendly and safe products to ensure their accessibility to the population;

(4) Control of the presence of a business system of social incentives for employees, including a material component for employees, as well as incentives related to personal and psychological characteristics;

(5) Development of a system of criteria (and a detailed scale), categorizing business as ESG responsible and, on its basis, implementing business incentives. The following incentives are possible for ESG responsible organizations:
   - Economic — e.g., providing organizations with any benefits that should differ according to the size of the enterprise. For example, the provision of financial benefits to enterprises (especially small businesses) for the implementation of activities within their organization aimed at increasing their ESG responsibility (e.g., waste recycling, cleaning of air (water) pollution, the production of environmentally friendly products, providing a social package, etc.). Such benefits can subsidize these costs or part of them (primarily for small businesses) and provides tax cuts for organizations that carry out their activities without violations and participate in environmental activities;
   - Moral — e.g., holding fairs among such organizations, forming a register of socially and environmentally responsible enterprises within each region (city). Such awareness of the population will allow people to give preference in choosing the products of these organizations, which will provide additional competitive advantages to enterprises. Organizations will be able to attract more qualified workers in view of the growth of their image.

These measures will contribute to the formation of organizations' understanding of the importance and benefits of a high level of ESG responsibility. Thus, these measures correspond to the interests of the main stakeholders and will meet their needs, which will ultimately contribute to the growth of ESG responsible businesses.

References

1. Chernysheva YG, Shepelenko GI. The social responsibility of the entrepreneur. *Financial Research*, 2015; 4(49): 271–276.
2. Chernysheva YG. Ecoanalytics as a new area of the analysis of environmental conditions at an enterprise. *International Business and Accounting Research Journal*. 2020; 4(1): 51–57. DOI: 10.15294/ibarj.v4i1.120

3. World Commission on Environment and Development (WCED). *Our Common Future*. 1st edn. Oxford, UK: Oxford University Press; 1987 Oct [cited 2022 Jan 10]. Available from: https://sustainabledevelopment.un.org/content/documents/5987our-common-future.pdf
4. Murzin AD, Murzina SM. Analysis of the practice of implementing regional environmental programs in Russia and abroad. *Economics and Ecology of Territorial Formations*, 2017; 2: 124–133.
5. S&P Global. S&P Global Trust has been assessing risks related to climate change, natural resource constraint, and broader environmental, social, and governance factors since 2000. Available from: https://www.spglobal.com/esg/trucost (accessed 27 December 2021).
6. United Nations. Sustainable Development Goals Report 2020. 2020. Available from: https://unstats.un.org/sdgs/report/2020/
7. Wittenberg EY. Environmental responsibility of Russian business. 2011. Available from: http://2info.ru/index.php?dn=article&to=art&id=25

Part 4

Environmental Marketing and Green Logistics of Social Entrepreneurship to Support the Sustainable Development of Territories

https://doi.org/10.1142/9789811264252_0019

Chapter 19

The Concept of Environmental Marketing in Companies' Activities as a Base for the Development of Green Economy in Russia

Olesya V. Ivanchenko[†], **Olga N. Mirgorodskaya**[*,‡], **Tatyana F. Romanova**[§] **and Tatyana A. Vysotskaya**[¶]

Rostov State University of Economics, Rostov-on-Don, Russia
[†]*iovkmr@mail.ru*
[‡]*olyana_mon@mail.ru*
[§]*kafedra_finance@mail.ru*
[¶]*mfrgeu@mail.ru*

Abstract: The chapter focuses on implementing the concept of environmental marketing in the framework of the development of a green economy in Russia to achieve sustainable development goals. In the current context, the idea of an ecological lifestyle is becoming not only a fashionable trend but also a behavioral norm; it is reflected by economic indicators of eco-product consumption. Consumers pay more attention to the climatic characteristics of products. The demand for low-carbon products has not yet formed in most industries, but end-consumer needs are increasing in line with the

[*]Corresponding author.

general rise in awareness of environmental issues. The authors consider the problem of greenwashing on the way of development of responsible environmental marketing. A considerable number of misleading advertising and unconfirmed promises make it impossible for the consumer to distinguish between the illusion of environmental friendliness and responsible environmental policies of companies. Responsible business management and an environmental marketing agenda can now significantly impact a company's reputation, its market capitalization, and the consumer behavior of customers. The positive effect of environmentally responsible behavior through the implementation of green marketing programs is the attraction of customers focused on eco-products and a new generation of investors who support the responsible investment trend. Promoting eco-innovations based on companies' active marketing activities is a prerequisite for developing a green economy in Russia. The results of the activities of environmentally responsible companies show the reality and relevance of the introduction of ecomarketing. The goal of implementing a green economy is to balance the interests of the economy and the interests of society in the long term. In turn, environmental marketing can implement this concept based on the offer of goods and services that consider the needs of consumers and the need to reduce the negative impact on the environment.

Keywords: Green economy; Sustainable development; ESG, Ecological marketing; Greenwashing; Eco-products; Ecological policy.

19.1. Introduction

Currently, the concept of the green economy as a resource-saving and socially responsible economy model is actively developing to increase social justice and solve environmental problems and deficits in world practice. Simultaneously, the development of a green economy is the basis for the sustainable development of regions and the world as a whole. In Russia, the stated goals of economic development for the next 10–20 years largely correlate with the ideas of a green economy. The main goal of economic policy in Russia is to move away from the raw material base, which is also the main task for the concept of a green economy [2].

Implementing the concept of environmental marketing in the practice of companies' activities can become the basis for the development of a green economy in Russia.

In recent research, the use of environmental marketing tools to solve environmental and social issues in the long term is widely studied and considered [3,5,9,10,16]. However, further theoretical research and analysis of the practice of using environmental marketing are needed.

Ecological marketing is the creation of goods and services focused on the consumers' needs, taking into account environmental security for the environment. "The criteria for the high environmental quality of a product are considered to be low consumption of non-renewable resources, minimal possible pollution of the environment and disruption of ecosystems throughout its entire life cycle from raw materials extraction, production of semi-finished products, products manufacture, their sale, and use until disposal (the assessment is made in comparison with the product of the previous generation)" [10]. That is, the product's environmental friendliness does not simply mean certain qualities; it is an integrated approach to the implementation of responsible environmental marketing [5]. Environmental marketing is not only offering the market a harmless product for consumers but also the strategic orientation of the company, business ethics, and internal processes.

Consumer behavior is currently characterized by an increased interest in a healthy lifestyle, while there is also an increased customer interest in "green" or eco-products. Consumers tend to pay attention to the environmental friendliness of products because they believe that these products are more useful [8]. However, recent business experience shows that instead of complying with eco-labeling criteria and real greening of production and a product itself, many companies implement "greenwashing," i.e., unreasonable positioning of the company and its products as being more environmentally friendly than it really is. Nowadays, greenwashing for Russian manufacturers is an acute problem and one of the most serious obstacles to developing responsible environmental marketing and the growth of the domestic economy.

Greenwashing involves creating the illusion of environmental performance for an organization or product using green marketing tools. Greenwashing involves using marketing communications tools to show the sustainability of a product or company rather than the actual activity. Thus, "the company shows the consumer that it is environmentally friendly but does not introduce any real eco-innovations into its production to reduce its environmental damage" [16].

Recently, especially often in the advertising of goods and services, emphasis has been placed on environmental safety and harmlessness.

"In particular, "green," "environmentally friendly," and "ecological" products are widely advertised in such market segments as food, goods for children, cosmetics, building materials, household chemicals, and other household products" [10]. Seeking quality and safe products, consumers choose products judging by these slogans. The question remains whether the manufacturers' statements about the environmental friendliness of these products have sufficient grounds.

The following main features of greenwashing can be distinguished:

- Use of green color in packaging;
- Advertising focused on the fact that the product contains natural ingredients;
- Inscriptions "organic," "eco," "100% bio," "does not contain parabens," "without GMOs," and others on the packaging.

These indicators are not necessarily the signs of greenwashing, but it is necessary to check the composition of such products. "There are cases of serious and even illegal greenwashing when a company prints an eco-certificate badge on the packaging, which it does not have. Moreover, if a Russian manufacturer assigns a certificate marking that it does not have, then the organization that developed the standard will most likely not be able to punish it or make any claim. In Europe and America, the situation is different — a brand risks to be punished by heavy fines in case of using the eco-certificate mark illegally" [14].

Various factors influence the rapid spread of greenwashing in the activities of companies. The lack of legal norms does not allow regulating the use of definitions such as "bio," "organic," "eco," "does not contain ...," etc. Another factor is the low environmental literacy of the population and specialists engaged in marketing communications (marketers, advertisers, and public relations officers). Another factor is the low level of state supervision of bodies responsible for environmental certification of companies and goods [7].

The use of unfair marketing policy leads to the fact that consumers no longer trust the truthful information about the greening of companies' production activities. Many misleading advertising and unconfirmed promises make it impossible for the consumer to distinguish between "green camouflage" and responsible environmental policies of companies.

Frequent greenwashing practices, combined with ineffective government oversight, lead to growing consumer skepticism about everything that is positioned as "green" and also do not encourage businesses to move towards the introduction of real green solutions.

The low level of consumer confidence in eco-products has a negative impact on the entire domestic market because those manufacturers who honestly invested in the greening of manufacturing processes and products are deprived of competitive advantages due to a large number of pseudo-ecological goods. As a result, "the development of environmental marketing aimed at environmentally competent production and consumption, reducing the environmental burden and negative effect on consumers' health slows down" [7].

Eco-consumption in Russia is beginning to take shape. There are great opportunities for domestic manufacturers to promote eco-innovations.

19.2. Methods

The informational basis of the research is the materials of Russian authors devoted to implementing the concept of a green economy in Russia based on the tools of environmental marketing, considering the goals of sustainable development and systemic problems of the negative impact of greenwashing on environmental marketing. Additionally, the authors analyzed secondary data from open sources on the Internet. The collected empirical data allows assessing the level of environmental marketing programs implementation by certain Russian companies and studying consumer behavior trends related to the environmental marketing agenda.

The tasks highlighted in the research were addressed based on general scientific methods of cognition: system analysis, comparative and logical analysis, generalization, synthesis of the information received, and the method of expert assessments. An analytical review of specialized literature, a comparison of secondary research data, own desk research, and synthesis of the obtained result was used in the research.

19.3. Results

In recent years, consumers have paid more and more attention to the climatic characteristics of products. Demand for low-carbon products is still low in most industries, but the needs of the end-consumer are increasing in line with the general rise in climate awareness. Thus, according to the Public Opinion Foundation (FOM), only 9% of Russians believe that there are no dangers to humanity arising from climate change for now; 41% think that such changes are happening and they can be stopped; 34% consider that it is already impossible to stop them; 49% of survey participants believe that living conditions on our planet will seriously deteriorate already in this century due to climate change; 31% believe that this can happen but later (Fig. 19.1). In general, 37% of the all-Russian FOM survey participants experience "environmental anxiety," 44% notice it around (1,500 respondents aged 18 and over took part in the survey).

According to the respondents, the most important environmental problems are water and air pollution, deforestation, an increase in the amount of garbage and waste, food quality deterioration, etc. (Table 19.1).

In the current context, the idea of an ecological lifestyle is becoming not just a fashion trend but a behavioral norm. It is reflected by economic indicators of the consumption of organic, environmentally friendly products.

Currently, more than half of consumers in Russia pay attention to the environmental friendliness of goods and are willing to pay more for environmentally friendly products. In 2021, the Russian Public Opinion Research Center (VCIOM) presented data from a survey of Russians on environmentally friendly consumption (1,600 Russians aged 18 and over took part in the survey). More than half of Russians (55%) more often consider the environmental friendliness of goods when buying, 40% more often do not attach importance to this (Table 19.2).

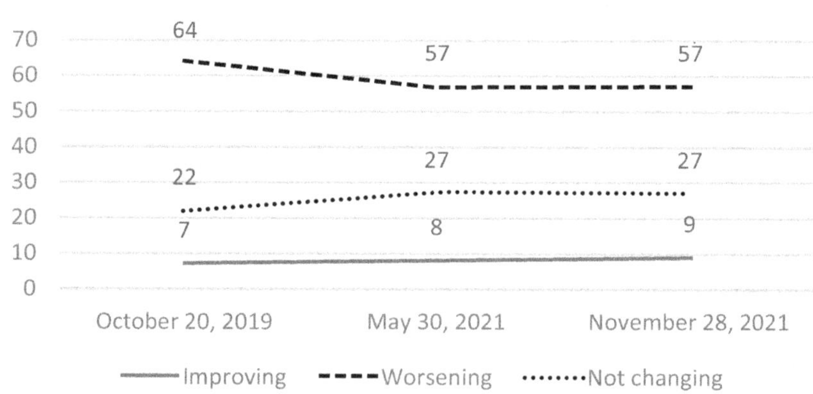

Fig. 19.1. Do you think the environmental situation in the world has been improving, worsening, or practically not changing in recent years?

Source: Compiled by the authors based on Ref. [11].

Table 19.1. Which of the listed environmental problems do you consider the most dangerous?

	October 20, 2019	March 14, 2021	November 28, 2021
Water pollution — rivers, seas, oceans, etc.	70	65	68
Air pollution	62	54	59
Deforestation	66	56	59
Growth in the amount of garbage and household waste, landfills: the situation with waste processing	49	54	51
Food quality deterioration (use of dyes, preservatives, harmful chemicals, etc.)	51	47	43
Growing number of diseases caused by adverse environmental conditions (allergies, skin diseases, respiratory diseases, etc.)	32	33	31
Irresponsible attitude of people to the environment, lack of environmental culture and education	25	36	29
Global warming, melting glaciers	20	14	24
Natural disasters (fires, floods, droughts, etc.)	24	17	24
Fossil resources depletion (oil, gas, etc.)	11	12	10
Reduction of flora and fauna species diversity	6	9	8
Other	0	1	1
Difficult to answer	3	3	2

Source: Compiled by the authors based on Ref. [11].

Table 19.2. When choosing a product, do you personally consider or not consider its environmental friendliness? (Closed-ended question, one answer, % of all respondents).

	All respondents	18–24 years old	25–34 years old	35–44 years old	45–59 years old	60 years old and older
More often, I consider it	55	40	58	54	58	57
More often, I do not consider it	40	59	40	41	38	35
Difficult to answer	5	1	1	5	4	8

Source: Compiled by the authors based on Ref. [17].

Table 19.3. What would you choose: To buy a product that is cheaper but less environmentally friendly or to buy a product that is more expensive but more environmentally friendly? (Closed-ended question, one answer, % of all respondents).

	All respondents	18–24 years old	25–34 years old	35–44 years old	45–59 years old	60 years old and older
A product that is cheaper but less environmentally friendly	25	39	21	24	24	24
A product that is more expensive but more environmentally friendly	64	51	68	64	63	67
Difficult to answer	11	11	10	12	13	9

Source: Compiled by the authors based on Ref. [17].

Two-thirds of Russians (64%) would prefer a more expensive product to a cheaper one if the expensive product is safer for the environment; one in four (25%) would choose a cheaper but less environmentally friendly product (Table 19.3). More than half of Russians (55%) believe that the quality of eco-friendly and non-ecological products is approximately the same, 26% consider that environmentally friendly products are of better quality, 3% have the opposite opinion.

During the COVID-19 pandemic, there has been a significant shift in the minds of consumers towards caring for the environment. Simultaneously, the two main environmental measures for buyers are reducing the amount of waste and moderate nutrition.

Consumers are becoming increasingly disillusioned with over-packaged e-commerce products, large amounts of disposable packaging in the catering industry, and materials that are not recyclable or compostable. Consumers want to get more environmentally friendly packaging. The labeling on the package goes from self-proclaimed to third-party certification, excluding “greenwashing.”

The higher the income of consumers, the higher their concern about the problem of excessive packaging of consumer goods. This trend is not surprising — in the marketing of products aimed at a more profitable audience, packaging plays a more important role than in the economic segment. Therefore, in the new realities, manufacturers of goods, focused primarily on more affluent consumers, should think not only about the environmental friendliness and recyclability of packaging of goods but also about minimizing packaging while maintaining the high perceived quality of the goods.

According to a survey conducted by Procter & Gamble in 2019, 55% of consumers actively inquire about the environmental standards of manufacturers before purchasing their products. Simultaneously, there is an increase in interest depending on the age of the respondent:

- 41% — among participants aged 18–30 years old;
- 52% — among respondents aged 31–40 years old;
- 61% — among respondents aged 41–50 years old;
- 66% — among respondents aged 51–65 years old.

Only 39% of respondents believe that the effectiveness of a product is more important than its environmental friendliness [12].

Russians consider those products to be eco-friendly that are made from natural ingredients (54%), safe for health (52%), the packaging of which is made from biodegradable raw materials or recyclable (49%), and produced without harm to the environment (40%). It is necessary to note that 80% of Russians agree that eco-products can cost more; 69% of Russians are currently willing to pay more for environmentally friendly products; 62% of Russians believe that products marked "Eco" are safe and healthy. However, 50% of respondents do not know the criteria by which a product can be classified as "Bio" or "Eco," or do not know what such labeling stands for [12].

Already, companies that use sustainable development approaches are more competitive. According to NielsenIQ, sales of consumer goods with eco-certificates are growing by 13%, and products without them, only 6%. The main channels for selling organic food in Russia are the following:

- Supermarkets, where most of the premium food products are sold;
- Specialized stores selling natural products;
- Direct sales through online stores to avoid retail margins;
- Pharmacies that sell a limited range of organic products.

These are mainly diabetic and low-calorie products, baby food, and cosmetics [9].

In a study of young consumers' attitude to eco-products (students of universities in Rostov-on-Don aged 18–25 participated in the survey, a total of 260 people were interviewed), when answering the question: “Do you pay attention to the environmental friendliness of products?”, 55.8% of students answered that they pay attention to eco-products (Fig. 19.2).

When answering the question: “Do you trust the advertising of eco-products?” it turned out that almost 70% of young people do not trust the advertising of green products, believing that advertising often misleads the consumer, namely, the properties of eco-products are exaggerated in advertising, and sometimes those properties that the product does not have at all are attributed (Fig. 19.3).

Fig. 19.2. Respondents’ answers to the question: “Do you pay attention to the environmental friendliness of products?” %.

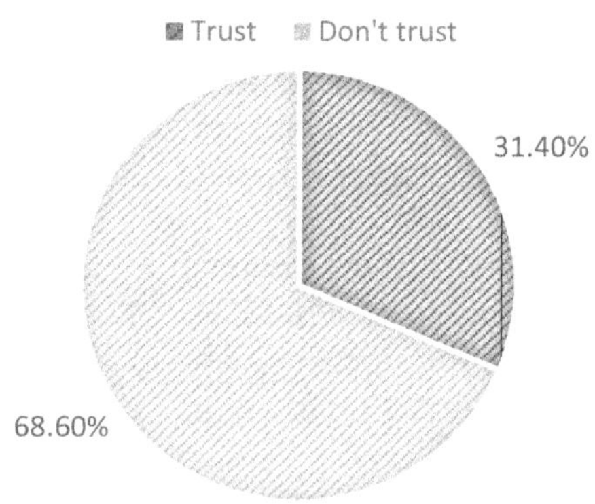

Fig. 19.3. Respondents’ answers to the question: “Do you trust the advertising of eco-products?” %.

The research results show that consumers in Russia are ready for responsible consumption and have a positive attitude towards the social and environmental activities of companies producing goods.

19.4. Discussion

Responsible business management and an environmental marketing agenda can now significantly impact a company's reputation, its market capitalization, and the consumer behavior of customers. The demand for minimizing the impact on the environment now comes from the outside (from investors, buyers of products, and local communities and regulators) and from inside in connection with the awareness of the impact of environmental risks on business efficiency and sustainability in the long term. The direct positive effect of environmentally responsible behavior through the implementation of green marketing programs on the financial results of companies is to retain customers in developed markets and attract new customers focused on green products and a new generation of investors who support the responsible investment trend.

The effectiveness of environmental marketing projects depends to a large extent on fixing the relevant company policy in an internal document that defines the goals and objectives of the environmental policy, the priorities of its implementation, management bodies and officials responsible for implementation, and the tools to assess its effectiveness. Because environmental issues are of strategic importance for companies, the environmental policy should contain strategic targets and be approved by the board of directors.

According to the "ESG issues in the practice of Russian public companies" study, conducted by the expert center of the Russian Institute of Directors in 2020, this approach is used by 27% of the companies in the sample (it should be noted that the experts considered not only a separate document but also a substantive section on the environment, within the overall strategy/policy of the company in the field of CSR and SD). In 20% of companies, an environmental policy is approved by the board of directors. However, targets for evaluating its effectiveness have not been defined. In 30% of companies, the environmental policy is approved by the sole executive body. In 23% of companies, there is no environmental policy. This group included not only financial companies (9%) but also industrial and non-industrial companies (14%) (Fig. 19.4).

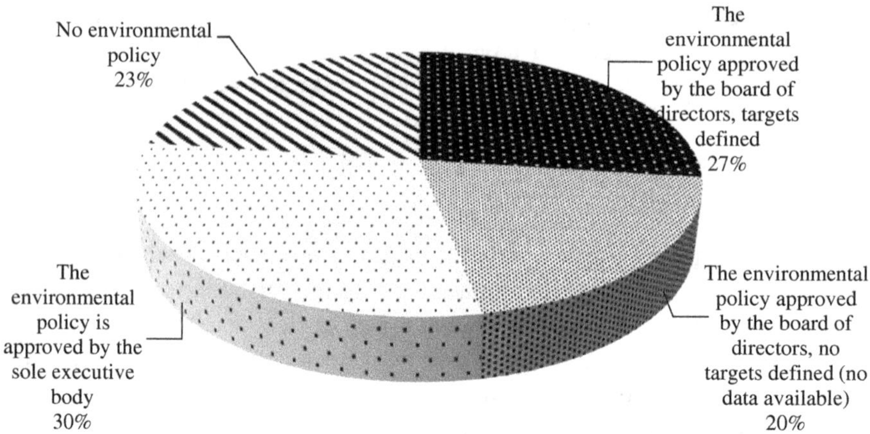

Fig. 19.4. Availability of an environmental strategy or policy.
Source: Compiled by the authors based on Ref. [13].

The study also underlines that the implementation of environmental marketing programs should not be limited to production and promotion and should concern the office divisions of companies. With the assistance of the World Wide Fund for Nature (WWF) and Greenpeace, businesses implement programs to reduce the negative impact on the environment at offices and buildings maintenance (Fig. 19.5). Such programs include a set of measures to save paper, water, and energy; minimize waste; sort household waste; and provide environmental education for employees.

According to Fig. 19.5, 27% of sample companies have implemented Green Office programs or their equivalents. These companies represent four industries — finance, retail, telecommunications, and the oil industry.

In 2021, the environmental agenda became an absolute focus for most Russian marketers, moving from the category of discussions and experiments to real communications and strategies. Interest in the agenda is confirmed by the growth of advertising budgets for environmental and social campaigns, the increase in the number of applications and relevant nominations at industrial marketing and advertising festivals, the emergence of new specialized conferences and workshops, and the dynamics of queries on the topic in search engines [4].

Greenwashing has traditionally been associated with industrial enterprises, whose activities are related to the environment and are often

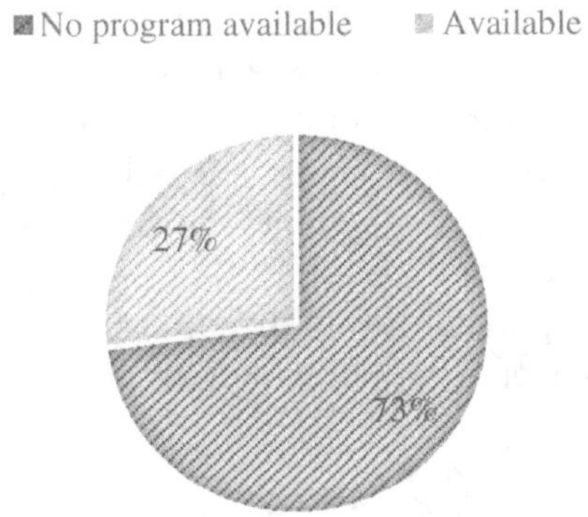

Fig. 19.5. Availability of the Green Office program.

Source: Compiled by the authors based on Ref. [13].

regulated by environmental standards, so the illusion of environmental friendliness is often created to comply with the requirements of the authorities. However, observing the environmental initiatives of Russian industrial companies, one can already see an honest environmental policy and a desire to contribute to the improvement of the biosphere.

For example, the environmental activities of the Taganrog Metallurgical Plant (TAGMET), one of the most high-tech pipe plants in the world, are based on corporate and factory environmental policy [15]. The TAGMET plant has the necessary permits in the field of environmental protection. Specialists of the factory environmental laboratory are constantly instrumentally monitoring the compliance with standards at emission sources, as well as the state of atmospheric air and the water area of the Taganrog Bay in the zone of enterprise influence.

The company's internal environmental marketing activities include the annual review — "The activities of departments to reduce the negative impact on the environment" competition. At the seminar dedicated to World Environment Day, the results of the competition are summed up, and the departments and workers of the plant who have made the greatest contribution to the conservation of nature of the Azov Region are awarded.

During the 15th anniversary of TAGMET, the enterprise organized an environmental educational campaign for schoolchildren. The main activities and results of responsible environmental policy are as follows:

- A new advanced steel-smelting complex DSP-150 is equipped with a highly efficient gas cleaning system;

- Water recycling and water treatment facilities were built;
- Advanced equipment of continuous PQF mill and OLIVOTTO thermal department were put into operation;
- The number of air pollution sources was reduced by 48 units;
- The number of pollutants emitted into the atmosphere decreased by six ingredients;
- Gross emissions of pollutants into the atmosphere decreased by 35%;
- The volume of seawater withdrawn from the bay of Taganrog Bay decreased by 13%.

Another example of a domestic industry eco-project is the production of biodegradable packaging by a resident of the port of Vladivostok. "The investment project of the company "ECO PACK" is to launch the production of biodegradable polyethylene bags and trays of polystyrene foam. The project involves the construction of a production and warehouse complex, where the production is located" [1].

Unlike plastic bags, which people have got used to enjoy, these products have an important advantage — they are absolutely safe for nature and do not require special conditions for disposal. The work of such an enterprise will improve the ecology of the Far East region and contribute to the development of the non-resource sector of the economy. The competitive advantage of this enterprise and products is based on the unique preferences provided by the residence of the free port of Vladivostok. Customs and tax benefits provide a serious incentive for production development. The proximity of the Asia-Pacific countries provides convenient logistics for the delivery of products to the buyer, which will make production cheaper and compete with large bio-packaging manufacturers [1].

Another example of a responsible environmental policy is juices, fruit drinks, and juice drinks for children from the "Spelenok" brand of the Russian company "Sady Pridonya," which has successfully passed the Leaf of Life environmental certification. For buyers, this is an independent guarantee that juices do not contain heavy metals, pesticides, artificial colors, flavors, preservatives, and other substances harmful to the child's body. Besides, the production of juices — "from growing fruits to choosing packaging" — is as safe for the environment as possible.

"Life cycle eco-certification is always an increased environmental obligation that a manufacturer takes on voluntarily. This is not only compliance with high requirements for the safety of juices but also the company's contribution to the environmental friendliness of production and drawing the attention of millions of families to responsible consumption and respect for nature" [6].

Due to excessive environmental pollution and the irrational use of non-renewable resources, the environment has suffered greatly. People now care not only about the efficiency and low price of the product but also about its environmental friendliness. There is a growing need for environmental goods and for the development and promotion of environmental projects based on environmental marketing tools.

19.5. Conclusion

The development of a culture of environmentally responsible consumption requires a marketing policy using various tools. For example, promotions, tastings, and free samples of products are effective channels of communication with the target consumer to attract attention to eco-products. Advertising of eco-products must contain truthful information about the impact of the production of this product on the environment and about the benefits that the consumer will receive.

The examples of responsible marketing environmental policy of industrial enterprises given in the research shows that the problem of greenwashing can be solved. Participating in a small environmental action can be the start of an environmentally responsible business. Russian and foreign businesspeople should realize that the economy and the environment should be united. Gradually, the market should include, and not exclude, the environmental component because, with the development of advanced information and communication technologies, the way the manufacturing company affects the environment will become of particular importance in marketing activities. Thus, the facts indicating that the company does not improve the quality of life and the environment of today's society can cause serious reputation damage.

The analysis carried out in the research showed that the active environmental marketing policy of companies forms the basis for the development of a "green" economy in Russia. The goal of the "green" economy is to focus the interests of counterparties on saving the biosphere in the long term. The task of environmental marketing is to organize this process in such a way that the producer, consumer, and society acquire significant benefits.

References

1. Biodegradable packages will be produced in Russia. 2018 Jan 25. Available from: http://brandingreen.ru/news/973.html
2. Bobylev S, Flight R. Sustainable development in Russia. 2014. Available from: http:/ecodelo.org/rossiyskaya_federaciya/27342-ustoychivoe_razvitie_i_zelenaya_ekonomika_v_rossii_aktualnaya_situaciya
3. Bondarenko VA, Guzenko NV. Possible ways to activate the sale of environmentally friendly sausage products. *Scientific and Methodological Electronic Journal "Concept,"* 2016; 2: 371–375.
4. Dentsu Russia. Sustainable Development & ESG Guide for Marketers. Moscow, Russia; 2021. Available from: https://assets-eu-01.kc-usercontent.com/296d8d4d-1c46-01bf-48d9-7c150d2fc3b5/c7d00561-f02b-4734-acd5-1b88ce215893/Dentsu%20Sustainability%20&%20ESG_2022.pdf
5. Ivanchenko OV, Bondarenko VA. Marketing of eco-innovations within the framework of the formation of a "green" economy. *Scientific and Methodological Electronic Journal "Concept,"* 2017; 31: 41–45. Available from: http://e-koncept.ru/2017/970023.htm
6. Juices and more of "Spelenok" have been assigned the eco-label "Leaf of Life." 2018. Available from: http://brandingreen.ru/news/965.html
7. Kalashnikova L. Why is it important not to let "greenwashing" on the window market. 2018. Available from: https://ardexpert.ru/article/11525
8. Kostoglodov DD, Bondarenko VA, Ivanchenko OV. "Green" branding and interest in environmentally friendly goods. Black Sea-Caspian Cooperation Forum: Security. Sustainability. Development: Materials of the International Discussion Platform. Rostov-on-Don, Russia: Publishing and Printing Complex of RSEU; 2017. p. 778. Available from: http://bscscf.rsue.ru/sbornik.pdf
9. Mirgorodskaya ON, Sagoyan AS, Dadayan NA. (2016). World experience and domestic prospects for the production and sale of organic products. In the collection: Russia and the EU: Ways of development and prospects. *Materials of the International Scientific and Practical Conference*, pp. 735–742.
10. Prituzhalova OA. True environmental marketing and "pseudo-green" marketing — Greenwashing. 2015. Available from: http://ecovestnik.ru/index.php/2013-07-07-02-13-50/nashi-publikacii/2324-istinno-ekologicheskij-marketing-i-psevdo-zelenyj-marketing-grinvoshing
11. Public Opinion Foundation. Ecology: General Situation and Acute Problems 2021. 2021. Available from: https://fom.ru/Obraz-zhizni/14659
12. Research Procter & Gamble. 69% of Russians are willing to pay more for eco-products. 2019. Available from: https://www.retail.ru/news/69-rossiyan-gotovy-platit-bolshe-za-eko-tovary-23-dekabrya-2019-189268/

13. Russian Institute of Directors. ESG issues in the practice of Russian public companies. Moscow, Russia; 2021. Available from: http://rid.ru/wp-content/uploads/2021/04/2021_РИД_Исследование_ESG.pdf
14. Shvetsova M. Be careful, Greenwashing! Available from: http://vegjournal.ru/etichniy-biznes/biznes-proekty/1592-ostorozhno-grinvoshing.html
15. TAGMET. Environmental Policy. Available from: https://tagmet.tmk-group.ru/tgm_eco_pol
16. Tsarev VE, Vershina DA, Novikov IV, Utkina VA. The problem of ecological entrepreneurship — "Greenwashing." *International Journal of Humanities and Natural Sciences*, 2017; 10: 178–180.
17. VCIOM (Russian Public Opinion Research Center). Analytical review: Eco-friendly consumption. 2021. Available from: https://wciom.ru/analytical-reviews/analiticheskii-obzor/ehkologichnoe-potreblenie

https://doi.org/10.1142/9789811264252_0020

Chapter 20

New Trends in the Sustainable Development of Logistics Systems During the Impact of COVID-19

Adam U. Albekov[*,†,§], Tatiana V. Parkhomenko[†,¶], Anna A. Polubotko[†,‖] and Venelin K. Terziev[‡,]**

[†]*Rostov State University of Economics, Rostov-on-Don, Russia*
[‡]*Kaneff University Hospital, Ruse, Bulgaria*
[§]*a2404929@yandex.ru*
[¶]*inrost@list.ru*
[‖]*annapolub@list.ru*
[**]*vkterziev@gmail.com*

Abstract: During the development of socio-economic systems with a certain periodicity, there arise crises initiated by the impact of political, financial, economic, epidemiological, and other nature events. Over the past few years, the global community faced the spreading and destabilizing effects of COVID-19 on all areas of life, business, production, commercial and non-commercial structures, and public administration. The chapter attempts to reveal and interpret current trends in the development of socio-economic and transport and logistics systems within COVID-19, revealing the reasons that characterize the emergence of

[*] Corresponding author.

imbalances in economic and transport and logistics systems. Within the framework of the studied topic, the chapter substantiates the necessity of forming forecast values for the sustainable functioning of supply chains, considering the possibility of interpreting the forecast in several variations. The basis for the formation of forecast values of development in the future is the fact that the value and volume of online commerce are already increasing every year. The unprecedented surge in online sales associated directly with the COVID-19 pandemic has brought volumes closer to the futures indicators of 2025. According to expert opinion, electronic sales have every chance to absorb 80% of the market by 2030. The research used classical methods of scientific knowledge, including system analysis, synthesis, graphical interpretation of the given data, comparative analysis, and abstraction. The summarizing part of the research substantiates the author's opinion on the formation of areas of sustainable operation of logistics companies in the medium term. It is necessary to invest in the development of IT technologies and transport and storage infrastructure of logistic complexes and form optimal paths of transport processes. Logistics companies that will adhere to these recommendations should make clear scripted forecasts in several development options, considering the emergence of crisis and force majeure situations. One of the conclusions of the research is the fact that competition within the framework of global logistics systems, which has expanded to all levels of their organization up to the local one, determines the main success parameters in today's business, not only the quality and value of the product but, to a greater extent, the time parameters of logistics services, the rapid development of last-mile logistics, and the optimization of intermodal and multimodal operations.

Keywords: Logistics; COVID-19; Forecast; Last-mile logistics.

20.1. Introduction

With the onset of the COVID-19 pandemic, forecasts of global economic development and the practical flow paths of transport and logistics systems have been substantially adjusted. Therefore, most leading economists and practitioners wonder whether it is possible to plan and predict the further sustainable development of socio-economic systems and develop logistics, avoiding the acute manifestations of crises, sometimes turning into chaos. Even at the beginning of 2022, it is impossible to say that the situation in the logistics services market in the world has stabilized.

Most expert opinions are that the crisis caused by the COVID-19 pandemic continues. The acute phase of this crisis has passed, but there are still limitations of transport communication, a high human factor associated with the disease, and a shortage of containers and drivers, narrowing the possibility of receiving and sending cargo [8,13,17,18]. Over the past few years, global trade has moved from the real sector to the virtual sector. Previously, the last-mile logistics was developing rather leisurely. Over the past two years, this direction has received significant preconditions for accelerated growth. Even competition in the field of retail has moved beyond the price range and availability of goods on the shelves — rivals are now fighting for speed of delivery and the ability to serve consumers quickly. The leadership in this competitive field lies in the plane of the last-mile logistics. According to the golden rule of logistics, companies that can deliver the necessary goods and proper quality in the specified time are fighting for the right of primacy in ensuring the effective transport and logistics process.

20.2. Materials and Methods

Within the framework of the research on the issues of socio-economic and transport and logistics systems development within COVID-19 and the reasons that predetermine the occurrence of imbalances in economic and transport and logistics systems, we have analyzed the views of leading Russian and foreign scientists on the sustainable functioning of supply chains and the formation of optimal trajectories of transport processes. We use such methods as literature search, comparison, system analysis, synthesis, graphical interpretation of the given data, and comparative analysis. The method of abstraction was applied to formulate conclusions.

20.3. Results

The rapid spread of COVID-19 on the planet has dealt a significant blow to all aspects of life, changing the world forever. Through integrated planning, organization, and management of flow processes, logistics in contemporary scientific and applied realities act as a major catalyst for changes occurring in social and economic systems. Modeling the network structure of supply chains and the configuration of logistics networks in the new realities, the response to the challenges of the COVID-19 pandemic as part of the confrontation with the destruction of the usual patterns of life, production, and distribution of products lies in the field of logistics. By initially distorting standard logistics activities and changing the paths of flows in established formats, the COVID-19 pandemic has changed most of the activities of logistics companies. Simultaneously, the market in general and logistics, as a key element of high commercial and social importance, got quickly used to the changes that occurred overnight, demonstrating the properties of adaptability, hybridization, and rationalization [1–3].

According to analysts, the value and volume of online commerce will increase each year and will significantly adjust the level of capitalization by 2030. Thus, companies that invest in developing electronic platforms, providing infrastructure for warehouse logistics complexes, and forming optimal trajectories of transport processes have all chances to be in demand and make a profit even in times of global crises. This situation can be illustrated by the identified imbalances initiated by the spread of COVID-19.

Thus, at the beginning of 2020, the demand for cars saw a significant decline. Simultaneously, the need for computer equipment increased because the COVID-19 pandemic and the lockdown affected the work processes and leisure activities of the society. The production of semiconductor components and microchips, concentrated in China, has also experienced restrictions from the USA [11,16]. Thus, as a result of fluctuating demand for components, computer hardware and automobile production worldwide faced essentially the same problems — a shortage of components. However, while demand for technology increased, the need for personal vehicles during the pandemic temporarily, for only a few months, decreased, with the decline in production. Some auto plants suspended production, resulting in disrupted production cycles. Looking at this example, we see a major imbalance in planning and forecasting, not so much in the lack of chips and semiconductors but in the organization of production and logistics processes. The result of this situation was the rise in prices for automobiles and computer equipment, whose long-term (more so for cars) production cycle demonstrated the need to build clear forecasting programs in several variations, linking demand fluctuations, the availability of insurance stocks of raw materials and supplies, and production and logistics processes into a single ecosystem.

20.4. Discussion

Listing the difficulties faced by today's logistics in maintaining the parameters of effective functioning, the provision of socio-economic and production processes is adjusted daily, both in the direction of the solution and due to the formation of new bottlenecks. Earlier, we could talk about the development of infrastructure support for logistics processes and the formation of clear movement paths [23]. In turn, in today's conditions, it is necessary to give these processes the properties of variability and adaptation to changing conditions of market reality. With the onset of the crisis, global transport connections have become considerably more complex, and even after the past two years, a certain range of problems remains unresolved.

The problem with the container shortage that emerged in 2020 has still not been solved. So far, the result is only an unprecedented increase in container prices (in some cases up to 300%) and a lack of quality logistics capacity. Moreover, the flow processes that function effectively have not yet been solved; there are risks of supply disruption and destabilization of international and local transport and logistics systems [7,21]. As properties of the last-mile logistics, relative stability and speed, realized only at the beginning of 2020 in the framework of the Russian reality, is the only indicator of the development of today's logistics in the next few years [14]. Decentralization of supplies across Russia, as a process initiated quite a long time ago, increasingly excludes the presence of the central region in the logistics schemes and transport arteries that supply the social and economic systems of the regions of the Russian Federation. In our opinion, this trend will become increasingly relevant every year. Focusing on this trend, let us present the prerequisites and forecasts for the growth of last-mile logistics in the world (Fig. 20.1).

Caring for the environment, green logistics, as part of the global trade process, is becoming increasingly important because certain European countries are already adopting or have already adopted a legal framework that does not allow the movement of vehicles with high levels of greenhouse gas pollution on the territory of these countries [12,22].

The situation related to the shortage of drivers is clearly illustrated in Table 20.1.

The cost of logistics and transport processes and freight traffic between Russia and European countries have increased. Over the last

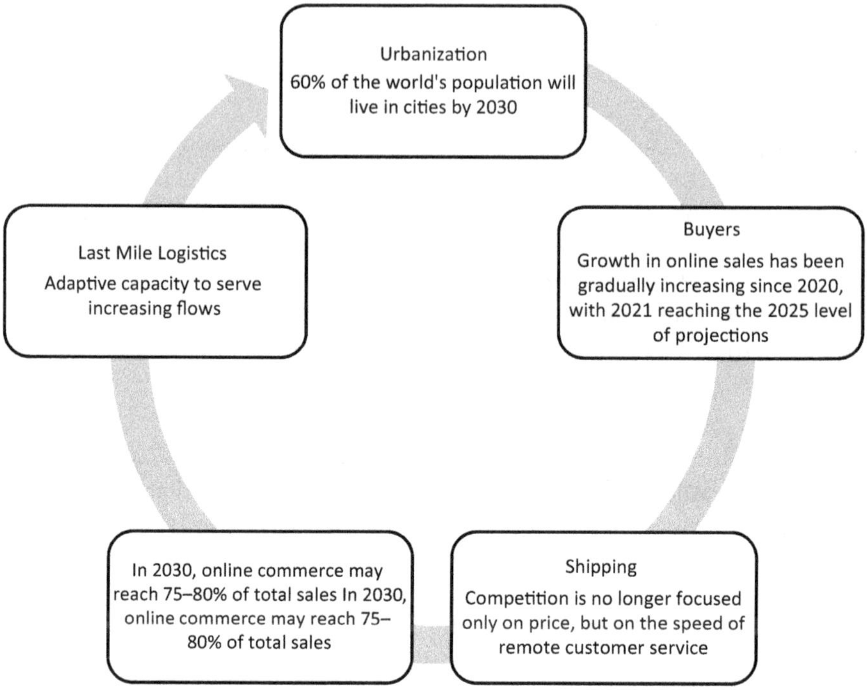

Fig. 20.1. Development of last-mile logistics in the world.
Source: Compiled by the authors based on Ref. [10].

Table 20.1. Data showing the shortage of drivers in the Government.

Government	Driver shortage indicator	Data submission period
Poland	123,842	2020
UK	60,000–76,000	2020
Germany	45,000–60,000	2020
France	43,000	2019
Spain	15,340	2020
Italy	15,000	2019
Sweden	5,000	2017
Belarus	4,500	2019
Norway	3,000	2017
Denmark	2,500	2017
Ukraine	12,000	2019

Source: Compiled by the authors based on Refs. [4,15].

year, these indicators increased by 10–40% [4,15]. An insufficient number of vehicles, high sickness rate of employees, shortage of drivers, and problems with the acquisition of new cars (the situation highlighted above as an example of a shortage of spare parts for the production of machinery and equipment primarily concerns the automotive industry, where the queue for the purchase of up to six months) has a negative impact on the activities of logistics systems.

20.5. Conclusion

In this regard, many representatives of the logistics business refused to renew the fleet of vehicles, losing the opportunity to carry out transport and logistics processes in Europe. The price of the purchase and the maintenance of vehicles and fuel has increased, which, as a result, was reflected in the growth of wages directly to drivers [5,6,24]. Additionally, although in 2021, logistics on a global scale has felt an increase in the volume of operations. Up to 30% of representatives of the logistics business faced a new problem — the inability to meet the increasing demand for integrated services. That is why the current trends in the development of logistics in Russia dictate the need for consolidation of companies and integration and consolidation of efforts.

Considering the indicators of logistics operations, it should also be noted that air transport in the context of the spread of COVID-19 for a certain period was the most stable option for freight transport between Europe, Asia, and North America [19,20]. However, while passenger lines are gradually recovering their service volumes, freight traffic is still significantly behind the 2019 numbers. Given the possible development scenarios, an optimistic forecast should assume that this unevenness will gradually flatten out. The gradual equalization of the situation and the restoration and formation of new logistics hubs will have a serious impact on the global economy [8,9,11]. Predicting future developments with accuracy is almost impossible because the limitations associated with COVID-19 created an initial chain reaction, leading to shortages and, as indicated earlier on the example of microchips, the imitation of products manufactured with these elements. Due to the redistribution of the supply chain on a global scale, it is impossible to speak confidently about any long-term prospects. Thus, the logistics business is focused on current operations, with planning ranging from three months to a year. However, it can be clearly understood that a new era of diversified logistics, which is multidimensional, complex, possessing a high property of adaptability and the level of implementation of information technology, has arrived.

References

1. Albekov AU, Parkhomenko TV, Polubotko AA. The logistics creation of ecological efficiency for the Russian economic under COVID-19. *European Proceedings of Social and Behavioural Sciences*, 2021; 116: 2754–2759. DOI: 10.15405/epsbs.2021.09.02.307
2. Albekov AU, Parkhomenko TV. Determinants of sustainable growth of logistics systems under pandemic conditions. In: Albekov AU (Ed.). Logistics vs. COVID-19: consequences, risks, new growth opportunities. *Proceedings of International Scientific-Practical Conference: XVI Southern Russian Logistics Forum*. Rostov-on-Don, Russia; 2020. pp. 11–15.
3. Albekov AU, Parkhomenko TV. Prospective directions for the development of logistics systems under COVID-19 pandemic conditions. *Bulletin of the South-Russian State Technical University (NPI)*. Series Socio-Economic Sciences. 2021; 14(1): 114–121. DOI: 10.17213/2075-2067-2021-1-114-121
4. Aristov VM. The problem of logistics quality in supply chains. *Economic Vector*, 2018; 1(12): 31–37.
5. Cherepovskaya YA. Digital twins for supply chain risk management in a COVID-19 pandemic. *Engineering Journal of Don*, 2021; 7(79): 304–310.
6. Chernikova SA. Methodological frameworks and prerequisites for the development of organizational — financial mechanism to ensure the strategic development of innovation and integration formations in the sphere of cooperative international movement in the context of sustainable development of the region's pro-structural and industrial structure. *Moscow Economic Journal*, 2020; 7: 18. DOI: 10.24411/2413-046X-2020-10526
7. Drobot EV, Makarov IN, Nazarenko VS, Manasyan SM. Impact of the COVID-19 pandemic on the real economy. *Journal of Economics, Entrepreneurship and Law*, 2020; 10(8): 2135–2150. DOI: 10.18334/epp.10.8.110790
8. Erokhina TB, Parkhomenko TV. Development of emotional background of the consumer personality in distribution logistics. In: Parkhomenko TV, Polubotko AA, Guzenko NV, Erokhina TB, Reznikov SN, Vanyushkina BB (Eds). Innovative achievements of green logistics: International Experience and Russian Practice. *Proceedings of the International Scientific and Practical Conference: XIII Southern Russian Logistics Forum*. Rostov-on-Don, Russia; 2017, pp. 164–167.

9. Hamadaqa E, Mulhem S, Mars A, Adi W. Clone-resistant joint-identity technique for securing fleet management systems. *NASA/ESA Conference on Adaptive Hardware and Systems (AHS)*; 2018: 327–332. DOI: 10.1109/AHS.2018.8541448
10. Heid B, Klink C. Rethinking last-mile logistics, post-COVID-19: Facing the "next normal." *Automotive World*, 2020. Available from: https://www.automotiveworld.com/articles/rethinking-last-mile-logistics-post-covid-19-facing-the-next-normal/
11. Ismailova DA. Theoretical foundations of international supply chain management for FMCG companies. *Economics and Business: Theory and Practice* 2021; 2-1: 83–87. DOI: 10.24412/2411-0450-2021-2-1-83-87
12. Kalitin DV, Kondratenko KA. Automation of information logistics. *Mining Informational and Analytical Bulletin*, 2011; 7, 331–333.
13. Kulikova OM, Suvorova SD. Designing an effective logistics supply chain. *RPPE*. 2021; 4(126): 122–129. DOI: 10.26726/1812-7096-2021-4-122-129
14. Kurbanov AKh, Plotnikov VA. Assessment of logistics development prospects in conditions of digitalization of economy and transformation of social sphere. *Izvestia SPbSEU*, 2020; 3(123): 94–101.
15. Noskov SV, Gumerov RH. The evolution of logistics from physical distribution to supply chain management. *Innovative Science*, 2020; 9: 52–53.
16. Ovechkina O. Virtual supply chains as a system of business functions. *Science and Innovation*, 2020; 1(203): 45–49.
17. Poleshkina IO, Vasilyeva NV. Use of blockchain technology as supply chain management system involving air transport. *Civil Aviation High Technologies*, 2020; 23(2): 72–86. DOI: 10.26467/2079-0619-2020-23-2-72-86
18. Riyadi MAA, Prastyo DD, Purnami SW. How SVM can compensate logit based response label with various characteristics in predictor? *Proceedings of ICITEE 2018: 10th International Conference on Information Technology and Electrical Engineering: Smart Technology for Better Society*, Kuta, Bali; 2018, pp. 615–620.
19. Rogulin RS. The place of ICT and entrepreneurship in shaping sustainable supply chains. *Economic Policy*, 2021; 4: 84–103. DOI: 10.18288/1994-5124-2021-4-84-103
20. Rosstat. Information about the total number and amount of contracts concluded with the only supplier (contractor, executor). Available from: https://www.gks.ru/statistic
21. SIGMA. Performance measurement. Public Procurement Brief. 2011. Available from: https://www.oecd.org/governance/procurement/toolbox/search/sigma-performance-public-procurement.pdf
22. Solodukha PV, Chernovalov PA. Logistics in crises (Crisis Logistics). *Bulletin of the Academy of Law and Management*, 2017; 2(47): 88–92.

23. Tkachev I, Galcheva A. Russia's state spending in 2020 is a record for the post-Soviet history. *RBC*. 2021. Available from: https://www.rbc.ru/economics/23/03/2021/60588a5c9a79476b862106ab
24. Zaripova RS, Rocheva, OA, Khamidullina FR, Arbuzova MV. Digitalization as a factor to improve the efficiency of transport and logistics systems. *International Journal of Advanced Studies*, 2021; 11(2): 100–114. DOI: 10.12731/2227-930X-2021-11-2-100-114.

https://doi.org/10.1142/9789811264252_0021

Chapter 21

Mechanism for Developing the Transit and Export Potential of the Southern Federal District Logistics System

Victor G. Khalyn[†,§], Tatiana V. Parkhomenko[†,¶], Natalia V. Guzenko[*,†,||] and Vladimir V. Klimuk[‡,]**

[†]*Rostov State University of Economics, Rostov-on-Don, Russia*
[‡]*Baranavichy State University, Baranavichy, Republic of Belarus*
[§]*v.khalyn@mail.ru*
[¶]*inrost@list.ru*
[||]*musamav@mail.ru*
[**]*klimuk-vv@yandex.ru*

Abstract: The development of the export potential of the Southern Federal District of the Russian Federation is associated with the justified need to increase the capacity of transport and logistics infrastructure of the studied region and make more rational use of its geopolitical potential. Using geopolitical potential, regions of the Russian Federation seek to optimize the development of competitive industries in areas of economic activity, expanding export potential and pursuing the objectives of government policy to increase the region's non-resource and non-energy exports, including from the perspective of the region's transit potential.

[*] Corresponding author.

In essence, the concepts of export potential and transit potential are interrelated and interdependent; In practice, the formation and development of one provoke the growth of the other. Transit and export potential are concepts based on export-oriented production and on the capacity of transport and logistics infrastructure. Investments in the construction of regional distribution centers, which are embedded in the distribution chains of industries operating in the region, have the greatest importance in developing the transit and export potential of the logistics system. The chapter identifies the need to transition logistics services provided in the Russian Federation to a new integrated level of service. The reason for this situation is the increasing demand for quality and accelerated time performance of services every year, as evidenced by the expansion of the very concept of fulfillment. The authors applied statistical analysis and comparison methods, sampling, correlation and regression, and horizontal and vertical analysis. Investments in the construction of logistics centers are objectively local in practice, i.e., they have a local character. The investor receives the necessary information via the relevant ministries and departments, and the possible benefits and threats in terms of production location and preferences are considered in the investment decision-making process. In this process, the agencies must be fully involved in preparing a package of information on the available transport and logistics options for the transport and marketing of products. Implementing an investment project is a lengthy process. By understanding the investor's needs, it is possible to offer solutions that are as attractive as possible for the investment. Since the necessary transport and logistics system will be developed by local businesses and logistics operators, the regional economy receives significant benefits realized in the creation of new jobs and increased revenues for the regional budget.

Keywords: Logistics; Export; Economic potential; Transit; Investment.

21.1. Introduction

Using its geopolitical potential and established specialization, each region of Russia is given the opportunity to develop competitive industries in areas of economic activity, expanding its export potential. However, in our view, while the export direction is essential, as stated in the national project "International co-operation and export," and the goals set to increase non-resource and non-energy exports are important, the issue can be considered more broadly — from the perspective of the region's transit potential. Transit and export potential are interrelated and interdependent. Export potential is based not only on export-oriented production but also on the capacity of the transport and logistics infrastructure [3].

Thus, "in January–October 2021, Russia's foreign trade turnover was, according to the Bank of Russia, $633.9 billion (138.0% compared to January–October 2020), including exports — $388.4 billion (145.3%) and imports — $245.4 billion (127.9%). The trade balance remained positive, $143.0 billion (in January–October 2020 it was positive, $75.5 billion)" [4].

The Rostov Region has a very good export performance in the region, focusing on the key areas of importance for the development of transit potential (and export potential, as its most promising part) and the overall improvement of the region's transport and logistics system.

21.2. Materials and Methods

Within the framework of the research on the development of the export potential of the Southern Federal District and the reasons that increase the capacity of transport and logistics infrastructure of the studied region, the authors analyze the point of view on the necessity of comprehensive involvement of departments in preparing package information on the available transport and logistics capacities for organizing transportation and sales of products [12]. Such methods as statistical analysis and comparison, sampling, correlation, regression, and horizontal and vertical analysis are used to formulate scientific conclusions.

21.3. Results

"In the south of Russia and in the Rostov Region, in particular, the volume of agro-industrial and agricultural production is growing, numerous research and development projects are being activated and successfully implemented, the capacity and turnover of enterprises are increasing, which implies the development of transport and logistics services. Therefore, there is an objective need to develop the transport and logistics system of the region. The realities of the development of global logistics systems as a mechanism for the functioning of commodity arteries allow prioritizing the development of territories that have the necessary resources to carry out logistics transit operations, have a favorable geographical location, and the ability to provide quality service for multidisciplinary material and associated flows passing through the Southern Federal District along the optimal trajectory from Asia to Europe. Our task is to make the Rostov Region a key link. The limited throughput capacity of regional markets and their transport connectivity determine the resources of export and transit potential, revealing shortcomings in the efficiency of logistics in the distribution system in the complex" [6,8,9].

The need for a range of services is evidenced by the market demand for service logistics and the increasing demand for quality and accelerated timing of service delivery each year. However, the situation in Russia

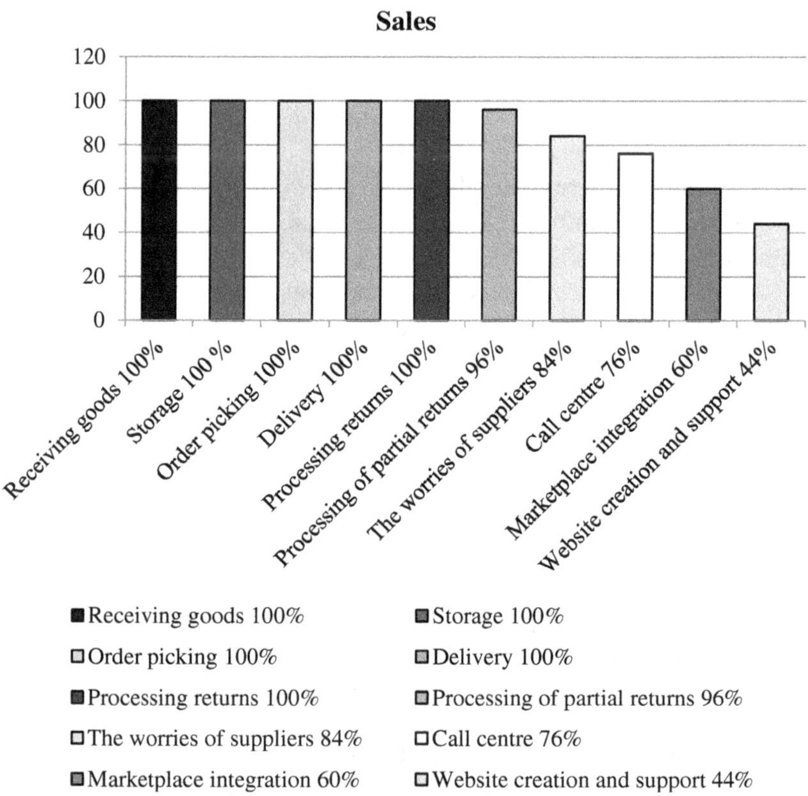

Fig. 21.1. Logistics service comprehensiveness indicators in Russia.

Source: Compiled by the authors based on Ref. [2].

does not look entirely favorable, as shown in Fig. 21.1, which characterizes the expansion of the very notion of fulfillment.

The function of transit potential is often more significant than the function of export potential. This can be seen in the example of grain exports. The Rostov Region, a leader in grain production, has the capacity to export even more grain than it produces.

21.4. Discussion

World leaders and large federal companies send products through the Rostov Region to all of southern Russia through several efficient logistics centers. However, the lack of such facilities significantly affects the volume of the region's transit traffic.

Globally investigated issues, including the export potential of the regional transport and logistics system of the Rostov Region, should be built "on the development of intermodal and multimodal logistics operations, actualized in the format of management cycle organization and transformed into the development of transit outsourcing, because the lack of development of logistics infrastructure is a significant factor limiting the development and export potential. Infrastructure needs to be developed, including transportation and distribution projects and the operation of storage facilities, but the primary objective is to expand the capabilities of logistics service" [7].

Additionally, the key to understanding the efficient development and effective operation of a transport and logistics system is the very notion of a system.

Practice, as we know, is the criterion of truth. Thus, let us illustrate the scientific findings by giving them an applied character.

The Rostov Region has created attractive conditions for investors, and PepsiCo Holdings LLC chip-making facilities have been deployed in the Azov Industrial Zone. There are only two such production facilities in Russia. There was the question of expanding production and building new lines. Market demand has given the manufacturer this opportunity. However, there was a question of where to build new lines — in Azov or Kashira. The question was decided in favor of Azov in the Rostov Region. This decision is based on the fact that a Class A logistics terminal using robotics and artificial intelligence has been constructed and is functioning effectively on this territory, allowing the company to provide the kind of product processing technology that no one in Russia has been able to provide. As a result, the new production facility is located in the Rostov Region, and the supply of products goes all over Russia through the Rostov Region, which also means new jobs and taxes in production and transport because the carriers are predominantly local, which also positively impacts the growth of transit potential.

Logistic technologies, certainly taking into account the geographical position of the region, have made it possible to organize exports to five countries: Uzbekistan, Kazakhstan, Georgia, Armenia, and Azerbaijan (not always even the favorable geographical position of the region plays a decisive role). The most important thing is the availability of logistics infrastructure.

"The region and the state as a whole can benefit enormously from logistics transit operations providing world-class service support to flow processes, which predetermines the relevance, timeliness, and need to activate the transit and export potential of the Rostov Region" [7].

In recent years, many warehouse projects have been implemented in the region. Plans for further development are being drawn up and implemented, which helps attract investment and create new jobs. These are distribution warehouses operating in the consumer market, which mainly serve the needs of e-commerce in terms of prompt delivery of consumer goods to the public. Goods are supplied in piecemeal form from different regions of the country and contribute neither to new construction nor to the localization and development of production facilities in the region, and hence to the development of export or transit opportunities in the region.

In the considered key area, in terms of the development of the Rostov Region's transport and logistics system and its export and transit potential [5], investments in the construction of regional logistics distribution centers, which are built into the supply chains of industries deployed or even planned to be deployed in the region, are important.

To consider the practical issues of development of this direction of logistics and their consideration in the formation of strategic issues of development of transport and logistics system of the region, it should be understood that, as experience shows, investments in the construction of necessary logistics centers are, as a rule, local investments [13]. The exception is large seaports, etc.

It would be useful to extend the industrial development fund not only to the construction of new production facilities but also to the construction of infrastructure logistics centers that provide such production with a distribution system and sales of finished products, as well as to extend the investment tax deduction for logistics infrastructure facilities [11]. This is because, as we have seen with investments (e.g., PepsiCo Holdings Ltd.), the decision to expand production is largely based on the capacity of the regional transport and logistics system, with the availability of logistics terminals for product storage and handling being a key indicator.

21.5. Conclusions

Based on the factors presented above, the following steps should be taken to further develop and strengthen the transit and export potential of the Rostov Region.

(1) The investor's entry procedure into the region. When making investment decisions, considering all possible benefits in terms of production location and the existing preferences in the region, the investor receives the necessary information through the relevant ministries and departments if they are attracted within the agency's project portfolios [15,16]. It is important that the various agencies are fully involved in preparing the package of information at the point of entry on the available transport and logistics capacities for organizing the transport and marketing of products, which is an important factor that will be considered when deciding on the location of production.

(2) The implementation of an investment project, especially when it comes to construction, is usually not a matter of one year [1,14]. Additionally, by understanding the investor's needs at the initial stage and in the implementation phase, it is possible to offer solutions to maximize the satisfaction of these needs so that by the time production begins, all or most of them will be met. There is another important aspect here. Since the necessary transport and logistics system will be developed by local companies, logistics operators, and centers, we not just help the investor but also develop the region's economy, create new jobs, and increase the region's budget revenues.

(3) Large investment projects are already implemented in the region. Knowing the information not partially, according to the profile of each ministry or agency [10], but as a whole, understanding the bottlenecks and relating them to the development of potential production

can either help find solutions based on the opportunities available or create appropriate conditions.

Additionally, when deciding on the functional zoning and development of the region's territories, we must consider which industries with what needs can be attracted and prepare the entire logistics infrastructure in advance, not separately for each area but comprehensively as part of a systemic approach. As both global and Russian experience shows, the mere availability of road and engineering infrastructure, without the organization of logistics services and the creation of advanced high-tech logistics centers for cargo storage and handling, has a greater or lesser impact on the investment attractiveness of the territory and reduces its transit and export potential.

References

1. Andreeva EL, Ratner AV, Sobolev AO. Impact of renewable energy development in Germany on Russian energy export. *Contemporary Europe*, 2021; 4(104): 71–82. DOI: 10.15211/soveurope420217182
2. DataInsight. Fulfilment for e-commerce 2020. 2020. Available from: http://logistics.datainsight.ru/fulfilment-dlya-internet-torgovli-2020
3. Erokhina TB, Parkhomenko TV. Marketing and logistics communications in the process of product distribution. *Vestnik of the Rostov State University of Economics*, 2019; 3(67): 66–70.
4. Federal State Statistics Service of the Russian Federation. On foreign trade in January-October 2021. Moscow, Russia: Rosstat; 2021. Available from: https://rosstat.gov.ru/storage/mediabank/227_22-12-2021.html
5. Jingwei W, Sazonov SL. Features of China's rail transport operations in the Euro-Asian transit space under COVID-19. *China in World and Regional Politics. History and Modernity*, 2021; 26(26): 387–395. DOI: 10.24412/2618-6888-2021-26-387-395
6. Khalyn VG. Development of distribution logistics systems based on activating the transit potential of the Southern Federal District (Synopsis of Dissertation of Doctor of Economics). Rostov-on-Don, Russia: Rostov State University of Economics; 2020.
7. Khalyn VG. Functioning of integrative logistics distribution systems in a pandemic. In: Albekov AU (Ed.). Logistics vs. COVID-19: Consequences, risks, new growth opportunities. *Proceedings of the International Scientific-practical Conference: XVI Southern Russian Logistics Forum*. Rostov-on-Don, Russia; 2020. pp. 164–169.

8. Khalyn VG. Innovative development of transit potential of southern Russia. In: Albekov AU (Ed.). *Market Infrastructure: Problems and Prospects*. Rostov-on-Don, Russia; 2018. pp. 27–31.
9. Khalyn VG. Logistics systems of warehousing and materials handling. *European Research Studies Journal*, 2018; 21(SI2): 893–902.
10. Kirillova AG. Actual aspects of the development of international transport corridors in Russia. Transport of the Russian Federation. *Journal of Science, Practice, Economy*, 2018; 2(75): 51–54.
11. Nikolaev VV. Aspects of customs control of transit of goods and vehicles moving through the territory of the EAEU. *Economic Vector*, 2019; 4(19): 55–58. DOI: 10.36807/2411-7269-4-19-55-58
12. Parkhomenko TV. Development of green logistics of energy systems in Russia. In: Parkhomenko TV, Polubotko AA, Guzenko NV, Erokhina TB, Reznikov SN, Vanyushkina BB (Eds.). Innovative achievements of green logistics: international experience and Russian practice. *Proceedings of the International Scientific and Practical Conference: XIII Southern Russian Logistics Forum*. Rostov-on-Don, Russia; 2017. pp. 111–115.
13. Stepanyan TM. Development of international transport corridors in the Eurasian space. *EESJ*, 2019; 4–7(44): 59–65.
14. Tikhomirov ME. Study of the role of customs and logistics terminals in the development of border regions of Russia (on the example of the Kursk region). *The Eurasian Scientific Journal*, 2018; 10(6): 48. Available from: https://esj.today/PDF/55ECVN618.pdf
15. Tsvetkov VA, Zoidov KKh, Medkov AA. Problems of economic security in Russian transportation and intermediate carrier infrastructure. *Regional Economy*, 2012; 1(29): 90–100.
16. Tsvetkov VA, Zoidov KKh, Medkov AA. Public-private partnership as the core form of the implementation of Russia's transport and transit potential. *Regional Economy*, 2017; 13(1): 1–12. DOI: 10.17059/2017-1-1

https://doi.org/10.1142/9789811264252_0022

Chapter 22

Medical Ecology and Organizational Marketing Solution Within the Smart City Concept Aimed at Improving the Quality of Life of the Population

Victoria A. Bondarenko[*,†,¶], Viacheslav A. Chisnikov[†,||], Natalya N. Zubareva[‡,] and Mikhail Yu. Zarubin[§,††]**

[†]*Rostov State University of Economics, Rostov-on-Don, Russia*
[‡]*Belgorod National Research University, Belgorod, Russia*
[§]*Kostanay Engineering and Economic University named after M. Dulatov 59, Kostanay, Kazakhstan*
[¶]*b14v@yandex.ru*
[||]*chisnikov7@gmail.com*
[**]*nzubareva73@mail.ru*
[††]*zarubin_mu@mail.ru*

Abstract: In this chapter, considering the focus of society on economic, environmental, and social efficiency, the authors discuss the need for medical ecology at the present stage of societal development and the original need for its inclusion in territorial development planning. The authors justify the thesis that there are additional risks of

[*] Corresponding author.

environmentally caused and environmentally dependent diseases when the population lives in urban agglomerations. The authors see the smart city concept as an organizational marketing solution that is initially oriented towards the needs of the area's target audiences. The chapter argues that health care should be fully integrated as a congruent module into the smart city concept to include the basics of environmental medicine and preventive health services that reduce risks to the population, thereby increasing life expectancy and the quality of life of the population.

Keywords: Sustainable development; Health ecology; Negative impacts; Risks; Marketing solution; Smart city concept.

22.1. Introduction

The evolution of economic activity, active development of the planet's resources by humanity, and the transformation of the environment, along with the positive effects on society, inevitably lead to an increase in negative consequences. Thus, scientific and technological progress, increased efficiency of production processes, the phenomenon of urbanization, and the increasing anthropogenic pressure on the surrounding landscape create additional risks for nature and the immediate human environment. These facts have led to a revision of the values of societal development, in which social and environmental effects have become predominant along with economic ones in the framework of sustainable development goals [4]. Solutions that combine economic, social, and environmental foundations are evident in various sectors and activities, such as construction, the creation of a comfortable urban environment [5], and hospitality and tourism [13].

In our opinion, these are not equally relevant in the framework of medicine and the functioning of the healthcare system that should increase life expectancy in the Russian Federation, which is associated with a reduction in mortality, disability, and disease and an increase in the quality of life [14]. In this context, our study focuses on the following Sustainable Development Goals (SDGs) [20]:

- Good health and well-being (SDG 3);
- Clean water and sanitation (SDG 6);

- Industry, innovation, and infrastructure (SDG 9);
- Sustainable cities and communities (SDG 11).

We highlight SGD 9 and SDG 11 because we believe that society's desire to innovate and provide advanced infrastructure, as well as the continued trend toward the enlargement of megacities and urban agglomerations, now seems to have no alternative.

In this context, we consider it relevant to investigate issues related to environmental medicine related to innovative urban development opportunities aimed at improving quality of life and reducing disability and mortality due to inadequate living and medical conditions. Since today's economy is client-oriented, combining a focus on citizens' needs and the introduction of appropriate innovation, it is reasonable to reframe this question by considering the concept of the smart city as an organizational marketing solution that demonstrates a focus on innovative development and societal needs.

22.2. Materials and Methods

Within the framework of research on the demand for medical ecology at the present stage of social life and the study of the "smart city" concept as an organizational marketing solution for improving the quality of life of the population, we have examined, to the extent necessary for analytical purposes, the evolution of ecology to medical ecology, the existing health risks of living in urban agglomerations, and the value of the "smart" city concept with an integrated healthcare element to reduce the destiny of the population.

22.3. Result

According to WHO data, confirmed by Russian experts, public health is largely determined not even by the existing health care system but mainly by the environment and lifestyle (Fig. 22.1), which makes the issues of environmental medicine, combining the above factors, even more relevant.

Of these factors, inheritance cannot be corrected. In contrast, lifestyles can be corrected through educational and preventive measures in the environmental medicine solution pool, and the environment (a factor

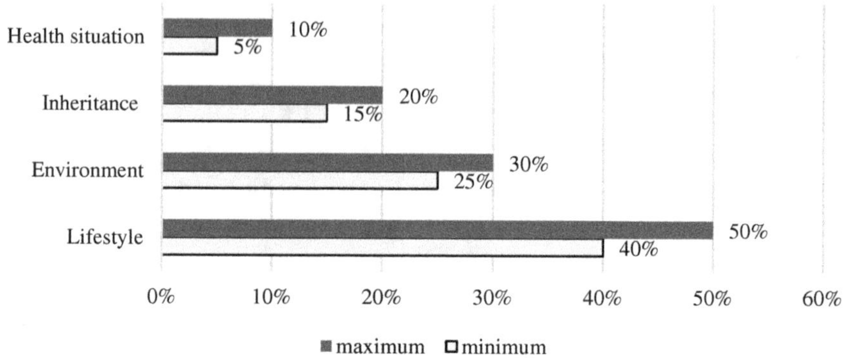

Fig. 22.1. Data on the contribution of determinants to health, %.

Source: Compiled by the authors based on Ref. [15].

of influence) can be mitigated by targeting sustainable development of the society in the smart city concept.

The urban landscape needs to be adjusted in terms of its orientation toward the needs of its inhabitants. This refers to the need to reduce noise levels in cities, decrease exposure to electromagnetic radiation, normalize the social microclimate, including through the development of appropriate, and provide a comfortable urban environment and preventive public health measures to reduce anxiety, stress, and the adverse effects of the built environment on the human body.

Interesting in terms of assessing the negative factors affecting the life of an individual in an average metropolis is the data from empirical research showing (according to respondents — medical students) a decrease in the value of a land plot when certain risks occur (Fig. 22.2).

Additionally, according to studies, ambient air temperatures are traditionally 3–5 degrees higher in urban agglomerations, and concentrations of pollutants of various etiologies are 5–25 times higher than normative levels [9]. In megacities, the biological rhythms of human life change, putting additional strain on the sensory, receptor, and analytical systems of the body and overloading the vegetative-somatic functions of individuals, contributing to environmentally induced morbidity [21].

People in megacities are in close contact in transport, closed workplaces, shopping malls, etc., which leads to the growth of the epidemic chain and the rapid spread of various diseases. The globalized COVID-19 pandemic is a clear visualization of the problem. In megacities, the problem of production of biosphere xenobiotics contaminants, which

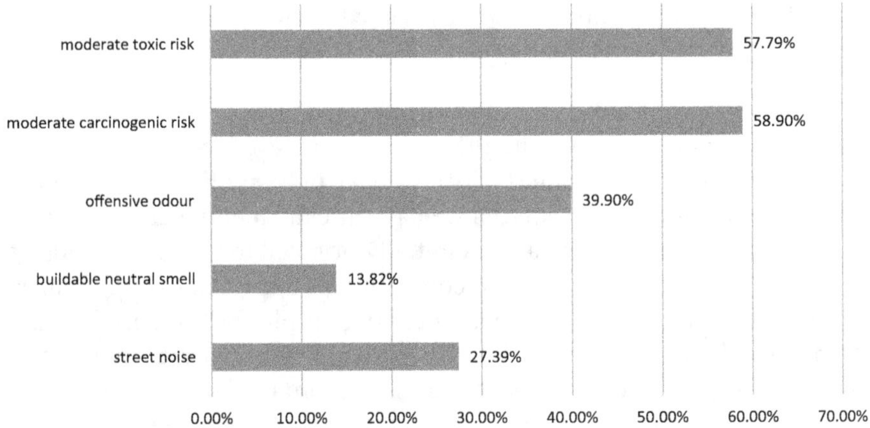

Fig. 22.2. Impact of risks on land value reduction (based on an empirical study), %.
Source: Compiled by the authors based on Ref. [21].

are mainly of anthropogenic origin (heat and power plants, processing and manufacturing plants, transport and domestic activities), is multiplying. Xenobiotics enter and accumulate in the human body through the respiratory tract, triggering allergic reactions, changes in organs and tissues, and inflammatory processes. They can become catalysts for cancer.

Such a complex environment poses challenges for public health in the primary prevention of pre-illness in individuals. It is also important to promote healthy lifestyles and develop health-oriented urban ecosystems, including opportunities for sports activities (not only in fitness clubs but also in outdoor sports grounds and parks created and maintained as part of the urban environment improvement project), healthy eating, and general health and well-being.

Preventive health care and counseling, as well as early case management, are also important to reduce the risks of disease development and increase the quality of life and life expectancy.

The traditional set of measures that should contribute to reducing the risks of living in a megacity include the following:

- The introduction of waste-free (ideally environmentally friendly) industries;
- Strategic spatial development planning with the allocation of water and green areas (as protective barriers), creation and development of a comfortable and safe urban environment;

- Application of sanitation solutions related to dust particle capture, air humidification, etc., based on innovative solutions.

It is also invariably important to set and adhere to standards of hygienic sanitation and hygiene [9].

To a large extent, the Smart City concept can be applied in solving the tasks at hand, which represents, as we have already mentioned, an organizational marketing solution, as it is initially oriented towards the needs of consumers (local businesses, local communities, and authorities). A smart city implements its solutions on a single digital platform focused on the coordinated functioning of various subsystems of the city economy and the possibility of remote access or at least a record to obtain the necessary services for the population. In implementing this concept, megacities and urban agglomerations, as part of their planning and adherence to the plan, move harmful industries and industries in general outside the city limits into appropriate industrial zones with a natural barrier (water, vegetation, etc.). Facilities are located in such areas, considering the windrose. As part of the strategy to build a smart city, urban agglomerations create landscapes closer to nature, greener, and equipped with water bodies to improve the environmental conditions and the psychological comfort of residents. Such decisions are considered in the planning of residential developments and the creation of new residential areas. An important part of the smart city concept is the functioning of the transport system, which ideally should be transformed into an environmentally oriented, predominantly clean energy (i.e., electricity and biodegradable fuels), which creates additional demands on the city's infrastructure. In foreign practice, the design of smart cities is related to ergonomics for residents, environmental safety, and the reduction of the burden on the environment from the very beginning [2].

Considering the above, we believe that when planning spatial development, forming, and implementing the concept of a smart city, an integral part of planning should be environmental medicine installations, allowing initially leveling out the possible negative risks and negative impacts that lead to environmentally caused and environmentally dependent diseases.

Since healthcare is an essential element of citizens' social welfare and evolves as part of the overall fairway of digitalization, it is only natural that the design of healthcare services for citizens, both online and offline, should be fully integrated into the smart city concept. This embedding and congruence of processes will, on the one hand, increase the convenience and accessibility of various health services and, on the other hand, encourage the involvement of the population in preventive health services and consultations prior to the development of the disease. As already mentioned, it is important to initially incorporate the provisions of environmental medicine (as a contemporary trend in urban healthcare) into the planning module of the smart city and its direct functioning as a system for the benefit of the target consumer audiences.

22.4. Discussion

Initially, ecology was understood as a body of knowledge characterizing nature within the framework of an analytical examination of the relations of animals with the organic and inorganic environment, as described, in particular, by E. Heckel's study "The general morphology of organisms" [6]. Furthermore, researchers such as R. Park and E. Burgess started to analyze the role of human communities (bioanthropocenoses) and their social relations in their interaction with the organic and inorganic environment, calling this complex of relations human ecology or social ecology [16–19], which is relevant for the current period.

Nowadays, some researchers interpret ecology as a specific general scientific method for studying nature and society [21]. It is also customary to consider community (population) health, mediated by the state of the environment, as an integrated indicator of the quality of life [23].

Researchers differentiate between individual health (related to the characteristics of the individual's body and life functioning) and population health, which characterizes the existing standard of living of a society [22].

In turn, specialists in the field of ecological medicine distinguish it as a narrower branch within social ecology, saying that the object of this area of scientific knowledge is the human organism, and the subject is the environment in interaction with this organism (organisms within society) [9]. Kartasheva *et al.* focus on environmentally dependent diseases of individuals in society and environmentally caused diseases also related to the specifics of current reality, in particular the phenomenon of urbanization [1,7–10].

The current view of scientists on the problem of ecological medicine, coupled with the reality characterized by the growing number of megacities and urban agglomerations, is important. In this regard, it is worth noting that the very concept of the smart city focuses on creating conditions for the sustainable development of territories and their host communities [11]. This concept, although a continuation of the urbanization trend that has created certain risks for the environment and biocenoses, nevertheless focuses on reducing negative pressure and minimizing possible risk situations for society and the surrounding landscape [3].

There is also a clear focus on the interests of target audiences living in a particular area and matching their future with it. As the researchers point out, the focus is on the residents (local community), the businesses involved in the positive transformation of the regional economy and society, and the regional authorities overseeing these processes [12]. This orientation of the smart city toward the interests of consumers in the megacity and the urban agglomeration should also be characteristic of eco-medicine. Additionally, the initial focus on the interests of the consumer community makes the smart city concept an organizational marketing solution.

22.5. Conclusion

In today's reality, in which the growth of megacities and urban agglomerations seems to have no alternative, including the articulated goals of sustainable societal development, there is an increasing interest in focusing on economic, environmental, and social efficiency.

Living in increasingly urbanized societies poses additional risks to individuals due to disturbances in the functioning of biocenoses in an anthropogenically modified environment. This mediates the need to develop the field of medical ecology, which promotes preventive counteraction against negative influences in megacities, communicating with individuals at a pre-disease stage. Moreover, in counteracting the damaging effects of urbanization, the solution can be found in the further innovative transformation of megacities and urban agglomerations based on the smart city concept. The smart city concept embodies an organizational marketing solution in the development of territories because it initially focuses on the needs of target consumer audiences.

In today's conditions, it assumes full integration of the health care component considering the basics of medical ecology in the general construction of a smart city to reduce the factors of environmentally caused and environmentally dependent diseases due to timely medical aid to the population and consideration and making decisions reducing these risks already at the stage of territorial planning and allocation of protective zones and zones of the comfortable urban environment. Such solutions, in our view, contribute to an increase in the quality and length of life of the population.

References

1. Agadjanyan NA, Radysh IV, Ermakova NV. Human ecology: Social and moral health. Environment and human health. St. Petersburg, Russia: SpecLit; 2003.
2. Belyaeva NB, Mingaleeva ED. Smart-city concept and its implementation in Russia and Northern Europe. *Izvestiya St. Petersburg State University of Economics*, 2019; 5-1(119): 95–98.
3. Boikova MV, Ilyin IN, Salazkin MG. The smart city approach as a response to emerging challenges for urban development. *Foresight and STI Governance*, 2016; 10(3): 65–75. DOI: 10.17323/1995-459X.2016.3.65.75
4. Bondarenko VA, Guzenko AV, Guzenko NV, Efremenko IN. "Green" economy: Theory, foreign experience, modern problems and prospects of Russia. *European Proceedings of Social and Behavioural Sciences*, 2020; 90: 174–182. DOI: 10.15405/epsbs.2020.10.03.21
5. Bondarenko VA. Development of a comfortable urban environment. In: Albekov AU (Ed.), *Complex Analysis of the Socio-economic Development of the City of Rostov-on-Don: Comparative Dynamics and Key Trends*. Rostov-on-Don, Russia: Rostov State University of Economics; 2019. pp. 492–513.
6. Haeckel E. Generalle Morphologie der Organismen. Bd. I. Allgemeine Anatomie der Organismen. Bd. II. Allgemeine Entwickelungsgeschichte der Organismen. Berlin, Germany; 1866.
7. Kartasheva NV, Bortnovsky VN. Contemporary hygienic aspects of children's and adolescent's health protection and improvement. *Health and Ecology Issues*, 2006; 4(10): 113–118.
8. Kartasheva NV, Bortnovsky VN. Hygienic bases of prevention of weather-dependent diseases. *Health and Ecology Issues*, 2007; 4(14): 117–123.
9. Kartasheva NV, Bortnovsky VN. Medical ecology. Legislative and legal bases of health protection. *Health and Ecology Issues*, 2009; 3(21): 128–132.
10. Klyuchenovich VI. Basic principles and methodological approaches for the implementation of social and hygienic monitoring based on a medical and environmental information system. Gomel, Belarus; 1996.

11. Kuznetsov YV, Kaisarova VP. Modernization of strategic management of a large city in the regional system of Russia. *TerraEconomicus*, 2012; 10(2–3): 31–35.
12. Maksimov SN. “Smart city”: On the question of the concept and concept. *Problems of Modern Economics*, 2017; 1(61): 117–120.
13. Meskhi B, Bondarenko V, Efremenko I, Larionov V, Rudoy D, Olshevskaya A. Technical, technological and managerial solutions in ensuring environmental safety. *IOP Conference Series: Materials Science and Engineering*, 2020; 1001: 012100. DOI: 10.1088/1757-899X/1001/1/012100
14. National project “Healthcare.” 2018. Available from: https://strategy24.ru/rf/health/projects/natsionalnyy-proekt-zdravookhranenie
15. Onishchenko GG. Actual problems of hygiene science and practice in the preservation of public health. *Hygiene and Sanitation*, 2015; 3: 5–9.
16. Park RE, Burgess EW, McKenzie RD. *The City*. Chicago, IL: The University of Chicago Press; 1925.
17. Park RE, Burgess EW. *Introduction to the Science of Sociology*. Chicago, IL: The University of Chicago Press; 1921.
18. Park RE. City: Proposals for the study of human behavior in the urban environment. In: Nikolaev VG, Transl. from English; Efremenko DV (Ed.) *Selected Essays*. Moscow, Russia: INION RAS; 2011. pp. 19–56.
19. Park RE. Human ecology. *Theory of Society: Fundamental Problems* (Ananyeva EV, Bankovskaya SP, Kovalev AD, Oberemko OA, Transl. from German and English). Moscow, Russia: CANON-press C; Kuchkovo pole; 1999. pp. 384–400.
20. United Nations. Sustainable Development Goals. Available from: https://www.un.org/sustainabledevelopment/ru/sustainable-development-goals/
21. Zakharchenko MP, Zakharchenko VM, Zakharchenko MM. Methodology of ecology and hygiene at contemporary stage. *Health and Ecology Issues*, 2007; 3: 140–146.
22. Zakharchenko MP, Maymulov VG, Shabrov AV. *Diagnostics in Preventive Medicine*. St. Petersburg, Russia: MFIN; 1997.
23. Zakharchenko MP. The problem of health monitoring in preventive medicine. *Hygiene and Sanitation*, 2004; 6: 8–10.

https://doi.org/10.1142/9789811264252_0023

Chapter 23

Issues of Involving the Potential of Environmental Marketing in Regional Development

Victoria A. Bondarenko[*,†,§], **Natalia M. Przedetskaya**[†,¶], **Tamara I. Razinkova**[†,‖] **and Khachatur Baboyan**[‡,**]

[†]*Rostov State University of Economics, Rostov-on-Don, Russia*
[‡]*M. Kotanyan Institute of Economics, National Academy of Sciences of the Republic of Armenia, Yerevan, Armenia*
[§]*b14v@yandex.ru*
[¶]*nvprv@bk.ru*
[‖]*tamara.razinkova@mail.ru*
[**]*xach-baboyan@mail.ru*

Abstract: The chapter examines the initiatives manifested in Russia for the sustainable development of the economy of the regions. The awareness of the importance of this direction for the transformation of the regional socio-economic system is emphasized. Conclusions are drawn about the need to involve the potential of environmental marketing in the issues of the socio-ecological and economic agenda. One of the

[*] Corresponding author.

significant tasks of environmental marketing in the positive transformation of the regional economy is the involvement of the population in the sustainable development agenda.

Keywords: Environmental marketing; Sustainable development; Regions; Engagement; Involvement.

23.1. Introduction

Nowadays, when planning their socio-economic development for the future, Russian regions rely on the fact that economic activity is already taking place and, in the future, this trend will increase within the framework of the sustainable development paradigm [14]. The adherence to the sustainable development targets can be traced, e.g., in the National Security Strategy of the Russian Federation, which defines strategic national priorities in terms of "ensuring national security and sustainable development of the Russian Federation" [2].

Several Russian regions also adopted policy and strategic documents predetermining the possibility of their sustainable development; this applies, e.g., to the Arctic and the Far North [3] and the Far East [1]. Other regions of the country also include the parameters associated with security and internal sustainability, and resilience to external influences in their social and economic development programs.

Although there are many Sustainable Development Goals (SDGs), they are in one way or another related to environmental protection, combating climate change, and adapting territories and their population to the new challenges posed by such change because the quality of life, education, and health services cannot be fully achieved without addressing environmental issues in a consolidated effort.

Security issues, in addition to possible direct military threats (resolved in terms of strengthening the defense capabilities of countries) and economic security, are linked to environmental well-being, which, in turn, largely determines the economic growth potential of a country and its regions. At the current stage of economic management, the marketing concept (in the broad sense) and the potential of environmental marketing as an integrator of supply and demand for green initiatives are appropriate to use for addressing the ambitious objectives set in the Russian regions because the overall effectiveness of the implemented projects depends largely on the adoption of management initiatives by businesses and the population.

For this reason, it seems relevant to investigate initiatives falling under environmental marketing in the socio-economic evolution of Russia's regions within the framework of their sustainable development targets that are being implemented.

23.2. Materials and Methods

Within the framework of the research on the issues of involving the potential of ecological marketing in the regional development, we analyzed the views of leading scientists on the construction of social and environmental-economic systems, understanding of the role of ecological marketing, its principles, and attitudes, and the significance of the involvement of business and the population in sustainable development. We applied such methods as literature search, comparison, and analysis and synthesis of data to formulate conclusions.

23.3. Result

According to established science and practice, economic marketing is the production and promotion of products that minimize environmental damage by reducing emissions and conserving resources [11,16].

In the format of regional sustainable development, it is important that environmental marketing focuses on several principles (Fig. 23.1).

The following areas of environmental marketing, which are applicable in targeting the sustainable development of Russian regions, are also currently highlighted [4], namely:

- Eco-sponsorship, which can be implemented by leading companies localized in the region and regional authorities encouraging environmental projects and innovations to solve regional problems related to environmental and social sustainability;
- Eco-timing, which aims to build an emotional connection between the authorities in the region, businesses represented in the region, and the consumers, the inhabitants of the area, forming in them a commitment to environmental values.

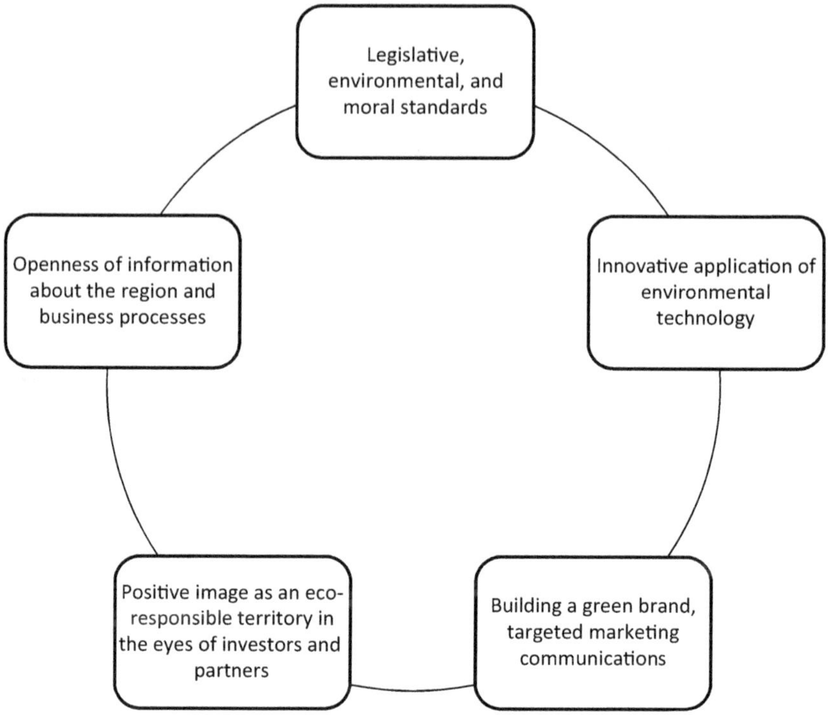

Fig. 23.1. Basic principles of environmental marketing implemented in regional development.

Source: Compiled by the authors based on Ref. [17].

An example of the authorities' encouragement of environmental innovations and solutions aimed at sustainable development of the regional economy can be considered the "Contest of projects of applied scientific research and experimental developments carried out by undergraduates, graduate students, and young scientists to ensure sustainable development of the Arctic and territories of the Far North" [10]. Within the framework of this contest, the scientific community, which largely influences the local community in the region and its environmental attitudes, develops ideas related to greening, effects of climate change, and sustainability [7,9].

According to empirical studies, the population's perception of the region's ecological restructuring and involvement in sustainable development processes allows for a more significant effect in terms of

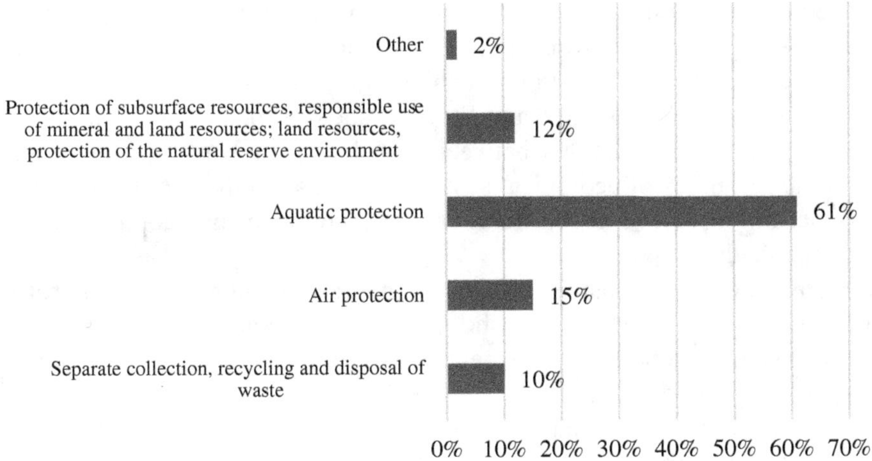

Fig. 23.2. Key areas of fundraising for environmental projects in Russian regions, %.

Source: Compiled by the authors based on Ref. [4].

ecological culture and investor relations, accelerating positive transformations [8].

In terms of the current situation, the Russian regions are characterized by the following key areas of fundraising for environmental projects (Fig. 23.2).

According to Fig. 23.2, activities related to the protection of the aquatic environment are in the lead. Other areas also receive attention.

In addition to investments from businesses and financing of sustainable development projects by regional authorities, the population's support has a significant resource. For example, according to VCIOM, in 2017, 32% of Russian citizens spent money on charity (the average size of such a donation was 900 rubles) [15]. In Moscow, e.g., the population donated about 3.6 billion rubles in 2017, which is more than 37% of the city's budget for landscaping [8].

23.4. Discussion

Within the framework of the study of the analyzed issue, we note that researchers such as Evgrafova and Kibitkin, speaking of the region, present it as a socio-economic system, which includes three specified subsystems: social, environmental, and economic [6]. The unity of these subsystems allows us to count on achieving the desired effects.

According to Strekalova and Frolov, "socio-ecological system refers to complex social relations between people (agents) and communities over the resources of ecological systems" [13]. According to the authors, this definition correlates the relationship of regional development with sustainable development.

Lukina connects sustainable development of territories with environmental marketing [8]. Thus, she proposes to conduct a social and environmental-economic assessment as part of the analysis of the regions' sustainability procedure.

Porfiriev attributes the principles of the green economy in sustainable regional development to such principles as "energy efficiency, resource conservation unity, and learning and formation of an ecological culture" [12].

We believe that the above points of view are correct. Nevertheless, it should be noted that within the current management paradigm adopted and implemented in territorial development, it is advisable to choose environmental marketing as the ideological basis for long-term relations, coordinating the interests of business, society, and government in choosing and justifying the desired trajectory of sustainable functioning [5].

23.5. Conclusion

At the present stage of economic development in Russia, there is an awareness of the importance of sustainable development of the regions, which is reflected in their socio-economic agenda, which has been transformed into a socio-eco-economic one. Environmental marketing acts as an integrator of alignment of interests between government, business, and local communities in finding reasonable compromises and achieving the desired interests of these audiences in terms of the environmental transformation of the social and economic system of the region. In addition to management initiatives and inclusion of business in the environmental agenda, to achieve the ambitious solutions, it is necessary to involve the population and ensure its involvement in the positive transformation undertaken, which is also part of the range of tasks to be solved within the ideological field of environmental marketing.

References

1. Government of the Russian Federation. Strategy of socio-economic development of the Far East and the Baikal region for the period up to 2025. Moscow, Russia; 2009. Available from: https://www.primorsky.ru/authorities/executive-agencies/departments/economics/development/strategy/dv-25.php
2. Presidential Executive Office. Decree No. 400 "On the National Security Strategy of the Russian Federation" . 2021 July 02. Available from: https://www.garant.ru/products/ipo/prime/doc/401325792
3. Presidential Executive Office. Decree No. 645 "On the Strategy for the Development of the Arctic Zone of the Russian Federation and Ensuring National Security for the Period up to 2035". 2020. Available from: https://www.garant.ru/products/ipo/prime/doc/74710556/
4. Badadyan LV, Pisareva EV. Development of environmental marketing in Russia. *Scientific Works of the Free Economic Society of Russia*, 2016; 201(4): 311–324.
5. Bondarenko VA, Guzenko NV, Romanishina TS. Marketing of spatial interaction in the socio-infrastructural development of the territory. *Bulletin of the South Russian State Technical University* (NPI). Series: Socio-economic Sciences. 2021; 14(3): pp. 116–125. DOI: 10.17213/2075-2067-2021-3-116-125
6. Evgrafova LE. Kibitkin AI. Application of scenario approach in management social-ecological-economic of systems of the fishery. *Modern Problems of Science and Education*, 2013; 6: p. 396.
7. Leszczynski NM, Sertakova EA, Pashova EV. Traditional economy of the indigenous peoples of Northern Asia, living in areas with extreme climate. *Siberian Anthropological Journal*, 2021; 5(1): 20–29.
8. Lukina AV. The green marketing mode in the management of sustainable regional development — is this a marketing matter? *Drucker's Bulletin*, 2019; 3(30): 336–350. DOI: 10.17213/2312-6469-2019-3-336-350
9. Medvedev SO. Development of cluster structures on the principles of sustainable development. *Fundamental Research*, 2019; 11: 106–110.
10. Ministry of Education of the Krasnoyarsk Territory. Contest of projects of applied scientific research and experimental developments carried out by undergraduates, graduate students, and young scientists to ensure sustainable development of the Arctic and territories of the Far North. 2020. Available from: https://krao.ru/publications/federalnyie-konkursyi/konkurs-proektov-prikladnyih-nauchnyih-issledovanij-i-eksperimentalnyih-razrabotok-vyipolnyaemyih-magistrantami-i-aspirantami-v-tselyah-obespecheniya-ustojchivogo-razvitiya-arktiki-i-territorij-krajnego-severa/
11. Peattie R. *Green Marketing*. London, UK: Pitman Publishing; 1992.

12. Porfiriev BN. "Green" economy: Global development trends and prospects. *Bulletin of the Russian Academy of Sciences*, 2012; 82(4): 323–333.
13. Strekalova A, Frolov D. Social and ecological system as an object of ecological territorial marketing: Analysis and synthesis of definitions. *Journal of Volgograd State University. Economics*, 2015; 4(33): 194–203. DOI: 10.15688/jvolsu3.2015.4.19
14. United Nations. Sustainable Development Goals. Available from: https://www.un.org/sustainabledevelopment/ru/sustainable-development-goals/
15. VCIOM. Analytical review: Charitable fundraising in Russia. 2017 Sept 15. Available from: https://wciom.ru/analytical-reviews/analiticheskii-obzor/blagotvoritelnyj-fandrajzing-v-rossii
16. Zaitseva DS, Krakovetskaya IV. Green marketing: Tendencies and perspectives. *Bulletin of Kemerovo State University. Series: Political, Sociological and Economic Sciences*, 2016; 2: 55–59.
17. Zakharova TV, Krakovetskaya IV. Environmental marketing: Market assistance, "green" advertising and other tools for promoting technological innovations in university cities of the world and Russia. *Tomsk State University Journal of Economics*, 2018; 42: 231–245.

https://doi.org/10.1142/9789811264252_0024

Chapter 24

Fundamental Aspects of Sustainability Reporting Based on GRI Standards: Evolution of Development, Substance, and Content of Integrated Reporting

Lyudmila N. Usenko[†], **Victoriya A. Guzey**[*,‡], **Natalia M. Usenko**[§] **and Svetlana S. Lavrenchenko**[¶]

Rostov State University of Economics, Rostov-on-Don, Russia
[†]*ln-u@mail.ru*
[‡]*79185140585@yandex.ru*
[§]*ln-u@mail.ru*
[¶]*thepop2010@mail.ru*

Abstract: The current conditions for the development of the Integrated Reporting Concept predetermine an increase in the efficiency and investment attractiveness of those companies that apply integrated reporting. This is true because the integrated reporting allows for a holistic view of the development of an economic entity, facilitates interaction with interested users, and attracts additional investment. The possibility of detailed disclosure of financial and non-financial information allows investors to study the organization's activities in greater depth and formulate the necessary conclusions in the context of the

[*]Corresponding author.

planned cooperation. Additionally, the formation of integrated reporting significantly increases the level of implementation of the financial risk management mechanism and operational control. Integrated reporting allows forming and interconnecting of information flows characterizing the performance of organizations in terms of their sustainable development. Taking this information as a basis, top management and investors will be able to minimize costs and existing risks and make informed decisions that are strategically important for the organization's development. High-quality information contained in integrated reporting will be in line with the current level of development of global economic relations. It will meet the needs of stakeholders to the fullest extent, given the development of opportunities for its standardization. Integrated reporting will need to establish a set of underlying indicators that need to be disclosed and then provide a format for the information provided. Nowadays, more and more organizations recognize the need for conscious forward-looking financial management based on scientific methodologies for predicting its direction, adapting it to the overall development objectives of the organization and the economic environment. This research reveals the evolution of development, substantive content, and content of integrated reporting in current conditions, including scientific research into the following issues: outlining the fundamental aspects of sustainability reporting based on GRI standards, studying the evolution of development, substantive content, and content of integrated reporting.

Keywords: Integrated reporting; Sustainability reporting; Stakeholders; Sustainability reporting guidelines; Economic; Social and environmental performance of business entities.

24.1. Introduction

At the current stage of development, the economy of Russia is affected by crisis phenomena, which is a factor stimulating business structures to carry out integration processes. Simultaneously, a stakeholder approach is of great importance within the framework of corporate governance. In the context of sustainability reporting indicators, information is generated in the context of the implementation of management approaches to the implementation of impact management in relation to the set of economic, environmental, and social components.

Significant interest on the part of scientists regarding the study of the essential content and content of sustainability reporting arose in connection with the aggravation of environmental, social, and economic problems about 50 years ago. These scientific studies are now actively conducted by both Russian and foreign scientists.

The scientific significance of the research lies in the analysis of the evolution of development and the study of the essence and content of integrated reporting. The relevance of comprehensive coverage of this issue is due to the need to study issues of sustainability reporting based on GRI standards, the underlying purpose of which is the need for detailed disclosure of financial and non-financial information, including information on the environmental, social, and economic components of the activities of business entities within the reporting framework.

The hypothesis of this research is based on the position that detailed research into the evolution of the development, substantive content, and content of integrated reporting will attract additional attention from the scientific community, business representatives, and the general public to enhance its implementation in the practical activities of business entities. The current conditions of functioning of enterprises are extremely dynamic and subject to the impact of internal and external factors in relation to the business entity. In this regard, detailed disclosure of the essence and content of sustainability reporting is an important aspect of improving the performance of today's enterprises by attracting interest to this issue and disclosing the prospects for organizations that form sustainability reporting.

The chapter investigates fundamental aspects of sustainability reporting based on GRI standards.

In connection with the formulated objective, the following tasks are set and solved in the present research:

- To present the fundamental aspects of sustainability reporting based on GRI standards are presented;
- To study the evolution of development, the essence, and content of integrated reporting.

The methodological basis of the research is the fundamental statements concerning the formation of the sustainable development paradigm and the main aspects of integrated reporting.

24.2. Methods

The present work is written based on recent scientific research by scientists concerning the evolution of development and the essence and content of integrated reporting.

The methodological basis for this research is the basic essence, principles, postulates, and sequence of integrated reporting formulated within the international community.

The following methods were used for scientific research: analysis and synthesis, content analysis of documents, and systematization and synthesis of the research results. Additionally, logical and systemic approaches were applied during the study of the main stages of forming the concept of sustainable development.

24.3. Results

In the context of sustainable development reporting indicators, a set of measures to improve the performance of the organization, within the framework of the following elements, is carried out:

- Ensuring occupational health and safety at production facilities;
- Taking measures for energy saving and energy efficiency of production processes;
- Creating conditions for the development of human resources potential in business entities;
- Creation of prerequisites for making its own contribution to the development of the regions where business entities are present.

For the first time, information regarding reporting on sustainable development was received in 1987 in the framework of the World Commission on Environment and Development. The Commission defined the concept of sustainable development as "... meeting the needs of the present without compromising the ability of future generations to meet their own needs" [11]. In general, each economic entity in the course of its functioning has positive and negative impacts on the economic, environmental, and social components, making it possible to identify positive and negative impacts on the achievement of sustainable development by economic entities. GRI is a so-called global reporting initiative, i.e., a not-for-profit organization that implements the principles of reporting by economic entities in relation to sustainable development. The stated principles are the most widespread. According to the GRI's vision, sustainability reporting is the practical aspect of generating information for a wide range of the so-called stakeholders about the economic, environmental, and social impacts each business entity has during its activities. At the same time, the environmental impact of an economic operator can be identified using sustainability reporting, which will enable maximum opportunities to be realized, considering the current internationally recognized rules.

The GRI carries out the process of creating the basic idea, principles, and rules of preparing reports on sustainable development that would be available for all users and also for the issuers and that would comply with the current achievements in this field. In today's society and dynamically developing markets, it is important to develop the content of sustainability reporting so that it is accessible to a wide range of users and becomes common practice in the economic life of countries rather than an uncommon event accessible to only a few companies.

The non-profit organization GRI has gradually and consistently produced the Sustainability Reporting Guidelines. According to the standards formed, it is important which aspect (economic, environmental, or social) has an impact, whether internal or external. Additionally, it is important to assess and analyze the extent of the impact, i.e., its reference limits. For example, within the environmental pillar, the level of greenhouse gas emissions in the course of the company's activities is important, which may impact internal processes in the context of operating companies and the interests of external stakeholders, which may include consumers, suppliers, or distributors. In the course of its activities, GRI has issued G1, G2, G3, and G4 standards. The essential difference between the latest G4 version and the G3 version is the fact that under the G3 version, only the impacts of factors controlled by a functioning economic entity had to be covered and reflected in the sustainability report. Under the G4 version, economic entities are advised to assess and analyze the broad range of impacts of the economic entity. This means that the company, preparing sustainability reports in the context of the G4 version, should prepare information in the reports which will contribute to creating an understanding of the boundaries of the impact of the economic entity on each of the sustainability components of the company, namely the economic, environmental, and social ones. Simultaneously, economic entities that do not have a mechanism for determining the impact they have had prior to the transition to the G4 version should form it within their activities, document it, and show it in the sustainability report to be formed. Additionally, business entities reporting on sustainability are encouraged to pay significant attention to the economic, environmental, and social impacts of their own supply chains, which is a key requirement of the new, broader substantive reporting requirements of the G4 version.

The GRI G4 Guidelines are currently implemented, providing a detailed guide to sustainability reporting. At the end of 2017, information about the preparation of GRI standards became available. This innovation was an important milestone in developing GRI guidelines because the non-profit organization GRI did not previously have standards. As of July 1, 2018, the G4 guidelines are no longer valid, and all companies that report on sustainability have switched to GRI standards. However, the most advanced organizations and those using sustainability reporting standards for the first time are advised to only report according to the new standards.

It should be noted that the set of disclosures in reporting under the GRI standards, in general, does not differ much from the requirements of the G4 Guidelines. Companies making the transition from G4 to GRI standards will not experience significant changes. The main essence of the difference lies in the change in the structural form of the GRI instruction and, in addition, in the transformation of the terminology used. The GRI standard positions itself not so much as an instruction for the formation of sustainability reporting but as a norm that companies have to comply with. It should be noted that the GRI standard is a set of linked standards to be used by organizations that prepare sustainability reports. The said set comprises 36 standards divided into four series: 100, 200, 300, and 400. The 100 Series are universal standards to be used by all sustainability reporting organizations. These standards provide information on common approaches and principles of sustainability reporting. Additionally, within the framework of these standards, it is necessary to specify a set of general information to be disclosed by all companies.

The 200, 300, and 400 series of standards are applied by companies at their discretion, depending on the aspects to be disclosed in the sustainability report. For example, the 200 series standards are aimed at generating economic information. This includes GRI Standard 202: Market Presence, under which a company has to form a picture of its own contribution to the economic development of the region of location or certain regions of the country.

As for the 300 series of standards, it requires a disclosure of information about the environmental component of a company's sustainability reporting. In the context of these standards, the following are distinguished: "GRI 301: Materials," "GRI 302: Energy," and "GRI 303: Water."

The 400 Series standards are the most comprehensive in that they include the requirements for the disclosure of issues in the context of the social component, which include approaches to the implementation of the employment and the implementation of the marking of goods to inform consumers.

This separation of the series of standards as stand-alone documents is of significant interest because all changes made will affect only the standard to be amended rather than the entire document, as was the case in the past when one had to amend the entire document. This measure will save as much as possible on the investment in the formation and implementation of the new standards. For example, two G300 standards were opened for revision on 16 January 2017: "GRI 303: Water" and "GRI 403: Health and Safety."

An essential aspect of the new GRI standards is the fact that companies can apply the standards individually and in combination to generate information about specific aspects of their operations without creating a full version of a sustainability report in accordance with the GRI standards.

For example, the company in question must report to stakeholders (activists) on its emissions of greenhouse gases and other substances into the atmosphere. In this case, the company may form the information only in the frame of the standard "GRI 305: Commission" to reflect the information in the frame of the required data. It is necessary to note that possibility of only partial use of GRI standards could be applied earlier. However, comprehensive instructions on such use of GRI standards appeared only in the last version, which, in our opinion, will be an impetus for the universal use of GRI standards.

With regard to the principles of the formation of sustainability reports, it should be noted that the new standards have retained them in their entirety. However, the said principles are now subdivided into principles for defining the content of the report and principles for defining its quality. Principles for defining the content of the report and, in particular, the emphasis on materiality are considered to be fundamentally new. This principle of materiality is a stumbling block in preparing a sustainability report.

The materiality principle implies that companies strive to optimize the content of the report in terms of the disclosure of the most material aspects of their activities, as well as to present only the key sustainability topics. Simultaneously, companies preparing sustainability reports should clearly understand what is material and what is not. An essential principle of sustainability reporting is the involvement of stakeholders in the process and the consolidation and consideration of their opinions. In accordance with the GRI guidelines, stakeholder engagement on a systematic basis enables a company to form preferences regarding the disclosure of information in the sustainability report, which, in turn, increases the credibility of the reviewed organization and its corporate reporting.

Applying the principles of GRI standards, the companies formulate specific topics concerning their own operation to be included in the sustainability report, namely market presence, energy use, waste management, human resources, training, human rights, non-discrimination, interaction with local communities, etc. As a continuation of the study, the company compiles information following the G200, G300, and G400 standards, according to the topics formulated.

Within each GRI standard, a set of indicators relating to specific topics (topic-specific disclosures) is generated. Each indicator is to be disclosed to a certain extent in the framework of the requirements and recommendations and clarifications contained in the GRI standard. In the case of a reporting organization, it has to disclose the information according to the GRI base case; the choice of one or more of the most significant indicators should be made. If the organization has chosen the so-called comprehensive option, to prepare a sustainability report, it is necessary to form a set of indicators included in the selected topics of the standard and include additional, comprehensive information on the organization's functioning, which is of a general nature.

Sustainability reporting can be a stand-alone document, or it can be part of other information sources. Nevertheless, it is also essential to have a GRI content index that will generate links to disclosing all elements of GRI standards. This will make it easier for Russian companies to cope with the changes as they prepare a sustainability report as part of their annual report.

The formation of public corporate reporting, including sustainability reports, can be considered one of the tools to ensure sustainability.

It should be noted that more than 7,000 companies worldwide publish such reports. The practice of preparing sustainability reports in Russia is about 15 years old, during which about 160 companies have prepared sustainability reports.

Increasing the qualitative and quantitative characteristics of the reporting information included in sustainability reports contributes to an increased level of transparency of business entities, which, in turn, has a significant positive impact on the degree of stakeholder confidence in the company in question (investors, consumers, suppliers, employees, public organizations, etc.). This is critical because stakeholders have a significant need for detailed information on the present and future impact of the company's operations.

Russian companies have applied sustainability reporting guidelines for about 19 years. Since 2000, due to the acceleration of the globalization process, the sustainability reporting guidelines have been continuously adjusted to achieve the greatest effect from their use and ensure the integration of information flows in terms of economic, social, and environmental performance generated by the non-financial reports of individual organizations. That is why, in our opinion, sustainability reporting is an integrated system containing several elements that ensure the achievement of the main goal, namely, the disclosure of information in the context of economic, environmental, and social performance for the needs of internal and external stakeholders, which can include managers, employees, federal and regional authorities, counterparties, and business partners.

This allows us to consider that the interconnection of information flows, formed within the framework of sustainability reporting, delivered to its internal and external users can be successfully used to form and make informed managerial decisions in the context of further prospects for the enterprise's functioning.

In January 2014, the GRI presented its fourth generation of G4 Sustainability Reporting Guidelines to the Public Chamber of the Russian Federation. Two years later, in 2016, the old versions of the GRI Guidelines were no longer applicable due to their irrelevance. The new version of the GRI Sustainability Reporting Guidelines has undergone the following changes.

Within the framework of this document, business reporting forms have been adjusted, which was facilitated by the investors' desire to have transparent information flows generated in an accessible form. Additionally, these changes in the reporting format have been driven by an increased level of social awareness. Stakeholders require not only financial performance indicators but also information on the environmental and climatic impact of the business entity in question and the company's respect for human rights.

In global practice, several organizations form standards for non-financial public reporting. The most applied are the so-called GRI Guidelines. About 80% of all public non-financial reporting in the world is formed using these Guidelines. The guidelines contain specific terminology, including the term 'materiality', which refers to how transactions carried out by companies can be classified as material, as well as being required to be disclosed. It is also a definition that considers the interests of all stakeholders, not just shareholders.

The GRI guidelines' main purpose for innovation is to meet the rapidly changing needs of the corporate sector. The GRI Guidelines have a modular structure, which facilitates adjustment of reporting methodology to the specific industry, thus facilitating the creation of tailored reports in any sector with a possibility of quick modification in the direction of reducing information disclosed or adding necessary items.

The practice of applying the Sustainability Reporting Guidelines is much more modest because most companies do not consider it necessary to draw up a report on sustainable development. However, the preparation and implementation of such reports is a significant breakthrough in achieving European business standards in the context of increasing the responsibility and transparency of economic operators. Drawing up such reports also constitutes an additional advantage for the company's reputation, constituting it before foreign investors because potential investors will become convinced that the economic operator plans long-term development and takes care of its positive reputation, which ultimately makes it more trustworthy as an investment object for investors.

The current conditions of economic development in Russia contribute to an increased interest in the study of the problems of achieving sustainable development within the business community. In this context, the growing importance of public opinion, legislative initiatives shaping environmental constraints, the increasing need for resources, the perception of their limited availability and constantly rising costs, and, in addition, the growth of competitors constantly shaping sustainability reporting with a market advantage contribute to the need for a sustainable development strategy.

The fundamental point here is that financial and investment decisions need to be made in light of the environmental and social impact generated by the company during its operations. In this context, the sustainability framework for a business is, in the long term, a critical factor in strategic development and increasing business reputation, market capitalization, and competitiveness.

In terms of sustainability strategy, the above has a decisive impact on the investment appeal of a company: a portfolio investor looking to acquire shares in a company needs to appreciate all risks involved, both financial and non-financial. For this reason, an investor evaluates the value of a company through the prism of reputational and environmental risks.

The issue of sustainability is particularly important for public and non-public companies. Nowadays, reputational risks largely depend on the company's level of social responsibility and the degree of its care for the environment. If the company in question generates transparent and comprehensible information within the economic, environmental, and social components of sustainability, it significantly increases the trust of counterparties, potential investors, and other stakeholders.

The need to achieve sustainability and translate it into a long-term development strategy is related to the fact that the problems it solves form the company's overall value chain, from the product design and production phase to the creation and growth of the customer base. These problems are systemic, involving the resolution of stakeholder conflicts of interest as part of achieving the company's financial and non-financial goals. Additionally, this involves interaction with stakeholders whose impact on the company's sustainability in the long term can have a significant effect. Decisions taken over the long term are implemented under conditions of uncertainty, which are shaped by climate change, transforming legislation, conflicting interests of customers and owners, and dynamically changing geopolitical events.

The practice of analysis identifies three fundamental pillars that constitute the three building blocks of long-term corporate sustainability, namely economic, social, and environmental responsibility. These three pillars of long-term sustainability are important aspects of stakeholder engagement. Therefore, they need to be integrated into companies' development strategies and business plans.

The G4 version of the Sustainability Reporting Guidelines has undergone the following significant changes. First, the new version has set a specific deadline for companies' transition to sustainability reporting in a two-year timeframe. Second, 27 new reporting elements were added. Third, there have been changes to the Sustainability Manual structure.

In general, the structure of the G4 Guidelines has been shaped in line with the objective of providing support for the preparation of sustainability reports. There are two parts to the G4 Guidelines. The first part, the Reporting's Principles and Standard Disclosures, sets out the principles and standard elements of the reporting process. The second part, called the Implementation Manual, focuses on implementation guidance. In general, sustainability reporting is an integrated system comprising a set of components that allow achieving its fundamental objective, i.e., providing detailed information on the economic, social, and environmental performance of economic entities for internal and external stakeholders (specialists and managers, federal and regional authorities, counterparties, experts, and business partners).

The above shows that the existing interrelation of economic, environmental, and social information generated by sustainability reporting on the one hand and internal and external stakeholders on the other provides the basis for the formation and making of management decisions concerning the future development of the organization in question.

The above allows concluding that sustainability reporting has come a long way in its formation and development. Each innovation that enabled the formulation of a new version of the standard allowed for the inclusion of all new indicators characterizing the sustainability of the corporate structure in terms of the underlying criteria of economic, environmental, and social responsibility.

Integrated reporting refers to the integrated production of financial and non-financial indicators within a reporting framework. The need for non-financial reporting is driven by the existence and dynamic development of globalization processes, the transformation of legislation, and increased requirements for the information generated by stakeholders. The formation of detailed non-financial information and its display in open sources of information allows us to talk about the evolution and development of various kinds of global ratings and sustainability indices, most of which significantly impact investment attractiveness and the shareholder value of corporate structures. The emergence of sustainability reporting has contributed to the attention of stock markets. Stock exchanges, representing around 70% of the securities market, are now proclaiming their intent to promote sustainability in their markets.

The practice of non-financial reporting has been used in Russia for 20 years. However, not more than a quarter of all Russian companies have adopted sustainability reporting. Each new version of the sustainability guidelines increases the requirements for non-financial reporting and, at the same time, acts as an important aspect of regulation in the global community. Since 2017, around 6,000 companies in the EU have been preparing and publishing sustainability reports. In Russia, mandatory non-financial disclosure requirements are now in place for specific categories of companies. The Concept for Developing Public Non-Financial Reporting, approved on May 5, 2017 [1], is significant support. This Concept should significantly improve the transparency of business conduct of Russian companies.

In general, the accounting (financial) statements of Russian organizations have specific features due to their diverse organizational and legal form. There are two main types of organizations in Russia: commercial and non-commercial.

Many economists pay attention to the essence and content of the generated accounting reports. A well-known academic economist Kovalev interprets the term "accounting reports" as follows: "Accounting reports and especially the balance sheet represents the best financial model of an enterprise" [7]. Describing the term "accounting," he echoes the Federal Law "On accounting," formulating the definition of accounting statements as follows: "Accounting statements are a system of indicators on the property and financial position of an entity, as well as on the financial results of its activities for the reporting period, presented, as a rule, in tabular form and formed directly as a result of closing the accounts in General Ledger."

Getman believes that the accounting (financial) statements imply information in the context of the financial position of the economic entity on the reporting date, the financial results of its activities, and cash flows for the reporting period, which is systematized in accordance with the requirements established by the Federal Law "On accounting" [4].

It is necessary to point out the fact that Kovalev identifies the shortcomings that exist in his own definition of accounting statements and formulates an approach to improving its concept. "Can any set of indicators be considered a system?" He then formulates a correction, "Of course not … In order for a set of indicators to be considered a system, it should have some "organizing principle," that is, something common, uniting the indicators. Establishing this "… organizing point is a fundamental step in the process of constructing an indicator system" [7]. In examining the underlying aspects of traditional reporting, problems have been identified with the logic and consistency of reporting forms, reflecting only certain aspects of the organization's functioning and forcing top management and potential investors to devote considerable effort to find the necessary data for management decision-making. This has been the driving force behind the need to develop a convenient and comprehensive tool for regulatory and control purposes, namely integrated reporting, which presents new opportunities for shaping the information provided on the functioning of companies in relation to stakeholder interests.

The need to develop and implement integrated reporting arises under the following conditions:

- It is impossible to obtain exhaustive information when using financial reporting due to the increasing need for awareness among stakeholders;
- Business entities become increasingly oriented toward social processes and requirements while assuming environmental responsibilities;
- Any business unit strives to achieve sustainable development; therefore, the achievements of the present and the future successes become important;
- Current non-financial reporting forms, both social and environmental, are a useful source of information, but they do not contain a mapping of the interrelationships between various aspects of a company's activity and its results, which does not provide exhaustive information on potential value creation over a long period;
- Nowadays, there is a significant need to gain comprehensive knowledge about the functioning of a business entity and about the possibilities of its development to make managerial decisions, which generates interest in the formation of more detailed studies [10].

In the framework of this research, the authors reviewed the views of economists on the formation of integrated reporting (Table 24.1).

In accordance with the authors' position, the Integrated Reporting Concept contains information about individual aspects of the organization's functioning. These reports are prepared considering the strategic objective and possible risks, which allows forecasting the organization's development and value creation opportunities in the short, medium, and long term.

Our research into the definitions of integrated reporting has enabled us to form our own view of the term. In our opinion, integrated reporting should be understood as an advanced tool for informing stakeholders

Table 24.1. Overview of existing perspectives on the concept of "integrated reporting."

No.	Author	Definition
1	International Integrated Reporting Council IIRC	Reporting that combines financial and non-financial information and reflects an entity's ability to create and sustain value over the short, medium, and long term [6]
2	V. G. Kogdenko, M. V. Melnik, and T. O. Khachaturova	Summary of how an organization's strategy and management methods, performance, and prospects (considering the external environment) affect the creation of value in the short, medium, and long term [9]
3	T. V. Malinovskaya	A new model of corporate reporting is based on the concept of integrated thinking, which implies the interconnection of financial and management reports, corporate management and remuneration reports, and sustainability reports [8]
4	V. G. Getman	Reporting that contains such information as is important for financial and other types of capital management. It is more transparent, revealing not only the data of the reporting period and the company's short-term prospects but also the opportunities arising in the medium and long term [5]
5	Ernst and Young	The process of assessing a company's ability to create value over time by collecting, consolidating, and analyzing qualitative and quantitative indicators of its performance in the reporting period to produce an integrated report [3]
6	Deloitte	Reporting that integrates different types of reporting into a coherent whole and explains an organization's ability to create and sustain value over time [2]

about the most significant aspects of the activities of an economic entity, as well as its position in the market for goods and services, expressed in financial and non-financial indicators, which allows formulating an idea of the results of activities already achieved and determine the prospects for its development.

The main objectives of integrated reporting are as follows:

- The formation of comprehensive information about the resources that have been used by the organization and its interaction with the external environment;

- Detailed disclosure of information to improve the quality of information for subsequent integrated reporting to investors, which will contribute to the efficiency of capital allocation;
- Creation of an effective integrated approach to the formation and implementation of corporate reporting, which includes a variety of reporting forms that provide a comprehensive picture to stakeholders and have a decisive impact on the creation of value for the company in the long term;
- Increasing the level of responsibility and improving the mechanism for managing resources and the organization's capital (financial, human, social, natural, productive, and intellectual). These types of capital must consciously interact within the organization to make management decisions in the short, medium, and long term;
- Raising the awareness of all stakeholders about the mechanisms of functioning and results of the organization's activities.

The International Integrated Reporting Council, an authoritative organization, has formulated the fundamental building blocks of integrated reporting. These blocks are as follows:

- Characteristics of the business entity that generates integrated reporting and its operating environment;
- Management structure of its impact on value creation in the short, medium, and long term;
- Existing opportunities and risks that allow threats to be explored in relation to the organization's activities.

The implemented strategy and resource allocation planning process provide insight into the organization's aspirations and ability to achieve them.

A view of the business model applied allows one to see the process of planning for value growth opportunities in the short and long term.

The performance of the studied business unit contributes to understanding the organization's success in achieving its strategy and the level of its performance.

Possible future prospects contribute to an understanding of the opportunities, threats, and uncertainties that the company will face in the implementation of its own strategy. Moreover, possible future prospects allow modeling the potential consequences of implementing the chosen business model of the organization and determining its results for the future.

Thus, integrated reporting contains constituent elements, which, on the one hand, characterize the organization's achievements in the present and, on the other hand, contain information about the forecast development of the organization in the aggregate, its development strategy, and information about the business model used, which will allow assessing its prospects for the future.

The current conditions of the development of the Integrated Reporting Concept predetermine the increase of efficiency and investment attractiveness of those companies which apply integrated reporting. This is true because integrated reporting forms a holistic view of the development of a business entity, facilitates interaction with interested users, and attracts additional investment. The possibility of detailed disclosure of financial and non-financial information enables investors to investigate the activities of the organization in greater depth and formulate the necessary conclusions regarding the planned cooperation. Additionally, the formation of integrated reporting significantly increases the level of implementation of the financial risk management mechanism and operational control.

Integrated Reporting allows forming and interconnecting of information flows that characterize the performance of the organization in terms of its sustainable development. By using this information as a basis, the organization's top management and investors will be able to make informed decisions that are strategically important for the organization's development, and that can minimize costs and existing risks.

In addition to its advantages, integrated reporting has some disadvantages caused by the transition of companies from traditional financial reporting to integrated reporting. The main difficulty is the cost, both financial, time-consuming, and personal, to be incurred in the preparation of reports. There is also a need for personnel training, software, etc. Given the high cost of the formation of integrated reporting, such an opportunity exists only for large economic entities. However, the formation of reporting for large companies that can bear the cost of labor, time, and financial nature, is associated with the emergence of problems of another kind: an increased level of risk of not keeping trade secrets, approximation of the values of predictive indicators, the lack of comparability of non-comparable information, etc.

This raises the dilemma of whether the organization has additional capacity to produce integrated reports or whether the financial, time, and labor resources required to produce them should be used more efficiently. This dilemma would apply to those organizations that have produced integrated reporting but have not received any significant investment.

In our view, the high quality of information contained in integrated reporting will be in line with state-of-the-art in global economic relations and meet the needs of stakeholders to the fullest extent, given the development of opportunities for standardization. Integrated reporting should formulate a set of underlying indicators that need to be disclosed and then formulate the information format to be provided.

24.4. Discussion

This chapter has revealed that the concept of sustainable development has emerged as a response to increasing environmental, social, and economic challenges, which has led to the gradual formation and development of the content and substance of integrated reporting. Nowadays, integrated reporting has been adopted by the global community as a tool to improve the transparency of business, disclosing information for all stakeholders concerning economic, environmental, and social components. The international community actively works to develop standards for integrated reporting. Companies leading in their industries successfully compile and publish the information displayed in integrated reporting. Following the principles of disclosure of information on social, environmental, and economic aspects of organizations' functioning will enable business community representatives to achieve positive long-term effects. Implementing the tenets of sustainability has contributed to the concept of corporate sustainability aimed at improving the performance of business representatives. As applied by business leaders in different economic sectors, the concept of sustainability becomes a new paradigm of their existence.

24.5. Conclusion

Nowadays, more and more organizations recognize the need for conscious forward-looking financial management based on scientific methodologies for predicting its direction and adapting it to the overall development objectives of the organization and the economic environment.

This study reveals the evolution of the development, essence, and content of integrated reporting in current conditions, including a scientific study of the following issues: fundamental aspects of sustainability reporting based on GRI standards, the evolution of the development, essence, and content of integrated reporting.

References

1. Government of the Russian Federation. Order No. 876-r "On the Concept of Development of Public Non-Financial Reporting and the Action Plan for its Implementation." Moscow, Russia; 2017. Available from: https://base.garant.ru/71673686/
2. Ageev AI, Galushkina MV, Kopkova EV, Smirnova VA, Stukelberger K. Integrated reporting: A challenge for management. Moscow, Russia: Institute for Economic Strategies, National Center for Scientific and Technical Information; 2017.
3. E&Y. Seven questions about non-financial reporting that CEOs should have an answer to. Available from: http://www.ey.com/Publication/vwLUAssets/Seven-things-CEOs-boards-should-ask-about-reporting-RU/$FILE/Seven-things-CEOs-boards-should-should-ask-about-reporting-RU.pdf
4. Getman VG, Polenova SN, Golysheva NI, Mislavskaya NA, Grishkina SN, Nurmukhamedova KSh *et al. Modern Accounting and its Problems*. Moscow, Russia: Financial University; 2014.
5. Getman VG. On the concepts and the structure of international integrated reporting standard. *Accounting. Analysis. Auditing*, 2014; 1: 74–85.
6. International Integrated Reporting Council (IIRC). International Integrated Reporting Framework. 2013. Available from: https://integratedreporting.org/wp-content/uploads/2015/03/13-12-08-THE-INTERNATIONAL-IR-FRAMEWORK-2-1.pdf
7. Kovalev VV, Patrov VV. *How to Read a Balance Sheet*. 3rd ed. Moscow, Russia: Finance and Statistics; 2003.
8. Malinovskaya NV. Integrated reporting: Theory, methodology, and practice (Thesis for the Degree of Doctor of Economics). Moscow, Russia: Financial University under the Government of the Russian Federation; 2016.
9. Melnik, MV, Kogdenko VG. Analysis of integrated reporting: The natural capital. *Economic Analysis: Theory and Practice*, 2016; 4: 72–84.
10. Novozhilova YV. Integrated reporting and its place in the system of corporate reports. *Social and Humanitarian Knowledge*, 2015; 1(4): 248–255.
11. World Commission on Environment and Development (WCED). *Our Common Future*. 1st ed. Oxford, UK: Oxford University Press; 1987. Available from: https://sustainabledevelopment.un.org/content/documents/5987our-common-future.pdf

https://doi.org/10.1142/9789811264252_0025

Chapter 25

Peculiarities of Planning and Neutralization of Risks in Logistics Distribution Systems

Darya V. Kozaeva[†], Tatiana B. Erokhina[*,‡] and Vadim B. Ukraintsev[§]

Rostov State University of Economics, Rostov-on-Don, Russia
[†]daria.ukraintseva@yandex.ru
[‡]tb.erohina@gmail.com
[§]rsue.spmes@bk.ru

Abstract: The chapter shows that the basic component of logistics management is the formation of specific objectives based on detailed planning and forecasting of organizational and functional complex activities that provide logistics processes that form a supply chain. The sections of the detailed plan must not contradict the dominant goals but identify the possible risks for new planned activities arising within the logistics distribution system. The systemic and consistent implementation of goals-dominants, covering the entire distribution system and forming a multi-level structure of supply chain management, is realized through the achievement of objectives planned at lower levels of planning. In summarizing the study, the authors formed the view that the

[*]Corresponding author.

systemic development of plans for logistics activities, covering procurement, production processes, and the area of distribution at the level of operational planning, contains certain guarantees of success in a changing external and internal environment. Logistics planning is differentiated by volume, territorial, and temporal scope. The emergence of crises leads to the need for program and strategic planning, as well as monitoring the implementation of plans.

Keywords: Logistics; Planning; Agribusiness; Distribution systems.

25.1. Introduction

The organization of material flow in logistics is the result of preceding sales planning, then production planning, and finally procurement planning. Each element involved in this chain usually has many private goals, which, in practice, are not always consistent with each other and may even contradict each other. Such a fact or imbalance can be eliminated if the identified situation can be subordinated to a system of goals or the main goal [1,4]. A typical global goal is to maximize profit, turnover, market share, economies of scale, and real benefits. The pursuit of reliability as a possible higher goal is based on the basic idea of preserving the existing potential.

Developing a system of goals is also possible using the mathematical method of weighting multiple goals, in which firm management decides to select one higher-level goal as the target function, considering other higher-level goals, which, however, should only be considered as concomitant conditions.

The following combinations of target functions and constraints are theoretically possible. Under the condition of a firm, profit or minimum rent should simultaneously maximize the turnover, market share, and equity or minimize costs. If these considerations transfer to logistics, then we can draw the following conclusion: logistics has the right to exist if the goals of its main spheres of activity, such as sales, production, and procurement, are in a state of competition with each other [3,5]. Since procurement logistics is designed to provide production with different materials in different quantities, the form of supply depends primarily on production goals. Production is primarily interested in the full use of its production capacity and, at the same time, to keep inventories of semi-finished products to a minimum, occupying accordingly small storage areas under unchanged conditions of agricultural production and achieving neutralization of risks in the logistics systems of distribution. The result of such aspirations would be the production of large batches of products with correspondingly large inventories of finished goods. Consequently, in this case, production would be focused not on the interests of the customer but on the creation of products for the warehouse. However, since the customers require their interests to be considered, production must consider the customer's desire to deal with production specifically aimed at this customer, which should have correspondingly decisive consequences for the closest logistics partners. Logistics must respond predominantly to the goals of other areas and define its own goals as inferior but oriented to considerations of prudence and balance. For warehousing, this may mean that the readiness of the distribution warehouse (distributor) for deliveries must adjust to customer requests, and the readiness of the purchasing (supply) warehouse must adjust to planned requirements or actual consumption of materials by cost centers. Two opposing logistical goals — high delivery readiness and low storage costs — when divided into target functions and parallel constraints, can be formulated as two possible combinations: for a predetermined delivery readiness, storage costs should be minimized; for a given storage cost, it is necessary to maximize delivery readiness.

Since neither of these two alternative goals in absolute form can be realized, each enterprise should choose an acceptable optimal option.

25.2. Materials and Methods

Setting goals will not work unless there is control, such as monthly variance analysis. Any planning must consider the possibility of such deviations before the sections of the plan are coordinated, and the individual targets for the relevant sections are recorded. Finally, the individual plans must be specified and checked for feasibility; this applies, above all, to budget planning.

The task of agricultural production planning is mainly to anticipate possible future changes in external and internal factors and consider their impact on the enterprise's activities to take timely countermeasures in the event of an unfavorable situation. The more reliable the decisions are, the better; decisions are reliable when their implementation leads to unambiguous and predictable results. A result, the probability of the occurrence of which is 100%, can be considered a reliable solution. However, such a solution in practice can be found only in rare cases. A reliable solution requires the analysis of a large amount of information. However, incomplete information is most often available in reality, and decisions can lead to different results depending on the overall situation. In such risky decisions, it is necessary to classify the results according to the degree of probability of their occurrence. If objective and subjective factors are such that the decision-maker has no data on the probability of events or cannot obtain them, then we speak of unreliable decisions. Production risk can be described more accurately using the formulas of probability theory, considering the expectation of risk. However, this does not help to find a solution.

An essential feature of production and economic activity is the principle of rationality, according to which a strictly defined goal is achieved with a minimum of means used or by maximizing the goal with the constancy of the means used. Risky situations must be avoided in both cases. However, if firm management makes risky decisions, it is because it hopes for a positive outcome. The higher the degree of risk with equal odds, the more difficult it is to make such decisions. Economic risk refers to the relationship between outcomes and inputs.

Plans record the targets to which all production processes are to be oriented. They also reflect the goals indicated by the management of the company as policy directives concerning the entire company and its individual enterprises, which are then elaborated in detail in private plans as private goals and implemented in the form of individual measures. It is important that the implementation of the latter lead to results that affect the achievement of the targets. Thus, the planning elements and individual private plans must be coordinated with each other and lead to the desired optimization of the firm's activities in the form of an overall plan.

The future is always fraught with uncertainty, and the necessary information about individual target values is either difficult to obtain or is purely estimative in nature. Therefore, any planning is associated with the risk, for example, that the profit received will be different from the planned. In a favorable combination of all circumstances, this risk is opposed to the chance of a deviation from the planned targets in the direction of their improvement, for example, getting a profit that exceeds the planned one.

The used planning methods can be reduced to two types. If individual private plans are formed and coordinated in a certain time sequence, then we are dealing with sequential planning. If all planning assumptions are consistent before planning begins (e.g., production capacity and purchasing volumes are consistent with the financial capabilities of the firm), then we are dealing with synchronous planning. Optimal planning in the firm is conducted with these features in mind. Gross planning errors in only one particular area can lead to the collapse of the entire planning process. For example, such a risk can be caused by the failure to solve capacity utilization problems even in one of the sectors having trouble. According to the law of balanced planning, this sector (production section) with the minimum output should be considered as a weak link in the production chain, although it is the sector that "dominates" the entire activity of the enterprise. Such bottlenecks reduce the productivity of other sectors in the agricultural enterprise and contribute to the emergence of idle capacity, which becomes redundant. Such a picture is observed in the absence of optimal planning.

In synchronous planning, considered cumulative, it is necessary to be particularly critical of the existence of bottlenecks. It is important to fix its shortcomings and prepare the ground for their elimination. In the framework of long-term planning, they can be eliminated by investments and full capacity utilization of other areas calculated on the production optimum.

Once target planning is completed, the production plan is determined as part of strategic planning. Planning for equipment, personnel, and research and development activities is carried out similarly.

The task of planning in industrial enterprises is to achieve coordination of quantitative and cost indicators to optimize the firm's activities. The planning of production and sales is based on volume indicators. The financial evaluation of production analyzes factors related to costs, prices, and exchange rates. Short-term planning is seen as an important component of management (regulation), and medium- and long-term planning — as a structuring moment of entrepreneurial activity. The longer the planning period, the more unreliable the information used in planning. Strategic framework planning is used to identify the main phases of logistics management, which serve as a guide for further levels of planning. The development forecasts of internal and external agencies and regional, national, and international development forecasts (estimates) are also considered. The planning of the firm of the respective industry must consider development trends and areas of activity, as well as social and political trends. The task of determining the area of use (sales) of the produced products falls on the share of long-term planning. Long-term and medium-term plans contain the necessary tasks for short-term plans, which, in turn, are necessary for the planning of production investments in the field of research and development and the financial support of the launch of new products, for which appropriate preparation of equipment and production technology is required.

25.3. Results and Discussion

When planning sales, production, and purchasing, the customer evaluations provided by the departments involved in customer contacts must be considered. This information is processed and considered in sales planning as information about the needs necessary for the production sector, where the actual production volume is determined. However, because of possible limitations, sales needs may not match production capabilities.

Production planning is completed by creating a demand plan for each item, from which forecasts for individual suppliers are determined. Next, a financial evaluation is required. Costs and profits are calculated, which could serve as a reason to revise the volume figures of the plans if it could lead to negative consequences for the company.

Finally, we note that planning that considers the interests of the enterprise can have an impact not only on internal affairs but also on external events.

The prerequisites for sales planning are the production program and the state of production capacity. When planning their development, attention should be paid to the volume indicators for each production unit for a long period. The decision-making process regarding products is of fundamental importance. Thus, it must be completed by the time of sales planning. The volume of sales as a prerequisite for any planning depends on many factors, such as trends in the economy or its individual industries, possible shifts in demand due to the appearance of substitute products, the behavior of competitors, and own participation in the market relations [7,8].

An elementary condition for any quality business planning is the consideration of exchange rate forecasts and the general economic outlook for the countries in which the firm operates or where it has important markets.

This refers to quotas, inflation, changes in demand, wage levels, material prices, and the presumed ratio between our own product prices and those of a competitor. We would like to emphasize that sales planning is a prerequisite for all other types of planning. If the distribution policy does not include warehousing, then changes in sales figures immediately affect the planning of production and purchasing programs. In reality, this leads to deviations in the planning figures. Therefore, the possibility of creating reserves (or a storage warehouse) must be considered. However, wastefulness is unacceptable in this case. In terms of production capacity and timing, it would be extremely risky to strive for 100% consideration of all reserves when developing plans. Either the production capacity will not be fully utilized, and the planning of deadlines will thus be flexible, or a constant change in the planned indicators as a response to deviations from the first days of work is necessary.

Planning without subsequent control and analysis of deviations is doomed to failure because, in this case, it is impossible to benefit either from subsequent planning or from actual production [2,9,10]. Under these conditions, the so-called budget planning is necessary, which is detailed monthly planning that covers all quantitative and cost production indicators. The basis of such work is the issuance of budgetary assignments for all production units. Therefore, constant contact of heads of production departments, through which the technological chain of product manufacturing passes, and with heads of corresponding controlling departments (planning and economic service) play a particularly important role because they allow timely and constantly evaluating and comparing the results of the current year with the approved budget indicators, which cannot be corrected retrospectively. Budget planning is a very effective tool of control in the hands of the firm's management. Constantly renewed short-term planning is an effective tool of adjustment. The planning allows us to forecast the future performance characteristics of the operation, taking into account the established indicators for the different time ranges. Such an updated budget allows taking countermeasures at the lower level of the production organization in case of undesirable deviations.

Planning and control should always go in parallel and complement each other. The task of control is to establish, by comparing the planned indicators with the actual ones, whether the planning is realistic, and if not, for what reason [6,11,12]. For better interpretation, deviations should be compared in absolute and relative forms. Additionally, the control calculations should be based not so much on quantitative as on financial indicators. When analyzing deviations of actual indicators from the planned ones and their consequences for production, the reasons for financial consequences, responsible persons, and corrective measures should be established. The control process is facilitated by the accounting within the budget planning and constantly renewed short-term planning of planned costs for each place of their origin and for each carrier. Depending on the causes of their occurrence, direct planned costs can be controlled by correlating them either with the production program or with the calculations for each area (workplace). Identified deviations may have different reasons: changes in prices or costs for materials or for the program due to manufacturing defects.

Costs in logistics are incurred primarily in the purchase, movement, storage, or distribution of materials and secondarily in the payment of services that are materially related to costs. This affects functions that have planning, management, coordination, and control as their primary focus, and it does not matter which section of the material flow is considered.

Costs in purchasing logistics begin with the shipment of materials by the supplier and end with their consumption at the customer's production site. Not all costs directly related to the procurement process and included solely in the purchase price are included in logistics costs.

Direct costs of raw materials and supplies can be attributed directly to the manufactured products without resorting to a roundabout way through a part of costs at the place of their occurrence. These costs directly depend on the volume of the production program. Thus, when analyzing the direct costs of raw materials and supplies, there are no problems that usually appear when controlling overhead costs. Nevertheless, their share in production is significant. Therefore, the analysis of direct costs is given special importance. Overhead costs are distributed in proportion to their size by sections and product types.

25.4. Conclusion

Supply and service flows can be generally described in terms of costs and profits using internal profit and loss calculations. Logistics costs consist of basic and handling costs. In internal profit and loss calculations, these costs are reflected in the items "Bank results" and "Special purchasing overhead costs." Logistics costs for cargo handling consist of indirect personnel costs, investment overhead costs, and balance sheet depreciation charges.

Planned costs are those that are set; that is, they correspond to a certain level of employment and consider all fixed costs and their corresponding variable costs.

Comparison of actual costs with planned ones is carried out according to their types, places of occurrence, and conversion factors. In this regard, it becomes clear whether deviations are random (and therefore can be excluded in the long term) or whether the trend of deviations is constant.

In order for controlling or firm management to be able to respond quickly to deviations, this type of analysis should be done as often as possible, but it makes the job of controlling more difficult.

Experience shows that at least a monthly analysis of deviations is necessary. The results of the analysis of deviations are presented to the responsible authorities as part of the production reporting, and their content and form should be focused on the intended purpose and the range of recipients. It is important that, in addition to the analysis of deviations, the documents submitted should contain specific proposals for solving the issue.

In terms of the cost-benefit ratio (i.e., given the great labor intensity of working with reports), the analysis of deviations should be limited to the essential items of deviations, which should be presented in order of importance to the enterprise, in absolute or percentage terms, in cumulative or free form.

References

1. Albekov AU, Parkhomenko TV. Prospective directions of logistic systems development in conditions of COVID-19 pandemic. *Bulletin of South Russian State Technical University (NPI)*. Series: Socio-Economic Sciences. 2021; 14(1): 114–121. DOI: 10.17213/2075-2067-2021-1-114-121
2. Boyko TS, Frolova NS, Gasanov EA (Eds.) Digitalization — the driver of economic growth in the post-pandemic period: Collection of articles on the materials of the All-Russian Scientific-Practical Conference with international participation: In 2 parts. Khabarovsk, Russia: RIC KSUEP; 2021. DOI: 10.38161/978-5-7823-0742-4-2021

3. Erokhina TB, Parkhomenko TV. Marketing and logistics communications in process of product distribution. *Vestnik of the Rostov State University of Economics*, 2019; 3(67): 66–70.
4. Erokhina TB, Parkhomenko TV. Scientific and applied synthesis of marketing and logistics in the processes of minimizing consumer risks. In: Kostoglodov DD (Ed.). *Market Infrastructure: Problems and Prospects*. Scientific Notes. Rostov-on-Don, Russia: Rostov State Economic University, 2020; pp. 62–65.
5. Kakajanov VM, Kudryavtseva SS. Using investments as a resource for the development of intelligent logistics. *Intellectual Logistics: Proceedings of the International Scientific-Practical Conference*, Astrakhan, Russia: Publishing House "Astrakhan State University"; 2021. pp. 102–105.
6. Khalyn VG. The significance of logistics in servicing growing volumes of e-commerce. *International Journal of Economics and Business Administration*, 2019 Nov; 7(SI2): 185–194. Available from: https://tinyurl.com/3vh9s6et
7. Levkin GG. Logistics in the *Agro-Industrial Complex: A Textbook*. 3rd edn. St. Petersburg, Russia: Lan Publisher; 2022.
8. Parkhomenko TV. Innovative solutions in green logistics of power supply systems. *Vestnik of the Rostov State University of Economics*, 2017; 3(59): 57–62.
9. Pochtarev TI. Supply chain management in the era of digitalization. In: *Scientific Search: Materials of the Thirteenth Scientific Conference of Postgraduate and Doctoral Students*. Chelyabinsk, Russia: South Ural State University; 2019.
10. Smirnova YA, Sadriev DS. Theoretical foundations for forming logistics and supply chain management. *International Journal of Applied Science and Technology "Integral,"* 2020; 2: 242–247. DOI: 10.24411/2658-3569-2020-10034
11. Turpak SM, Taran IO, Ostrohliad OO. Improvement of a system controlling a process of railcars unloading in the context of changes in temperature mode while operating. *Radio Electronics Computer Science Control*, 2018; 1(44): 183–191. DOI: 10.15588/1607-3274-2018-1-21
12. Vorontsova OV, Ukraintsev VB, Sedykh YA. Innovative energy producing structures in Russia. *Proceedings of the International Science and Technology Conference "EastConf" 2019*, Vladivostok, Russia; 2019. pp. 1–4. DOI: 10.1109/EastConf.2019.8725426

https://doi.org/10.1142/9789811264252_0026

Chapter 26

Review of the New International Scientific Journal on the Economics of Climate Change

Elena G. Popkova

MGIMO University, Moscow, Russia
E.Popkova@inno.mgimo.ru

Abstract: The chapter aims to justify the feasibility of combating climate change in the economy. To support cutting-edge research in this area, a new international scientific journal on the economics of climate change has been created, the relevance and review of which is the subject of this research. The research results contribute to the theory of sustainable development in the environmental economy, substantiating the systemic nature and close interdependence of economic growth and combating climate change. This emphasizes the relevance of a new international academic journal on the economics of climate change. The journal has been launched by a respected publisher Frontiers, in the series Frontiers in Environmental Economics. The new journal focuses on the economics of climate change, which refers to the totality of economic and environmental processes, linkages, and relationships arising in combating climate change in the economy. The uniqueness of the journal lies in its original subject area: the economics of climate change. The journal is notable for its multidisciplinary research on the economics of climate change. The research resolves the contradiction between the interests of society, the economy, and the environment by proposing a new scientific concept and a new promising area of research — the economics of climate change. The new international scientific journal on the economics of climate change has been created to stimulate the application of scientific thought to current issues in this subject area. The value of this new journal is that it pushes the boundaries of the study of climate change from ecology to environmental economics and breaks down the barriers to combating climate change in the economy.

Keywords: Economics of climate change; Fighting climate change; Economic growth; SDG 13; Sustainable development; Environmental economics.

26.1. Introduction

Climate change is occurring worldwide, and no territory or country can remain aloof from the global effort to slow it down and mitigate its negative effects [1,11,18,19,21]. Numerous recent studies [2,10,12,13,17] indicate that climate change is a common problem faced by humanity because it served as one of the causes of the COVID-19 pandemic (according to one of the main versions, COVID-19 is a zoonotic disease, that is, it has a natural-biological origin).

As climate change progresses, the interests of the environment (related to reducing the environmental costs of economic growth) are becoming increasingly divergent from the interests of society and the economy (related to accelerating the rate of economic growth). This contradiction of interests leads to the fact that the fight against climate change is carried out within a narrow ecological framework. The problem is that this framework hinders the fight against climate change. A growing number of scientific studies [4,5,7–9,14,15,20] confirm that the use of economic opportunities and tools can achieve impressive results far superior to those achieved within ecology.

Nevertheless, the theoretical and methodological basis for linking the economy to climate change is not strong enough; there is a lack of empirical research on this link, which is a gap in the literature. In this regard, the purpose of this research is to justify the feasibility of combating climate change in the economy. To support cutting-edge research in this area, a new international scientific journal on the economics of climate change has been created, the relevance and review of which is the subject of this research.

26.2. Materials and Method

The author applies an econometric methodology to determine the relationship of the economy to the fight against climate change. A correlation analysis is used to assess how closely the results of Sustainable Development Goal (SDG) 13 (climate change) are linked to the other 17 UN SDGs. The research is conducted separately on the example of dynamically developing BRICS countries and developed G7 countries, a group of which is selected by the International Monetary Fund [6]. Table 26.1 presents the empirical basis of this research.

Based on the statistics in Table 26.1, the author assesses the correlation of the results of the implementation of SDG 13 with the results of the implementation of other UN SDGs. The correlation coefficients are compared with each other in the considered categories of countries, which reveals the influence of institutions (economy) on the fight against climate change. The author also applies regression analysis to estimate the impact of climate change mitigation (SDG 13 outcomes) on the overall economic growth rate in a sample of countries in 2021. This allows the author to conduct a systemic study of the causal links between sustainable growth and economic development in the fight against climate change.

26.3. Results

The link between the economy and the fight against climate change and its differences between the BRICS countries and the G7 reflects the cross-correlation of the results of the implementation of SDG 13 with the results of the implementation of other UN SDGs in 2021 (Fig. 26.1).

The systematization of the results of the correlation analysis (Fig. 26.1) showed that seven SDGs are positively associated (as indicated by positive correlation coefficients) with SDG 13 in the G7 countries; in the BRICS countries, only five SDGs showed a positive relationship with combating climate change.

Table 26.1. The results of the implementation of 17 UN SDGs in the BRICS and G7 countries in 2021, points 1–100.

	Country	Goal 1	Goal 2	Goal 3	Goal 4	Goal 5	Goal 6	Goal 7	Goal 8	Goal 9	Goal 10	Goal 11	Goal 12	Goal 13	Goal 14	Goal 15	Goal 16	Goal 17
BRICS	Brazil	87.0	69.9	77.8	87.7	70.3	86.2	94.8	65.3	59.7	12.4	75.9	77.4	93.9	57.7	59.5	61.5	75.8
	China	98.6	81.1	81.7	97.5	76.2	68.6	78.2	71.6	73.0	30.7	78.0	87.1	87.1	54.1	49.6	69.9	42.1
	Russia	99.9	57.5	78.8	99.7	66.4	72.0	90.8	75.4	67.7	64.9	85.9	76.7	73.4	52.3	66.2	55.8	70.3
	South Africa	44.2	58.6	51.9	81.1	84.0	64.0	81.3	60.6	61.4	0.0	78.9	81.5	79.4	64.6	59.0	58.6	74.5
	India	59.6	52.4	58.0	86.5	34.1	56.1	69.9	71.1	42.2	27.9	53.2	91.7	96.1	62.2	50.7	58.9	50.7
G7	Canada	99.5	67.4	94.0	99.6	82.4	85.9	94.9	81.5	85.6	83.2	92.7	51.0	47.6	63.7	59.9	84.4	72.6
	France	99.7	73.7	92.5	99.7	87.0	86.7	97.0	82.4	87.4	84.3	89.3	57.7	72.4	61.4	70.8	75.1	71.2
	Germany	99.5	72.4	93.8	98.8	80.7	84.7	93.6	87.4	93.0	86.5	91.3	54.9	60.7	62.6	79.7	84.7	77.8
	Italy	98.1	71.0	94.0	96.7	72.8	82.1	93.8	76.6	83.6	71.5	82.3	63.6	76.8	53.5	80.2	79.0	63.0
	Japan	99.2	75.2	94.1	99.7	61.5	84.9	93.7	86.8	89.5	75.3	85.8	66.6	66.4	51.7	63.9	91.6	71.5
	UK	99.7	67.3	92.8	98.4	83.0	92.3	93.8	80.5	89.8	66.3	93.3	53.3	57.8	73.1	76.7	83.1	58.2
	USA	99.2	69.1	88.7	99.2	74.4	84.3	93.5	76.6	93.9	47.0	92.6	53.6	52.7	64.6	60.6	73.3	68.8

Source: Compiled by the author based on UNDP materials [16].

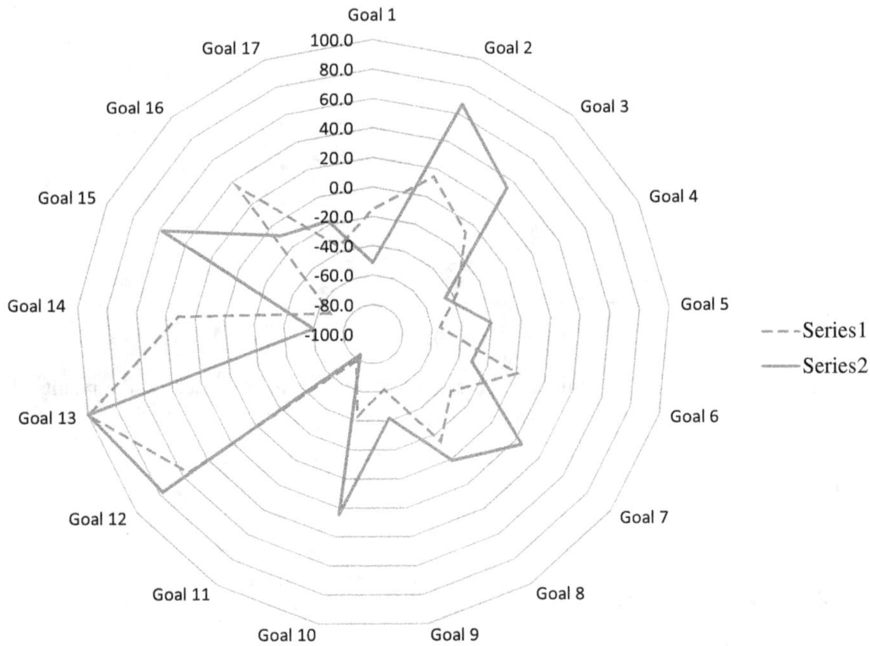

Fig. 26.1. Cross-correlation of the results of the implementation of SDG 13 with the results of the implementation of other UN SDGs in 2021 in the BRICS and G7 countries.

The arithmetic mean of the positive correlation coefficients of the results of the implementation of SDG 13 with the results of the implementation of other UN SDGs in 2021 in the G7 countries was 41.08% ((66.98 + 34.10 + 25.12 + 1 + 24.38 + 77.63 + 58.35)/7); in the BRICS countries, this indicator was 48.83% lower — 27.60% ((14.9 + 0.2 + 55.8 + 31.9 + 35.2)/5). The difference between the countries of these categories lies in the effectiveness of institutions. Consequently, institutions (economics) strongly influence the results achieved in combating climate change. The opposite effect is evidenced by the results obtained in Fig. 26.2.

The regression model from Fig. 26.2 showed that a one-point increase in climate change outcomes in 2021 provided a 0.0547% acceleration in the rate of economic growth. The change in the economic growth rate in 2021 by 15.91% was due to the results of the implementation of SDG 13. Consequently, the fight against climate change strongly impacts today's economy.

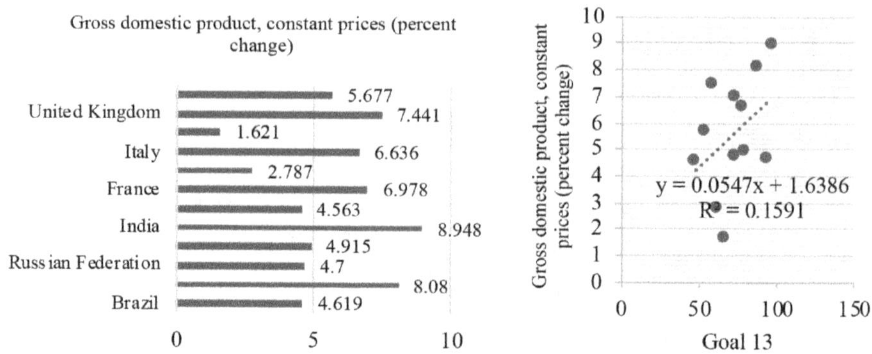

Fig. 26.2. The rate of economic growth and its regression dependence on the results in the BRICS and G77 countries on SDG 13 in 2021.

Source: Calculated and compiled by the author based on the materials of the International Monetary Fund [6].

26.4. Discussion

The obtained results have contributed to the theory of sustainable development in the environmental economy, substantiating the systemic nature and close interdependence of economic growth and the fight against climate change. This emphasizes the relevance of a new international academic journal on the economics of climate change. The journal has been launched by a respected publisher Frontiers, in the series *Frontiers in Environmental Economics* [3].

The new journal focuses on the economics of climate change, which refers to the totality of economic and environmental processes, linkages, and relationships arising in combating climate change in the economy. Specialty Chief Editors of this journal are Elena G. Popkova (Moscow State Institute of International Relations, Russia) and Xunpeng (Roc) Shi (University of Technology Sydney, Australia). All articles in this journal are published in open access and indexed in CLOCKSS, CrossRef, Google Scholar, and OpenAIRE.

The uniqueness of the journal lies in its original subject area — the economics of climate change, which covers a wide range of promising areas of research, including the following:

- Green growth and sustainable development of the ecological economy;

- Social entrepreneurship, nonprofit marketing, and corporate environmental responsibility;
- Green finance in support of climate change;
- The regional economy of territorial inequality in a changing climate;
- Climate-smart technologies and smart environmental innovations, etc.

The journal is notable because it publishes multidisciplinary research on the economics of climate change at the interface of climate science, environmental science, economics, business, and the social sciences and humanities (philosophy, education, cultural studies, law, and sociology). To support multidisciplinary research, the discussed journal encourages methodological pluralism, allowing for the application and combination of quantitative and qualitative research methods.

26.5. Conclusion

This research resolved the contradiction between the interests of society, the economy, and the environment by proposing a new scientific concept and a new promising area of research — the economics of climate change. The new international scientific journal on the economics of climate change has been created to stimulate the application of scientific thought to current issues in this subject area. The value of this new journal is that it pushes the boundaries of the study of climate change from ecology to environmental economics and breaks down the barriers to combating climate change in the economy. The journal systemically reveals the direct and inverse effects of climate change on the economy.

The new scientific results obtained in this research deserve further discussion and in-depth elaboration in studies that may be published in the new journal. The institutional differences between the results of the implementation of SDG 13 and the implementation of other UN SDGs between developing and developed countries (shown in this article using BRICS and G7 as examples) are only the tip of the iceberg; the nature of these differences determines the great potential for further research.

In turn, the identified significant contribution of climate change control to post-crisis economic recovery in the face of the ongoing COVID-19 pandemic in 2021 reflected climate change control in a new light, demonstrating its potential for economic crisis management. This should also be the focus of further studies, which are welcomed in the *Journal of the Economics of Climate Change*.

References

1. Buhvald EM, Larionova EI, Avkopashvili PT, Adamyants ST, Alekseev AN. Post-economy of AI: New challenges and perspectives of sustainable development of socio-economic systems. In: Popkova EG, Ostrovskaya VN (Eds.). *Meta-Scientific Study of Artificial Intelligence*. Charlotte, NC: Information Age Publishing; 2021, pp. 445–452.
2. Carlson CJ, Albery GF, Merow C, Trisos CH, Zipfel CM, Eskew EA, *et al*. Climate change increases cross-species viral transmission risk. *Nature*, 2022. DOI: 10.1038/s41586-022-04788-w
3. Frontiers in Environmental Economics. *Economics of Climate Change* Available from: https://www.frontiersin.org/journals/environmental-economics/sections/economics-of-climate-change (accessed 12 May 2022).
4. Furlan M, Mariano E. A confirmatory factor model for climate justice: Integrating human development and climate actions in low carbon economies. *Environmental Science and Policy*, 2022; 133: 17–30. DOI: 10.1016/j.envsci.2022.03.004
5. Golovchanskaya EE, Strelchenya EI, Popkova EG, Leonenko OV. The key role of intellectual resources in the economic growth models in the institutional environment of innovative activity of the Republic of Belarus: Theory and practice. *International Journal of Trade and Global Markets*, 2018, 11(3): 213–227. DOI: 10.1504/IJTGM.2018.095813
6. International Monetary Fund. World Economic Outlook Database 2022. Available from: https://www.imf.org/en/Publications/WEO/weo-database/2022/April (accessed 12 May 2022).
7. Jiang Y, Chen M, Zhang J, Sun Z, Sun Z. The improved coupling coordination analysis on the relationship between climate, eco-environment, and socio-economy. *Environmental and Ecological Statistics*, 2021; 29(1): 77–100. DOI: 10.1007/s10651-021-00516-1
8. Khanna M, Gusmerotti NM, Frey M. The relevance of the circular economy for climate change: An exploration through the theory of change approach. *Sustainability*, 2022; 14(7): 3991. DOI: 10.3390/su14073991
9. Liang Z, Qamruzzaman M. An asymmetric investigation of the nexus between economic policy uncertainty, knowledge spillover, climate change, and green economy: Evidence from BRIC nations. *Frontiers in Environmental Science*, 2022; 9: 807424. DOI: 10.3389/fenvs.2021.807424
10. Manik S, Mandal M, Pal S, Patra S, Acharya S. Impact of climate on COVID-19 transmission: A study over Indian states. *Environmental Research*; 2022; 211: 113110. DOI: 10.1016/j.envres.2022.113110
11. Ngo Q-T, Tran HA, Tran HTT. The impact of green finance and COVID-19 on economic development: Capital formation and educational expenditure of ASEAN economies. *China Finance Review International*, 2022; 12(2): 261–279. DOI: 10.1108/CFRI-05-2021-0087

12. Popkova EG, DeLo P, Sergi BS. Corporate social responsibility amid social distancing during the COVID-19 crisis: BRICS vs. OECD countries. *Research in International Business and Finance*, 2021; 55: 101315. DOI: 10.1016/j.ribaf.2020.101315
13. Popkova EG, Bogoviz AV, Lobova SV, Chililov AM, Sozinova AA, Sergi BS. Changing entrepreneurial attitudes for mitigating the global pandemic's social drama. *Humanities and Social Sciences Communications*, 2022; 9(1): 141. DOI: 10.1057/s41599-022-01151-2
14. Rhodes E, Hoyle A, McPherson M, Craig K. Understanding climate policy projections: A scoping review of energy-economy models in Canada. *Renewable and Sustainable Energy Reviews*, 2022; 153: 111739. DOI: 10.1016/j.rser.2021.111739UNDP
15. Styles D, Yesufu J, Bowman M, Williams AP, Duffy C, Luyckx K. Climate mitigation efficacy of anaerobic digestion in a decarbonising economy. *Journal of Cleaner Production*, 2022; 338: 130441. DOI: 10.1016/j.jclepro.2022.130441
16. UNDP. Sustainable Development Report 2021. Available from: https://dashboards.sdgindex.org/ (accessed 12 May 2022).
17. Wei L, Lu Z, Wang Y, Liu X, Wang W, Wu C, *et al*. Black carbon-climate interactions regulate dust burdens over India revealed during COVID-19. *Nature Communications*, 2022; 13(1): 1839. DOI: 10.1038/s41467-022-29468-1
18. Winkelmann R, Donges JF, Smith EK, Milkoreit M, Eder C, Heitzig J, *et al*. Social tipping processes towards climate action: A conceptual framework. *Ecological Economics*, 2022; 192: 107242. DOI: 10.1016/j.ecolecon.2021.107242
19. Zhang R, Tang X, Liu J, Visbeck M, Guo H, Murray V, *et al*. From concept to action: A united, holistic and one health approach to respond to the climate change crisis. *Infectious Diseases of Poverty*, 2022; 11(1): 17. DOI: 10.1186/s40249-022-00941-9
20. Zhao L, Saydaliev HB, Iqbal S. Energy financing, COVID-19 repercussions and climate change: Implications for emerging economies. *Climate Change Economics*, 2022; 2240003. DOI: 10.1142/S2010007822400036
21. Ziaja S, Chhabra M. Climate adaption for Energy utilities: Lessons learned from California's pioneering regulatory actions. *Frontiers in Climate*, 2021; 3: 718472. DOI: 10.3389/fclim.2021.718472

https://doi.org/10.1142/9789811264252_bmatter

Conclusion

Fighting Climate Change by Social Entrepreneurship for a Sustainable Ecological Economy

Elena G. Popkova

MGIMO University, Moscow, Russia
E.Popkova@inno.mgimo.ru

Climate-smart innovations enable successful adaptation to climate change and long-term climate resilience. This book formed a systemic theoretical view and offered comprehensive practical recommendations for implementing climate-smart innovations in social entrepreneurship to support a sustainable ecological economy. However, this is only the first stage in the development of the economics of climate change; the practical implementation of the scientific developments and recommendations proposed in this book will allow us to move to the next stage, which will be related to combating climate change.

Adaptation allows entrepreneurship to reduce climate risks, but they are still periodically exacerbated, and new risks arise. The potential of climate-smart innovations is very great — to adapt and prevent further climate change and, in the long term, even to achieve reverse climate change (recovery). Through this, the sustainable development of the ecological economy can move to a new level where a stable and favorable climate will be achieved. Social entrepreneurship can and should play a leading role in this process.

Thus, while this book answered the research question of how to use climate-smart innovation to adapt social entrepreneurship to climate change (in a comprehensive way), it led to a new research question of how to achieve preventive climate risk management and combat climate change in social entrepreneurship through climate-smart innovation. It is suggested that further research be devoted to the scientific study of this question and the search for an answer to it.

https://doi.org/10.1142/9789811264252_bmatter

Index

www.ingramcontent.com/pod-product-compliance
Lightning Source LLC
LaVergne TN
LVHW011700200926
848484LV00004B/1006
9789811264245